DATE DUE

PRAISE FOR TERRY FREI

HORNS, HOGS, AND NIXON COMING

"We had a few friends over who thought we had lost our minds as we whooped and hollered through a football game so exciting it was billed as the Game of the Century. For a few hours, we were innocent again, totally caught up in the contest. The game and its cultural contexts have been beautifully chronicled by Terry Frei in his book *Horns, Hogs, and Nixon Coming*."

— Bill Clinton, from *My Life*

THIRD DOWN AND A WAR TO GO

"Many times you hear athletes called heroes, and their deeds and accomplishments on the field are characterized as courageous. After reading *Third Down and a War to Go*, I am embarrassed to have ever been thought of as brave or courageous. . . . Enjoy this adventure in history, life, and courage and take it from a so-called tough guy—keep the hanky close by."

— Dan Fouts, Hall of Fame quarterback and CBS sportscaster

"*Third Down and a War to Go* will put you in the huddle, in the front lines, and in a state of profound gratitude."

— Neal Rubin, *Detroit News*

"Brings to life, in shades of black and blue and blood red, the idea that certain things are worth fighting for."

— Rick Morrissey, *Chicago Tribune*

'77: *DENVER, THE BRONCOS, AND A COMING OF AGE*

"Ahh the memories. And they all happened right here in the forgotten time zone. Those magical moments came back with a rush last week reading *'77: Denver, the Broncos, and a Coming of Age*. What a fantastic read . . . '77 is more than just a Bronco football memoir. It was a time when our Centennial State exploded on the national scene. . . . [T]hanks to Terry Frei's wonderful work, we get to live that magical moment all over again."

— Dick Maynard, *Grand Junction Sentinel*

"A must-read for fans of the NFL, of the 1970s, and of the American West. You didn't have to live through it in Denver to appreciate this account of the flowering of a franchise and its love affair with a town, but this book takes those of us who did straight back to those thrilling days of yesteryear in unforgettable fashion."

— Michael Knisley, senior deputy editor, ESPN.com

THE WITCH'S SEASON

"Events carry the story forward swiftly, and that alone would make it a good read. But Frei has a larger point to make. It's during times of upheaval, when the very foundations of normalcy are being shaken, that personal courage, honor and the willingness to stand fast on principle matter most. All of the central characters in Frei's story will have to decide whether to make that stand, and if so, how to make it. Frei has written three nonfiction books, most notably *Horns, Hogs, and Nixon Coming*. This book proves he can write fiction too."

— Ken Goe, Portland *Oregonian*

"Frei combines his passion for college football, politics, and the turbulence of the 1960s into a classic. The recipe works, as *The Witch's Season* is a compelling page turner."

— Doug Ottewill, *Mile High Sports* magazine

PLAYING PIANO IN A BROTHEL

PLAYING PIANO IN A BROTHEL

A Sports Journalist's Odyssey

TERRY FREI

TAYLOR TRADE PUBLISHING
Lanham · New York · Boulder · Toronto · Plymouth, UK

Published by Taylor Trade Publishing
An imprint of The Rowman & Littlefield Publishing Group, Inc.
4501 Forbes Boulevard, Suite 200, Lanham, Maryland 20706
http://www.rlpgtrade.com

Estover Road, Plymouth PL6 7PY, United Kingdom

Distributed by National Book Network

British Library Cataloguing in Publication Information Available

Library of Congress Cataloging-in-Publication Data
Frei, Terry, 1955–
    Playing piano in a brothel : a sports journalist's odyssey / Terry Frei.
        p.   cm.
    Includes index.
    ISBN 978-1-58979-459-7 (cloth : alk. paper) — ISBN 978-1-58979-460-3
(electronic)
    1. Frei, Terry, 1955– 2. Sportswriters—United States. 3. Sports journalism—
United States. 4. Sports—United States I. Title.
    GV742.42.F74 2010
    070.4'49796092—dc22
    [B]
                                                                    2010008847

Printed in the United States of America

CONTENTS

PART FIVE: DANCING HALL OF FAMERS

PART SIX: COLLEGE FOOTBALL

PART SEVEN: PUCKS

PART EIGHT: BOXING

PART NINE: OLYMPIC FLAMES

PART ONE

PLAYING PIANO IN A BROTHEL

It is partly on account of last summer that I am writing this book for the benefit of the 100,000,000 boobs and flatheads that swallow down everything they read in the papers, in particular the writing of Krazy Kress in *The Star-Press*.
  —New York Mammoths pitcher Henry Wiggen in
    The Southpaw by Mark Harris

MIKE
TYSON
FRANK
BRUNO
Saturday · February 25, 1989
⟨ LAS VEGAS HILTON
MEDIA

PORTLAND OREGONIAN
TERRY FREI

S
5
6

PRINT MEDIA
TERRY FREI
DENVER POST
DENVER, CO

GAME **1**
The
1992
NBA
Finals™

TERRY FREI
OREGONIAN

WORKING MEDIA

A PAIR OF TWOS

W HEN MY FATHER, Jerry Frei, finished up his seventeen-season stay at the University of Oregon as the Ducks' head football coach from 1967 to 1971, he and my mother, Marian, hosted social receptions at our home for assistant coaches, boosters, university officials, and members of the media after games in Eugene. I was twelve when they began, and that's the way I met most of the major members of the Oregon sportswriting community.

Those experiences were the basis for a scene in my novel and screenplay, *The Witch's Season*. A 1968 college football team's radical linebacker goes to the post-game reception at the coach's home to apologize for an antiwar protest at the game that got out of hand and embarrassed the university, and the linebacker discovers that the embattled university president is at the party. There's another scene in the novel where the coach eloquently philosophizes to reporters after a bitter loss as his young son sits in a corner listening. The words the coach uses in the novel are word for word from a clipping detailing my father's reaction to an especially heartbreaking defeat, and in reality I was indeed sitting in the corner of the tiny coaches' dressing room at Oregon's Autzen Stadium that day, glaring at reporters' backs and waiting for them to leave my father alone.

I now understand that the sportswriters respected my father and generally were fair and sympathetic. My father considered many writers who covered the Ducks to be his friends. One of the "worst" things they and others said about my father was that he sometimes seemed "too nice" to be a head coach. I'll trade that for knowing at the time and also being told later how influential he was in the lives of so many young men—stars and scrubs alike—and in the development of many young assistant coaches who went on to great accomplishment. He was not just a coach; he also was an educator, earning roughly the same money as an English professor. I still remember being startled when his head-coaching salary—$17,600—was published in the paper, for all (including *my friends!*) to see, and his perks included $100 a week during the season for a television show and the use of an Oldsmobile.

He was in the local spotlight and with it came scrutiny. I understood that. At my own football, basketball, and baseball games, I was "Frei's son." Intensely loyal, I had a low tolerance for anything remotely critical of my father, his coaches, or his players. Simply stating that Oregon lost was "negative" enough to make me mad. And fans? My parents finally decided I would be better off standing on the sidelines than sitting in the stands, because I argued with those critical of the players or the coaches. At a 1970 game in Corvallis against Oregon State, I sat in the designated visitors area of Parker Stadium, and it wasn't easy for me because I had just had anterior cruciate ligament surgery and was in a cast from toe to hip and on crutches. Down the row, an obnoxious guy—I'm guessing now he was in his mid-thirties—spent the entire game, a wrenching Ducks' loss, blasting the players. Several times, I told him to shut up and said such things as, I bet he had never put on a jock in his life and the players on the field were better men than he was. Yes, that's how naive I was. Near the end of the game, he walked down the row, where he had to pass me. He said something about hoping that my recovery went well. Next, I did something I regret to this day. No, I didn't haul off and punch him. I said I was sorry for mouthing off at him. As he passed me, he said, "That's okay. You'll understand someday."

I have to concede he was right. I understand. That's the way it is. What my father and his family went through is mild compared to what coaches and their families experience today. Fans pay their money or support sports in other ways, and they passionately follow them. Criticism, even bitter denunciation, is part of the dynamic that fuels American sport. There are many more outlets for that now. The media are not just a part of that but also at the leading edge. Sportswriting is parasitical; I wish we would acknowledge that more often.

In speeches, I often have told a fact-based joke about how those young assistant coaches on my father's staff who were barely making a living wage scrambled to get to our house to play poker with the reporters.* I explain that the off-season card games were designed to be relationship-building experiences for the coaches and influential writers who, along with many folks who bragged of being "influential boosters," sometimes questioned

---

* By "fact-based," I mean it's closer to the truth than most "true" sports-themed movies. Which isn't saying much, I know.

whether the Oregon staff was too inexperienced. When the young assistants left, one by one, counting their winnings, I asked each why they were so eager to socialize with the writers. In succession, each of them laughed and said to ask the next coach coming out of the door.

The first was John Marshall, as of this writing a veteran NFL defensive coordinator with the Oakland Raiders.

The second was Ron Stratten, who became the head coach at Portland State, a respected NCAA executive, and finally a highly successful businessman.

The third was Gunther Cunningham, who went on to be the Kansas City Chiefs' head coach and the defensive coordinator for the Chiefs and several other NFL teams.

The fourth was Bruce Snyder, who later was the highly successful head coach at California and Arizona State University and who came within one play of winning a national championship at ASU.

The fifth was George Seifert, later the head coach of the Super Bowl champion San Francisco 49ers and Carolina Panthers.

Only one assistant coach remained. That was John Robinson, eventually the head coach of a national championship team at the University of Southern California and of the Los Angeles Rams. When I told Robinson he was my last chance to find out why the young Oregon coaches so enjoyed socializing with the sportswriters, he—"Robbie" to all of us—laughed and put his hand on my shoulder. He looked me in the eye and said, "Terry, here's a lesson to remember. Always make room at the poker table for the guys who keep raising with a pair of twos."

Telling this story was more about poking fun at myself for being in the profession than about criticizing the writers who had preceded me.

When I worked part time at the *Rocky Mountain News* while attending the University of Colorado, and after when I joined the *Denver Post* following graduation, I was in the final days of rattling typewriters and wire-service teletype machines*; pneumatic tubes carrying copy from the sports department to the printers in the back; headline "counts" to determine if "Buffs Rout Huskers 28–27" would fit in the allotted number of columns, and, yes, the occasional Jack Daniels bottle stashed away.

I've witnessed the changing sports journalism scene in my two separate stays at the *Post*, at the *Oregonian*, and in an enjoyable hiatus from the newspaper business at the *Sporting News*. Much of the change in the business

---

* When the bells rang, it meant somebody better run over there immediately and see if Mickey Mantle had been killed in a car crash, although there wasn't a lot we could do with breaking news, other than put it in the next morning's paper.

has been for the better. Much has not. When I told friends that I would include a frank assessment of my own profession and express some disagreements with my own newspaper in this book, I was asked variations of, "You sure you want to do that?" One reason I got into the business was that I took seriously newspaper journalism's reputation as a marketplace of ideas, not just in the newsprint pages, but also in the workplace. That's a reputation its leaders courted and bragged about. I make no pretense that this is anything other than one man's opinion. I know that some will conclude that I am a traditionalist resistant to change who also probably believes that we should go back to typewriters, 33⅓ rpm albums, and rotary phones. That's not true. Yes, I would prefer that baseball players wear their pants as something other than full-length slacks and that NBA players actually move without the ball, but I do have a cell phone, iPod, and computer, and I embrace most modern advancements. Why, just the other day, I learned how to text! (I think.)

So here goes.

Nationally, in sports and the other sections, reporters, writers, copy editors, layout designers, and especially editors have become specialists. Sports editors at major papers usually don't write and are office-bound administrators with little contact with the teams and people we cover, and their decisions and expectations sometimes reflect a lack of understanding about reality in the field. They do get out to the Associated Press Sports Editors Conventions, but that's where they compare notes and come back with copycat ideas that tend to make sports sections look alike from coast to coast.

The separation of duties also has encouraged a blinkered attitude among writers, who have little clue about how difficult it is to get a newspaper out every day—especially in the sports department.* We also used to be "sportswriters," or generalists who not only accepted but also sought periodic shifts from beat to beat or covered them all, at least to some extent. Now, while there is some shifting—and we do occasionally help out on all beats— specialization is the norm. We have "football writers" or "baseball writers" or "hockey writers." That can lead to increased familiarity and knowledge about the specific teams and sports, but less rapport with the general sports fans who follow all sports and teams.

This is an issue on all the beats, but especially so in pro football, where the one-game-a-week routine means there are six days of "off-day" stories.

---

* Every Election Night, you can count on the city room congratulating itself for handling a huge rush of copy and live news on deadline. There's a saying in sports departments: *Every night is Election Night.*

Beat writers know that the way to gain favor and get the so-called scoops about signings, player moves, or other details is to make tacit deals. Some have allowed coaches and team officials to dictate when a story will be written, how the story will be spun, and what will be underplayed or swept under the rug altogether. A few reporters around the country whom I personally like made those deals, flourished, and moved on to bigger things. Those deals probably even can be justified because of the scoops they produce—even if involves merely being tipped off about what is about to become public knowledge anyway. The reporters who don't make those deals can find themselves at a competitive disadvantage in multiple newspaper markets or when NFL coaches find sycophants in the national media to feed this information. While often stonewalling the Colorado media after Denver became a one-newspaper market, Josh McDaniels, after taking over as the Broncos' head coach, quickly developed that knack for locating sympathetic national reporters to feed material that served his purposes.

In baseball writing, we unquestionably buy into the modern devotion to pitch counts; the division of relievers into long, set-up, and closer roles; ridiculously detailed statistics that increasingly prove little except that computers are amazing; and the premise that as long as managers memorize the "book" and can pull off the double-switch in the National League, they're brilliant. Too often, seamheads are writing for seamheads. I love baseball, but we've turned the diamond into an Excel spreadsheet.

An alarming number of NBA beat writers are "house voices" for the league and teams and are far too close to the players. Editors don't seem to mind the all-too-common occurrence of NBA beat writers high-fiving and embracing players on teams that they cover or coming off as star players' personal press agents.

The NHL? Like other leagues, the NHL has an obsessed wing of fandom that thirsts for minutiae—who's playing left wing on the fourth line tonight?—rather than human-interest stories the general sports fan also would read. In no other sport does the print media now cater to the fringe as much as we do in hockey coverage. Yes, even more so than in baseball.

The coverage of college sports, especially football, is increasingly formulaic and predictable. Newspaper beat writers or national college sports specialists learn quickly to fixate on whether a coach is "safe" or "in trouble," to write about quarterbacks whenever possible, and to consider handicapping the Heisman race more important than assembling a delegate count during the presidential primaries.

On all beats, we've too often forgotten that the best stories often are profiles that let our readers learn about the players and coaches they're watching: *What's his (or her) story?* Editors would counter that they ask for them and want them and even come up with the ideas for subject matter at times, but they generally want them in nice little formulaic packages.

It also is true that sportswriters sometimes are allowed to tackle big subjects beyond profiles. The catchword of the past few years in sports departments has become "enterprise." They must have talked about it at the Associated Press Sports Editors Convention. The definition is vague, and it's difficult to come to an agreement on what's interesting. Editors are big on "concepts" and "trends"—anything that is fodder for a few charts or lists. They *love* charts and lists ("Three Things to Look For" "Ten Key Plays" "Five Key Dates").

Regardless, major profiles and enterprise stories are more frustrating than fulfilling for the writers and readers, because each year, sports editors are more reluctant to clear the space to do them right. Narrative journalism—creating scenes and telling a story from interviews, research, and observation—is virtually impossible. It's not only space, either; it's also philosophy. The trend is toward using snappy, "sound bite" quotes, rather than allowing those whom we're writing about to actually *talk*. Editors tend to think a perfect sports profile is one that quotes the main figure, a coach or two, a couple players, a network game analyst, and a family member for one or two sentences apiece, and all in a story that runs less than a thousand words—but preferably shorter.

Many of those stories *can* be told well in today's desired lengths, especially if reporters know how widely to cast their net when interviewing. With limited available space, reporters can let only the most important figures actually speak without crowding the story with too many other "voices." Conducting eight hours of interviews with sixteen people in order to pick eight great quotes from four people and using some of the rest as background sounds possible in theory, but it's a great way to anger everyone and also a waste of time for all involved. It's also maddening because so much good material ends up on the cutting room floor.

Many of those stories *can't* be told well in those desired lengths. But every story is subject to the one-size-fits-all and one-approach-fits-all standards. An "enterprise" story touches up the formula only slightly. (But don't forget the charts and lists!)

"Writing coaches," whether in-house or independent consultants, emphasize the formula also should include a summary "nut graf," which essentially means readers must be told very very early in the piece why this is an important story.* If it's allowed to be only artful foreshadowing that helps draw readers deeper into the story, it can work. More often, though, the formula leads to an insulting spoiler that implies that readers are so impatient and unintelligent that they need to be told what they're about to be told or they won't keep reading.

I don't completely buy the industry excuse that "the news hole has shrunk," meaning we have less space and every inch is precious. We do have less space and every inch is precious, but if it means getting away from the daily formula approach and leaving out one or two of the eleven stock elements on the baseball team's eighty-seventh game of the season, that's a small price to pay to clear room for exceptional stories. I don't mean to make light of human suffering, but every sportswriter will nod in agreement to this: Our best shot at getting more space is if a player's family member has a life-threatening illness. Editors also *love* those kinds of hooks. I wish they were as open-minded about clearing space for exceptional stories that don't involve tragedy.

For many years when I spoke to high school and college classes or at conferences, I emphasized that writing is largely a self-taught and intuitive craft, and it also requires ancillary skills—such as observation, curiosity, and interaction—that are sharpened through a broad base of life and educational experiences. I told many young men and women that although some might consider a journalism degree to be essential on a resume for those seeking a newspaper writing position, they would be better off carrying double majors—I ended up with degrees in journalism and history—or possibly not majoring in journalism at all. But if young men and women said they hoped to go into the newspaper business, I said, "Go for it."

My position has evolved, and not only because of newspapers' endangered status and the shrinking of the job pool. Now I tell sharp young men and women that even if newspapers survive, they might be too smart for the business—perhaps now, but certainly in the future, if the dumbing-down trends continue. Sadly, the industry's status as the great nurturer of writing talent in this nation already is waning, and talented young writers are ill-advised to consider the business as even a temporary stepping-stone avocation. The industry soon will be—and in many ways, already is—best suited for those who consider 300-word stories, 140-character Tweets, and lightweight blogs to be fulfilling.

---

* For some reason, whenever I hear the term "writing coach," I think of Robert Preston in *The Music Man.*

Newspapers' online sites raise interesting possibilities, and we're still feeling our way. Currently, the usual (but not universal) practice is to simply transfer the print story to the online site, where it joins all online-only bells and whistles, including blogs, slideshows, and video. In theory, it would be great to run two versions of ambitious stories—a short version in the newspaper and a longer, more comprehensive version online, where there are no space limitations. Yes, we have added additional online-only coverage for beats in blogs and stories. But we accelerated the abandonment of the paid print product by not only giving away the online product, but putting more resources and energy into it long before it made financial sense.

I've stopped counting the number of people who have told me that they stopped subscribing to or buying their local paper because they read it online. For free. The newspapers that tried to make their online sites fee-based—including giving it free to paid subscribers—encountered great resistance, in part because they were in the minority. There are indications that there might be another wave of newspapers trying to charge for "premium content," but I wonder if the precedent needed to be set years ago. The hope is that increased online advertising will bring us closer to the free but profitable television and radio models. As of this writing, we're getting there. When that corner is completely turned, if it ever is, I will acknowledge that those who decided to invest so much money and energy in the Web version of the newspaper had foresight. I also will continue to argue for making online the outlet for not just additional minutiae and bells and whistles but also for longer and more in-depth stories that can't be wedged into the paper.

The other extreme is riskier but also worth considering. What about making the print product a daily magazine with longer, high-quality stories, plus only news digest material? The news digest approach is close to what we're doing anyway, so it wouldn't be a drastic change to relegate the more detailed news stories to the Web. You can't get everything in the paper anyway, so why even try—and why not use the limitless online space that way? I realize that one's a long shot, but newspapers should take better advantage of the Web's limitless space one way or another.

What has happened now, though, is that many writers have stopped asking the sort of questions that could lead to bigger stories and instead just focus on the daily grind. That's too bad, and it's our fault, too.

Here's one on me. Defenseman Alexei Gusarov, a Leningrad native, played several seasons with the Colorado Avalanche before I finally got around to asking him about the horrific Siege of Leningrad during World War II. As it turned out, his parents went through it. His father was in his early teens; his mother was a young girl. Although Gusarov's English was limited, he related what he knew of their experiences. In all his years in North America, nobody had ever asked him about it. Until that point, I had been more worried about how he and his defensive partner, Adam Foote, did on the penalty kill.

In the *Post* sports department, the last outlet for stories of exceptional length and outside-the-envelope subject matter was the excellent, beloved, and a bit quirky *Baseball Monday* section, which was killed several years ago. Now even the separate NFL and college football preview sections each week are subject to length and subject constraints that aren't much different than those in the daily section, and that's a lost opportunity. For the most part, we're just giving readers more of the same. That's at the *Post*, but it's my impression that the pattern is repeated at most major sports sections.

Granted, the newspaper business always has been about grind-it-out, nuts-and-bolts news stories as well as ambitious pieces, whether profiles or narrative journalism. It's hard to craft something memorable in 250 words and on deadline about city council meetings or a high school basketball game. I concede that. Plus, looking back over newspapers from the "old days" in my book research, I've been reminded that the general quality of writing and certainly the depth of reporting in sports sections significantly improved in the 1970s and 1980s. Yet it's sad that many of the men and women who had a hand in that or who got into the business because of that chance to do quality work now are made to feel like typewriter repairmen. Their skills are obsolete. And almost as unfortunate, others have completely abandoned that quest to produce memorable work and now are more concerned with their next Tweet or getting to the radio or television studios on time.

I still believe it's a pragmatic goal to occasionally set aside our preoccupation with the daily grind and to give a niche of our readership an exceptional story, one they'll remember, as often as possible. If it deeply affects a portion of our readership—the segment not prone to react with e-mails or letters to the sports editor or comments online—and lives on through Google and other means, it's important in other ways.

Here's an example of the philosophical gulf. I recently did a feature on former major league first baseman Mike Epstein, who owns and runs a hitting school in the Denver area. Ted Williams was one of his managers when he played for the Washington Senators. Epstein was a member of the 1972 World Series champion Oakland Athletics in their brawling days and was their leading home run hitter that season with 26—one ahead of Reggie Jackson. He told wonderful stories about Joe DiMaggio, Ted Williams,

Charlie Finley, Reggie Jackson, and others. The story was transformed into: *Hey, this former major leaguer has a hitting school!* One anecdote that bit the dust in the original story: Epstein played in the Yankee Stadium Old Timers game on the fiftieth anniversary of Lou Gehrig's "Luckiest Man" speech, and he spoke of the emotionalism of lining up on the foul lines with so many great players. As the Yankees played the film of the speech on the scoreboard, Epstein realized that he was standing a few feet away from where Gehrig spoke. Epstein said that in the clubhouse, Joe DiMaggio looked down the hallway and told Epstein that he could still see Gehrig walking down the corridor with a towel around him and smoking a cigarette, as if it were yesterday.

I damn near cried when I transcribed the tape and then typed the passage in the story. I could *see* DiMaggio looking down that hall. I could imagine him seeing Gehrig. I regretted leaving out a lot of other great material, but not even that anecdote made the paper. I was given the impression that I should have gotten Epstein to talk more about techniques for hitting the curveball up the middle and then asked three local high school coaches for comment to make it that tight story focusing on the present and avoiding historical anecdotes. I would like to think that baseball also is figuratively sitting around the cracker barrel and telling stories, not just pitch counts, OBP, batting averages with RISP,* and dissecting inside-out swings. I bring up the Epstein story not to antagonize those who made those decisions— they're entitled to their opinions, too, and they are in positions of power— but to emphasize that such decisions are typical of the philosophies gaining influence in the business. And that's everywhere, not just in Denver.

I'm often asked about the perceived "liberal bias" in the media or in the newspaper business specifically. I'm convinced that major newspapers strive to be objective with such issues as covering political races, and they try to have a balance of views on the op-ed pages and other sections. What's more striking to me than the liberal/conservative distinctions, which have become harder to define, is the unmistakable acceleration of the trend for writers and editors to prove how "sensitive" they are. The beliefs behind that stance can be sincere, but unfortunately it also frequently involves calculated devotion to Political Correctness, not because all wholeheartedly subscribe to the beliefs involved, but because anything else can stamp you as "insensitive" in

---

* On-Base Percentage and Runners In Scoring Position.

the newsroom—and that's a damning label in internal office politics and maneuvering. If that's a liberal bias, yes, major newspapers generally have a liberal bias, and those who try to say it's not true are not being honest—even if that means they're not being honest with themselves.

I'm a Democrat and generally (though not always) vote a straight ticket. Under most standards, my beliefs—both in years past and current—would qualify me as a card-carrying liberal. *The Witch's Season* has what most would consider a definite left-wing bent. Many of the Oregon football program's critics in Portland during my father's coaching tenure were racists and believed he was too "permissive" with his black players. The truth was, he treated them as adults and with respect—as he did all his players—in part because he had been flying an unarmed P-38 fighter reconnaissance plane over Japanese targets at their age. When you've flown in combat at age twenty, are you going to treat twenty-year-olds as "kids"? At least in my father's case, the answer was an emphatic "no." I used my father's philosophy about that "kids" issue as the basis for one of the novel's plotlines. The book also has an anti–Vietnam War theme, although it is tempered by the implication that the 1960s activist movement's lack of civility was both polarizing and counterproductive. I was barely a teenager at the time, but that radical linebacker on the 1968 football team in the novel has a lot of me in him.

My major problem with mainstream media newsroom sensitivity is that it's so selective. For example, if you snidely mention spaghetti and checkered table cloths and use wise guy vernacular in a passage about an Italian American such as troubled NFL lineman Richie Incognito—no problem. Hey, that's funny. If you use corresponding food references and vernacular in a discussion of Hispanic or African American athletes, the paper is being picketed in the morning and your coworkers are demanding an apology. I can argue this both ways, saying: (1) The former is just as offensive as the latter, and one of the weaknesses of conventional liberalism is this tendency to divide society into those we can poke fun at with impunity and those we can't; or (2) Everybody needs to lighten up and learn how to take a joke. I'd also argue that we should pick one of those stands as the societal standard and lobby for its consistent application. We can't tell Italian Americans they need to lighten up and take a joke and then react to a parallel insensitive remark about another ethnic group as if it's an affront that should cause the writer or broadcaster to be fired.

That desire to be stamped "sensitive" shows up in many other aspects of media coverage. The most glaring example in sports is the discussion of the racial makeup of the coaching community. There haven't been enough football coaches of African American descent. That's a given. But the coverage and discussion of the issue highlights how so much phony sensitivity comes into play and how the standards of assessment often are presumptive, inconsistent, and cynical.

Richard Lapchick is chair of the DeVos Sport Business Management Graduate Program in the College of Business Administration at the University of Central Florida. He also is director of the Institute for Diversity and Ethics in Sport.* He has made much of his reputation by categorizing, counting, and issuing annual report cards about the percentage of minorities in coaching. I agree with his basic point but not with his reliance on presumptive racial categorization and measuring "fairness" with numbers. Lapchick wrote pieces in the past for the *Sporting News* and has become a frequent contributor to ESPN.com. He states his case in such predictable terms that it can come off as satire, along the lines of *Politically Correct Fairy Tales*. This was in his ESPN piece after Louisville hired Charlie Strong as head football coach in December 2009: "With several coaching positions remaining to be filled, there are 11 African-American head coaches, and 13 coaches of color among the 120 (Football Bowl Subdivision) schools."

On the surface, that might seem reasonable. I still identify men and women as African American or black if it seems pertinent, but I have done so less frequently as time went on. Now I wince when it gets into official categorization and scorekeeping, because it's insulting and condescending to those being "counted." I believe that's the prevailing attitude, even among liberals, and they're not ashamed to admit it—except perhaps if they work in newsrooms. Plus, it's tricky: if we're counting, what *officially* qualifies as an African American or a minority (a term Lapchick also uses), especially in a quickly evolving and changing American society? Who decides? Is self-declaration enough? Don't you have to have some standards if you're trying to neatly categorize? And if you do, doesn't it begin to sound more like the Nuremberg Laws than the basis of justice? Why isn't an Eastern European immigrant a "minority"?

Wait. It all comes down to *color*? Doesn't anyone else find that offensive? Isn't that what we were trying to get away from?

Tough-guy winger Sandy McCarthy, who played for six teams in an eleven-year career, often was included when well-meaning journalists compiled lists of black NHL players. In fact, as a member of the Mikmaq First Nations Tribe in Canada, McCarthy considered himself an indigenous North American. The eyeball test didn't work.

---

* I wonder if he ever considered becoming a writing coach.

I'm all for proudly declaring your own heritage and reveling in it. But there's a difference between that and others making presumptive judgments for you. There's a difference between that and officially bringing self-declaration into scorekeeping and preferential hires, which opens the doors for opportunistic ethnic elasticity. We were reminded of that by notorious University of Colorado professor Ward Churchill, who would have been anything he needed to be. Another of our weaknesses has been our fear of challenging the phonies, opportunists, and those who want to manipulate the system and play whatever "card" seems likely to work. The "race card" is the most obvious, but only one of many available.

I was an advocate of affirmative action as a means of compensating for past exclusionary policies and of gathering momentum for fairness. I still am in favor of it, as long as it's allowed to evolve into an instinctive concept. I'm proud that my father hired Ron Stratten as his defensive line coach in 1968, both because Ron was and is a terrific man but also because he was the first African American assistant coach in a major program on the West Coast. That was more than forty years ago. I believe that we're past the point of needing to officially define everyone and, more so, past the appropriateness of counting. I can't tell you *when* we got past that point; I just know that we have.

If I were an employer or a supervisor making hiring decisions in either the public or private sector, I would define diversity myself by feel—and not through questionnaires, categorization, and percentages. I know what diversity is, and I know it by instinct not by counting on my fingers, assessing pigment, or asking questions about family trees. Diversity is energizing, educational, and smart business, because I'm convinced it makes everyone better. Diversity means a cross section of personalities, of beliefs, of background, of everything—but not just of what you see when you look at a person.

That's where we should be by now. Including in the discussion of the heritage of major college football coaches.

Put away the questionnaires and calculators.

I did one of the very first stories in the 1980s about how Tony Dungy, then the Steelers' first-year defensive coordinator, was clearly NFL head coach material. By 1994, when he still hadn't been hired as a head coach and was the defensive coordinator of the Minnesota Vikings, I brought him up again in a couple of *Sporting News* stories—one in January about the pool of hot head coach candidates and one in November about Dungy specifically. We talked about his long wait to be a head coach and how long I had been writing about the issue, and he joked, "At least you've still got your hair." The point was that he was a great coach waiting to happen. It demeaned him to make race the primary issue. I concluded, "Expect him to be the head coach at Carolina, or Detroit, or Houston, or Tampa Bay, or Somewhere in 1995." I was off by a year. He went to the Buccaneers in 1996. Was racism involved in his long wait? Probably, but it's impossible to state that as fact because of the myriad factors—not all of them sensible—that go into coaching hires. By now, we should be beyond an insipid scorekeeping paragraph in every story about the hiring of a perceived minority coach. Taking the lead from Lapchick, often before also quoting him in the story, writers give us: "Jones becomes the XXth African American head coach in NFL history. . . . The XXth current African American coach in the NFL. . . . The XXth African American coach in the NCAA's Football Bowl Subdivision."

Yes, I know that some argue that the reason we're not beyond that kind of scorekeeping is because there haven't been enough black coaches. But wasn't our goal as a society to reach the point where we didn't need to officially classify people for purposes ranging from who could sit at lunch counters, be considered for jobs, or even have a realistic chance of being elected president, *because it shouldn't matter?*

Another deterrent to media members taking carefully reasoned, non-bandwagon, sincere, and fair positions on diversity matters is that they're scared to death that moronic, hateful, ignorant racists might voice agreement without being intelligent enough to understand the distinctions. We're paranoid about knowing that if racist scumbags are among those who praise a stand, some will consider us racists by association. Political writers can shrug it off and plow on; sportswriters tend to self-censor themselves because of that fear. In newsrooms, that increasingly irrational fear of being accused of being insensitive or even bigoted drives our decisions and coverage more than common sense.

This desire to avoid being labeled insensitive is so ingrained in me as a journalist that I often caught myself being careful when typing those previous passages about selective sensitivity. And, yes, I felt the need to establish my "liberal" *bona fides.* I'm laughing at myself, but I'm leaving that in.

Bottom line: I've come to grips with the fact that the way we in the media cover the diversity issue is laughably cynical.

All of that made the coverage of the University of Colorado football "scandals" of the mid-2000s a study in contradictions. We were faced with the dilemma of prioritizing our sensitivities, and we reached the conclusion that it was more important to appear sensitive on gender issues than on race issues—and it affected our coverage to the point of *unfairness.*

As Bruce Plasket pointed out in *Buffaloed*, a book my profession generally ignored, the coverage even had a tinge of racism. The media—including me—botched it, too often assuming the worst about allegations and not backing off or apologizing when they were shown to be overreactions and ultimately unfair. Even looking back at the stories now—about mostly wild allegations that proved to exaggerated or unfounded—I am embarrassed about the assume-the-worst tone of the coverage, locally and nationally. I said "including me," mainly because I wrote an ESPN.com column that, while carefully nuanced, called for Coach Gary Barnett's firing when he was suspended for impolitic—but accurate—remarks about placekicker Kate Hnida, who had been welcomed into the program when Rick Neuheisel was the Buffaloes' coach.* My point was that CEOs commonly take the fall in the business world when they are no longer effective, even for unfair reasons, and that it was time to take that approach with Barnett. I shouldn't have said that. I've admitted my mistake and apologized many times publicly; I'm doing it again here. The posse mentality infected me. Barnett's reputation was unfairly tarnished and, more important, so were the players', because they were all under that blanket of suspicion. CU alum Rick Reilly's *Sports Illustrated* column about Hnida was irresponsible. He allowed her to accuse an unnamed teammate of rape and was unwilling to scrutinize her story or point out how indirectly connected to the football program it was, even if what she said was true. The alleged rape took place at an off-campus apartment during the summer. She never reported it to police or told Barnett about it. Even if it happened, as abominable as that would be, it would be ridiculously unfair and unrealistic to consider it part of his watch, especially when he wasn't aware of it.

There were flaws in the CU recruiting process, and they were addressed, including reforms that other schools adopted. There was an ugly incident at an off-campus party involving prospects on recruiting visits in 2001 that led to a lawsuit. None of it was as simple as the media coverage would have had you believe. Nobody at that party, including the hosts, was wearing a halo, and it's not "insensitive" or "blaming the victim" (if there was a victim) to point that out. It's also not insensitive to argue that the lawsuit against the university—and, by extension, against the taxpayers—that resulted from the party ridiculously stretched the parameters of Title IX, making it a catchall

---

* Although she ended up in the University of New Mexico football program, Hnida was not a good enough kicker to be on a Division I-A roster. I'm convinced that in the near future, a young woman soccer player is going to be a star college football kicker. But it wasn't going to be Hnida.

for any perceived transgressions against women. The lawsuit was thrown out, then reinstated and eventually settled because of fear of a runaway jury.

The same men and women who label stereotypes abhorrent see nothing wrong with buying into the jock stereotype, often not even noticing when it has racist undertones, as it did in the CU imbroglio. Crosscurrents were involved in the "sensitivity" issue, but what won out was the ridiculous conclusion that these horrible jocks routinely were running wild and maltreating women— and that it didn't involve the renegade actions of a few but was a program-wide plague and one of the condoned perks of being a CU football player. That was the tone of most of the city room coverage. I believe many of the writers involved in Colorado and national coverage unquestionably bought into every overwrought generalization about those who were talented enough to play major-college football. One reporter covering these issues told me he'd never allow his daughter to go to a university with a major football program. I'm pretty sure his attitude predated his coverage of the story. That's the type of prejudice we wouldn't allow in coverage of anything else; he would have been taken off the story. I assume that meant he would tell his daughter to turn down scholarship offers to attend not just Colorado, but also such terrible universities as Stanford, Duke, Northwestern, Wisconsin, Michigan, California-Berkeley, and Texas, among so many others. It reminded me of when the *Oregonian* ran an editorial about a college football funding issue that included this line: "What about those who go to college for an education?" To its credit, the *Oregonian* ran a rebuttal column written by my father's Oregon predecessor and mentor, Len Casanova, arguing that the editorial insulted the many former Oregon football players who had obtained degrees and gone on to productive careers in such endeavors as business, education, and law—or anything else. The equivalent argument could have been advanced—and still can be—for every football program in the country.

In the CU case, we repeatedly got carried away. My *Post* colleague Mark Kiszla, whose writing and work ethic I respect tremendously, wrote: "But it's pretty difficult to deny women have been served up like steaks on the football training table." There are several ways to interpret that sentence. Many reasonable readers drew the inference that Mark was accusing the coaches of acting as pimps. That was unfortunate.

Also, the Denver and Boulder papers never sufficiently criticized or scrutinized CU regent Cindy Carlisle for remaining on the board when her husband, attorney Baine Kerr, agreed to represent Lisa Simpson in that Title IX–based lawsuit. They emphasized that they separated their professional and personal lives and that Carlisle wouldn't vote on issues related to the lawsuit. That was laughably insufficient. As an alumnus, I was offended that Carlisle was in a position to indirectly reap the benefits of her husband's representation of the recipient of a major settlement from CU. As a journalist, I was embarrassed that we essentially shrugged about the obvious conflict of interest. Again, it was a double standard. The merits of the case aside, if Kerr had been representing an athlete suing the university, there would have been relentless examination of the Kerr-Carlisle connection, and Carlisle would have been forced to resign.

The media also let hapless Boulder District Attorney Mary Keenan off virtually scot-free for her ridiculous, agenda-driven statement that the CU football program used sex as a recruiting lure.

What is never brought up when discussing the slide of the CU football program, including during its struggles under Dan Hawkins, is that the Colorado media was culpable in unfairly tarnishing the image of the school and the program, and those effects still are being felt today. The assume-the-worst coverage lives on in Internet searches, and the conclusions drawn from it persist as myths in the minds of many.

It all showed that liberals are capable of virulent racism, cloaking it in sensitivity about other issues.

WE'RE SUPPOSED TO BE BETTER THAN THAT

SPORTS COLUMN WRITING can be a craft, involving storytelling, reporting, and versatility of approach. Now, not only is all of that undervalued, it's even discouraged. It's "boring." Today, Red Smith, the great Pulitzer Prize–winning New York columnist, would be told, "Get to the point! Give us opinion!" Jim Murray, the terrific *Los Angeles Times* columnist, would be told, "Those are nice lines, but where's the *attitude?*" Exaggeration and contrived controversy are the trends, and that approach is rewarded.

The explosion of cable television and the Internet has made all of that worse, because now more than ever, the goal is to attract attention in the crowded marketplace and draw as many online hits as possible—by any means possible.

Journalism is supposed to be better than that.

Unfortunately, those who try to treat column writing—and not just in sports—as a craft rather than a sideshow now are considered "soft." (Yes, I have been accused of that, so that's my axe.) Yet the best columnists make readers think, cry, laugh, and, yes, get angry—whether in a single column or, ideally, in columns of different approach throughout the week. They don't write one way; they vary their deliveries. When they seem angry or indignant in print, you know they *are* angry or indignant, because they don't try to manufacture it in every column. Some days, they take you places, tell you stories, introduce you to people. They're supposed to be the best writers on staff, and that calls for versatility—with broad-based knowledge, relentless inquisitiveness, and even a willingness to subjugate their egos and simply tell a story and enlighten when appropriate. If it produces fewer coveted hits online, it also produces more memorable columns that contribute to a writer's and a newspaper's credibility. It's too easy to write column after column that not only cover the obvious subject areas, but also involve the familiar stands.

(*Fire the manager! Bench the quarterback! Steroids are bad!*) That approach produces columns that could have come from fill-in-the-blank templates.

Columnists should be seen everywhere, not just in the press boxes at the games. They should show up on campuses and at team headquarters, not always because they're going to get a column out of it that day. It can be networking and establishing credibility with those we cover. There still are some columnists who do that, but their ranks are dwindling. It's a shame when columnists spouting off about college football coaches, for example, never have had an intimate, behind-closed-doors conversation with the coach they're ripping—or, even worse, are just doing it from the comfort of their homes without having been in contact with him for weeks.* I'm the first to admit—and I've even used this rationalization myself—that skyrocketing coaching salaries have changed the rules of the game; the intense scrutiny, high expectations, and considerable pressures are all part of the system that leads to coaches making ten times more than a tenured physics professor. But that doesn't excuse laziness. *Chicago Sun-Times* sports columnist Jay Mariotti drew the ire of White Sox manager Ozzie Guillen in Chicago for what Guillen perceived as cheap shots, but what was more interesting was that Mariotti's colleagues disowned him—not so much for what he wrote, but because he was such a phantom and minimally accountable.

"Provocative" is the buzzword, but what editors forget is that it can mean provoking something other than anger—including thought. But what we have now is an emphasis on melodrama and "strong stands," and those who are the most proficient have the ability to start with a reasonable thesis, work themselves into lathers as they write, distort that thesis as they go, and believe their exaggerations by the time they're done typing. Acknowledging that everything in the world isn't black or white and that there are gray areas enhances rather than diminishes the credibility of a column or commentary. But that's considered indecisiveness.†

Intelligent readers lose trust in the relentless desk-pounders. Once trust is lost, it's difficult to regain it. When they're tackling the occasional subjects that call for genuine outrage, or they're occasionally skipping the contrivances

---

* Almost all major columnists work out of their homes in this era.

† I mostly agreed with Jon Stewart's blistering assessment of the Crossfire format as "partisan hackery" and more theater than journalism. But I will say that staking out extremes in a back-and-forth television format—Hannity/Colmes, Novak/Kinsley, ESPN analyst versus ESPN analyst, or even Aykroyd/Curtin—tends to be accepted for what it is, and it can be more effective and credible than a contrived, extreme view standing alone in print.

and making a very well-reasoned argument, their impact is diluted. Even the reasonable columns can draw this reaction: *There he goes again. . . .*

True, some readers take the bait and make noise about the contrived extreme positions, most recently in the various forms of anonymous "feedback" that we shamefully not only allow but encourage. That gives editors the impression that those columnists are effective. Perhaps when judged in the context of a marketplace jammed with mindless reality shows, they *are* effective, if the only criteria is attention. Loudmouth writing and pandering to the lunatic fringe gets a lot of attention and even praise for "courage," but often it's actually gutless because it takes more courage to say that the loud bandwagon view is wrong.

I had considerable respect for broadcaster Howard Cosell, but it's amusing that although he disdained most sports columnists, his bragging motto ("telling it like it is") has become distorted as a rationalization for laziness in column writing. Any alleged strong stand, regardless of its justification, is said to be "telling it like it is," when it actually can be the opposite. It often is gutless and the easy way out.

Journalism is supposed to be better than that.

This is an outgrowth of my position about longer stories and narrative-style pieces, whether about conventional subjects or something perhaps a bit quirky. I'm in the minority here, but I also think that sticking to that high-minded principle, in all sections, would be a pragmatic business decision. Technologically, we—or the newspaper industry's techies, at least—have done an amazing job of adapting to the 24/7 news cycles and putting together Web sites, essentially by trial and error and on the fly. I marvel at how fast it has happened, and writers and editors have adapted to the need to get news online as soon as possible while still putting out a newspaper. Journalistically, though, we've botched the transition. In the name of "keeping up with the times," including the staggering improvements in communication technologies, newspapers have too enthusiastically lowered their standards and mimicked the "new media" with its fixations on such things as Britney Spears's travails. Newspaper competition has thinned, leading to many single newspaper markets, including in Denver, where the *News* folded in 2009. A better strategy than pandering to the lowest common denominator would be to emphasize the difference between traditional journalism and the new media by zealously maintaining—or reinstating—high journalism standards.

Consumers have hundreds of media alternatives today. If a newspaper mimics all the others, from the surprisingly good to the laughably amateurish or outright bad, it cannot claim to be more authoritative and credible than the other media, and we especially have no right to belittle the upstarts. The newspaper industry's survival depends on many things, but I'm convinced that it's crucial, especially for full-size broadsheet papers, to maintain that image of being better and more authoritative. We seem to be trying to imitate celebrity-driven Web media, but we never will be as "good" at that approach, and for newspapers, that's the worst of both worlds. If that's what consumers are seeking, they'll always find outlets better than newspapers for that kind of coverage. We also will be losing the discerning readers who give up on newspapers being above the inanity (and insanity, too). Yes, that's even true in sports coverage, because if we emulate the passionate amateur fans with blogs in the way we cover teams, we're not taking sufficient advantage of our access to coaches and players and seats in the press box.

Standards for filtering comment on newspaper stories posted online vary widely. The *New York Times* attempts to maintain decorum by moderating comments to ensure that what follows an online story amounts to more than drunks screaming at each other in a bar. In the *Denver Post* and other newspapers with lower standards, anonymous comments often make intelligent readers feel stupid or slimy for reading the paper (or at least the online version). Count on finding, among other things, racial stereotyping and mindless and predictable back-and-forth yammering from right and left wings. In any case, anonymity is a great enabler for idiots. Only the most tasteless is censored or eliminated, often after it has been online for a while. Many of the comments that remain online are, regardless of political affiliation or sentiment, moronic. In the newspaper buildings, Web-savvy young men and women with little understanding and appreciation of true journalism too often are making the decisions about online policies.

The inconsistency makes no sense. We have scrupulous standards, including sensitivity parameters, in the stories themselves, but below the stories, despite the requests to keep it civil, virtually anything goes. *And it's still the same site!* If the writers cross the line in the stories, their names are on them and they're accountable. There is little or no accountability at all in the commenting forums, short of programs that reject the words on George Carlin's list.

The articulate comments from either side of the spectrum come from folks who wouldn't mind standing behind them with their real names. It's true that sometimes insiders who are involved in an issue and who have intelligent viewpoints couldn't risk posting under their own names, but raising the bar for civilized dialogue would more than compensate for losing their input.

That's all bad enough. But anonymity has spread into the pages of the newspaper itself. We have the ludicrous contradiction of requiring not only real names on letters to the editor published in the editorial pages, but also phone numbers to confirm the identities, while in other parts of the paper, we routinely have comments attributed to, for example, "Spiked Punch." Again, even if the comments are intelligent, who's to say we didn't just make them up if there's no name attached to them? It's not a "dialogue with our readers" unless we know whom we're talking to and ask them to stand behind what they say with a confirmed identity. It would be easy enough to do that by charging a $5 annual fee for the right to comment online, under a full and confirmed name and city of residence, with the proceeds donated to charity. The quality of the discourse and dialogue would improve immediately, and the ripple effect would be noticeable. Intelligent dialogue begets more intelligent discourse.

In journalism, we used to be good at spotting those spouting off as the lunatic fringe and waving them off as unimportant. Now, we act as if those nuts are the most important voices on the planet. We react to them, giving them far more influence than they deserve, and pander to them.

I admit that not long ago, I tended to be disdainful of much of the new media, including amateur bloggers, writers for specialized Web sites, and especially those gadflies who haunt the message boards. I've come around. There are excellent amateur bloggers and excellent blog sites out there offering opinion but usually without the benefit of official access or accreditation. (Those who write under their own names and provide contact information immediately enhance their credibility.) If generalist newspaper columnists are simply spouting off from an armchair—or from a seat in the press box—without doing their homework, chances are at least one amateur with specialized interest has done a better opinion piece on that subject, even if it's an account manager writing on his lunch hour at the power company. That's the challenge. That's why it's so perplexing to see so many mainstream media columnists backing off from energetic exploration and networking, who see nothing wrong with becoming increasingly lazy after their reputations are established. Of course, many (though not all) of those with television or radio gigs write their columns almost as afterthoughts. But editors increasingly care more about columnists' celebrity status than the quality of their newspaper work.

There often is entertaining banter on message boards, including from those who remain anonymous. On some sites, the discussion can be high-minded, whether analyzing T. S. Eliot's *The Waste Land* or trying to devise constructive solutions for the Palestinian refugee problem. On others, it's mindless venom, but we don't have to visit those sites, and there is no expectation of quality.

We're supposed to be better than that.

The vast majority of intelligent readers, the constituency we should be seeking to retain, *wants* us to be better than that. But to varying degrees around the country, we continue to pander to that lowest-common-denominator mentality with breathless Twitter and blog updates about such things as which defenseman is going to be scratched from the hockey team's lineup that night, the cab ride in Detroit, the great catch on the sideline in practice, and the food in the Dallas press box. I know some writers, including some who lament the lowering of standards in the business, who seem incapable of functioning for five minutes without Tweeting or blogging. At national events, it's common to hear writers say, "Oh, I'm gonna put that in my blog!" after a mundane conversation about something such as the oatmeal in the coffee shop.

The more blog responses, we're told, the better we're doing in steering readers to the newspaper's Web site. Well, I could post a blog saying, "I think the coach should be fired. What say you?" That blog would generate many, many responses. But then I've become nothing more than a message board administrator. There are plenty of other outlets for that, even on the newspaper site.

We're supposed to be better than that.

Yes, it's our job to cover the news and also to uncover it. But some of it has gotten ridiculous. We have an entire generation of reporters, also outside of sports, who believe that being tipped off about what is going to become public knowledge shortly is a scoop, and they equate this with poring through piles of documents obtained through the Freedom of Information Act and then other tireless detective work to discover and document malfeasance. We're racing *ESPN*, *Fox Sports*, and other outlets—both television and Web sites—to claim that we "learned" something first. Sourcing? I'm not saying the standards should be as high as for coverage of national security matters, but in sports coverage, all you have to do is say the tip came from "a league source," (or even just "a source"), which doesn't enlighten readers one iota. Yet that's good enough, even if, as often is the case, the real source is one of the individuals in the story who had no comment on the record. When that happens, it's an out-and-out lie, but it's one of the staples of the business. I'd rather have us write what we know to be fact as fact than to indulge in that often disingenuous source attribution.* Unfortunately, that's becoming more common, and I'm waiting for a "crawl line" across the bottom of the screen that says, "The Steelers beat the Cardinals 31–27 on Sunday, ESPN's John Q. Broadcaster reports." Or for a newspaper story to begin: "Veteran quarterback Paul Passer threw for 337 yards and four touchdowns to lead New York to a victory over Philadelphia, according to multiple NFL sources. One source close to the teams confirmed the score was 24–17." Or for editors to suggest that we could save space in the paper and stay in tune with our readers by typing "u" instead of "you" and "r" for "are."

This is heresy, but I don't really care that ESPN.com "first reported"—by 78 seconds—that an offensive coordinator signed a contract extension, that Nick Saban is going to Alabama, or, for that matter, which outlet first had confirmation of Michael Jackson's death.

I was going to find out soon enough.

I'm loyal and I'm grateful, but this is different than a typical private sector employment situation, where airing disagreement with a company's policies and practices in public usually is considered disloyal. I'm idealistic enough to believe that public trust is involved, and that newspapers' very reasons for existence are rooted in that aforementioned concept that they can and should be a marketplace of ideas. Plus, in a business that thrives on scrutinizing and often criticizing public figures and policies and in a time when that criticism, especially in sports, is more acerbic than ever, thin skin in the newspaper industry is inappropriate.† This famous quote from *Post* cofounder Frederick G. Bonfils runs every day on the editorial page: "There is no hope for the satisfied man." That ideal isn't embraced everywhere; it still is in Denver.

I am thankful that sportswriting has afforded me a chance to write and to cover events in the United States and around the world, including Super Bowls, NBA Finals, Final Fours, World Series, Stanley Cup Finals, bowl games, championship fights, and Olympics. I am thankful that it has opened doors to the book business. I am thankful, too, that I have been able to meet, talk with, and write about people whose names might never be mentioned in print again, in small towns and big cities alike. What follows are glimpses of what I've encountered. I'll introduce you to such figures as Lieutenant Colonel John Mosley, a football star and Tuskegee Airman; a former small-time boxer, Oscar Smith, trying to get up from the canvas after the San Francisco earthquake; and Antonia Traga, who tended to her beloved wild

---

* Often, editors insist that some sort of attribution—however vague or even disingenuous—must be inserted.

† That's a fancy way of saying if we can't take it, we shouldn't be dishing it out.

cats as the Olympic marathon passed her by. Yes, the "famous" are in here, too. I make no claim to have chronicled anyone's career in biographic detail. Not even the careers of John Elway, Jerry Rice, Emmitt Smith, Patrick Roy, Lou Holtz, Nick Saban, Muhammad Ali, Matt Holliday, or any of the other prominent figures I came across.

I'm going to show you where I dropped in, and my perspective on it. It is a cross section, and I decided against including pieces on such obviously memorable events as Michael Jordan's incredible 35-point first half barrage against Portland—one of the two teams that passed on the opportunity to draft him—in Game 1 of the 1992 NBA Finals, where I was courtside in the Chicago Stadium, watching him shrug after hitting yet another three-pointer.

I'll bet you figured out the book title's meaning, but just in case, I often feel that the old joke about lawyers applies to my situation: I'm a sportswriter but don't tell my mother. She still thinks I play piano in a brothel.

PART TWO

PREDOMINANTLY ORANGE

When the Broncos switched to their Nike-designed, new-wave uniforms in the late 1990s, owner Pat Bowlen deflected some of the criticism about the switch to the blue home jerseys with the comment that the color scheme still was "predominantly orange."

The Broncos immediately won consecutive Super Bowls following the makeover, and maybe it was karma. They occasionally wear orange "alternative" jerseys now, in part because NFL Properties loves having additional lines to sell— including those generally horrific throwback uniforms teams often wore in the 2009 season.

I still consider orange the Broncos' color. Including on John Elway, whose two Super Bowl victories came after the redesign and color-scheme change.

Working Press
Main Box Second Level

SUPER BOWL
XXI

PRESS
ENTRANCE: GATE F

Auxiliary/Table
West/North Stands
Loge Level

343	10	14
SECTION	ROW	SEAT

SUPER
XXIV
BOWL

PRESS ENTRANCE:
GATE A
GROUND LEVEL   752

University of Northern Colorado
Athletic Field Pass

Event BRONCOS TRAINING CAMP

Date JULY 12-AUGUST 18, 1983

Authorized
Signature Charles Lee

THE ELWAY EFFECT

I N 2006, WHEN FORMER AVALANCHE goaltender Patrick Roy was about to be inducted into the Hockey Hall of Fame, the *Post* assigned me to select the top athletes in Colorado history. I tweaked the assignment and the list ran with the preamble describing it as a list of the "top twenty Colorado athletes who have had the greatest impact. The rankings involve gut-feeling judgments, admittedly variable definitions, and no right and wrong answers."

Roy was number 7.

Number 7 was number 1.

Virtually everyone with even a tangential connection to Colorado immediately knows what (and who) "number 7" is. That's testimony to the magnitude of John Elway's effect on Colorado sports—and, yes, even on Colorado in general. One irony is that Craig Morton, the quarterback of the 1977 Broncos, the team that had the most impact on Colorado sports, wore that number 7 during his tenure in Denver. But Elway took the Broncos to five Super Bowls—including three times his team had little business going that far. It would demean others on the roster and display ignorance about the dynamic of the sport to say he did it virtually alone. That said, this is the rare instance of a much-honored, much-revered athlete whose contributions, if anything, have been underappreciated.

Yes, *under*appreciated.

To this day, Elway has been *under*rated, if not as a quarterback, certainly as a difference-maker. Steve Young, or perhaps even a journeyman quarterback, could have stepped in sooner for Joe Montana, and the 1989 San Francisco 49ers still would have been one of the top teams in NFL history. Troy Aikman deserved the accolades he received, but those Cowboys teams of the early 1990s were so elite that it took the implementation of the salary cap to prevent a dynasty, and it's not out of line to wonder if they could have won with a decent-or-better starter taking the snaps. Yes, those San

Francisco and Dallas teams *won* Super Bowls, and it wasn't until the final two seasons of his career that Elway would hold the trophy up—and by then it was apparent that he was past his prime.

Yet this is the bottom line on Elway's career:

- He was indispensable and irreplaceable in the Broncos' rise to the league's elite level, and he took teams to Super Bowls after the 1986, 1987, and 1989 seasons that even in the uncapped era of the NFL never threatened to go down as elite teams. (And that would have been the case even if they had managed to win one of those games.)
- Despite some of the historical revisionist blather, Elway *still* caused his teams to overachieve in the Super Bowl championship seasons of 1997 and 1998.

On May 2, 1983, I was finishing up my first season as the beat writer assigned to full-time coverage of the Denver Nuggets. Denver had lost the first three games of the Western Conference semifinals to the San Antonio Spurs, and that night they faced elimination in Game 4 at McNichols Sports Arena.

The morning of the game, there was a major football story in the Denver papers, but it had nothing to do with the Broncos. On Sunday, May 1, at Mile High Stadium, the United States Football League's New Jersey Generals got a late 80-yard touchdown run from Herschel Walker and came back to beat the Red Miller–coached Denver Gold 34–29.* There was nothing in print or on the airwaves about the Broncos being on the verge of making the blockbuster trade that would so affect the franchise's future.

By that night, though, the big story was making the rounds, and amazingly it broke because a Houston radio announcer phoned a Denver sports talk show and said the Broncos were about to acquire the rights to Stanford quarterback John Elway, the first overall pick in the NFL draft on the previous Tuesday, from the Baltimore Colts. It's surprising that the lid stayed on that long, because the talks actually began informally before the draft and then more seriously the day of the draft. Still, Broncos coach Dan

---

* I was in the New York area for the Stanley Cup Finals and covered the May 11, 1982, news conference at Club 21 in Manhattan, at which plans for the USFL were unveiled. With former Broncos coach John Ralston doing much of the planning, the USFL was a sound idea that would have worked—if only the league had stuck to its original cost-controlled, spring-season model. Thanks, Donald Trump. You're fired.

Reeves showed up at the Nuggets' game and sat across from the benches and press row. He left the building during the game. Believe me, we noticed.

The Nuggets got 37 points from Kiki Vandeweghe and stayed alive in the series, winning 124–114. But my story ended up jammed into the bottom right-hand corner of page 1 of the sports section.

The Broncos held a 10:30 p.m. news conference at the team's Adams County headquarters to announce the trade and Elway's signing to a series of five one-year contracts. I was one of the few Denver reporters attending the Nuggets game who stayed behind at McNichols, only a few miles away from the Broncos' offices at the time. The game ended a few minutes before the news conference began. Broncos owner Edgar Kaiser, who lived in Vancouver, opened with these remarks: "What I'm not going to say is that we have a deal in the works. We have made a deal with Baltimore and we have signed John Elway." With the deal closed that afternoon, Elway took a flight from San Jose to Seattle, where he boarded Kaiser's private plane and came to Denver, and he signed the contracts shortly before the news conference.

"I'm definitely thrilled to be here," Elway told all those other reporters. "It was something I wasn't expecting to happen. I'm just glad to be playing in the NFL and glad to be playing for the Broncos."

It's universally remembered that the Colts took Elway as the first overall choice that year, after being warned against doing so. The Elway camp—including John's father, Jack—dug in its heels and re-emphasized that John would skip football and concentrate on his professional baseball career if the Colts took him.

What was underplayed was that it had nothing to do with Baltimore. Baltimore fans neither believed nor accepted that, but it's the truth. Although cantankerous owner Robert Irsay didn't help matters, his presence wasn't insurmountable.

Jack, and by extension, John, had little respect for the Colts coach, Frank Kush—and that might be the polite way to put it. Kush was not just out of step with the times with his military-discipline bent, but he was a detestable human being. Some of Kush's former players would be offended by that assessment, arguing that his belief that football was Camp Lejeune benefited their development as young men, but the fact of the matter was that he was not only inappropriate for college football by the 1980s, but he was also ridiculously out of place in the NFL. He was fired at Arizona State *during* the 1979 season because, ASU officials said, he was trying to influence players and coaches to clam up about what had happened in his dealings with punter Kevin Rutledge, who was suing the school for $1.1 million. The Colts hired him in 1982, and they promptly went 0–8–1 in the strike-shortened season.

Jack Elway was about to embark on his fifth season as the head coach at San Jose State, but he had been a fixture in the West Coast coaching ranks for many years, including at Washington State as an assistant and then at Cal State–Northridge as head coach. The West Coast coaching fraternity, at least among its veteran members, was a tight-knit group, and Kush was despised. Jack also had coached with Kush in an all-star game, and nothing he saw there changed his mind.

The Colts were bad, but it wasn't as if Elway could have expected to go to the Los Angeles Raiders, who had gone 8–1 in the 1982 season, or either January 1983 Super Bowl team—the Redskins or Dolphins. Part of the price of going first overall was the knowledge that you almost certainly would end up on a rotten team. The Broncos hadn't exactly steamrolled anyone in 1982, either, slipping from 10–6 during Reeves's first season to 2–7 his second. So it wasn't a case of the Elways manipulating the system to force a trade to a top team.

The great what-if was what would have happened if the Colts held their ground and insisted that if Elway wanted to play in the NFL, it would be with Baltimore. John had played one season of minor league baseball as a New York Yankees farmhand, with Oneonta of the short-season New York–Penn League, where he hit .318 in 1982. Given the extraordinary circumstances, and the likelihood that there would have been pressure and reasons to accelerate his advancement through the minor leagues if it could be at all justified, speculating on a time line is perilous. But I'll do it, anyway. It likely would have taken at least three more seasons for Elway to reach the major leagues, if he reached them at all. He would have been at least twenty-five when he joined the Yankees or whatever team held his rights by then.

Even if it had taken a year or two for Elway to relent, the Colts would have been better off waiting. But the Colts were the Colts, and Kush and Irsay were the types to urge the franchise to react with "to hell with him" petulance rather than pragmatism. The Colts caved. They sent Elway's rights to the Broncos for quarterback Mark Herrmann, tackle Chris Hinton (Denver's number 1 choice in that 1983 draft), and a future draft choice.

That summer, I was part of the *Post* entourage at Elway's first training camp at the University of Northern Colorado in Greeley. Only five and a half years earlier, the paper sent just a few writers to New Orleans to cover the Broncos' first appearance in the Super Bowl. Shortly after that, it became fashionable for papers to send armies to such major events if their local teams were involved. The champions of this approach were the *Boston Globe*, *Los Angeles Times*, and the Dallas papers, but the *Post* jumped into it, too, and we covered Elway's first training camp as if it were a major event at the top of the Nielsen ratings. With Greeley only an hour's drive away, that added to the temptation. In later years, when the *Post* was both admired and ridiculed for its major-event approach ("Geez, is there anyone back at your office? You guys doing a sidebar on every starter?"), I could look back and identify the Elway training camp as the turning point.

I was part of the *Post* mob coming at Elway in waves. Rick Reilly, Gene Wojciechowski, and Michael Knisley are now all with ESPN. David Von Drehle, then a part-time reporter attending the University of Denver, wrote a few stories coming out of the bullpen. He has gone on to cover, among other things, the White House for the *Washington Post* and to author, among other best-selling books, *Among the Lowest of the Dead*, a landmark look at capital punishment.* I spent several stints in Greeley, too.

When I started at the *Post* in late 1976, my father was coaching at Tampa Bay. He then spent three seasons with the Chicago Bears before returning to Denver to be Reeves's offensive line coach in 1981. After two seasons in that role, he went into scouting with the Broncos, a switch that eventually led to him becoming the team's director of college scouting and put him in roles he loved up until the day he died. But in 1983, the reality still was that I was a sportswriter whose father now worked for the biggest team in town, so we all knew that it could be awkward if I did too much on the Broncos. That didn't get me completely out of Elway's first training camp. I periodically was on the Elway Watch, too—and I mean that literally, because in addition to the stories and columns about him, we also did a daily boxed graphic called, yes, the Elway Watch. One day, after we sent in our stories, the office called us and pointed out we hadn't sent in the Elway Watch. I think I said that we indeed had forgotten about it, but there really wasn't anything else notable about what Elway had done that day. It was a slow camp day, in other words. But we were told that we still needed to turn in that box, so I wrote what I thought clearly was poking fun at the concept. Several of us contributed items, and mine was about what Elway wore to lunch. It ran the way I turned it in, and I never heard a word about it. The lesson was that in the era of overkill, there was no such thing as excess in coverage of the hot topics or big events. (Among all the meaningless detail, there rarely was one great story.)

---

* Dave did great work, but his best pieces in that period were his hilarious, in-house parody columns about the Denver sports scene and our coverage of it. He went to law school before getting into journalism full time.

Elway was one of six quarterbacks who went in the first round that year, and they would be forever linked as the Class of '83. The others include Kansas City's Todd Blackledge (number 7), Buffalo's Jim Kelly (number 14), New England's Tony Eason (number 15), the New York Jets' Ken O'Brien (number 24), and Miami's Dan Marino (number 27). Their careers were a mixed bag, but early on, they all suffered in comparison to Marino, an immediate sensation. Thrown in as the starter, in part because of the immense pressure on Reeves to do so, Elway struggled as a rookie, completing only 47.5 percent of his passes and throwing twice as many interceptions (14) as touchdown passes (seven). Veteran Steve DeBerg started five games in a 9–7 season that at least represented a recovery after the strike-year disaster. Meanwhile, in Miami, Marino took over as the Dolphins' starter from David Woodley for the sixth game in 1983, a 38–35 overtime loss to Buffalo, and never looked back.

Late in the 1984 season, when the Dolphins still were undefeated, I was sent to the Meadowlands for a Jets–Dolphins game. After the Dolphins won, remaining undefeated at 10–0, I was told to follow the Dolphins back to Miami. The Dolphins were playing the Eagles that week, and Ray Didinger of the Philadelphia *Daily News* nicely consented for me to join him for a prearranged Tuesday afternoon interview session with Marino.* The main thing I remember about this was sitting outside the Dolphins' locker room at St. Thomas College in the sun and realizing that the scramble to change my schedule and come to Florida was going to prevent me from voting in the general election and in the Reagan–Mondale presidential race. The Marino story ran in the paper the next morning.

Marino's success early in his career was especially pertinent in Denver because the natural question had been: if Marino—who mysteriously almost fell out of the first round altogether—could do it so soon, why couldn't Elway? By the time I was dispatched to do the Marino story, though, it was nearly a moot point because with DeBerg gone and Elway the undisputed starter, the 1984 Broncos had lost only once themselves—they were 9–1 on Election Day—and it seemed entirely possible that a Denver–Miami AFC championship game was in the offing.

One of the theories floating around was that Reeves mishandled Elway as a rookie by not allowing him to work his way in gradually. Dolphins coach Don Shula shot that down in his media session when I asked him about it,

---

* Those sorts of private sessions, especially for outside newspaper writers, are rare these days. It's catch-as-catch-can or get what you can at the star quarterback's appearances at the podium in the pressroom.

pointing out that Marino was starting by the sixth game of his rookie season, so it wasn't as if he had served a lengthy apprenticeship. But then he seemed to contradict himself, saying the wait enabled Marino to listen to the play calling and soak in a few things. "In talking to Dan Reeves, they felt it took a long time [for Elway] to learn what those numbers meant as opposed to learn the numbers, call the play, and know where everybody was," Shula said.

Marino told us it was a matter of perceptions. "The difference was the contrast between me and John Elway," he said. "He was the first player picked, and everyone expected him to play. I was drafted later on in that round, the Dolphins went to the Super Bowl the year before, so I guess the expectations were different for me. But I don't think of situations in terms of pressure. I don't worry about that."

That season, the Broncos finished 13–3 but lost at home to the Steelers in the divisional playoff round. The Dolphins then beat Pittsburgh in the AFC title game before losing to the 49ers in Super Bowl XIX at Stanford Stadium. Marino never played in the Super Bowl again.

By the end of Elway's career, of course, the Denver quarterback had been on two Super Bowl winners, Marino none. When nothing else is going on, an easy time-filler for talk show hosts is to say that a great player's credentials are incomplete until he wins a championship—or to say he can't even be considered a great player until he does. Most understand it's ridiculous to belittle Marino because his teams didn't win a Super Bowl. It would have been just as ridiculous to say the same with Elway if he had retired at thirty-five and finished 0–3 in Super Bowls.

Elway's critics distort the argument, saying he didn't win a Super Bowl until the Broncos were a more well-rounded team, including when Terrell Davis provided an elite running threat. That both implicitly underestimates Elway's contributions with the two title teams and actually buttresses the point that he was the indispensable element in the three teams that made the Super Bowl and lost.

Once again, the Broncos had good (but no more than good) teams during Elway's first three Super Bowl seasons—and Elway got them there. His strengths were varied, but the one I believe he doesn't get sufficient credit for was his ability to find a way to keep the play alive—sidestepping, scrambling, fighting off an arm tackle, or bouncing off a hit—until he could find someone open. There have been other excellent scrambling quarterbacks, from Fran Tarkenton on, but none with Elway's arm. His most breathtaking passes were those thrown back across the field, against the grain, after he moved around. Those are the perilous throws others couldn't get away with, but he could.

Here's an irony. The only Broncos' Super Bowl I've missed was Super Bowl XII. That was the one the 1977 Broncos lost to Dallas after giving the entire Rocky Mountain region that first-time, never-again-to-be-experienced feeling that wasn't ruined by the 27–10 defeat in New Orleans—or even by the realization that Denver was overmatched against Roger Staubach, Randy White, and the Cowboys. It was such a notable experience for the region, and it came in such interesting, pivotal times for the Denver market, I saw fit (with some encouragement) to look back on it and write '77: Denver, the Broncos, and a Coming of Age.

Elway wasn't infallible, the Broncos weren't a dynasty, and he was part of a few embarrassments. One was in January 1988, when the Redskins blew out the favored Broncos 42–10 on the strength of meteor-striking-earth performances from quarterback Doug Williams, who threw for 340 yards, and tailback Timmy Smith, who ran for 204. Denver's defense turned from decent to inept in the span of a few minutes, and the Redskins scored 35 points in the second quarter. Elway was only 14 for 38 for 257 yards, but the defense's collapse was the difference.

Elway's *worst* moments came in that 55–10 loss to the 49ers in January 1990 in New Orleans. For the third time in four years, the Broncos beat Cleveland in the AFC championship game to get to the Super Bowl. That's the game that's rarely remembered, in contrast to those featuring "The Drive" and "The Fumble." The Broncos simply rolled 37–21, with Elway throwing for 385 yards and three touchdowns. But even that day, they were confronted with the issue of whether it would be better *not* to make it to the Super Bowl again because the consensus was that they'd just get whipped again. The AFC had lost five consecutive Super Bowls at the time.

"Here we are going to the Super Bowl and not many people thought we'd be better than 6–10," Elway told us that day from the middle of the locker room at a time before the practice of sending quarterbacks to separate rooms and podiums after games became the norm. "It's great to win the AFC championship, but unless you win the next one, it doesn't mean a whole lot. We're going to be underdogs. We can go in and let it fly. We have to go in and have fun. We have to realize that, hey, you have to go to bat. Only one other team has a chance."

That was the one rout we saw coming.

George Seifert's 49ers dismantled John Robinson's Rams 30–3 in the NFC championship game and the San Francisco staff also had two weeks to break down the Broncos' defense.

In that Super Bowl, Elway, who was fighting a cold, had a horrible game. Before or since, I never saw him flinch in the face of a rush as he did that night in the Superdome, and for whatever reason, he never could get outside the pocket to work his improvisational magic. But even a superlative night from him would have done nothing but keep the score a little closer for a little longer. The organization had done a great job of rebuilding on the fly, given the considerable turnover since the Super Bowl loss two seasons earlier to Washington. Also, there was much criticism of the AFC as a wimpy conference, but during that season, the Broncos—with Elway's presence as the difference-maker on most Sundays—were as good as anyone on the second rung below the 49ers. Their five regular-season losses were by a total of twenty points. But then they ran into a great team that played its greatest game.

"You start questioning why we can't play better in the Super Bowl because we've played so poorly in the three times I've been out here," Elway told us in New Orleans that day, between coughs. "We're going to go back to the drawing board."

There was a seven-year span between Super Bowl seasons. The tension between Elway and Reeves became toxic. The problem there was that they were too much alike—exceedingly stubborn. Reeves, by God, had his ways, and as great of a job as he did during his Denver tenure, he wasn't flexible enough to suit Elway or for that matter a lot of others around him. I personally owe Reeves considerable gratitude for bringing my father back to Denver. His stubbornness in appropriate situations was one of his strengths; in others, it was his Achilles' heel. It certainly also affected his relationship with Mike Shanahan, eventually fired as offensive coordinator because of what Reeves considered insubordination and surreptitious plotting with Elway behind his back.

By the time the Broncos made it back to the Super Bowl under Shanahan, they had evolved. Behind the Alex Gibbs–coached zone-blocking schemes—often featuring the cut blocks so many in the league detested, then emulated—Terrell Davis was a marvel. Elway had decent running backs behind him in the past, including Bobby Humphrey, but never a difference-maker. Davis's speed, but more important his vision and judgment, made him the perfect complement. The offensive line was solid, and Rod Smith and Ed McCaffrey were the best blocking wide receiver tandem in the league. Offensively, at least, it was the perfect formula. Those who diminish Elway's importance in the two championship seasons are exactly right when they say that he wasn't capable of being as heroic as he was earlier in his career. To the Broncos' credit, he didn't need to be. Yet he was every bit as important in the overall picture as he was before because of his leadership and set-the-tone qualities.

I'm typical, I think, when I say the play I remember most from the breakthrough win over the Packers in San Diego was Elway's eight-yard run for a key first down. With the score tied 17–17 in the third quarter, the Broncos faced a third-and-6 from the Packers' 12. Elway scrambled to the right, decided to run, was hit hard, spun in the air like a helicopter's blades, and came down at the 4. The Broncos had their first down and Terrell Davis scored from the 1, two plays later.

That helicopter spin was John Elway's signature play. Not any of the across-the-field or long throws. Not the pass to Mark Jackson at the end of "The Drive."

After the game, in the middle of the field on the hastily constructed stage, Elway had to slam down the game ball, with smiling and heartfelt emphasis, to accept the Lombardi Trophy from Broncos' owner Pat Bowlen and hold it overhead. Elway's grin, the feeling of triumph, the latest moment of exultation with the world watching and a region celebrating, was fifteen years wide. It stretched back to when the Class of 1983 quarterbacks had fewer lines on their faces, when all of them were playing, when none of them owned car dealerships or were pitching home-equity loans or doing television analysis with network symbols on their blazers.

"This is indescribable," Elway told us a little later standing at the podium and wearing a Super Bowl championship T-shirt and hat. "You can't put words to it because you work so hard to get to this game and to finally come out as champs is unbelievable. Those were the ultimate losses and this is the ultimate win. This one erases those other three, no question. . . . There's been a lot of things that have come along with losing three Super Bowls and playing for fourteen years, and kind of being known as the guy who's never been on a winning Super Bowl team. The NFC–AFC thing, you take that for a long, long time. And all those things we've been asked questions about for the last umpteen years, well, that just makes it that much sweeter. It doesn't matter what happened before. This kind of wipes my slate clean. It doesn't matter that we've lost three now. We do have the one."

Elway's passing numbers—12-for-22 for 123 yards and no touchdowns—weren't great that day, but this was the reprise of The Drive: Elway stepped into the huddle with the Broncos and Packers tied 24–24, with Denver beginning a possession at the Packers' 49 with 3:27 remaining. It is one of those moments children dream about in backyards; as he had in Cleveland years earlier, Elway got to live it again.

"Everybody knew we had three minutes to go," Elway said, "and the thing is, I said, 'We need seven points. We can't afford three, we have to get this one in the end zone.' We were going to continue what had been working all day, and that was running the ball."

Elway got to celebrate a championship with Jack, by then a longtime professional personnel scout and executive for the Broncos.

"My dad's my hero and my best friend," he said. "To be on the same team and to accomplish this together, I can't put words to that, either. He's been my mentor and the reason why I'm standing here right now. He's the best and I'm just so glad he was there."

There was some talk at the time that Elway might retire on top. Well, he did retire on top, but he came back for another season.

The next year, the Super Bowl was in Miami, and it would have been a far better matchup if the Atlanta Falcons hadn't upset the Minnesota Vikings in the NFL championship game. But that did create an intriguing story line, with Elway and Shanahan going against the Reeves-coached Falcons. Elway's 80-yard touchdown pass to Rod Smith opened up a two-touchdown lead in the second quarter, and there was little doubt from then on, and the Broncos won, 34–19.

Against Reeves, Elway this time was 18 for 29, for 336 yards and one touchdown, was named the game's most valuable player, and even got to run for a touchdown himself on a quarterback draw called from the sideline.

"It was Mike's call," Elway told us with a grin. "But I liked the call."

The run put the Broncos ahead 30–6 and after he landed over the goal line guard Mark Schlereth fell on him.

"Hello, John," Schlereth said dryly. "How are you?"

Elway was pretty darned good, as a matter of fact. "He made me laugh," Elway said later as he stood at one of the Broncos' mini-podiums in the bowels of Pro Player Stadium.

In retrospect, I came to conclude that the sneak call on the goal line at that point was a "so-there" statement to Reeves by both Shanahan and Elway. But nobody would say that after the game.

By then, after back-to-back titles, it was even more pertinent to home in on the possible retirement angle in the aftermath. Before the official media sessions, I was interested to hear Fox's Terry Bradshaw interview Elway, this time in the on-field trophy presentation and celebration. It wasn't much of a secret that Elway had a long memory and still harbored resentment toward

Bradshaw because of Bradshaw's frequent negative comments about Elway, as far back as when Bradshaw—then still playing with the Steelers—blasted Elway for refusing to play for the Colts. Bradshaw asked Elway if he would retire, and Elway gave a noncommittal answer, an approach he repeated to us in the interview area a few minutes later.

Bradshaw was one of the few quarterbacks who led his team to two straight Super Bowl titles. The list: Bart Starr, Terry Bradshaw, Joe Montana, Troy Aikman, and then John Elway.

Would he return to seek an unprecedented third straight? That would surpass, among others, Bradshaw.

"I'm not even going to talk about that," Elway told us. "We'll cross that bridge later on. I don't even want to talk about retirement right now."

A few moments later, though, Elway said that the possibility of holding that Lombardi Trophy for the third consecutive year "definitely will go into the thinking, throw a kink into the thinking, about what I decide to do."

Elway was answering a question when a man in a gray and black polo shirt stepped unobtrusively to the side of his podium. Elway didn't notice him. The man waited patiently.

Finally, during another Elway response, the man stepped onto the platform as Elway spoke. Elway saw the man, but the identity of his visitor didn't register immediately. I'm guessing he assumed it was a league official, about to tell him he could go back to the dressing room and continue celebrating with the other guys in those championship hats and T-shirts. Those to the side of the platform, watching his eyes, could follow his reaction—and his surprise. He was face-to-face with Dan Reeves, who shook his hand, congratulated him, and said to give his best to John's wife, Janet, who had had health problems in the previous year.

There was no heartwarming storybook reconciliation between the quarterback and the coach who had been through so much—success, failure, exhilaration, and enmity—together. That happened a few years later. But at least they talked that day, Elway said thanks, and Reeves was gone.

One of the catches of winning the Super Bowl MVP award is the obligation to appear with the winning coach the next morning—early the next morning—at a wrap-up news conference, in this case at the Hyatt Regency in downtown Miami. Elway and Shanahan had been at the team's victory party in Fort Lauderdale, with Big Bad Voodoo Daddy playing, until the middle of the night. The *Post*'s Woody Paige and I had been at the gathering, too, and we didn't get much sleep, either, before going to the news conference together. The funny part about it this time was that Elway already was an automobile dealership entrepreneur in Denver, so giving him the choice of the Ford Mustang or the Expedition was like giving Bill Gates his choice between two free computers.

"I still feel like this morning's last night," Elway told us. "I haven't even had a chance to lie down and change days yet."

He again said he wasn't ready to make a decision.

"I said all week, I said this year, that there was a 90 percent chance I would retire," he said. "But the last thing I want to do is shut the door. I don't want to say I'm done and then get into April, May, or March, and say I can play one more year. I just want to take some time and do that and not close the door."

Elway said it "would be great to come back and three-peat. But also, it would be nice to walk away at the level that I'm playing right now. . . . I don't want to walk away too late, but I also know if I can play like I played [in the Super Bowl], I can play a little longer. There will be a bunch of different things that go into the decision, and it's just a matter of taking that time."

I was convinced that Elway would talk himself into playing one more season and going for that three-peat.

I was wrong.

He retired that spring, delaying the official announcement until a few weeks after the Columbine High School shootings in April 1999. The news conference was in a ballroom at the Inverness Hotel, and it would be the same room where Avalanche captain Joe Sakic announced his retirement ten years later at age forty. In retrospect, their reasons were similar: they both thought they could still play, but neither was certain he was capable of the full-time, year-round physical commitment especially necessary as players get older. In Elway's case, the consistent pain and the long recovery time between Sundays was the tiebreaker.

Elway's effect on Denver sports was the major reason for raised expectations and standards. By the time he was going to the Super Bowl, Denver had changed considerably from those wide-eyed, collegiate zeal times of 1977. The notion that Denver shouldn't even want the Broncos to go to the Super Bowl against a favored opponent because they might decisively lose was raised by some fans and media in January of 1990. Yes, the three previous Super Bowl losses had a lot to do with that, but it was interesting to think of what the reaction would have been in 1977 if anyone argued in public that Broncos fans shouldn't hope for a Super Bowl appearance because they probably would lose, perhaps even decisively. Elway's Broncos teams were part of a loss of innocence that also raised levels of cynicism across the board in the Colorado sports scene. Winning was expected and old hat, and falling short was to be derided.

He spoiled us.

But the Broncos' continued success and the unrelenting interest in and support for the franchise—it wasn't Orange Crush maniacal and naive, but it was as intense in other ways—kept Colorado in the national sporting spotlight, which probably was one of the factors that led Major League Baseball to finally award Denver an expansion franchise to begin play in the 1993 season. That seems a no-brainer now, but considering that Colorado periodically seemed on the verge of getting a franchise since—yes—1977, the wait was agonizingly long.

———◆———

At the memorial gathering following my father's February 16, 2001, death, Jack Elway was one of many who stood up and asked for the microphone. Jack told about how he and Jerry Frei always shared a golf cart and a dormitory suite at the Broncos' training camp in Greeley and hosted the informal staff happy hour each night. (Like at TGI Friday's, this happy hour could begin late and last until closing time.) Jack loved his Sky vodka; Jerry, who was seventy-six when he passed away, was partial to Black Velvet.

Jack said, "Every morning I'd ask Jerry, 'How many people do I have to apologize to?' And he always had a list ready for me."

At the Broncos, nobody had to use their last names, and they tended to be mentioned in tandem, so much so, that they deserved an ampersand.

Jack & Jerry.

They became close friends fairly late in life, although they had known each other for many years and their shared background as former West Coast college head coaches and their many common friends gave them a natural starting point for discussion. Jack came into the Broncos organization as a pro scout, evaluating and judging talent on other teams around the NFL, and eventually added the title of pro scouting director before retiring in 1999. Jerry was semiretired and working part time when Shanahan asked him to become director of college scouting and to groom his successor, Ted Sundquist, which he did for a couple of years before stepping back again and becoming a consultant. He couldn't walk away from the game completely, and he enjoyed the consultant's role, too.

When Jack and Jerry both were working during those years, they shared an office on the second floor of the team's Dove Valley headquarters, and other staffers became accustomed to hearing big band music—they were big fans of Rick Crandall's popular "Breakfast Club" on Denver's KEZW-AM—and laughter coming from the office. When they could, they took road trips with the Broncos and sat together in the press box. If they were in town for home games, they sat together in the second row of the Mile High Stadium press box or sometimes in one of the tiny coaches boxes on the front of the top deck. I sat with them one game, and while I prided myself in understanding football better than the average scribe, that afternoon reminded me that what I knew was minimal compared to what these two longtime football men knew. They'd both be reacting, positively or negatively, to what they saw as the Broncos came out of the huddle, and I'd be trying to figure out what the hell they saw.

Around 1997, Jerry—yes, this was my father, but it always sounds right to call him "Jerry" in any shared context with Jack—asked me to call Jack. I did. Jack asked if we could meet for lunch. At the restaurant, Jack asked if I would be interested in collaborating with him on a book. He noted that he'd had an interesting life in the game and had stories to tell. Jack was a funny and very intelligent man with a dry sense of humor, and I knew that his memoir—dating back to his high school coaching days and his climb up the college coaching ranks—would be fun to help write and certainly entertaining for readers. He did say that he understood any publisher would want him to write about his perspective on John's life and career, and he was fine with that. We quickly got an offer and even a proposed contract with Sports Publishing of Champaign, Illinois, and we were dealing with former University of Illinois sports information director Mike Pearson, the company's vice president of acquisitions. The advance money was minimal, and I considered my involvement as a favor to Jack and Jerry, as well as a potentially enjoyable experience because I knew I would spend a lot of time laughing during my discussions with Jack.

Jack had second thoughts, though, and we never signed the contract. It wasn't money, because if that had been the case, he would have told me— or an agent—to keep shopping the project to see if we could get a higher advance. I didn't press him, but I'm pretty sure he realized that his best stories had foils, and he might make some enemies. Plus, it might have made it awkward for John if he frankly discussed some issues, including John's relationship with Dan Reeves, who by then had departed the Broncos. At the time, I was putting the finishing touches on about the seventeenth draft of *The Witch's Season,** which had drawn some movie interest, and I hadn't yet completely accepted the fact that I would be better off turning to nonfiction

---

* *The Witch's Season* has been both a screenplay and a novel. The book finally was published in 2009.

to establish myself in the book business. So I wasn't at all heartbroken that the collaboration project fell through, just a bit disappointed that I didn't get to hear all of Jack's stories.

Jack Elway died on April 15, 2001. He was only sixty-nine years old. He had an apparent heart attack at his and Jan Elway's second home in Palm Springs, California. At Jack's service, Pat Bowlen noted that the organization had lost the two close friends only two months apart, and proposed a toast. We went to John's Cherry Hills home after the service, and John and I briefly talked about the mutual experience—and pain—we had gone through, but the memories we treasured. And about how lucky we were.

HAVEN MOSES: A MAN OF COURAGE

HAVEN MOSES CAREFULLY CLIMBED out of bed and thought of how much effort it would take to perform everyday tasks he previously had taken for granted. Getting dressed. Brushing his teeth. Walking. Everything.

He looked at his wife, Joyce.

"I wouldn't wish this on my worst enemy," he told her.

Joyce wanted to cry, but didn't. She couldn't. Haven's battle was just beginning.

As chronicled in '77: Denver, the Broncos, and a Coming of Age, Moses was quarterback Craig Morton's favorite big-play target during the Broncos' energizing first Super Bowl season. They became, and in Broncos lore always will remain, the M&M Connection.

When I began the book research, Haven was in the early stages of his recovery following a 2003 stroke and experiencing the daily challenges of not just his body but also his spirit. His left side still was severely affected. His frustration sometimes showed. We stayed in touch as the book's publication approached and then after it came out. His steady progress was heartening. Haven and 1977 Broncos head coach Red Miller appeared with me for a signing in Blackhawk, and Haven and I also signed books in an afternoon session at our Cheers-style hangout, My Brother's Bar in Denver's South Platte area. With good humor, the balding Haven took and even encouraged the teasing about how his hairstyle had radically changed since he sported an Afro on his football cards and in other 1977-era pictures.

One day, we sat down to lunch—okay, it was over beers—at My Brother's to talk. "It's that old saying, 'You've come a long way, baby,'" Haven told me. "I really feel blessed to be at the point I'm at now. Two years ago, if you had asked me that same question, I would have said I was fine but with reservations. The neurological damage certainly presented challenges about

Haven Moses has come a long way in his recovery from a 2003 stroke. Here, I'm having lunch with him at Denver's landmark, My Brother's Bar. Bartender extraordinaire Jimmy Hayde took the picture. *Source*: From the author's collection.

how I could function with my left side. What I was able to conjure up from sports—that work ethic that pushes you to know that you can get better at what you're doing—helped me tremendously. I have applied a lot of that to my rehabilitation, reading up on it to better understand what happened to me, and I've visited with a lot of people who suffered the same kind of setback."

The support he received from the public, as well as his family, was crucial.

"A lot of people continue to have that picture of me in the orange," Haven said. "That hasn't diminished any. This is another game for me. They're cheering for me again. I'm not going to let them down."

Haven had lost a lot of weight since the interviews for '77. He wasn't deteriorating; he was getting back in shape.

"People ask me if I have a therapist," he said. "I'm the therapist. I know my body better than anyone. I just do the things that I know are stretching my limits. When I walk, my pace is so much better than before. Going up stairs can be difficult, but I look for difficult things to do. I have to retrain my brain to work, so I even pick the hardest things to do in reaching and scratching."

Haven gradually lengthened his walks on the State Capitol grounds or along Cherry Creek. He pushed himself with considerable help, most notably from Joyce, and their two sons, Bryan and Chris.

"I had heard that it's so easy to quit," Haven said. "It's so easy to drop into depression and try to find blame and ask, 'Why me?' If I had broken a leg or arm or had a knee replacement, I would have had a better fix on this. But when the neurological issues and the disconnect from the brain came into play, all of a sudden I was at a loss. I know there are a lot of experiences in life that help us keep things in perspective, and I feel pretty good about my life and my relationship with my family and friends and this community. No, this hasn't been a pleasant experience, but it helps me to feel strongly about who I am as a person and what I can do. I wasn't going to allow it to change me in any way. The fact that I may have a limp wasn't that important. That's just physical. I'm still the same person I've always been.

"The support of Joyce was the key, because things like this can tear apart a family. With their help, I've really come to look at this as a positive, as setting up the next phase of my life, the fourth quarter of my life, which is going to be that much more special. I'm not going to be able to run any 'go' patterns anytime soon, but I had to make sure that my right side was intact and build on that foundation, and then begin working on my left side. It's fallen into place. The first four years, the only thing I could think about was not being as fluid or graceful and not doing the things that I took for granted before."

A few days later, I spoke with Joyce, who met Haven when both were students at San Diego State and married him in 1968.

"In all of this, his spirit has further transcended into my spirit," Joyce told me. "He's my hero, as well as a lot of others' hero. We've done a lot of praying and a lot of drawing on faith. We've been together a long time, since we were youngsters, and that's helped. We've been able to get through this through the grace of God and friends, and there never has been a moment where he's said, 'I can't do this.'"

The Hell's Kitchen–raised Jimmy Hayde is the day bartender at My Brother's and one of Haven's closest friends.

"There are mornings you don't want to get out of bed," Jimmy told me. "There are mornings you don't want to work out. Then you look at a guy like Haven, who could have rolled over and relied on his fame and renown here and have people take care of him. He's never stopped for a day trying to get better. And for a man who played the roughest sport on the planet, he is one of the kindest, gentlest, and most sincere souls I've ever known in my life."

Before the stroke, Moses was a regular at Lakewood's Fox Hollow Golf Course, where he became friends with the resident pro, Craig Parzybok. After the stroke, he didn't take a swing at a golf ball for four years. He finally returned to the driving range in 2007.

"I said if there was one place I probably would be comfortable, where I wouldn't feel self-conscious about how I looked, it would be there," Moses said. "I tried to pick a day when I didn't think anybody would be out there on the driving range.

"I took a couple of swings and I thought, 'I'll probably not do this again.' I sat down and looked over the driving range and reminisced about the way it used to be. I tried to comfort myself. And then I got back up and started swinging again. I used one hand. The other hand wouldn't release for me. But I kept working on it. I said, 'I can do this.' I had seen handicapped people play golf. I'd seen people with one arm play golf. That inspired me. Then I started making one or two shots, and it started firing me up."

Haven began playing full eighteen-hole rounds, mostly at Fox Hollow but without keeping score. He set his own standards—occasional good shots, redeveloping his touch, and getting the exercise.

"He will not give up," Parzybok told me. "It has been a long, hard battle for him, especially being a superstar athlete and being unable to do the types of things he could do. We all get older, and you and I can't do the things we could do when we were younger, but to have such a huge gap between being a wide receiver in the NFL and now just struggling to have normal functions, it must be very dramatic. And yet he keeps plugging away. He keeps working. He keeps trying. At least outwardly, he doesn't get discouraged. To talk to Haven, he's such a class act. He's just so warm with people. He's remarkable. He's absolutely an inspiration to me."

When he suffered the stroke, his speech wasn't affected. But the physical toll on his left side was unmistakable.

"When we went and saw him in the hospital, we didn't know if he was going to able to walk," Parzybok said. "Now to look at him and talk to him and watch him move, you can tell if you look real close, but to the average person, you see very little effects of the stroke. He does whatever he can to make everybody's day a little more enjoyable."

I also spoke with Tom Graham, the former Broncos linebacker who had played for my father at Oregon and is the father of Broncos tight end Daniel Graham. Tom was raised in Harbor City, California, and said he sneaked in to Harbor City Junior College games to watch Moses, the Los Angeles native, star there for two seasons before heading off to San Diego State.

"You had this guy with this huge Afro, and he was a bigger-than-life figure for us," Graham said. "When Haven was traded here from Buffalo [in 1972], I walked up to him and was looking at him as my hero. I told him, 'I used to watch you when I was a kid!'"

Graham burst out laughing and added, "Haven said some things to me that were not nice. But I finally met my hero."

Tom's admiration grew while watching Haven's recovery.

"He's still the same Haven," Graham said. "We hook up over at Stanley's Barber Shop, and when we get in there, we talk about each other for a minute and a half, 'Where you been? . . . You were supposed to call me. . . . Blah, blah, blah.' And then we sit down and really talk, and he's very positive. He struggled with this at first, but now he is very upbeat."

On his sixty-third birthday in 2009, Haven played twenty-seven holes at Fox Hollow—and kept score for the first time since his stroke. A couple of days later, as Jimmy Hayde and I waited for Haven at My Brother's Bar, we mused about what his score for the first eighteen holes had been. To make it interesting, Jimmy set the over-under at 86 and gave me my choice for a dollar.

When Haven arrived, he showed us his scorecard. He had shot an 87. I considered that as amazing as anything that happens in a PGA Tour event every weekend.

But I took Jimmy's dollar.

"O" LINEMEN: BREAKING THE SILENCE

FROM THE TIME TOM NALEN settled in as the Broncos' starting center in the late 1990s until his retirement in 2009, he was the enforcer of a silence-is-golden policy for the Denver offensive linemen. Veteran tackle Gary Zimmerman, who felt he had been burned by the media in Minnesota during his days with the Vikings, was the inspiration. Nalen was the one who tried to make sure the offensive linemen followed Zimmerman's lead, even after Zimmerman retired following the 1997 season, when the Broncos were celebrating their first Super Bowl championship victory over the Packers. It was a bonding experience, and part of the motivation was to collect fines for violating the policy to fund a postseason party. As time went on, several of the linemen didn't necessarily agree with the no-comment standard, and it never was quite as universal as some have portrayed it to be. Also, after games, league policy mandated that they be available for comment, even if the comment was monosyllabic or calculatingly boring. At Super Bowls XXXII and XXXIII, the Broncos' lineman had to speak at the mass media sessions as part of mandated league policy. When Roger Goodell took over as commissioner in 2006, one of his early mandates was that players must be available to the media. The linemen found it harder to avoid talking on the occasions media members bothered to seek comment from the men who opened the holes (or in the Broncos' case, created the seams) and protected the quarterbacks.

The funny part of all of this was that some of the linemen during the "silent years" were, and are, both funny and eloquent, as former guard Mark Schlereth has proven in his broadcasting career with ESPN.

When the Broncos released their fiftieth anniversary all-star team in 2009, Nalen, Zimmerman, Schlereth, and Matt Lepsis—linemen who joined the team in the nineties—were on it. Zimmerman was inducted into the Hall of Fame in 2008, and Nalen should be there someday.

Nalen came to the Broncos as a 1994 draft choice from Boston College, and he was a native of Foxboro, where the Patriots play. He settled in as the starter at center during his second season, made All-Pro five times, and arguably was the Broncos' best player for long stretches following Zimmerman and Elway's retirements. He left the Broncos quietly, officially announcing his retirement—via a team press release—after he sat out the 2008 season due to a knee problem. That followed his absence for most of 2007 with a bicep injury. He was the last link to the Broncos' back-to-back championship teams.

He decided he wanted to remain in the Denver area and coach—volunteering as an offensive line coach at the high school level. I caught up with him one day at Denver South High School after being assured by South head coach Tony Lindsay Sr. that he would convince Nalen to talk with me for the good of the program and for Denver Public Schools football.

When I arrived at South, the sprawling building just off of I-25 near the University of Denver, a player walking out to the practice field gave me directions to the dressing room.

I walked into the hallway and there was Tom Nalen, walking toward me.

I stuck out my hand and reintroduced myself.

"Now, Terry, why would you possibly think I would do this?" Nalen asked, not at all malevolently. "You know how I feel about those of your ilk."

I stated my case. I came to realize later that he probably already had decided to cooperate, but he wanted to make me squirm a bit. We talked at length, and then I watched a practice. One of the first things I asked him was how much weight he had lost, because he was noticeably leaner than in his playing days. He put it at "thirty, thirty-five pounds," and then added, "My joints feel better. My knee doesn't feel as bad. Then again, I'm not playing football and that might have something to do with it."

At one point as we talked before practice, a baby-faced lineman approached Nalen. "Coach," he said, tapping his sternum, "these pads just don't feel right."

Nalen lifted the player's practice jersey and began tugging, adjusting, and tightening the young man's shoulder-pad straps. Nalen looked at me and said he already had learned and accepted that such tasks come with the territory. He was coaching many inner-city young men who hadn't played football until they decided to give it a try at the high school level.

The player looked at me, nodded at Nalen, looked back at me and asked, "He's rich, isn't he?"

I dodged the question, saying that he wasn't making much as a coach.

He was making nothing.

Nalen's reward was the invigorating feeling he got from coaching young players at the Denver high school, which is a magnet for students for whom English is their second language—and Spanish isn't their first language. I heard many languages even in the parking lot and at the soccer, cross-country, and football practices on the fields behind the school. The most common language of the boys on the cross-country team, for example, was an African dialect.

Nalen began working with the Rebels, under Lindsay Sr., in early 2009, with the eighth-grade team in a "futures" program sponsored by the Broncos and the NFL.

"We had an awesome eighth-grade team, and most of those guys are out here now," Nalen told me. "I've been telling people that after those three months, I feel like I wasted fifteen years of my life in the NFL and feel so much better about where I'm at as a person, contributing to society as opposed to playing football."

I was surprised that he had to talk his way into the unpaid job and that other high school programs around the Denver area could have gotten him but didn't step up. Perhaps other coaches didn't believe he was sincere or would have felt threatened by the presence of a former Broncos star. But after his retirement, he and his wife, Denise, and their three children were committed to remaining in the Denver area. He began contacting area high school coaches, making it clear money was no object, because he didn't expect to be paid.

"I didn't want to be a head coach," he said. "I just wanted to coach the offensive line."

The initial responses were lukewarm.

Bronco tight end Daniel Graham intervened after Nalen told him of his desire to coach in the Denver public school system. Graham had played for Lindsay at Thomas Jefferson High. He told Nalen to give his old coach a call. Nalen left a message for Lindsay, and the South coach confessed to me that he thought it was a joke and didn't return the call. The next call was from Graham, and Lindsay laughed as he related the rest of the conversation.

"Coach, did Tom call you?" Graham asked. "He said he called you!"

"Tom who?" Lindsay asked.

"Tom Nalen."

"So that really *was* him?"

Lindsay and Nalen quickly reached an agreement.

"Last year, I started thinking about it, and for some reason, I wanted to coach in the DPS," Nalen said. "The coaches seem to have a lot more authority here as opposed to the parents in the suburbs. Maybe it's [that] you eventually can become a mentor to some of these kids and make sure they get to college."

At practice, Nalen sounded like a veteran line coach. At one point, he hollered, "I want him driven out of here! Out of here!"

To one player, he talked about what kind of initial contact he wanted. "I don't want *that*," he said, demonstrating one move. "I don't want *that*," he said, showing another move. "I want *that*!" he said, demonstrating that initial "pop."

He also painstakingly went through blocking scheme "calls" on certain plays, a concept that seemed Greek to some of the Rebels.

"These kids are learning, I'm learning," he said. "A kid came up to me yesterday and said, 'You know, I wish you would explain more things.' I think I go too fast and expect things a certain way, and I know I need to slow down a bit.

"Some of these kids aren't used to working hard. Some of them are. Some of them are great kids that know what's going on. But there are some kids who need some prodding, and I'm going to provide that for them and teach them to be accountable. As offensive linemen, I don't think they've grasped the concept yet of communicating with each other, working with each other, and those lessons go on for all your life. I hope I can accomplish that by the end of the year."

What else was he doing?

"Nothing," he said. "Mowing my grass. Pulling weeds. I mean, my kids aren't in school yet, so it was three months with them, and that was fun. It's been awesome not having football."

Nalen said this coaching position wouldn't be a brief interlude.

"This *is* a job for me," he said. "When people ask me what I do, I say I coach football. Regardless of what level it's at, this is what I do. I'm pretty jaded with the NFL right now. I love my family, I love spending time with them, and college and the NFL is not the place to be if you want to spend time with your family. It's too much of a time commitment, and I'm not ready for that.

"This is something I want to do. I told the freshmen, 'Learn these [blocking] calls, because until they fire me, these are going to be your calls, so you better learn them.'"

Nalen said he couldn't envision himself as a head coach, though. "Oh, God, no," he said. "Tony has to put up with a lot of stuff. I respect what he does. It's a big headache for the head coach and I don't want headaches now."

So Nalen was committed to remaining a position coach. And would his linemen be allowed to speak to reporters?

"I hope they get an opportunity to talk to the media," Nalen said. "I hope they're doing that well. But if the chance comes, there's no way they're talking."

The Rebels had their best season in years in 2009, going 6–4 overall and finishing fifth in the ten-team Class 4A West Metro League. They beat Green Mountain, Adams City, Lincoln, Denver North, Denver West, and Kennedy. In the final game of the regular season, they fell to my alma mater—the defending 4A state champion Wheat Ridge Farmers—56–13 and didn't make the state playoffs. But Tom Nalen and the Rebels did themselves proud, and I imagine that would have been the case even if the record hadn't been as good as it was.

———

At least I recognized Nalen.

In September 2009, a couple of weeks after talking with the former Broncos center, I waited for Matt Lepsis in a Starbucks in Southlake, Texas, near Dallas–Fort Worth International Airport. A tall, lanky guy approached the front door. I thought, *Could this be him?* He waved. I didn't want to respond too demonstrably, in case it wasn't Lepsis and he was waving to someone else behind me.

It *was* Lepsis, the ex-Broncos tackle.

He was listed at 290 pounds in the eleven-season career that ended when he walked into Mike Shanahan's office on December 31, 2007, and said he was retiring.

"I'm about 245," Lepsis told me after we shook hands and he sat down. "I got down to about 235 a month ago, but once I got back to school, I was busier. In the summer I ran every day, three miles a day, and that really helped me to lose weight."

Lepsis was not proud of his reliance on recreational drugs during part of his final season in the NFL, but he was proud of his life since. He and his wife, Shana, and their two children moved in 2008 from Castle Rock to the Dallas area, where Matt was raised in the suburb of Frisco. He enrolled in the nondenominational Dallas Theological Seminary and hoped to receive a ThM degree—a master's in theology—in 2012 or 2013. He had no vocational goal when he enrolled, but he has started to consider starting his own ministry, becoming an ordained pastor, or serving as a chaplain in sports.

"I've learned there were a lot of things I was given, a lot of abilities I was given, that I kind of took for granted and used kind of loosely in a lot of ways," he said. "I learned that God forgives us for things like that. He's ready to accept us with open arms if we give him a chance. It's definitely been the craziest two years of my life. I sit in class and every day I'm in there, at some point I stop and I just kind of laugh to myself. I'm in a seminary! You know? I just can't believe it, and I still can't. So, yeah, I've had a radical transformation."

John Hessler roomed with Lepsis at the University of Colorado and has been through considerable adversity after suffering brain injuries in a 2003 automobile accident. After his accident, Hessler told Lepsis that he had come to accept what happened because God had a plan for him. When Lepsis went through his religious conversion, Hessler told Lepsis that God had a plan for him, too. Hessler jokingly asked Lepsis to hurry through the seminary so he could officiate at Hessler's wedding, but they settled for Lepsis being a part of his former roommate's wedding party. "He's made a great turn in his life," Hessler said.

Kicker Jason Elam, Lepsis's mentor and confidant during his transformation, continued to follow Lepsis's transformation after leaving the Broncos and signing with Atlanta before the 2008 season. "Matt was kind of the last person you'd expect to go the direction he has," Elam told me on the phone from Atlanta a few weeks before the Falcons released him. "You felt like he wanted nothing to do with God. He wanted to do what he wanted to do. It was just kind of the way Matt was. Since I'm a Christian, it's always exciting to see some step away from the things they were doing and see things the way we really think they are."

Lepsis played tight end at the University of Colorado, where he and Hessler shared a Boulder apartment with linebacker Matt Russell, who became the Broncos' director of college scouting in 2009, and quarterback Koy Detmer. "He was very laid-back," Hessler said. Lepsis was painfully shy and uncomfortable around people he didn't know.

The future NFL tackle had a beat-up little blue car his roommates made fun of, and they went to Hessler's parents' home in Brighton to get their laundry done. Lepsis went to the Broncos' 1997 camp as a free agent but sat out that year, the first of Denver's two consecutive championship seasons, with a knee injury. He was a backup on the second title team. From 1999 on, he started all but one game until he suffered another season-ending knee injury in the sixth week of the 2006 season.

"I had taken painkillers and I had done other drugs in the past, but this was different this time," he said. "I'd always used alcohol in any kind of social setting to allow me to relax and be able to talk with people. That turned into popping a few Vicodin and then drinking, and then popping more Vicodin and drinking, but it all stemmed from my insecurities in social settings."

As the 2007 season approached, he said, "I started doing some other stuff and I found that it really, really helped me with [insecurities]. It was like medicine made for me. I thought I had found the answer to all my problems. It got its hooks in me big time."

Lepsis told me what drugs he used but asked that they remain off the record. But if you're guessing, you're probably in the ballpark. He played high in the first three games of the 2007 regular season—against Buffalo, Oakland, and Jacksonville.

"I would like this to help people who are going through this, but what happens with people who do drugs, it's, 'Oh, he's doing that, he's not doing this,'" he said. "I would rather just not say, not because I'm embarrassed to say it or anything like that, but because I think it would have a negative effect on some people I would like to help through my story."

Lepsis said he first would get high before meetings on days the team didn't practice. "I'm back there going 'Blah, blah, blah,' talking away and laughing," he said, meaning that it was uncharacteristic of the shy tackle. "Nobody noticed. So I wondered, 'Can I actually get by in practice? Can I actually play when I'm high?'

"I was high all the time because I loved what it was doing for me socially. I loved what I thought it was doing even for my marriage. I was able to communicate with my wife a lot better. I thought, 'Well, maybe it will make me play better.' So I got high before a practice and practiced. I didn't get yelled at, I didn't make many mistakes or anything, and I thought, 'Maybe I can do this.' So I did it before practice a few more times and practiced while I was high. The next step was, 'I'm going to try this in a game.'

"If we had a road game, I would bring it with me and do it in the hotel before we got on the bus to go to the stadium. At home, I'd be in the parking lot at the stadium and do it then. Before, other than game day, I would do it as soon as I woke up in the morning, and I would try to continue that all day long if I could, depending on my schedule. It had totally taken over my life for sure, in a short period of time."

He watched film and decided it wasn't affecting his play. His opinion changed during the 24–13 loss to Jacksonville in the third game.

"I started thinking about a million things at once right before the snap," he said. "After that game, I decided I was never going to mix this with football again." He didn't stop using drugs immediately. "Just not for the games," he said.

Lepsis was adamant that none of his teammates were aware that he was practicing and playing high and that he knew of no teammates doing the same thing. He said the only ones who knew were his wife and "one or two close friends" who weren't teammates.

Early that season, Lepsis was in his yard, playing with his son, Hayden, then five, and daughter, Jordan, then two. "I was on top of the world," he said. "I felt like this [drug use] was the answer to a lot of my problems. I was having a great time and starting to open up to people."

His cell phone rang. He discovered nobody was calling him, but his phone was playing a Dave Matthews song, "#41." "It was the part of the song that said, 'The difficulty is coming,'" Lepsis said. He had the song in his extensive collection on his phone, but he would have had to get past a keyguard to play it. He said it struck him as weird but nothing more.

"Then a couple of days later, we're getting ready to play a game, and I'm in my locker and listening to music," he said. He went to have his ankles taped and came back and heard music coming from his earphones, which surprised him because he believed he had turned it off. He said he put on the earphones and heard, "The difficulty is coming."

He was high at the time.

The next week, as the Indianapolis game approached, Lepsis and his wife were on the way to a friend's thirtieth birthday party. His phone vibrated. It wasn't a call. It was music. The same song. The same line. "The difficulty is coming."

"Not only is it playing the music," Lepsis said, "but on the cover of my phone is the album 'Crash.' So it says 'Crash' on the screen and I'm freaked out. Someone's trying to tell me I'm going to die in a crash."

The team flight to Indianapolis was coming up, plus he also had arranged for a chartered plane to take him and his wife to the Los Angeles area for a Dave Matthews concert the next week.

At the birthday party, he told the small group of his concerns. The birthday girl told him to stop worrying, that it was silly. He said she told him, "God's in control of everything. If it's your day to die, it's your day to die. If you're going to die in a plane crash, you're going to die in a plane crash. If not, you're going to die some other way. Stop worrying about it."

Lepsis said, "It was the first time I started to even put God into the equation."

He thought of telling Shanahan that he couldn't take flights to games and of the reaction that would trigger. He told several teammates he was starting to think about God and that he might talk with Elam on the trip to Indianapolis. Under Shanahan's assigned seating, he always sat near Elam. The kicker said he got a hint when Tom Nalen told him, "Wait 'til Matt gets on the plane. You're in for it."

Lepsis approached Elam and asked if he could sit with him, not just near him. He said he told Elam, "I don't know why I'm talking to you right now, but I'm freakin' out. I feel like maybe God is trying to get my attention or something." He didn't tell Elam about his drug use, just about his confusion. At the end of the flight, Elam suggested that Lepsis attend the team chapel on the morning of the game. A local pastor conducted the service and delivered a sermon about fear. "It was like the guy was sent there for me," Lepsis said. "Everything he was saying was happening in my life. I'm blown away."

The next week, he said, he told Elam about the drugs and tried to rationalize his drug use, saying it had made him a better person, before adding that he wanted to "become a Christian." Lepsis said Elam showed him Bible passages that indicated Christianity and drug use shouldn't mix.

"I just tried to listen a lot and be a friend," Elam said. "I asked him some questions, to make him think about some things. I think he knew the drug thing was wrong, but he was trying to justify it. But I have to say it didn't take much, just a few questions, and he was, 'You know what? You're right.' It wasn't me so much as it was making him step back a little bit and look at it in a different way."

At home, Lepsis talked to his wife, updating her, and then walked into his closet, closed the door, got down on his knees, and prayed. He said the prayer went something like this: "I feel like you're pursuing me, I want to do this, but I'm having a really hard time with what I'm doing. So if there's any way you can somehow give me what I'm getting from the drugs and give me what I'm looking for, I need your help."

He said that the next day was the first time in a month when he hadn't gotten high in the morning and that he had a "horrible" practice. Shana told him not to give up, and he went in the closet and prayed again. He felt awful again the next day, and a couple of younger linemen sat next to him and asked him why he was talking with Elam so much.

"In the middle of sharing with these guys what I felt God was doing in my life, it was like God right at that moment answered my prayers," he said.

"I knew at that moment that the feeling that I got from sharing with those guys was the same feeling I'm getting talking to you. . . . I was thinking, this is how God is going to help me to get over the drugs, to get over the issues—all the issues."

Sharing his story was a natural high.

In the next few weeks, he read several books Elam recommended. He stopped using drugs.

On the morning of the October 29 *Monday Night Football* game against Green Bay in Denver,* Lepsis showered in his room at the hotel where the Broncos stayed the night before home games. "The whole time I'm in the shower I'm praying for all my family, for my friends, saying, 'God please show them what you've shown me,'" he said. When he got out of the shower, he saw the word "Jesus" on the mirror.

"Somebody had written this before and the steam brought it out," he said. "Shanahan was superstitious. I stayed in room 4060 at the Inverness Hotel for eleven seasons. I'm sure a maid who was a believer wrote it on there, but what are the odds after I'd been praying at that moment, in the shower all this time—and still at that point I could count my number of prayers on one hand—that it's there on that mirror at that moment?"

Lepsis said he had an awful 2007 season. "I was feeling my age [and] two knee surgeries," he said. "I got called out three times by Shanahan. I'd never been called out by him before in eleven years. Never. I was trying my hardest. I just couldn't do it. I wanted to do it, but I didn't have it to give."

The day after the final game, against Minnesota, he thanked Shanahan for all he and the organization had done for him but said he was retiring. "He wasn't shocked," Lepsis said. He assumes that if he hadn't retired, he might have been released or at least asked to accept a pay cut, since he did have nearly $10 million and two years remaining on the deal.

"I get in the car and I'm like Jerry Maguire, yelling and singing Tom Petty and pumping my fists, driving," he said. "All of a sudden, *ba-ring, ba-ring,* my phone's ringing and I look at it and it says, 'December 31. Freedom has arrived.'" He had forgotten that at the start of the season, he had set his phone to go off with that message at noon on the day after the final regular season game. He said he "wanted to start crying when I was driving."

Soon, he decided he wanted to attend a seminary and started checking around and heard about the Dallas Theological Seminary. He took a trip to Israel with former teammates Dan Neil, Tom Nalen, Jason Elam, and Ben

---

* It would have been the same night as Game 5 of the Red Sox–Rockies World Series at Coors Field, but Boston finished off the four-game sweep on Sunday.

Hamilton. The tour leader had attended Dallas Theological Seminary, as well. Shana Lepsis also had become a Christian and supported the move to Lepsis's home state. They bought a home in Southlake. Lepsis began attending classes in 2008, and he started passing along his message in isolated public appearances.

"The number one thing, obviously, is their salvation through faith in Christ," he said. "But it's also that God can help you through things. If you put your trust in God and put your trust in Christ, he can help you through these things. He helped me through it."

His second point: "In our society today, it's like making a lot of money, being famous, that's all there is. You've got that, you've got it made. I tell people, no, some of my happiest days in my life were when I was living in a two-bedroom apartment with Koy Detmer, Matt Russell, and John Hessler, in the same room with beds pushed together because we were getting $300 stipends a month.

"I'm telling you, the fame, the money, is nice. I'm not saying it's not nice to have and I'm not saying it's inherently evil, but it easily can become what you live for."

He doesn't subscribe to the belief that his current stance excuses everything in his past. "A lot of people will share their testimony in church and say, 'I was in a Harley gang and killed people for a living and I found Jesus and now I'm perfect,'" he said. "That's not the case at all, obviously. I still struggle every day."

When Lepsis got the word that he was selected as one of the tackles on the Broncos' fiftieth anniversary team, he was both suspicious and sheepish.

"I was at school and [Broncos executive] Jim Saccomano had called and told me, and I went, 'Is this a joke?'" Lepsis said. "He told me that Gary Zimmerman and I were the first team tackles. I thought this has got to be wrong. I don't know a whole lot about a lot of the tackles who played before me, but I do know I played with Tony Jones and he was one of the best players I've ever seen at the position."

Lepsis also joked that after eleven seasons of being Nalen's teammate, he felt even more awkward to be honored.

"I think a lot of this comes from Tom Nalen, who's beating me up on this whole thing," Lepsis said. "And not only Tom, the whole offensive line mentality of Denver that you are not to be proud of anything you do. Which is good. It's good and it's bad. If you're just beating yourself for no reason, it can be a double-edged sword, I think. So when I heard that, I didn't tell anybody, because that's not what we do. Bronco offensive linemen don't tell anybody about any accolades they receive. My brother called and told me, 'I just heard you were named to some all-star team with the Broncos,' and I said yeah, and he said 'What's up with that?' I said it's wrong, first of all. Tony Jones deserves to be on that list way before me."

Jones, though, played only four seasons for Denver, from 1997–2000. Lepsis was with the Broncos' organization from 1997–2007.

The irony of all this, given Lepsis's comments?

Nalen was on the fiftieth anniversary team, too.

———— ◆ ————

I first spoke with Mark "Stink" Schlereth at the Super Bowl buildup in January 1992 in Minneapolis, when he was with the Washington Redskins and had just been selected to the Pro Bowl for the first time. In the years since, or at least after he lifted the curtain of silence and became an analyst on ESPN, I've spoken with him many times when serving as a radio cohost. I gained even more respect for him when I was helping a remarkable young man, Columbine survivor Patrick Ireland ("The Boy in the Window"), with his memoirs. Patrick told me that Schlereth and Dan Neil were among the first athletes to visit him after the April 20, 1999, shootings, and I was at the Denver studio with Patrick in 2009 when he taped a segment for ESPN's *Outside the Lines*. Schlereth also appeared to eloquently express his admiration for Patrick and assert his belief that the story of Columbine is now one of recovery and community support, not of tragedy.*

I sat at Schlereth's table at one of the two game-week sessions in the Redskins' New Orleans hotel.

Schlereth was a University of Idaho lineman from Alaska. In Anchorage, the youth football opportunities were few, but Schlereth used the game as an outlet for frustrations. Schlereth's classmates would tease him, often turning mean, about his reading problems. Later, specialists determined he was dyslexic.

"When you're young, it's very embarrassing being made fun of like that because you can't read," he said. "We'd be playing football and I'd just point somebody out and run over him. That was all you had to do. You didn't have to throw any punches, and if he had to go to the nurse's office, he got hurt playing football."

He could read, but with great difficulty and without great speed. He told me he received a degree, with a B-average, at Idaho after reading only one book, and he scouted out professors who loved to lecture.

---

* Patrick's recovery from his wounds has been miraculous, and despite a bullet fragment still in his brain and slightly impaired physical movements, he is a success in the business world.

"Teachers would say 85 percent of this course is on the notes, 15 percent is the book," he said. "And I'd say, 'Well, I'm going to be in class every day because I hate to read.' I would try and listen and focus and take my notes and know that if I aced that part of it, I'm going to have a B."

When he was in college, his knees already looked like a road map of Europe with scars both old and new. He and his wife, Lisa, had a son, Daniel, and a daughter, Alex. (They later would have a second daughter, Avery.) Most of his Idaho coaches begged him not to play his senior season. By then, he had had six knee surgeries and one elbow reconstruction, so his coaches were like fight managers, begging the heavyweight to let them throw in the towel and end it before he really got hurt. He played anyway.

In the spring of 1989, the NFL scouts were coming to the Idaho campus to take private looks at Marvin Washington, a Vandals defensive end who ended up with the New York Jets. "I'd go up there with Marvin and say, 'Hey, can I run for you; can I do the test for you; will you take a look at me?'" Schlereth said. "It's no sweat off those guys to time one more guy in the forty, or do one more guy in the bench test, and if they find a sleeper, they get a pat on the back. They were very cooperative."

For his size—six feet three, 285 pounds—Schlereth was fast, agile, and strong. He wasn't unknown to the scouts because all of that had been in the computers for a couple of years, along with notations about his operations, but these private predraft workouts gave many of them cause to look at him again. They'd go to the Vandals' offices, look over the game tapes once more, and say, "well, maybe."

"Out of the twenty teams that expressed interest that way," said Schlereth, "eighteen of them took the next step of looking at my medical records and saying, 'Don't call us, we'll call you. Good meetin' ya.'"

The Redskins took him in the tenth round of the 1989 draft, which probably means somebody suppressed his medical records—or the Skins decided they had reached the "what-the-hell" point of the draft.*

Schlereth was a starter by the end of his rookie season and entrenched by the time I talked with him at that Super Bowl. He also was a curiosity as the league's first Alaska-born player.

"It's not like I'm from Mars or anything," he said. "But it's kind of funny. When I first moved to the East Coast, I guess I was as naive about being on the East Coast as people are about Alaska. There's always the dogsled

---

* By 1994, the draft was cut back to seven rounds, so by today's rules, Schlereth wouldn't have been drafted at all.

questions and the igloo questions. I envisioned the East Coast as New York City, up and down, everything. I didn't think I'd ever see another tree."

We never got to the igloo question.

Schlereth signed with the Broncos as an unrestricted free agent in 1995 and started on both Denver Super Bowl championship teams. By the time he played in the second of Denver's back-to-back winning bowls (and fell on John Elway in the end zone) in Miami in January 1999, he was up to twenty-two operations. There at one of the interview sessions, I laughed when he showed off by rattling off the names of the surgeons for all but his kidney stone operation. "I haven't had a lobotomy yet," he said. "That's coming."

So what kept him going?

"Stupidity," he said. "Pretty much every morning, I wake up and I say, 'What am I doing playing this game?' But I just love playing it, I really do."

He talked of the linemen's kinship, whether in collective silence during the regular season or any other time.

"For us, it's just important for us to go out and play hard for one another," he said. "Every guy in the room feels that. If I needed help at three o'clock in the morning from any of those guys, I wouldn't hesitate to call, and I think they feel the same way about me. There's a special relationship there, and it doesn't matter who plays beside me, that's just how we operate as an offensive line."

Schlereth played through 2000 before physical problems forced him into retirement. He now spends much of his time traveling back and forth from Denver to ESPN's Connecticut headquarters or to watch son Daniel pitch.* His "Mark Schlereth's Stinkin' Good Green Chile" is a major hit. Because of his frequent television and radio appearances and his recurring role as Roc Hoover on *Guiding Light* before the soap opera's cancellation, it's fair to say that "Stink's" profile is far higher than when he played.

---

* Daniel played at the University of Arizona and for the Arizona Diamondbacks before going to the Detroit Tigers in a trade following the 2009 season.

PART THREE

COLORADO CHARACTERS

Many times, I've been struck by the richness of Colorado sports tradition and regretted that so many of the state's transplants—and I'm one of them—for whatever reason generally have limited knowledge of it. I've greatly enjoyed exploring it, and that includes such experiences as the "Bell Game" between Pueblo Centennial and Pueblo Central, the oldest high school football rivalry west of the Mississippi. When I put together that highly subjective list of the twenty men and women who have had the most impact in Colorado sports,* it nudged me to explore even more, including when I decided to figure out just how tightly connected to Colorado famed boxer Jack Dempsey really was. I've also served on the Colorado Sports Hall of Fame selection committee, which has broadened my horizons and knowledge, too.

I've realized that history is being made every day.

---

* The top twenty: John Elway, Jack Dempsey, Byron "Whizzer" White, Floyd Little, David Thompson, Randy Gradishar, Patrick Roy, Joe Sakic, Rich "Goose" Gossage, Hale Irwin, Earl "Dutch" Clark, Alex English, Larry Walker, Amy Van Dyken, John Stearns, Walter "Bus" Bergman, Dave Logan, Peggy Fleming, Bobby Anderson, Frank Shorter.

Denver Nuggets

1983-84 WORKING
MEDIA PASS
NON-TRANSFERABLE

Denver Nuggets

TERRY FREI

Issued To: _____

Organization: ___ DENVER POST _____

No. 178   _Tom Holmen_
                 Authorized Signature

DENVER
NUGGETS

1999-2000
Denver Nuggets

MEDIA

TERRY FREI
DENVER POST

ACCESS TO: PRESS ROOM,
HOME VISITING LOCKER ROOMS,
PRESS BOX

21

"Chopper" 1932-1999

This Pass Does Not Guarantee A Seat And Is Not Transferable.

Denver Nuggets

1984-85 WORKING MEDIA PASS
Full Season

NON-TRANSFERABLE

Denver Nuggets   NBA
Issued To:_____ Terry Frei _____

Organization:_____ Denver Post _____

Number:_____ _Tom Holmen_
                 Authorized Signature

CHOPPER, THE BIG STIFF, AND THE NUGGETS

A FTER THE DENVER NUGGETS ADVANCED to the Western Conference finals against the Lakers in 2009, Doug Moe—a coaching consultant under head coach George Karl—got a lot of face time on the national television broadcasts. It was noted that he was the Nuggets coach in 1985, the last time they had gotten that deep in the playoffs—also against the Lakers—and that the "retired" number 432 banner hanging from the Pepsi Center rafters represents the number of Denver victories during his 1981–1990 tenure as head coach.

Moe himself represents a period when the Nuggets were refreshingly different, from the bellowing coach on the bench, to the self-taught character named Chopper hustling in his role as trainer and traveling secretary, to a cast of players that didn't always win, but usually managed to put on a good show.

I was fortunate enough to be part of the traveling circus.

After the NHL Rockies were sold and moved to New Jersey in 1982, I was told I would be switched to the Nuggets beat. (More on my Rockies adventures later.) I immediately was sent to Coronado, California, for the NBA meetings. Unfortunately, some of the first stories I had to work on involved confirmation that Nuggets star David Thompson had a cocaine problem and that the team had hired an off-duty police detective to follow him around and document it, apparently in an effort to void his contract. Thompson was traded to Seattle and eventually got his life straightened out, and he was the last athlete with a drug problem I ever felt sorry for.

Chopper, the Nuggets' renowned trainer and traveling secretary, was Bob Travaglini. The beat writers—Kevin Simpson covered the team for the *Rocky Mountain News*—traveled with the team on commercial flights, so Chopper handled lining up our boarding passes and checking our luggage. One of

In the days I covered the Nuggets, the media still was on press row, next to the Denver bench—and within earshot of the entertainment provided by Doug Moe and the caustic comments from trainer "Chopper" Travaglini. Here, I'm watching a game with (to the right of me) Kevin Simpson of the *Rocky Mountain News* and play-by-play broadcaster Jeff Kingery of KOA Radio. Simpson later became a *Denver Post* colleague, and Kingery switched sports to become the longtime voice of baseball's Colorado Rockies. *Source*: From the author's collection.

the first things he told me was, "Piss me off, kid, and your bag's in Taiwan." One of the next things he told me was that because I liked greyhound and, especially, horse racing, there would be cities in which he would "ask" me to rent a car so we could go to the track. Often, center Dan Issel, Chopper's close friend, would join us.

But that's getting ahead of myself.

I enjoyed being around Moe from the start. He had been a victim of a 1961 basketball betting scandal. During his senior year at North Carolina and after completing his four seasons of eligibility for the Tarheels, the scandal broke and Chancellor William Aycock threw him out of school. "Suspended" was the polite word used, but the message was unmistakable. Moe was in negotiations with the NBA's Chicago franchise. But the NBA blackballed him. Over $75. This was a decade after a point-shaving scandal involving thirty-three players and seven schools,* which had rocked college basketball, so all were conscious of the potential problem. A gambler named Aaron Wagman met with Moe, the Brooklyn native, in New York in the summer of 1960, offering him money to throw games the next season. Moe said no. His mistake was accepting $75 in expense money and failing to report the bribe attempt. The meeting had been set up by a UNC teammate.

In the eyes of the NBA, in the eyes of Chancellor Aycock, and in the eyes of much of the public, Moe deserved condemnation.

"I thought I was making a pretty good deal," Moe told me. "Here I had turned him down cold. He said, 'This is for your trip back to school, whatever.' I said, 'Sure, great.' I figured I had turned him down."

When an ambitious New York district attorney, Frank Hogan, got into the act, Moe's name was dragged through the mud. Tony Jackson of St. John's didn't report a bribe attempt because, he said, he thought it was a joke. He was blackballed, too. Connie Hawkins of Iowa suffered the same fate. The players weren't indicted. The gamblers involved were. None of that prevented Aycock from summoning Moe to his office and telling him that he was being tossed out of school.

"He gave me some very good advice," Moe said. "When something happens to you, you can react to it negatively, accuse people, whatever. He said he was doing his job, that I shouldn't do anything bad, regardless of how I felt. The papers interviewed me, and I said the chancellor was doing his job, he felt he had to suspend me, that he was right."

The NBA followed suit. Because Moe and Jackson hadn't reported the contacts listed in the indictment, the league shunned them.

"It was a very difficult time," Moe said. "My whole life was basketball. It was hard to adjust. That's where my personality helped. I screwed up, I was a happy-go-lucky guy, and I guess I didn't realize that some people round Carolina thought I might have done something."

Donnie Walsh, who later coached with Moe and now is the New York Knicks' president and general manager, was Moe's teammate at North Carolina. "We knew it was all totally B.S.," he told me. "We knew Doug, we played with him. I remember when the chancellor threw him out of school. The students marched on his office."

Moe ended up finishing school at tiny Elon College, and he was shocked—and chalked it up as part of a lesson—that Chancellor Aycock told Elon officials that Moe should be admitted.

---

* The seven schools: City College of New York, Long Island University, Manhattan College, New York University, Bradley, Kentucky, and Toledo.

"'The president of Elon said, 'What did you do to the chancellor?'" Moe said. "I thought, 'Oh, shit.' But then he said, 'I've never got that good of a recommendation from anybody. He was going on and on.' You know, earlier it might have been easy to say the chancellor screwed me. When something like that happens, you can look for excuses. When things aren't working out right for you, instead of blaming someone else, maybe you should look at yourself and find out if it might be partly your fault."

Moe was at Elon for two years, finishing his degree and serving as assistant coach for the basketball team. After playing four years at North Carolina, he still had much work to do before getting his diploma at Elon. "I used to tell people that Doug was so lazy, that if they were handing out A's at the administration building, Doug would ask one of us to go over and pick them up for him," Walsh said.

At Elon, he started taking school more seriously, at least during certain times of year. Moe's photographic memory impressed a history professor for the first part of a term. But then the professor noted a change and called Moe into his office. Describing the meeting, Moe adopted a prim English accent, "'Mr. Moe,' he said to me, 'you had a Harvard A in my class, but then basketball season started and your interest began to decline.' I said, 'If you think it's that way here, you should have seen me before [at North Carolina].'"

Moe went to Padua, Italy, and played there until the American Basketball Association opened shop in 1967. He was one of the upstart league's top scorers for five seasons, and he and Hawkins—another ABA star—sued the NBA and settled out of court. "I got to finish school at Elon, and playing in Italy [with Padua] in 1965 and 1966 were the two best years of my life," Moe said.

Walsh got letters from Moe from Italy. "He used to send us clippings, and the headline would say, 'El Grandioso Moe,'" Walsh said. "And he was the best. Compare him to Jerry West, Oscar Robertson, all those guys. That was about the same time Bill Bradley went over there, too, and I knew Doug was better than Bradley. That was heresy then. Then the ABA got started."

Moe said he might not have returned to North America to play in the ABA if his sons, Doug Jr. and David, hadn't been approaching school age. "The ABA was great, a lot more fun than the NBA," he said.

When Moe was the head coach at San Antonio, before moving to the Nuggets as first an assistant and later head coach, he took note of his coaching brethren sending out Telexes telling where they could be reached on Draft Day. Moe sent out a Telex saying he would be on the ninth tee. "That might have been the best one I've ever done," he said, chortling. "Naturally, some of them thought it was true."

When I covered the Nuggets, Moe seemed entrenched on the bench, coaching a highly entertaining passing game that called for constant movement from all five players, both with and without the ball. The image was that the Nuggets, who led the league in scoring, did it with classic fast-break basketball, but that was inaccurate. Rather than the conventional, fill-the-lanes running game, the Nuggets relied on fast pace in a half-court offense. You rushed the ball up the floor, you passed, and you moved.

Although the Nuggets had a bombastic coach, attention-getting style, and three of the league's top scorers in Alex English, Dan Issel, and Kiki Vandeweghe, Bob Travaglini was as well known as any of them within the league itself. Skycaps and bellmen on the circuit could quickly tell how he had done at the tracks so far on the trip. If he had run out of tip money, they knew the horses or dogs he had bet on hadn't come in.

He already was a legend when he came to the Nuggets. The most famous story involved a plane trip when he was with the Virginia Squires of the ABA. Al Bianchi, who was the Squires' coach at the time, told me about it, and I was originally skeptical, but I received confirmation from others who were there and swore it really happened.

Bianchi said that the Squires rushed to the gate at the Pittsburgh airport but discovered that the plane already had pulled away. Chopper ran out of the terminal door, through the snow, in front of the plane. Travaglini got the pilot to stop and let the Squires' traveling party climb up the stairway in the tail.

"The pilot asked me if I was crazy," Travaglini told me. "I said no, I just had twenty people I had to get on the plane."

Chopper always had a scheme going. He was a throwback—an uncanny, gravel-voiced, hyperactive, self-educated survivor in an era of licensed therapists.

A New Jersey native, Chopper was a quality control inspector for Chrysler and a volunteer trainer at a Catholic high school before he became the trainer for the Philadelphia Bulldogs of the Continental Football League in 1961. Bob Brodhead, the Bulldogs' quarterback, went on to become the athletic director at Louisiana State. "Lo and behold," Brodhead told me, "here enters the Mandrake the Magician of trainers. He was amazing."

Chopper worked for the Squires and baseball's minor league Tidewater Tides in the early 1970s and was a full-time resident of the Admiralty Hotel in Norfolk. Most visiting teams stayed at the Admiralty, and his room became the gathering place for card and craps games as well as conversation. The games of chance, he said, were "nothing big," but there was another reason he didn't worry about a raid. Some of the rollers were policemen.

When he had a persistent sore throat, Travaglini worried he might have cancer. Dave Rosenfield, the Tides' general manager, and team director Marvin Lucas called Chopper's doctor, who told them that Travaglini was healthy. Rosenfield and Lucas put a "rest in peace" wreath in Travaglini's room and a dead fish on his pillow. "You talk about a guy being mad," Rosenfield told me. "He sent me a cement block of the Mafia's Black Hand. To get back at Marvin Lucas, he went to a different florist every day. He sent two dozen red roses to Marvin's wife every day and billed it to Marvin."

Bianchi hired Travaglini to work for the ABA's Washington Capitals. The franchise moved to Virginia but remained financially troubled. Dave Twardzik was a Virginia guard. He said Travaglini told the players to "cash your check at one bank and hurry and deposit it at another." One night at the Chicago airport, Twardzik said, broadcaster Marty Brennaman teased Travaglini about "saying one thing about the owner, Earl Foreman, to his face, another thing behind his back. Chopper exploded. He had one hand around Marty's neck and I thought he was going to kill the guy. Al had to come over and separate them."

Larry Brown, a Capitals' guard in Travaglini's first year, brought Travaglini to the Nuggets in 1976. In an ironic twist, Chopper was diagnosed with throat cancer early in his tenure with the Nuggets but went into remission. As he had at Virginia, Chopper moved into a hotel in Denver, this time at the Holiday Inn–Sports Center, the round high-rise next to Mile High Stadium and within walking distance from McNichols Arena.*

He defied convention by treating racing greyhounds on his training table. It's wrong to say he also watched them race. Although Chopper was a regular at Mile High Kennel Club (in addition to all the tracks on the road), he didn't watch Mile High races live. He would go to the bathroom or walk around, then check the tote board after the race and flip through a thick stack of mutuel tickets to find the winning one to take to the window—if he had one. Chopper spread out his wagering on each race, and he was known to hold tickets on a two-dog quiniela that paid $200 for a $2 bet and still lose money on the race.

With the team still traveling on commercial flights, he pulled enough travel strings to qualify as a puppeteer. He held court in his second office, the Three Sons Italian restaurant on Denver's North Side. He tirelessly promoted a "magic potion" analgesic, Flexall 454, and unfortunately didn't retain his financial interest in it. Against largely younger competition, he was the ace pitcher for the Nuggets' slow-pitch championship softball team.

---

* It's now the VQ Hotel.

Above all, he inspired incredible loyalty from players. When Julius Erving, who began his career with the Squires, made his retirement tour stop in Denver, he presented one of his championship rings to Travaglini in the pregame ceremony. The close friendship of Issel and Travaglini was unique in professional sports. Off the court, Issel had two hobbies: horse racing and "arguing" with Chopper. On the court, until the day he retired as pro basketball's number five career scorer, Dan had two tricks. One was his pump fake. The other was remaining on the floor after getting knocked down during televised games to get his trainer camera time.

Chopper deserved it, and he made covering the Nuggets even more fun.

Early during my time on the beat, Lakers coach Pat Riley, whom Moe despised (almost as much as he did the pompous Hubie Brown), caused controversy when he announced he was closing practices to the media. Until then, practices traditionally were open. The NBA office and the NBA Writers Association tried to fight the trend, but it turned out to be spitting into the wind. Moe's practices remained open, which during the time of a newspaper war in Denver meant that Kevin Simpson and I had to be at the practices from start to finish, out of self-defense. If something bizarre happened and only one of us was there, the writer present had a huge exclusive and the unfortunate absent scribe might be covering Regis College lacrosse the next week. When we jokingly asked Moe to follow Riley's lead and close practice, which would have meant that we didn't need to be there until they were over, Moe's response was derisive. "If I have to watch this shit, you do, too," he told us.

At practice one day, he climbed to the top of the Regis Field House bleachers, put a bag over his head—in homage to frustrated fans of the New Orleans "Aints" and to the Gong Show's "Unknown Comic"—and sat down.

"You better cut a nose hole in that thing," yelled Issel, "or you'll suffocate."

I spent a lot of the time at practices talking with Gus, assistant coach Bill Ficke's five-year-old golden retriever. Now, NBA coaching staffs seem as large as playing rosters. There are about eleven guys in suits on the Denver bench attempting to look indispensable as they hold clipboards and perhaps tell the television interviewers at halftime that the Nuggets need to hit the boards harder. During the 1983–84 season, Moe had one assistant coach— Ficke, a former Air Force man who owned an athletic shoe store and was one of Moe's best friends. Bill knew basketball, but even he admitted he was an unconventional hire. Ficke brought Gus with him to practice, and the dog— the son of a Westminster Kennel Club champion—was well behaved on the sideline. Moe and Ficke were inseparable on the road. Once, they decided they both wanted to lose weight and were going on a chicken-only diet on one extended road trip. One afternoon, I joined them in the hotel coffee shop, where the waitress brought them order after order of baked chicken. The famous wrestler Andre the Giant couldn't have eaten as much chicken as Doug and Bill that day. On their "diet."

During my two seasons on the beat, the Nuggets went 45–37 and then lost to San Antonio in the second round of the 1983 playoffs, and then went 38–44 and fell to Utah in the first round in 1984.

With the Big Three—Issel, Vandeweghe, and English—piling up the points, the Nuggets were highly entertaining.

Vandeweghe was from a wealthy family—his father, Ernie, played for the Knicks before becoming a physician, and his mother, Colleen, was a former Miss America—but he almost always wore athletic shoes, gold corduroy pants, a white cardigan sweater, and his UCLA letter jacket. In October 1982, he lost his head and donated the white sweater—by then notorious—to a charity auction to benefit the Special Olympics. He had second thoughts, though, and approached auctioneer Ron Zappolo, the local sportscaster, and bought it for $500 before it could be put up for bid. "It's the only sweater I have," he told me. "What could I do? I wouldn't have had anything to wear the rest of the year."

The Nuggets' deficiencies on the boards and on defense had less to do with Moe's push-the-pace passing game than it did with the fact that Issel was trying to play center with a power forward's body and that the silky English and Vandeweghe were virtually incapable of getting physical inside. To this day, I'm convinced that English—whose number 2 also hangs from the Pepsi Center rafters—is the most underappreciated athlete in Denver professional sports history.

Moe had learned to carefully pick his spots to get on English, whose pride bruised easily and whose game deteriorated when it did. He was one of the "quietest" prolific scorers in NBA history, gliding and flashing around until the scorebook had him for 30 points in the third quarter. His teammates called him "Pink," after the furtive Pink Panther cartoon character. Away from the arena, he wrote poetry that tended to make even the most worldly readers blush, and his first collection was published in my first season on the beat. "I feel like my stuff is pretty good," he told me. "A lot of people appreciate it. If it became a Book-of-the-Month Club selection, I'd be just as thrilled as making the All-Star game. My poetry is the way I see life."

The ringleader in any shenanigans often was Glen Gondrezick, who came from Boulder and then was a star on Jerry Tarkanian's first Final Four team in 1977 at Nevada–Las Vegas. He constantly engaged in games of one-upmanship with Chopper. He exasperated Chopper by coming down the luggage chute once; after all, Chopper was in charge of keeping these guys in line while making all the arrangements with the airlines. During training camp in Alamosa, Chopper once returned to a completely empty hotel room. Gondo had removed every bit of furniture, including the bed. And the verbal barbs never stopped coming; as tough as Chopper was, when he got in wars of words, he often got frustrated and sputtered and stuttered.

The most memorable events of my tenure on the beat didn't always involve anything on the court, and that included being snowed out of Denver for Christmas in the great Christmas blizzard of 1982.

The Nuggets beat the Detroit Pistons 135–127 in the Pontiac Silverdome on December 23. Snow started falling in Colorado late that night and forecasters were calling for ten to sixteen inches of accumulation. At the Northfield Hilton near the Silverdome, Chopper checked with United and was told that it looked bad in Denver but that since the flight was scheduled to land early—9:15 a.m. Mountain time—we might beat the worst of it. We left for the airport at 7:00 a.m. Eastern time.

Moe was a nervous flyer under the best of circumstances. Walking from concourse to gates, he would ask flight attendants and pilots coming the other way how the flight conditions were—and he really wanted to know. He tested the seatbelt regulations on every flight, because he couldn't relax enough to stay seated, and he often stood in the aisle and talked with anyone, whether a player, reporter, or accountant from Sheboygan. On this Christmas Eve in Detroit, he was the first off the bus. He charged into the terminal, looked at the screens and as we caught up with him said, "Canceled! I knew it." Stapleton was shutting down.

Chopper and an agent at the group counter tried to sort out the alternatives. Vandeweghe decided to go to Los Angeles. Issel headed off to meet his family in Kentucky. Backup center Rich Kelley got on a flight to Phoenix. Soon, the party was just eight players, Moe, Ficke, Travaglini, and six members of the media, including radio play-by-play man Jeff Kingery, later the longtime radio voice of the Rockies baseball team, and television analyst Irv Brown. We left the airport and checked in at a Detroit airport hotel. Next, Chopper ordered us to meet in the lobby at 2 p.m. The plan was to head to Chicago, spend the night there, and then go on to Denver on Christmas morning.

At the baggage claim area in Chicago, a television news crew was doing a story on travelers stranded at O'Hare because of the storm in Colorado and Wyoming. Gondrezick eagerly talked with the reporter on camera.

At the O'Hare Marriott, where Chopper set up a "Snow Central" command post at a desk in the lobby, we watched the five o'clock news. The curly-haired guy was identified onscreen only as "GLEN GONDREZICK, DENVER." (For all Chicago viewers were told, he could have been a carpenter.) "I was planning on spending Christmas at home," he said. "I'm disappointed. I had a brother coming in from L.A., and he didn't make it into Denver, either."

The players had Chopper paged, and Gondrezick identified himself on the phone as another United official and told Chopper he could only guarantee the Nuggets four seats on the first flight out the next morning. After Chopper told the other players the news, they interrogated him about which four he would send first. As Chopper hemmed and hawed, their laughing gave them away, and they confessed to the joke. Chopper might have been just going along with it, but if so, he did a great job camouflaging it.

Chopper called us all in our rooms shortly after midnight. (No, the bar was not open.) He told us there was no way the Denver airport would reopen until at least Christmas night, so he had canceled our wake-up calls and we could sleep in.

On Christmas morning, Moe had gotten word that because of the weather, neither Denver paper had published that morning. Moe greeted Simpson and me with a cheery, "I loved your stories today! Best ever!"

Our Christmas was card games involving players, coaches, and media members; meals in the hotel coffee shop; and two movies at nearby theaters. Moe went to both movies with us—*The Verdict* in late afternoon, *Tootsie* at night. Moe had seen *The Verdict* before and recommended it, but he took a nap during the show. His explanation? "I can't ever sleep in the room or on planes," he said. When the group gave *The Verdict* thumbs-up, Moe gloated, saying, "You have taken the recommendation of the world's greatest movie critic." (Doug always thought he should be the third wheel on *Siskel and Ebert*.)

I recall the card games as a bit like "Tegwar" or "The Exciting Game without Any Rules," in the baseball novel and movie *Bang the Drum Slowly*. The rules were what the game's organizers decided they were at any given time. I don't remember if I claimed my losses on my expense account.

Finally, Chopper told us we were booked on a 10:10 a.m. flight to Denver on the next morning.

At O'Hare the next morning, the scenes at the gates for the Denver flights were chaotic, with travelers from two days of canceled flights begging to get out. Chopper procured boarding passes, and we didn't ask how. "Guard these with your lives," he said. "They'll kill you for one." As we pulled away from the gate, the pilot congratulated us—"you lucky 254 people."

When we landed at Stapleton, Denver, which had recorded 23.6 inches of snow in a twenty-four-hour period with high winds, it was still a mess. Chopper approached a tour bus driver, flashed bills, and soon was waving us onto the bus. (Nobody asked if this was prearranged or whether Chopper had hijacked somebody else's bus.) The ride from Stapleton to McNichols Sports Arena, normally no longer than fifteen minutes, took an hour and forty-five minutes. Even the freeways took Herculean effort to navigate, and the bus driver got a standing ovation when we made it to the arena. Fair or not, the city of Denver's snow removal response was so criticized that it cost the longtime mayor, Bill McNichols, his job in the next election to upstart Federico Peña. The next night, December 27, the Nuggets beat Golden State 130–128 at the arena named after the soon-to-be ex-mayor.

Much was made of Moe's verbal assaults on the players, whether during time-outs or even as the game continued, but the point was that he knew who could handle it—and who needed it. He was merciless on Vandeweghe, trying to prod him into abandoning his placid personality and becoming tougher. It was a losing battle, but Moe knew he had to try and got about as much out of Kiki as was possible in the high-paced game. At one point, Moe confessed that he had a fantasy: that Vandeweghe finally would decide he had heard enough.

"I want him to tell me, '[bleep] you!'" Moe told me. "I want him to get mad enough where it hurts him, to where he wants to knock someone's butt off. He can do it. But it's just because of his lifestyle, his personality."

I asked Vandeweghe whether Moe's screaming bothered him. "Sometimes it upsets you, right at that second," he told me. "Then you realize it's because he cares about you. I'm lucky to be here. This offense fits me well. Doug has been good to me, even though he yells and screams at me. So I can't be too unhappy with him."

The possibility that Vandeweghe later would become an NBA general manager and the New Jersey Nets' head coach, albeit on an interim basis, was unfathomable.

Moe also picked on Gondrezick and reserve forward Bill Hanzlik, ultimately a Nuggets head coach himself and now a television analyst. The six feet seven guard-forward once got so exasperated with Moe's tirade during a time-out that he started to yell back. The problem was, he had a mouth full of water, which ended up being sprayed everywhere as he delivered his retort to his coach. Moe got the most out of Hanzlik, though, even using him to guard the Houston Rockets' seven feet four Ralph Sampson, frustrating Sampson because Hanzlik refused to back down, figuratively or literally.

Moe didn't get on Issel much and realized that English, the poet off the court, was hypersensitive and screaming at him was counterproductive. Still, despite that relative kid-gloved treatment, English's relationship with Moe was strained when he left as a free agent in 1990.

Gondo was gone after my first season on the beat. The Nuggets decided not to sign him for the 1983–84 season, and after he signed an offer sheet with the Indiana Pacers, I received a phone call at the office from someone who identified himself as "George" and said he was a Nuggets season-ticket holder on a temporary job assignment in Portland. He said he was a Gondrezick fan and wanted to know why the Nuggets had given up on him. I said something innocuous, and "George" told me he read my stories "all the time and really like them."

Aw, shucks, I said—or something to that effect.

An instant after I hung up, it hit me.

It was Gondo.

The Nuggets had a couple of notorious regular season games in my second season on the beat.

On November 22, 1983, the twentieth anniversary of the John F. Kennedy assassination, the Nuggets—who came in with a three-game winning streak—were getting blown out at Portland and the fans in Memorial Coliseum were informed that the Trail Blazers were on the verge of a single-game record for points scored. With 1:12 left, the Blazers had 146 points, four short of the record. The crowd was clamoring. Moe called a twenty-second time-out. Angrily, he told his team that since they hadn't played any defense all night, there was no sense starting now, and he ordered the Nuggets to not even *pretend* the rest of the way. They were to stand aside, allow the Blazers to score, and let the fans celebrate the record.

I was sitting near the bench and could hear the exchange during the time-out. Frankly, I thought it was funny. Portland coach Jack Ramsay, whom I later came to know and greatly respect, considered it an affront and glared at Moe as he walked off the court.

After the game, Moe sarcastically explained, "Our defense was getting so tenacious there, I was afraid they weren't going to get 150. I really was scared."

The Blazers were favored by five and won 156–116, so Moe's decision didn't affect any wagers. Yet the NBA's preoccupation with avoiding any hint of gambling scandal was reflected in its decision to fine Moe $5,000 and suspend him for two games. Moe's one-time banishment for not reporting the bribe attempt also might have made the league incapable of having a sense of humor about the Portland incident. Regardless, it was all about image, not reality. The NBA statement was that the "*no mas*" defense was "contrary to the very essence of sport, which demands a full effort for the entire length of the game."

The embarrassed Nuggets also had won the next night, beating Bill Walton and the San Diego Clippers. "I knew what I did and why I did it," Moe said. "In this business, you're worried about winning games and you keep your job depending on how well you do."

A few weeks later, another game drove all of that into the background.

Before the Pistons faced the Nuggets on December 14, 1983, in Denver, Detroit coach Chuck Daly was sitting in the pressroom when Moe stuck his head in.

Daly saw him and said, "First one to 140 wins."

Moe laughed. "Hell, we won't even make it through the third quarter," he responded.

The game lasted through three overtimes. I started and junked about twenty "ledes," or the first few paragraphs of a story, before finally writing about the Pistons pulling out a 186–184 victory. Vandeweghe had a game-high 51 points, and English and the Pistons' Isiah Thomas both had 47. The 370 points shattered the league record of 337, set in another triple-overtime game (San Antonio beat Milwaukee 171–166) in 1982.

It was the last Nuggets game worked by strikebreaker referees before the regulars, who finally had settled with the league, went back to work. If the regular referees had worked it, regardless of what had happened, Moe might not have said what he said when it was over, mostly referring to a missed call near the end of the first overtime: "It was a great game, but we got screwed." The funny thing was that one of the strikebreakers, Joe Borgia, ended up becoming a longtime NBA referee and now is the league's vice president for referee operations.

Tiring after seven years of travel in winter pro sports with seasons of eighty or more games, I became the national football and basketball writer, just when the Nuggets improved, thanks to the trade of Vandeweghe to Portland in May 1984. With Fat Lever, Calvin Natt, and Wayne Cooper coming over in the trade, they adapted, became tougher defensively and on the boards, and made it to the Western Conference finals in 1985 before losing to the Lakers.

But they weren't as much fun as they had been before.

When Chopper died in 1999, Issel delivered the eulogy in a packed Denver church. When the service ended, the music that accompanied the carrying of the casket to the hearse was "The Call to the Post." I swear I could hear Chopper saying, "Gimme a 1-2-all trifecta."

JACK DEMPSEY AND DAMON RUNYON

FOR MUCH OF THE ROARING TWENTIES, Jack Dempsey and Babe Ruth arguably were the most famous men in the country. Damon Runyon, the raconteur/scribe who brought the streets of New York and its characters to the rest of the nation in his journalism and his great short stories, hung out with the boxer and baseball player—and, in fact, gave one of the two his famous nickname.

No, not "Babe."

Runyon was the first to call Dempsey the "Manassa Mauler," coming up with it after Dempsey's devastating knockout of heavyweight champion Jess Willard in Toledo on July 4, 1919.

Like Dempsey, Runyon was raised and began his professional career in Colorado, so if Runyon hadn't come up with that nickname, perhaps nobody would have. What other influential Dempsey chronicler would have known that when Manassa had a high school, its teams were called the Maulers? Who else would have been struck by the appropriateness, given Dempsey's savagery in the ring? Dempsey remained world champion until Gene Tunney dethroned him in 1926 and was legendary as a New York restaurateur and celebrity until his death—and beyond.

Wherever he went, he was the Manassa Mauler, even to folks who had no idea what that meant.

Dempsey and Runyon's Colorado hometowns, Manassa and Pueblo, are 142 miles apart. They are linked by not only roads, but also by the intertwined stories of the two men.

Sheepish confession: because I knew that Dempsey had bounced around Colorado mountain towns in his early boxing days, for a long time I assumed that Manassa also was in the Rockies. Eventually, I learned that it's in the

San Luis Valley, not far from Alamosa, and not long after, I visited the Jack Dempsey Museum and Park in Manassa.

It wasn't hard to find. I went down Manassa's Main Street, past the best (and only) restaurant, Val's Place, and came to the museum across the street from the post office, city hall, and the kids' shaved ice stand. If I had kept going, as I did later, I would have come across the Church of Jesus Christ of Latter-Day Saints and Bond's Manassa Market.

Michelle Richardson, curator of the town-owned museum, told me that visitors come in streaks during its open months—Memorial Day through late September. "July's our busiest month, and we can get up to fifty people in one day," she said. "I have had days when nobody walks through the door."

The town's identification with Dempsey, she said, "has started to fade a little bit, and I think that's sad. I tell people I wish everybody loved it as much as I do, but you can't expect everybody to."

The modern population is barely one thousand, and it was less than seven hundred when the future world champion was born in 1895. He was the ninth of eleven children born to Hyrum and Celia Dempsey. There is some dispute about how long Jack and his down-on-its-luck family lived in Manassa before the start of a series of moves that took the Dempseys to a handful of other Colorado towns. Dempsey himself contributed to the confusion with inconsistent remembrances, but Mormon Church records show Jack was in Manassa at least as late as 1903. In one of his autobiographies—1977's *Dempsey*, written with his daughter—he said that the wandering family settled in Uncompahgre, between Telluride and Montrose, shortly after his ninth birthday in June 1904.

In a 1960 interview with writer Roger Kahn, a friend who eventually used the material in the highly sympathetic 1999 book, *A Flame of Pure Fire*, Dempsey said he hated leaving his native town.

"All the kids were upset," Dempsey said. "Manassa was what we knew of home." He told Kahn, "It was terrific growing up in the Wild West. I learned to shoot, not for fun, but for food. I liked to go with my father on hunting trips. Sometimes he'd run out of ammunition, but there always was plenty of game. I learned how to set traps. I could follow deer tracks through scrubby brush. I fished in the Conejos River. . . . I could handle horses before I was ten."

The home on the grounds of the park doesn't much resemble the ramshackle stucco structure in which Jack—officially William Harrison Dempsey—was born. In the mid-1960s, the town bought and moved the home several blocks to the park, also renovating it. Area residents were thrilled when Dempsey consented to be grand marshal of the town's annual

Pioneer Days celebration in July 1966 and preside over the official dedication of the Jack Dempsey Park and Museum.

A monument on the front walkway to the house includes a bronze sculpture by Bob Booth of Dempsey in full fighting pose. It officially is dedicated to Dempsey's mother—she and Hyrum were divorced long after Jack left the nest as a teenager—and carries this quote from Jack: "My mother was the most magnificent woman I ever met. I knew from the time I could walk that she deserved a better break. And I swore or vowed or prayed, or whatever it is a kid does, that I would someday make it up to her."

Inside the house, when Richardson gave mini-tours to visitors—"mini" because the house, after all, is only six hundred square feet—she could include her remembrances of Dempsey's 1966 visit, featuring his ride in the parade down Main Street on a horse.

"Being nine and a girl, I didn't really know what was going on," she recalled. "My paternal grandmother was born in 1910, so she knew exactly who he was. As he approached her, she was waving a white handkerchief and she dropped it. He stopped his horse and climbed off, picked it up, returned it to her, and kissed her hand. She was impossible the rest of the day. Just impossible. I was standing there, too, and he told me I was a pretty little girl, wished me a good day, and got back on his horse.

"That's my Dempsey story. And it took me a few years to realize that not everybody has one."

Many do, though, and now that everyone who knew Dempsey from his childhood has passed on, those stories either have been handed down through generations or come from Dempsey's 1966 visit or both. News stories of the time emphasize that Dempsey met with dozens of his childhood friends on the visit, and the implication seems to be that he played along with whatever stories anyone told, whether they were about fighting him when they were kids or about swimming in the Conejos.

Raised on a family farm five miles outside of Manassa, in the Los Rincones ("the corners") area, young Ken Salazar used to think of Manassa as the big city.

"It had lights!" Salazar, who was a Colorado U.S. senator at the time, told me with a laugh.

Before attending Centauri High School in nearby La Jara, the nearest high school after Manassa shut its doors for good in 1964, Salazar went to elementary school in Manassa. "There was a teacher named Mrs. Joyce, who has passed away," Salazar said. "I remember she talked at some point about Jack Dempsey beating up her brother—sticking his face in a mud puddle."

Salazar also was on Main Street on July 23, 1966, and he vividly recalled Dempsey waving. "I thought it was pretty cool," he said. "Here is a person who has been heavyweight champion of the world, and here he is in our little town."

Salazar said he has visited the birthplace and museum several times, including with then-Governor Roy Romer in 1987.

During my visit to Manassa, I also stopped at city hall. Town clerk Evelyn Tibbets wore a Dempsey Museum and Park T-shirt.

"I'm amazed at how many people do come, and how much they know about Jack Dempsey," Tibbets said.

Within a few steps of her office, in the entranceway, a painting showed Dempsey in the ring. It was a curious choice: in what many consider the most action-packed title fight of all time—Dempsey's second-round victory over Luis Firpo, the "Wild Bull of the Pampas," in 1923—the champ has been knocked through the ropes into the arms of the writers at ringside in the first round. They shoved him back in the ring, and many argued he should have been disqualified.

Controversy tended to follow him. He was married four times. He was (apparently unjustifiably) accused of being a "slacker" and manipulating the system to avoid World War I service and for dodging noted black heavyweight Harry Wills. He wasn't above pushing the envelope of the looser boxing rules of the time.

A few hard knocks were nothing for a man who, often calling himself "Kid Blackie," literally fought his way through Colorado mining towns and saloons to get started as a professional boxer. In fact, Dempsey's final fight, the infamous "Long Count" loss to Tunney in their 1927 rematch, in some ways sent him out of the ring as a sympathetic victim. After knocking down Tunney in the seventh round, Dempsey for several seconds didn't heed the new rule requiring him to head to the neutral corner. In his book on Dempsey, Kahn implied that referee Dave Barry was crooked and that he should have picked up the knockdown timekeeper's count at five instead of starting a new count when Dempsey finally went to the neutral corner. Tunney got up at the referee's count of nine. No credible evidence of referee funny business has been unearthed, though it raised eyebrows that Barry started counting immediately after Tunney later knocked down Dempsey before Tunney went to a neutral corner. Yet there is universal agreement that Tunney otherwise dominated the fight.

After retiring, Dempsey presided over one of Manhattan's most famous watering holes, Jack Dempsey's Restaurant, which in its later years was at

1619 Broadway, between 49th and 50th streets. He joined Byron "Whizzer" White and Earl "Dutch" Clark as the inaugural inductees in the Colorado Sports Hall of Fame in 1965, and he maintained a touching and lifelong friendship with Colorado boxing mogul Eddie Bohn, who owned the Pig 'N' Whistle motel and restaurant on West Colfax in Denver. At Times Square's low ebb, Dempsey's restaurant closed in 1974—three years before my first trip to New York. Over the years, though, I located where the restaurant was and bought some menus and vintage postcards on eBay; I almost feel as if I've been there.

Dempsey died in 1983, and stories the next morning said the end came shortly after he assured his fourth wife, Deanna, "Don't worry, honey, I'm too mean to die."

Thanks to Runyon, Dempsey forever will be the Manassa Mauler.

Runyon never owned a place, but I did make it to both incarnations of the Manhattan restaurant that bore his name and was a hangout for journalists and media personalities—the great original downstairs joint on 50th Street in Midtown East, and the newer (and too darned antiseptic and generic) place around the corner on Third Avenue. His spirit haunts the Denver Press Club, my after-work hangout, especially during my part-time years at the *Rocky Mountain News* while I was in college and in the early stages of my *Denver Post* career. And I made several pilgrimages to Runyon Field, the baseball park just south of downtown Pueblo and adjacent to Interstate 25. In Pueblo, all you had to do was say you were headed to Runyon and most knew what you meant—even if they didn't know Damon Runyon's background and the history of the park.

Bleachers were moved from another local park to the site along the railroad tracks in 1934, and the "new" stadium was variously called County Park and Merchants Park. Major league players, the House of David's famous team, and former stars made appearances on barnstorming tours. Babe Ruth showed up for a game in 1938.

There is some dispute about how the name Runyon Field came about. The story that makes the most sense is that in 1947, when the Pueblo Dodgers entered the Single-A Western League, the name Runyon Field was selected for the ballpark in a contest. Runyon had died the year before.

Before the Western League folded in 1958, many of the Dodgers' top prospects, including Maury Wills, Ron Fairly, John Roseboro, and Jim Gentile came through Pueblo. So did manager Walter Alston. After the golden postwar era of minor league baseball ended and the Dodgers departed, Pueblo's youth baseball program stepped in. Runyon Field became a complex in the mid-1980s, when two more fields were added. As part of the fund-raising effort, each diamond was offered for sponsorship; the original stadium is officially Oneal Hobbs Field, honoring a Pueblo baseball pioneer. The entire complex is known as Runyon Field, but—no knock on Hobbs—most still refer to the main diamond as "Runyon," too.

Visitors who come in from out of town to American Legion games at the Runyon complex tend to be astounded to discover they can buy beer to wash down the kielbasa.

Runyon wouldn't have had it any other way.

The name of the field alone triggered an urge to use the present tense, append many explanatory phrases beginning with "which," compose long sentences, and plug in words favored by Runyon and other scribes of yore. Also, on one on my visits, it conjured an apparition, which is a fancy way of saying it inspired me to piece together a short story set at Runyon Field using the Runyon model and some of his words:

A dapper guy plops himself at the picnic table next to the Runyon Field concession stand. This guy is called Obadiah Masterson on the birth certificate but goes by the moniker of Sky. He is visiting his southern Colorado hometown, which has been hinted at in the famous Runyon story, "The Idyll of Miss Sarah Brown."

Sky places two of Runyon Field's famous kielbasa sandwiches, which are known to be wonderful brain food, in front of him and carefully arranges his paper napkin in the fashion of a baby's bib. He must chomp with great caution, for if he does not, he could deposit mustard all over the front of his dark blue pinstriped suit jacket and a tie as white as the lights on Broadway on a Saturday night.

It is 95 degrees in the middle of July, but nobody remarks upon the peculiarity of Sky's impeccable wardrobe.

Sky is asked if he cares to place a little scratch on the proposition: Which does the concession stand sell more of, kielbasa or frankfurters?

Sky allows that such propositions quite often intrigue him and thicken the bankroll in his pocket, but he will pass on this one before he heads to Las Vegas to roll dice, when he is not reading the Gideon Bible in his hotel room.

Nothing personal, says he, but when he was a young guy about to venture forth beyond the basement dice games, his father pulled him aside and allowed to him that he did not have sufficient scratch to stake his son, and all he could offer was advice.

The advice, Sky says, went thusly, as reported in "The Idyll":

"Son, no matter how far you travel, or how smart you get, always remember this: Some day, somewhere, a guy is going to come to you and show you a nice brand-new deck of cards on which the seal is never broken, and this guy is going to offer to bet you that the jack of spades will jump out of this deck and squirt cider in your ear. But son, do not bet him, for as sure as you do, you are going to get an earful of cider."

So, no bet about the kielbasa or frankfurters?

No bet, says Sky.

Sky gets up and strides toward the parking lot, singing as clear as a bell and a tenor in a church choir, "Luck Be a Lady Tonight."

He sounds nothing like Marlon Brando, which is a good thing.

Then he disappears, as if it all had been a dream. Which, of course, it was.

Alfred Damon Runyan was born in 1880 in Manhattan—the Kansas college town, not the $24 New York island. His father, a printer, moved the family to Pueblo, hoping to find a climate suited to his wife's battle with consumption, yet Libbie Runyan died when "Alfie" was seven.

Alfie moved around, once even living in an abandoned shack. He most often was on the streets, left alone to his own devices in a rough town. Pueblo had smelters, railroads, several newspapers, many bars, and a few brothels. It also had a library, and Alfie was a frequent visitor there, showing a precocious fascination with the works of Rudyard Kipling.

His storied career started with a poem, "Creede," that ran in the *Pueblo Chieftain* on February 6, 1892. He was eleven. (Later, a printer's error altered the writer's name to "Runyon." It stuck.) He became a reporter at the *Pueblo Evening Press*. He was only twelve, but it didn't stop him from becoming a regular at the Home Cafe's raucous bar and at the brothels.

In Pueblo, he covered everything from a lynching near the railroad station to *Gunfight at the OK Corral*, which is the name that famous sheriff-turned-boxing promoter Bat Masterson gave his boxing card's matches at Pueblo's St. James Hotel. Sky and Bat's common last names are not coincidence. Runyon already was mentally taking notes about the cast of characters that became the basis for *Guys and Dolls*, and Bat Masterson would become the model for Sky Masterson.

He finagled his way into the Army in 1898 and was with the 13th Minnesota Volunteers fighting in the Philippines. His major weapon was a typewriter, since he wrote for soldiers' magazines and newspapers. When he returned, he bounced around the newspaper business, going from Colorado Springs to St. Joseph, Missouri, back to Pueblo, to Trinidad, and finally to Denver in 1905, where he landed a job at the *Denver Post* and took to hanging out at the Denver Press Club.

Even in an era when whiskey was as much of a tool for a reporter as pad and pencil, Runyon was over the top. He was farmed out to the sports department, where he often ghostwrote sports editor Otto Floto's column. But the *Post* fired Runyon in 1906. Legend has it that the firing involved a prostitute typing a story on behalf of Runyon in the newsroom while he was "indisposed."

After Runyon served a short stint with the *San Francisco Post*, the *Rocky Mountain News* hired him on a make-good basis and then embraced him as a star in the ongoing newspaper war with the *Post*. He wrote about politics, sports, and business, and led a campaign to erect a statue of Kit Carson at Colfax Avenue and Broadway.* One of his final acts in Colorado was his ill-fated attempt to form a new Colorado State Baseball League. It never played a game, but Runyon did a season's worth of traveling and drinking up and down the Front Range trying to promote it. (At least that was his excuse.)

He still was drinking at the Denver Press Club, and he almost ruined his chances with society writer Ellen Egan—his future first wife—when she spotted him at a Cheesman Park concert with two women who were well known as members of the world's oldest profession. Runyon's bender that night ended in delirium, and a doctor told him his heart couldn't hold out if he continued his self-destruction. He promised himself that he was done with alcohol.

A sober Runyon moved to New York in 1910 and wound up working for the *New York American* as a sportswriter. On his first story, he typed his usual byline: "By Alfred Damon Runyon." The sports editor scratched out "Alfred." That stuck, too.

In the Roaring Twenties, when he wasn't writing about Jack Dempsey or Babe Ruth, he wrote piece after piece about lurid courtroom cases. He hung around with guys and dolls who became the basis for such Runyon characters as columnist Waldo Winchester, bookie Sorrowful Jones and his Little Miss Marker, Brandy Bottle Bates, Nicely-Nicely Jones (Broadway changed it to Johnson), Dream Street Rose, Harry the Horse, Madame La Gimp, The Lemon Drop Kid, and famous horse handicapper Unser Fritz.

---

* The statue is still there within a few feet of the entrance to the new *Denver Post* building.

The description of Fritz in *All Horse Players Die Broke* is quintessential Runyon.

"In his day," wrote Runyon, "Unser Fritz is a most successful handicapper, a handicapper being a character who can dope out from the form what horses ought to win the races, and as long as his figures turn out all right, a handicapper is spoken of most respectfully by one and all, although of course when he begins missing out for any length of time as handicappers are bound to do, he no longer is spoken of respectfully, or even as a handicapper. He is spoken of as a bum."

By today's standards, Runyon's character, especially during his Colorado years, might seem as questionable as his characters are enduring. That's unfair. His was a rogue time, and the journalists and chroniclers of the era reflected it.

The Runyon name will live on, and not just because of the stage revivals of *Guys and Dolls* or the movies made from twenty-six of his short stories. In Pueblo, it will be because of baseball.

DAVE LOGAN: A MAN FOR ALL SEASONS

One play baby, one play. Fourth and six. And I know I'm supposed to be objective but I can't help it. Fourth and six with thirty-two seconds to go. One play to the championship. Freeman and Mays wide left, Chmura inside of Mickens to the right side, Favre with Levens behind him. Fourth and six from the 31. Blitz is on. Favre hit as he throws. Pass is gonna be incomplete! Denver holds! Denver's gonna win it! Oh, baby, they're gonna win this thing! Are you kidding me? Bronco players are all over the field! Oh, man! You can stand up and salute in Denver. You got the World Champions that live in your town.

—Dave Logan, KOA Radio, January 25, 1998

ON THE THIRTY-YARD LINE at Invesco Field after Denver's Mullen High School Mustangs won the first of its two consecutive 5A state championships in 2008, coach Dave Logan finished a television interview and turned as I called out to him.

"Hey, T-Bone," he said.

The only people in the world who call me that went to high school with me.

Logan is among the highest profile figures in Colorado. The former University of Colorado All-American and longtime Cleveland Browns receiver is the longtime radio play-by-play voice of the Denver Broncos, a rare responsibility for a former player. There are those who knock him because he doesn't indulge in celebratory screaming when the Broncos score or make a big play that draws guffaws when replayed on such shows as *SportsCenter*. (The rule of thumb is that when your home-team broadcasters are ridiculous-sounding cheerleaders, they're doing their job, and it doesn't sound at all strange; when another team's broadcasters do the same thing, they're "bush-league homers"—i.e., embarrassingly partisan and unprofessional—and worthy of derision.)

Also on the flagship station on the Broncos' network, Denver's KOA, he is cohost, with Lois Melkonian, of the afternoon talk and news show, "The Ride Home."

On the side, Logan is the top high school football coach in the state, having spent successful stints at Arvada West and Chatfield in Jefferson County and now at Mullen, the Catholic school tucked into Denver's southwest corner. He also is a television commercial spokesman for a regional bank and also the voice for a natural energy drink and for TeamDaveLogan .com, a contractor screening and referral business.

The day I was on the field with him at Invesco, Mullen had just beaten Cherry Creek for the state title. I asked Dave why he still was doing this. After all, he—we—weren't getting any younger, and his range of responsibilities was dizzying.

"I love working with kids," Logan said as he stood back and allowed his players to celebrate on their own. "It's been a passion of mine since I started coaching in 1993. I know some people thought it would be a one- or a two-year deal, but as long as I'm healthy, it's what I want to do. I get a lot from these kids, I really do."

Dave and I go back to February 1972, when he was a high school senior and I was a junior. My father returned to Eugene from a house-hunting trip to Denver, where he had just become the offensive line coach under new Broncos coach John Ralston. In mid-February, Dad handed me a student manual and told me, "Son, you're going to be a Wheat Ridge Farmer." The caricature on the cover was of a man in overalls holding a pitchfork. *So much for moving to the big city*, I thought. Even worse, the manual listed dress code and personal appearance standards that made me think I was headed for West Point. Most of them turned out to be out of date and no longer were enforced in 1972, but I didn't know that. I was coming from South Eugene High, which had an open campus and self-policed attendance that didn't require notes from parents excusing absences.

After adjusting from a virtual collegiate atmosphere to suburbia, I ended up enjoying my year and a half as a Farmer.

The day I reported for school, I gave myself a guided tour of the trophy cases outside the gym adjacent to the student lot. Among other things, I noticed the pictures of Freddie Steinmark, the former Wheat Ridge star who had been a starting safety on the Texas Longhorns' 1969 national champions

After moving to Colorado in the middle of my junior year, I was the Wheat Ridge Farmers' catcher in 1972. I'm kneeling third from the right in the middle row in this photo taken by the area's legendary sports photographer Bill Worthen, a familiar face and friend to multiple generations of Colorado high school athletes. One of the pitchers I caught, or tried to catch, was Dave Logan.He's fifth from the left in the back row. Back row: Mike Miller, Tom Waring, Mike Clark, Bob Krause, Dave Logan, Steve Cribari, Gary Denkler, Chuck Rasey, Reid Gamberg, and head coach Steve Bell. Middle row: Mike Shanahan (no, not that Mike Shanahan), John Teilborg, Jim Livingston, John Milow, Rick McCoy, me, Mike Sottler, and Greg Holley. Front row: Pete Morton, Dan McCord, Martin McCoy, and Steve Larsen. *Source:* Photo by Bill Worthen.

and died of cancer in 1971 after drawing national attention for his courageous battle.*

At the time, the Farmers still were alive in the state basketball playoffs, and I quickly figured out that it was a team with three senior stars—Dave Logan, Jeff Fosnes, and Steve Cribari. A couple of weeks later, the Farmers lost to Denver's Manual High in the state finals, and Wheat Ridge ultimately came away with three near-misses and no state championships in Logan's three seasons.† The end of the basketball season freed Logan and Cribari to join the baseball team, and they were our top two pitchers.

---

* The seed for my 2002 book *Horns, Hogs, and Nixon Coming* was planted.

† Eventually, Fosnes ended up an All-Southeastern Conference player at Vanderbilt and turned his back on a chance to try the NBA, eventually becoming a pediatrician. Cribari was a standout at the University of Denver.

I was a catcher with a great arm—in terms of velocity, not accuracy. Good behind the plate. Decent hitter, but only until the other team discovered one of the curveball's amazing properties: it never hit my bat. With Dave's help, I probably set a Jefferson County record for passed balls my junior season.

The park where Jefferson High used to play its games was next to the King Soopers grocery store on West 20th Avenue in Edgewater. The park had two diamonds. The smaller Little League field was down the left-field line of the main diamond. In the 1972 season against Jefferson, Logan hit a ball to left field, driving it over the other diamond and across a street. As time went on, the distance grew to about 600 feet in my mind, but when I went back and more carefully took stock, I'm guessing it was about 430 feet.

We finished third in the league that season, but we had our moments. Dave threw a five-hitter as we beat the eventual league champion, Lakewood, 4–1. He had 15 strikeouts and allowed only four hits as we beat Bear Creek 3–1. And he threw a no-hitter in our 4–2 win against Alameda. The *Denver Post* reported: "Logan, who starred on the Wheat Ridge football and basketball teams, lost his shutout in the last inning on three walks and an error."

We also were teammates in American Legion ball that summer. When you played with Logan, what you remembered was his competitiveness. Baseball wasn't his number one sport, but if you weren't into it, he'd kick your butt until you were. Peer and parental pressure being what it is, he had to put up with much abuse from the stands and the other dugouts. Occasionally, he would talk back. Then he always delivered.

I've often wondered if he would have made it in major league baseball. When I asked him that, he answered with a challenge. "Well, you caught me," he said. In other words, what did I think?

He was raw in baseball, but that made him even more of a prospect. Cincinnati drafted him as a shortstop in 1972, after his senior season at Wheat Ridge, but I'm convinced his best shot would have been either as a Goose Gossage–type pitcher or in the outfield. If he had signed with the Reds and given up football and basketball altogether to concentrate on baseball, he would have made the major leagues. Later, after his senior seasons at Colorado, the NFL's Browns and the NBA's Kansas City Kings also drafted him. The only other man drafted in all three of the marquee sports was Dave Winfield, a pitcher-outfielder at the University of Minnesota, who at times was baseball's best outfielder with the Padres and Yankees in the 1970s and 1980s. While Logan probably wasn't on a par with Winfield in baseball, they were men with similar abilities who took different paths. Logan turned down the Reds and never played baseball at Colorado. Football and basketball were enough, and even two sport athletes had become rare by then. He did play baseball for a couple of collegiate summers with the semipro Englewood Redbirds.

"There was a lot I needed to learn to be on the major league level," he told me years later. "Possibly, in the right environment, with the right coaching, I would have had a chance. A lot of players get lost in the minors and never surface after spending eight, nine years down there.

"I didn't want to take the chance of anything like that happening. I don't even know what the Reds' intentions were. They drafted me as a shortstop and I think I beat more balls into the ground than I caught there. I certainly don't know if I could have played baseball as a shortstop, but I would like to think I might have been able to pitch."

Actually, if it was about pure enjoyment, and this might be hard to believe today, Logan preferred basketball. In the mid-1970s, he would come out for Colorado's team after the football season ended, and he and future NBA star Scott Wedman were standout forwards on an otherwise shaky team.

He stopped playing baseball in the summer after his junior year at CU. Playing on the side wasn't satisfying. "I stopped when I served up three consecutive home runs to the Boulder Collegians, including one to Mike Miley," he said. (Miley was considered a future major league star but drowned in 1977.) "They had guys from Arizona State, and they had a great team. For about a couple of innings, I could just throw hard and get by. But by the third, they were ready, and they deposited three over the fence."

The Nuggets were set to sign and suit up Logan as a late-season, emergency eleventh-man in the early 1980s, when rosters were only eleven men, but Kansas City, which still held his NBA rights, wouldn't cooperate.

"Realistically, I don't think I would have been a great player in the NBA," Logan said. "But I feel like I could have played somewhere and filled a role somewhere. I was an in-between size at 6-5, and too small to play small forward, too big where you're going to have to cover quick people. But given the right situation, I could have played."

Logan spent eight productive seasons with the Browns, mostly as Brian Sipe's go-to receiver and then played for the Broncos in 1984 before retiring. He didn't enjoy being a spare-part receiver for Dan Reeves, and it showed.

A quarter century later, he is a fixture in Colorado, and I am an occasional guest on his radio show. We run into each other in situations both professional and personal.

One time, when his KOA cohost, Melkonian, asked me to tell a story on the air about Dave as a high school athlete, I spoke of our school pictures with long hair and then brought up the time when we finished our Wheat Ridge regular season with a game at Golden. The way I remembered it, he had a 2–0 count on the opposing pitcher, a hot dog–type who wore sunglasses on cloudy days and just rubbed me—and everyone else—the wrong way.

Dave called me out to the mound and announced that since he probably was going to walk this guy anyway, he might as well try to scare him. On the next two pitches, he succeeded, brushing the hitter back with high and inside pitches that weren't dangerous but might have succeeded in grazing the hitter if he wasn't bailing out before the ball left Dave's hand.

On the air, Dave protested that he wouldn't do that. He clearly didn't remember the incident.

I told Dave the Golden pitcher's last name.

There was a pause.

Finally, Dave responded. "He had it coming."

FOURTH DOWN AND A WAR TO GO

I N *THIRD DOWN AND A WAR TO GO*, I told the story of my father's college football team, researching the Wisconsin Badgers' successful 1942 season in a final-fling atmosphere on campus the year following Pearl Harbor, and their wartime and postwar experiences. Several times, I came across references to Colorado and Colorado A&M (now Colorado State) players whose paths had crossed those of the Badgers, especially former Buffalo Bob Spicer and one-time Aggie Walter "Bus" Bergman, who both served in the Sixth Marine Division with Dave Schreiner and Bob Baumann, two Wisconsin stars killed in the Battle of Okinawa. That made me curious about the CU and A&M teams from the World War II era, too. Although Bergman already had graduated and was in the Marines by then, I first homed in on the 1942 CU–A&M game on October 24 at A&M's Colorado Field in Fort Collins.

The Game

Like the Badgers and all the players around the country, the 1942 Aggies and Buffaloes followed the mostly discouraging war news in the year after Pearl Harbor. Virtually all of the schools were in the Enlisted Reserve Corps, meaning they had signed up and were awaiting their call-ups.

Both schools were members of the Mountain States Conference. CU's big rival was the University of Denver. "They always looked down on CSU . . . just like they do now," Perry Blach, an Aggie sophomore lineman in 1942, told me with a laugh as he sat in the living room of his Yuma, Colorado home. "They were a bigger school and they thought we were just a bunch of farmers."

For the 1942 season, the conference was one of a handful that lifted the previous ban on freshman participation in varsity football, so some of the players on both rosters had been in high school when the United States entered the war. A&M came in with a 2–1 record under first-year coach Julius "Hans" Wagner. CU was 3–1 in their second season under coach Jim Yeager.

The week of the game was eventful. The continued bloody fighting in the Solomon Islands was in the headlines. A Washington communiqué announced: "Our land, sea and air forces of the Army, Navy, and Marine Corps are engaged in meeting a serious enemy assault, the outcome of which is still undecided." In the Soviet Union, the latest German attempt to take and secure Stalingrad was in its second week. The British were taking on General Erwin Rommel's German forces in North Africa with U.S. naval and air support, and most Americans assumed that U.S. troops soon would invade North Africa.* The House of Representatives passed legislation to lower the draft age from twenty to eighteen. The Senate passed it, too, with many revisions. While the legislation was headed back to the House as the weekend began, it was obvious the change was inevitable—and imminent.

Army advertisements in papers encouraged older teenagers to beat the rush by enlisting and choosing one of the Army's thirteen branches, including the Army Air Forces. The message in the *Denver Post* ad was: "A new and glorious chapter of American history is being written. It is a chapter of adventure—the supreme adventure of all time for young Americans. On its pages will be the names of millions of young men who now accept the challenge thrown in our free American faces by Hitler, Mussolini, and Tojo—accept it and ram it down their cruel throats!" A Damon Runyon syndicated column, bannered across the bottom of the *Post* front page that week, supported lowering the draft age and argued against the continued acceptance of "middle-aged" men. The upper end of the draft age at the time was forty-five. Runyon began, "General Marshall and other high military authorities confirm what I have been telling you all along, that those middle-aged fellows they have been taking in the army are not worth a dime a dozen as combat soldiers simply because they cannot stand up under the grind. The spirit is steel, the flesh is putty."

Eleanor Roosevelt arrived in London, settled into Buckingham Palace, and prepared to tour the city to assess the damage.

Scrap metal and rubber drives were the patriotic rage, and if players and students could afford to go to the movies, their top choices were the war sto-

---

* It happened two weeks later.

ries *Wake Island*, Humphrey Bogart in *Across the Pacific*, and James Cagney in the flag-waving *Yankee Doodle Dandy*.

The Buffaloes weren't even the only football team on the CU campus. The Navy had taken over several campus buildings and dormitories so its recruits could train and study, and the naval students had their own "CU Navy" team that played a limited schedule against Regis and other area schools.*

The young men on college campuses at the time realized they likely would be in other uniforms before long.

A&M had mixed news on the injury front. Star fullback Lewis "Dude" Dent, the senior from Craig, Colorado, had missed the previous game because of an infected elbow, but he was expected to return against the Buffaloes despite suffering a broken nose in Tuesday's practice. The *Rocky Mountain News* put it this way: "The Craig socker . . . will be in there Saturday and promises to dish out plenty of trouble to the visitors." The *News* quoted CU's coach, Yeager, as saying, "He doesn't run with his nose." A&M's Julius Wagner, though, switched Dent to halfback because starting halfback Chet Maeda suffered a neck injury in practice, spent the night in a hospital, and wasn't going to be able to play against CU. (Wagner apparently ran tough practices.) In what was common for the offenses of the era, Maeda, although a halfback, threw most of the Aggies' passes, and the quarterback called the signals and was mostly a blocker. So Wagner wanted Dent at halfback to replace Maeda as the passer. Dent was banged up, Maeda was out, and the Aggies' other senior leader, guard John Mosley, the Mountain States Conference's first black player, was hoping to leave Fort Collins with a win against the Buffaloes. CU hadn't lost to the Aggies since 1933 and came into the afternoon with an eight-game winning streak in the rivalry.

A foot of snow fell Friday in the Fort Collins area, and it was even worse with nineteen inches in Boulder. At A&M, athletic director Harry Hughes asked students to bring shovels to Colorado Field at 8:30 Saturday morning to help clear off the field. The field was in surprisingly good shape for the 2:30 p.m. kickoff.

Wartime bus availability was iffy, so the Buffaloes caught scheduled bus service to Fort Collins on the morning of the game, transferring in Lafayette.

---

* By the next season, military men training and studying on campuses played for the schools themselves, which is why many men—stars and scrubs alike—played for two different universities during the war years. Many of my father's 1942 Wisconsin teammates played for Michigan in 1943, when they were studying and training in the Marines' V12 program.

Attendance was sparse. The *Fort Collins Express-News* estimate was 2,300. Attendance was down all over the country because of the somber wartime atmosphere as well as travel restrictions, even within states. Originally scheduled as the Aggies' homecoming game, those plans were scrubbed because of the restrictions. All of these issues resulted in a lot of fans staying home. In Denver, that meant listening to the play-by-play broadcast on KOA. Some listeners might have switched to the game from KVOD's "Defense and You" while others, perhaps, hoped the game would be over in time for KLZ's airing of "The Kate Smith Hour" with guest Veronica Lake, the glamorous movie star.

"I can remember that A&M treated us really well," Paul Briggs, the huge CU left tackle from Grand Junction, told me with a laugh from his home in Santa Ana, California. "They put us in a shed out there, with hurdles in it, and you hung your clothes on a twenty-penny nail driven into a four-by-four."

One of the Buffaloes' other standouts was center Don Brotzman, a senior from Merino. His teammates called him "Meatnose," because of all the shots he took to the nose as the center. From his home in Alexandria, Virginia, he vividly remembered the game's opening kickoff, because he looked downfield and spotted his buddy, Aggies' star Lewis "Dude" Dent.

The previous summer, Brotzman worked on a state highway department crew on the Western Slope. "We laid oil roads over there, and I was the night watchman for all the equipment," Brotzman said. "I also drove a state highway truck." Dent was driving a truck for an oil-drilling operation in the same area and living in Craig. Their paths crossed. "Dude was a really good athlete and he had a hell of a lot of character," Brotzman said. "He kind of took me under his wing and we went to a lot of dances over there on the Western Slope."

All summer, they teased one another about their upcoming meeting on the field that fall, and they popped off about who was going to hit whom first—and how hard.

When the kickoff dropped right into Dent's hands, Brotzman had a free run at his friend. "Man, I hit him a good shot," Brotzman said. On the ground together, they laughed about it.

The Buffs blocked a Dent punt late in the first quarter and recovered on the 5. Two plays later, sophomore halfback Carl Stearns scored from three yards out, and Bob Knowles kicked the extra point to make it 7–0.

The big play on CU's next scoring drive was a long run by Stan Hendrickson on an end-around that got the Buffs to the Aggie 3. John Mosley stopped CU's Walt Clay on the next play, and I mention that in part because the *Fort Collins Express-News* referred to the tackler as "John Mosley, dusky Aggie guard." John Ziegler went over for the touchdown from the 3 on the next play of the second quarter and Knowles made it 14–0. The Rams got within 14–7 by the half, after Johnnie Speas threw a 12-yard touchdown pass to James Riggenbach and Dent kicked the extra point.

CU was up 28–7 after three quarters, adding to the lead with Clay's 60-yard interception return, Stearns's 2-yard run, and two more Knowles conversions. Ziegler added the final touchdown on a 27-yard run.

Playing both offense and defense, as did all starters in the era of one-platoon and limited-substitution football, Brotzman had a terrific afternoon, and he was awarded the game ball. Mindful of the Buffs' need to catch the bus back to Boulder, Brotzman hurried out of the dressing shed to meet with Dent. They had a nice talk. It was the last time they saw one another.

A&M: Dude

Number 1, Lewis "Dude" Dent, Halfback

Dent starred in everything at Craig High, graduating in 1939. At A&M, Dent was the region's best fullback—his switch to halfback for the rivalry game was only temporary—and he also played basketball and ran track for the Aggies. He worked as a busboy in a campus cafeteria.

Perry Blach said of Dent, "We looked up to him, and he was always there when we needed him." John Mosley added, "I did a lot of blocking for him. We had a great experience together. He was a great friend in showing that I didn't need to fight all my battles all by myself."

While at A&M, Dent married Mildred Bach, a fellow student from Denver. In 1943, when athletic directors voted Dent the best all-around athlete in the Mountain States Conference, he was in the Army reserves and serving as a physical training and commando tactics instructor on campus. He had taken field artillery instruction in advanced ROTC. When he was called to active duty in May 1943, he was four hours short of receiving his mechanical engineering degree.

"There's plenty of chances for glory in the armed services," he said in an Associated Press story. "As a matter of fact, if the Army looks as good to me from the inside as it does from the outside, and if I'm any good as a soldier, I'll probably make it my life career. . . . If the Army doesn't like me, or I don't like it, I'll come back after the war, make up the four hours and go on with my engineering."

Four other products of A&M's Advanced ROTC program—Wayne Seaman, Al Hoffman, Irv Ferguson, and Gordon Rutherford—went through training with Dent at Fort Sill, Oklahoma. "After that, some of us got into a battery executive school for a month, and Dude and I were in that," Seaman told me from his home in Evans, Colorado. "We'd had a lot of experience with live ammunition, more so than a lot of guys in the division we ended up with. After that, you had a list of choices where you could go, and the Fourth Armored Division was getting ready to go overseas, and we were kind of gung-ho. A bunch of us signed up for that, and they took the five of us from A&M. Dude, Al, and I went into the same battalion, the 94th Armored Artillery Battalion."

Ferguson was assigned to a tank battalion and Rutherford went to another artillery battalion.

The 94th Battalion arrived in Europe in late 1943. "Dude and I had one leave together in London," Seaman said. "We went our separate ways once we got there, but we went back and forth together."

Lieutenant Lewis S. "Dude" Dent was killed in action near Troyes, France, in August 1944.

When I talked with them, his teammates didn't know any details about his death, but they had heard that he had been awarded the Silver Star. A photo taken at the couple's northwest Denver home accompanied the vague news story in the *Denver Post*. It showed his widow, two-and-a-half-year-old son Richard, and infant daughter Cheryl.

Wayne Seaman and Roger Boas, an eighty-seven-year-old retired car dealer and political figure in San Francisco, filled in the blanks about Dent's death when I spoke with them in 2009. Boas explained that he and Dent were in a pool of forward observers with the 94th Armored Field Artillery Battalion as the unit moved toward German-occupied Troyes. Boas, who served as the battalion adjutant, said Dent was told the night before the battle that it was his turn in the forward observer rotation.

"He said, 'I'm going in on the attack tomorrow and I know I'm going to get killed, I'm not going to make it,'" Boas told me. "We had done a lot of fighting to get to Troyes, and Dude had done his share of the forward observer work and done it well. He was not a shirker or a complainer. . . . There was nothing cowardly in this. He just had an instinct that his time was up."

Boas told Dent to convey his premonition to Bob Parker, the battalion's operations officer. Parker told Dent he couldn't change the rotation. The next day, Dent and his driver were in an open jeep, ahead of the U.S. forces advancing toward Troyes over huge expanses of open ground. Boas was back at the command center. "We heard Dent give firing coordinates on the radio, or try to, and all of a sudden, we heard him scream," Boas said. "That was when the bullets hit him."

Seaman said, "I was in a tank. We were in what I call desert formation, spread out, going into this town. A German popped out of a foxhole and sprayed Dude across the stomach. I heard he jumped out of the jeep and said, 'Keep going.' But that was hearsay because I was nowhere near him at the time. We went into Troyes and I heard about Dude there."

In the Pacific, CU star Don Brotzman heard about Dude's death. "I just felt terrible," he said. "I felt like I had lost a great friend. I had lost some others, of course, but I thought about it a lot. I still remember hearing it, so precisely."

Of the original group of five Aggies, Rutherford also was killed in action. Ferguson later became A&M's baseball coach. Hoffman was killed in a plane crash shortly after the war. Seaman worked for the Colorado Game and Fish Department for thirty-one years, primarily as a fish biologist and researcher.

Dent first was buried in France. His remains later were brought back to the United States, and he was re-interred in the Golden Gate National Cemetery near San Francisco. His widow, Mildred, married former Aggies teammate Bob Hess.

CU: The Congressman

Number 60, Don Brotzman, Center

After that season, "Meatnose" ended up in the Army, going through Officer Candidate School at Fort Benning, Georgia, and eventually was with the 81st Infantry Division in the Philippines.

"We were getting ready to launch an attack on Japan when the atomic bombs were dropped and the war ended," Brotzman said. "I jokingly have told people that I guess I should have been a Democrat because Harry Truman saved my life."

Instead, Brotzman was a Republican. After attending law school and going into private practice in Boulder, he became a state legislator and was the Republican candidate for governor in 1954. He lost to Ed Johnson, then ran for Congress and served five terms as a U.S. representative before Democrat Tim Wirth unseated him after the Watergate backlash. He was president of the Rubber Manufacturers Association for ten years before retiring.

Brotzman died in 2004, and I never got to take him up on his offer to treat me to lunch in the House of Representatives dining room.

A&M: The Tuskegee Airman

Number 14, John Mosley, Guard

Many of the players in the 1942 game came from Denver, and one of them was a trailblazer. Aggies guard John Mosley was raised in a home on Marion Street, across the street from Whittier School. John Sr. was a porter on the Union Pacific Railroad and his wife, Henrietta, was a housewife.

"The old expression was that it takes a village to raise a child," John Jr. told me. "Denver was actually a village at that time, so all the neighbors and community people in the area helped raise the children. We couldn't go two or three steps without someone saying a word of encouragement or criticizing us for what we were doing or not doing."

They don't take "publicity" photos like this anymore: Here, John Mosley is a sophomore "Aggie" at Colorado A&M, now known as Colorado State University. Significantly, the Aggies' program was integrated long before the University of Colorado's. I came across Mosley while researching my book *Third Down and a War to Go.*

At the time, covenants and standards essentially prevented black families from living anywhere other than extreme northeast Denver. "The types of things going on in Denver were quite similar to what was happening down South, in terms of drinking fountains and the various department stores," he told me. The segregated lunch counters in downtown Denver included those at Kress and Woolworth, and he took pride in being part of the movement that led to their integration in later years.

I asked how those experiences couldn't have left him embittered.

"I didn't look at it that way," Mosley said. "I looked at it as an opportunity to move ahead. I really didn't have any bad feelings about who was responsible for the segregated activities and the types of discrimination we experienced. I was too busy trying to ensure that I got everything I possibly could out of school and also to participate in athletics."

Mosley also was active at his church and with the Boy Scouts, the all-black Troop 150, and sang in a quartet called the "Junior Mills Brothers." The quartet appeared in many of the Denver theaters and also on KLZ radio. Mosley laughed and remembered with wonder that they once were paid $5 for each gig.

He often went fishing for crawdads at City Park, using pieces of liver as bait. "We'd go down to Lafayette Street and sell crawdads to people," he said. "Crawdad meat was considered very tasty at the time." He also visited the old National Guard field on what is now Park Hill Golf Course and watched planes land and take off. "I pretended I was flying," he said.

A National Merit Scholar at Manual, Mosley went to Fort Collins with his childhood buddy, Charles Cousins, also the son of a Pullman porter, and enrolled at A&M. "I wanted to go to school with my buddy," Mosley said. "He went up there with the intention of going to veterinary school." Mosley was an all-city fullback at Manual, but he wasn't pursued to play collegiate football, even under the limited recruiting practices of the times.

There were nine black students at the school. Most of the time, six men shared a small house off campus. Four of Mosley's housemates were Harry Martin, Eugene Combs, Jesse Douglas, and Junior James. "We called ourselves, 'The Lonesome Boys,'" Mosley said.

Most of the Fort Collins restaurants wouldn't serve blacks. "We would load up on food in Denver, as we came down on weekends," Mosley said. "Our whole existence was cooking for ourselves. We could eat at the student union and there was an ice-cream parlor where we could get ice cream. All the rest had signs up. Some of the things were so demeaning, I didn't want to recall them, but I do remember, 'No Niggers allowed,' or, 'We don't serve Niggers here.'"

Cousins and Mosley went back and forth from Denver to Fort Collins during their college years. "As a result of working on the Union Pacific railroad in the summertime, Charles and I were able to acquire Model A Fords," Mosley said. "We went up in tandem because if one broke down, we were able to have the other pull or shove or render some help to make sure we made it down from Fort Collins to Denver or back up."

Housemates nicknamed him "One-Tea Bag Mosley," because he tried to nurse a single bag through a month. They saw no humor in him trying out for football as a freshman in 1939. "I just showed up and asked for a uniform," Mosley said. To reemphasize: before that season, there wasn't a single black player in the Mountain States Conference, which included CU.*

Nearing his thirtieth anniversary as the Aggies' head coach, Harry Hughes welcomed Mosley. "I guess he felt that he knew he was retiring soon and to have a black on his football team was no big deal because they couldn't do anything to him," Mosley said. "And he recognized that I could contribute to the team."

His teammates' reactions, especially at first, were mixed.

"I had to sell myself not only to Harry Hughes and the coaches but to the players," Mosley said. "There were many players from Texas and the Western slope, farmers and so forth, who didn't like black people. That was quite an experience to gain the support of my teammates. My first night out for football, one of the players from the Western Slope tackled me, and in doing so, he slapped his hands down on my helmet at the ears. That actually knocked me out. When I came to, Eugene Combs was there on the sidelines watching and he was laughing. He said, 'I *told* you not to go out for football. I *told* you these guys weren't going to treat you right.' But the fact that I could play football and block and tackle was productive in showing what I could offer to the team. I won't call out any names now, but there were several players on my team who never accepted me. But most did."

He played fullback until he was switched to guard as a senior.

"Naturally, there was name-calling and that type of thing," he said. "I had no problem in my responses, because I didn't respond. It was my teammates, Dude Dent and Woody Fries, who were quite vocal in ensuring that those voices didn't get out too much. The way I responded was through my ability to tackle and to run the ball hard. I never had to 'fight my own battles' on the football field. There were some things that were said, and that was constant, but if anyone tried to challenge me any other way, all my teammates would

---

* The CU program wasn't integrated until the mid-1950s.

come and get in their way. I always backed off. I got several awards for being a good sportsman, and that was one thing I didn't have to worry about. The way I got around that was on the next play or subsequent plays, if I was blocking someone or tackling, they knew that they got hit and blocked. So you always had a chance to get back at those who weren't too polite."

During the 1940 season, when Mosley was a sophomore, the Aggies traveled to Salt Lake City to play Utah. On Friday, they went to a movie theater. An usher told Mosley he would have to sit in the balcony.

"As the team went in, Coach Hughes asked the players, 'Hey, where's Mosley?' Somebody said, 'They sent him upstairs.' He told the assistant coach, 'You go in there and make this announcement: All Aggies, get the hell out of this damn theater!' The team came out and they were asking, 'What's wrong?' And Coach Hughes said, 'We're not going to that damn theater because they wouldn't let Mosley sit downstairs.'"

By the time the 1942 season began, Mosley was down to one roommate, Harry Martin, who was majoring in chemistry and went on to be a physician. They lived near the campus. Mosley considered CU the enemy on the playing field and noted that while the Buffaloes' football program hadn't yet been integrated, he had friends attending the school. "We used to go down to visit them, and they were restricted, as we were," Mosley said. "They were off campus, on Water Street. That was the black district down there and they lived with black families."

At A&M, Mosley was named vice president of his class as a junior and senior and hoped to become the first black in Advanced ROTC at A&M. "I had the correct academics and was well-known on campus, and I thought it was a shoo-in for me," he said. He took a physical at Fitzsimons Army Hospital. "Understand, I had been playing football for six years and wrestling and taking physical exams every year," he said. "I went back up to Fort Collins and was awaiting my assignment for Advanced ROTC, and they said, 'Sorry, you didn't make it; you didn't pass the physical.'"

Doctors told him he had a heart murmur.

I asked Mosley if he was an angry young man at that point, given what he was going through in Fort Collins and in football and wrestling. "Very definitely, but I had had some very good white friends and buddies up at CSU," he said. "I certainly wasn't angry at them. I was angry at the system. The president up there was a guy named [Roy] Green. I never will forget Green. He was a racist S.O.B."

When the door was shut to Advanced ROTC, Mosley sought an alternative.

"They were starting up a program called civilian pilot training, and it was at most of the colleges around the United States," he said. The civilian pilots ferried military aircraft to bases around the country or even to bases overseas. "So I decided, 'This is the way I am going to beat this game,'" Mosley said. "You had to get your own flight physical and pay for it. I got my money together, went to the flight physician, and he examined and passed me."

He started taking flying lessons in Fort Collins.

"When you signed up for civilian pilot training, you had to either sign up for the Army Air Forces or the Navy," he said. "At that time, the Navy wasn't even thinking about having blacks fly their airplanes. The only thing that was left was this experimental group, down in Tuskegee."

The all-black 99th Fighter Squadron was formed at Tuskegee in June 1941. By late 1942, the 332nd Fighter Group was considered the umbrella organization for the Tuskegee Airmen. Mosley made it his goal to join the Airmen.

After taking civilian flying lessons and campaigning to be included in the program, John Mosley, at left, became one of the famed Tuskegee Airmen during World War II. *Source*: Denver Public Library, Blair-Caldwell Dept., John Mosley Collection, ARL-214

Before he entered the service, an experience as his graduation ceremony approached left him reluctant to return to Fort Collins for many years. Fort Collins businessman "Sparks" Alford clumsily tried to congratulate Mosley.

"Sparks was really the sponsor of the team," Mosley said. "He went on all of our trips and he owned the Burlington, the bus run from Fort Collins to Denver. He did give me a job of mopping up the bus station, which was just a little cubbyhole down by the train station. I worked for Sparks for two years, I guess, maybe three, and we were good friends because he was a sponsor of the team. Whatever the team needed he would certainly work very hard to try and give the team that type of support. In getting my diploma, I was the happiest person in the world, thinking, 'Boy, I really have it made,' and that type of thing. I saw Sparks, and Sparks came up to me and said, 'Hey, John, very good, if you ever get in jail just give me a buzz and I'll get you out.' That to me was the most disappointing thing, to suggest that I might be a candidate for jail. I'd never been to jail in my life and certainly hadn't been involved in any problems up in Fort Collins. For him to think that the only thing I could do was to get involved in trouble some way left a very bad taste in my mouth."

Mosley was astounded when he wasn't drafted after graduation. "My peers were given their degrees early so they could go in," Mosley. "I got my degree, and my process was sitting and waiting. September came along, and nothing. I thought for sure I would be going down to Tuskegee." He complained to the draft board, and he was told that there had been a mix-up and his draft board believed he already had been called up. Soon, he was called in to the Army.

Instead of being sent to Tuskegee to fly, however, he was dispatched to a segregated field artillery unit at Fort Sill.

"I started writing letters, along with my parents, to congressmen and the White House," Mosley said. "I said, 'Look, I have actually been trained in flying, and why haven't I been sent down to Tuskegee?'"

He got his wish two months later.

"When I was going through," he said, "they didn't graduate any more pilots than they needed with the 99th [Fighter Squadron]. If they lost two people in the 99th, two people would graduate. They would eliminate you for anything—shoes not shined or for any attitude you had that wasn't appropriate. I often tell people I'm the best pilot in the world, but there were pilots better than I was who got washed out for nothing because they didn't realize they had to demonstrate they could out-strategize their white instructors. Those were the kinds of things we had to go through.

"The one goal I set for myself was I wanted to get those silver wings. I knew I had to do everything in the world to scrap and to prove myself. Although we had black instructors through primary training, they were all white instructors at basic and advanced. That's where the washouts were frequent. We used to say, 'How many did we lose in Europe, three or four?' And three or four would graduate from the next class. It was that sensitive and [there was] quite a bit of trying to outdo your fellow classmates so you would be selected to advance. That wasn't very pleasant, either, because you were fighting against other blacks down there trying to make it. I didn't tell my flight instructors that I already knew how to fly."

Why not?

Mosley said the word was that instructors would feel threatened by that and find a way to "wash out" that Airman.

Following pressure from black-owned newspapers and from the White House, the first black airmen served in combat, flying fighters in North Africa and Europe. In 1945, Mosley was one of the first blacks trained to be a bomber pilot. "They didn't trust us with B-17s, with bombs," Mosley said. "They thought the first thing we'd do was head for 1600 Pennsylvania Avenue. They really had to sell Congress with 'we think we can trust those guys now,' so we were permitted to fly B-25s."

Part of the training was at Tucson, and then at Freeman Field in Indiana. "They had a provision that there would be no black officer above the rank of captain, and there wouldn't be any white officers below the rank of major," Mosley said. "The white officers were all considered instructor personnel, and they had an officers' club they called the Instructors' Club. To ensure that we as black officers recognized that we weren't supposed to use it, they had two MPs standing up there. We discussed this and said, 'This is not right.'"

The angriest was pilot Daniel "Chappie" James. Mosley said James announced that the pilots should just storm into the officers' club. Eventually about forty of them did just that and were arrested, but Mosley was on a training mission to South Carolina at the time.

"The commander of the airfield used to carry around a swagger stick and put it under his arm," Mosley said. "We used to mock him by picking up a stick and carrying that. He decided to court-martial everybody involved. He had issued a statement that we were supposed to sign, that we understood we were not supposed to go into the officers' club. Of course, nobody signed it. We were sent back to Kentucky by Fort Knox. They thought by moving us back there, it would be a more secure thing. They thought there might be a revolution."

While the insurrectionists were awaiting their court-martials, Mosley said, they were under confinement at the Kentucky airfield in a barracks behind barbed wire. "German prisoners also were housed there, and they had the complete run of the base," he said. "They could use the PX. The airfield was somewhat separate from the Fort Knox unit, but the Germans had assignments over there, picking up the trash and things like that. It was most embarrassing to watch those German prisoners and then to look over there to the barracks that housed the guys who were under arrest, and the German prisoners had the full run of the base, it seemed like. So you knew what they thought of us. That was really disturbing."*

Mosley said that the court-martial was held in the base's theater. Future Supreme Court Justice Thurgood Marshall was one of the defending attorneys.

"It was a comical show for all of us blacks on base because we had to get there at six in the morning to get in line and get in the theater, because everyone wanted to crowd in there to watch this court-martial," Mosley said. "It really was the white base commander who was on trial. It was embarrassing to him and to the armed forces and the War Department, and following that, only about four people received a very minimal reprimand and letters in their files."†

By then promoted from copilot to pilot, Mosley and others were ticketed to fly in Pacific combat had the war continued into late 1945. As a reservist after the war, he was asked to write a position paper about the possible integration of the armed services and was told it would reach President Harry Truman's desk. He doubts that it did. But that report also is part of the reason why he always felt he had at least a small role in Truman's decision to integrate the military.

"The integration of the armed forces was really a prelude to all the kinds of civil rights activities that took place in this country," Mosley said. "That's why I use the Tuskegee Airmen as being the basis for all of this developing and making America what it should be. You asked why I wasn't bitter. It was because I was part of the movement to prove that we were capable of making a contribution to the development of this great nation. We had the foresight

---

* I thought of all of that when I read James McBride's novel, *Miracle at St. Anna*, and saw Spike Lee's film version. In the book and movie, during their training in the United States, African American soldiers of the 92nd Division encounter German prisoners of war and their guards eating ice cream in a cafe. The African American soldiers are told they must go to the back if they want to be served. That was a novel, but unfortunately it wasn't really fiction. In our great cause, that was our blind spot.

† The insurrection leader, Chappie Jones, became the Air Force's first black four-star general.

to know that this would be the best nation in the world. And it is the best nation in the world. The Armed Forces would have never been integrated had it not been for the Tuskegee Airmen proving they could fight, wanted to fight, could be relied on to fight, and were not afraid of giving their lives to accomplish their missions and goals."

During the Cold War years, Mosley spent reserve stints in the new U.S. Air Force flying supplies to West Germany and North Africa and also worked for the YMCA. During the Vietnam War, he was an operations officer in Thailand as U.S. pilots flew bombing missions over North Vietnam. He retired from the Air Force in 1970 as a lieutenant colonel and served as special assistant to the undersecretary in the Department of Health, Education and Welfare in Washington before returning to Denver. He worked at the regional office for the Department of Health and Human Services until he retired.

Mosley was inducted into the Colorado Sports Hall of Fame in 2009, and I was honored to introduce him at the banquet.

CU: Tex

Number 33, Maurice "Tex" Reilly, Quarterback

The Buffaloes' quarterback came by his nickname honestly.

"Tex came off of the King Ranch in Texas," teammate Paul Briggs recalled. "His dad was a foreman."

"Tex was my best friend in college," said Dick Woodward, the Buffaloes' right end. "He was all Texas from head to foot. He invited me down for a period of time to join him on his ranch, and that's where I got my cowboy training."

"Tex was a big redhead, a good passer, a neat guy," recalled Carl Stearns.

"He was a heck of a student and a good head to have out there," recalled CU guard Don Creese.

In the war, Reilly, who commanded a bomber in the Pacific, flew several missions over Japan, returned to CU to play one season after the war, then re-entered the Air Force and retired as a major general.

CU: The Kicker

Number 5, Bob Knowles, Halfback/kicker

Like Dude Dent, CU's Bob Knowles—the Buffalo from Sterling who successfully kicked four extra points against A&M—died in Europe during the war. It was classified as a non-battle death, which usually means a training exercise or another sort of accident.

A&M: The Rancher

Number 42, Perry Blach, Tackle

Perry Blach's family had been ranching in the Yuma area since his grandfather came over from Austria and homesteaded, building a two-room sod house in 1887. His father, Ambrose, was born there in 1889. Perry starred in sports for Yuma High School while participating in 4H and Future Farmers of America activities.

In 1941, Blach went off to A&M. The next year, he was a sophomore lineman, not starting but getting a lot of playing time, including in the loss to Colorado.

Blach was called up from the Army Reserves in May 1943, but was granted a four-month extension to help his father farm that summer. After his September induction, he was attached to the newly formed 738th Field Artillery Battalion. "We had eight-inch howitzers and all the trucks and equipment that went with them," Blach told me. "I was in firing direction. I figured the firing data for those guns."

Blach went ashore with his unit on Normandy's Utah Beach about a month after D-Day. "Everything was quiet at that time there, but all the wrecked landing craft were still in that harbor," he said. "We were on a three-quarter ton, what we called a 'carry-all.' It was a big pickup and we pulled a trailer behind that with a lot of our equipment on it."

On the first night and the next day, the 738th moved 178 miles, much of it under German shelling. "We ended up in a little town, and by that time, the Allies had so many prisoners, they didn't know what to do with them," Blach said. "They pulled us off the road and gave us barbed wire. We strung barbed wire and we guarded prisoners for five or six days. You take everything away from them. I still have some of their pocketknives down in the basement. Then the rear echelon caught up with us and took over the prisoners. They put us with the 4th Armored, the 80th Infantry, and the 35th Infantry, and that was in Patton's Third Army."

After about three weeks of rough going, Blach and his buddies arrived at the Moselle River, near the German border. "Tanks were ahead of us, but if they ran into something they couldn't soften up, we'd pull the eight-inch howitzers off and blast 'em and go on," Blach said. "My job was to figure the range and the altitude. I enjoyed that part of it because I always knew where we were, because we had good maps. When we got to the river, we were out of gas and out of ammunition. If the Germans had known that, they could have walked back across that river and taken all our equipment. We drained the gasoline out of everything but four trucks to be able to send those trucks back to Paris for supplies."

After the infantry division was pulled out to help in the Battle of the Bulge, Blach's group moved from Luxembourg into Germany and went all the way across the country, including through Frankfurt, well to the south of Berlin. They were fired upon by artillery and snipers, and the closest Blach came to getting killed was when he attempted to repair a generator in the open and was subjected to fire from 88-caliber artillery. At one point, a muddied and fatigued Blach was crossing a road in Germany when he heard a jeep racing up behind him. He turned and saw stars—three stars on the jeep. Blach saluted General George S. Patton, and as he passed by, Patton saluted back. The forces moved into Czechoslovakia, where Blach was amused to hear natives ask, "You going to fight the Russkies?" Then the Germans surrendered. "The Czech people rolled out the beer every night and had big dances to celebrate and invited the GIs to join them. They made us pull out and turn it over to the Russians, and everybody was sick. We really felt sorry for them."

After German occupation duty, Blach was switched to the 945th Field Artillery and had orders to go with that unit through the Suez Canal to the Pacific to join in the war against Japan. "We were still in Germany when they dropped the first bomb on Japan," Blach said. "They put us on hold and dropped the second bomb, and the war ended."

When Blach was discharged, he bought the ranch next to his parents' outside Yuma in 1946 but returned to school and played for the Rams again in 1946 and 1947. "School was easier because I was older and I knew what I wanted," he said.

Blach served on the CSU alumni board for twenty-four years, became a major financial booster for the university and the athletic department, and renowned for his Hereford cattle. He and his wife, Teresa, had nine children. His cousin from Yuma, Leonard, became a veterinarian and was co-owner of 2009 Kentucky Derby winner Mine That Bird. Perry admitted he hadn't bet on his cousin's horse, a 50 to 1 longshot that went on to finish second in the Preakness and third in the Belmont Stakes.

CU: Bomber Pilot

Number 38, Glenn Hedgecock, Halfback

CU captain Glenn Hedgecock, the starting right halfback, came from Denver North High and had wrestled Manual High's John Mosley several times. By 1942, Hedgecock was the president of the CU student body. He lived in the Pi Kappa Alpha fraternity. His wife and high school sweetheart, Virgeen, was living with her parents in Denver. "We got married that year and we kept our marriage a secret," Virgeen told me. "People didn't get married in college in those days. My family, his family, and a few close friends knew. That's it."

Virgeen believed she attended the CU–A&M game with Hedgecock's parents and celebrated. But she also said the big party came at the Brown Palace Hotel, after a season-ending 31–6 rout of DU left CU with a 7–2 record.

Soon, Hedgecock was in training with the Army Air Forces. He commanded a B-17 bomber, and he flew missions from England over Germany. At least one of his missions was to Dresden, where approximately twenty-five thousand German civilians died in 1945 bombings.

Making his living selling insurance, he raised a family with Virgeen, unsuccessfully ran for the state legislature, and worked the small ranch he bought. "He was a peace activist," Virgeen said. "He just felt there had to be another way to resolve problems."

The Hedgecocks went to most CU games until Glenn's death in 1998.

A&M: The Vet

Number 7, Chet Maeda, Halfback

Maeda, who hadn't been able to play in the 1942 game because of his injury, arrived in Fort Collins after starting out at Los Angeles City College; his intent was to attend the veterinary school. His father was half Japanese and half Hawaiian, and his teammates remember occasional remarks directed at him by fans after the war began. Maeda told me that during the 1941 CU–Aggies game, won by the Buffs 26–13, a Buffalo challenged him to a fight.

"John Mosley was on the bench at the time," Maeda said from his home in San Bernardino, California. "John saw what was going on, and he immediately got up and started running toward the field. One of the fans told me later that Coach Hughes got up and started yelling, 'Mose, come back! Mose, come back!' They got him back, but if they got me in a fight, he was going to get in it, too."

Maeda had stood up for Mosley, and Mosley was going to return the favor.

After the 1942 season, Maeda was commissioned as a first lieutenant in the Veterinary Corps. "They took some of the top students, and some of the rest of us were put in the reserves and were on call to go into active duty at any time," Maeda said. "For a few months, I went to Nebraska and did some practice with dairy cattle, and it kind of bothered me. So I went back home to L.A. and investigated the possibility of going back into active uniform. After a few months, I went into the active Veterinary Corps. I was stationed in Alabama, at Fort McClellan, then went to Fort Lewis, Washington, where I served my three years. Most of the work was meat and dairy inspection during the war."

He ended up in private practice after the war and retired in 2001.

CU: Anchors Aweigh

Number 66, Paul Briggs, Tackle
Number 18, Stan Hendrickson, End
Number 31, Don Creese, Guard

Briggs already was wearing a Navy uniform to class that fall of 1942 as a member of the Navy ROTC. He was the rare Buffalo who played again for CU in 1943 while getting his commission before leaving campus.

Later, as an ensign and a lieutenant, Briggs was assigned to a destroyer, the USS *Daly*, in the Pacific. "I was 6-5 and 270," he said, laughing. "The only thing worse for me would have been a submarine. But I saw everything from New Guinea clear to Tokyo. I never missed anything. I had the privilege of getting close to the shoreline at Okinawa, I got close to the shoreline at the Philippines, and got damn close to Iwo Jima. We became the destroyer squadron that went with General MacArthur whenever he decided he was going to move from one island to the other."

Briggs knew he didn't have it as tough as did Stan Hendrickson, the Buffalo end who lined up next to him on the left side of the line in 1942—and who had come ashore at the Philippines ahead of MacArthur's troops. "Stan was a guerrilla fighter," Briggs said. "He came off a submarine with a life jacket. He lived off the land. He became a communicator in the Philippines."

Off Okinawa, Briggs's destroyer took a hit from a kamikaze plane. "One of them lit between the number-one and number-two stack," he said. "They put a couple of [landing-craft carriers] next to us, and we were able to get back into dry dock for the repair work right there."

Briggs was on the *Daly*, next to the *USS Missouri* when MacArthur signed the armistice with the Japanese on the *Missouri* in Tokyo Bay.

He returned and played another season with CU, with another veteran 1942 lineman, right guard Don Creese, who had been a physical instructor at Navy boot camp during the war. Briggs played one year with the Detroit Lions before becoming a high school teacher and coaching at Rocky Ford, Colorado; Casper, Wyoming; and Bakersfield, California. He had one of the top high school programs in the nation at Bakersfield from 1948 to 1983, and he retired in 1983. He also was a full commander in the Navy Active Reserves.

Creese, meanwhile, coached and taught at Boulder's Fairview High School, then was a counselor at nearby Centaurus High School until retiring.

A&M: Torpedoed

Number 15, Duane Warnock, Tackle

A&M's starting left tackle, sophomore Duane Warnock, was from Longmont, Colorado. After entering the Army, he was headed across the English Channel in a troop carrier on Christmas Eve 1944 when the ship next to his was torpedoed and went down, killing more than one thousand. The troops had been ticketed to join the Battle of the Bulge in Belgium. "We didn't go [on] because we were no longer what they called 'battle-ready' after we lost those men," Warnock told me shortly before his death. "I lost a lot of friends. I wound up stationed in Austria. I was in France for a long time."

Warnock played again at A&M in 1946 and 1947, then was a coach and administrator at Loveland and Fort Collins high schools in northern Colorado.

CU: Bad Dude's Dad

Number 29, Carl Stearns, Halfback

CU left halfback Carl Stearns, who scored twice against the Aggies, came from Denver East High, was a sophomore in the 1942 season, and was in the Army Air Force reserves. After being called up, he spent a short time in a holding pattern on the Michigan State campus, in what was a common procedure designed to space out pilot classes and also give them additional academic training. His flight training was in B-25 and B-26 bombers, but late in the war, he and other young pilots were diverted to learn how to fly the new A-26. "It was twin-engine, and you had three in your crew with you—a navigator, a bombardier, and a gunner," he said.

The war ended while he still was in training.

Stearns reenrolled in college at the University of Denver and played football for the Pioneers. He had a teaching career in the Denver public schools, including a long stint in coaching at his alma mater, Denver East, and retired in 1980. His son, John "Bad Dude" Stearns, was an all-American football and baseball player at CU and had a long major league career, most notably with the New York Mets.

An Aggie and a Buffalo on Okinawa

CU: Number 36, Bob Spicer, Guard
A&M: Number 15, Walter "Bus" Bergman, Halfback

CU's Spicer and A&M's Bergman played in a game against each other during World War II, but it wasn't in Fort Collins in 1942.

Spicer came to Boulder from Leavenworth, Kansas. In 1942, he was a sophomore reserve lineman and got in for mop-up duty in the easy win over A&M. After call-ups to reservists in college went out, he was in the Marines by early 1943. As a sergeant, he came ashore at Bougainville, the largest island in the Solomons, in November 1943. "We secured part of the island to build a landing strip," he told me. His unit moved on to another island, Emeru, by then calm, but went back into action on Guam. After fighting there, Spicer ended up on Guadalcanal, which U.S. forces had taken in 1942 and were using as a staging area for further movement in the horrific Pacific fighting. The Sixth Marine Division was re-formed there.

Bus Bergman was on Guadalcanal, too.

Raised near the original Elitch Gardens in northwest Denver, Bergman was a three-sport star at North High. At A&M, he earned ten letters in football, basketball, and baseball, and he was the school's student body president in the 1941–1942 academic year. In February 1942, Bergman and Aggies teammate Red Eastlack drove to Denver to enlist in the Marines. The Marines' preference was for upperclassmen to stay in college long enough to graduate. To publicize the officer-training program, the Marine brass had the star athletes "sworn in" a second time at midcourt during halftime of an A&M–Wyoming basketball game. Bergman and Eastlack were playing for the Aggies in Fort Collins, so they toweled off the sweat and raised their right hands.

As he finished his classes, Bergman didn't respond to an eye-popping $140-a-game contract sent by the Philadelphia Eagles. After receiving his degree, he went to boot camp and Officer Candidate School and then joined the 29th Regiment at Camp Lejeune. He got wind of the Buffaloes' 1942 romp over the Aggies while in the Marines but had more important things on his mind than disappointment over the loss. By August 1944, he was on Guadalcanal, where the 29th Regiment became part of the Sixth Division.

Bergman, former Notre Dame star George Murphy, and former Boston University tackle Dave Mears were the platoon leaders in D Company of the 29th Regiment's 2nd Battalion. The three lieutenants shared a tent and trained. Looming over the Marines was the likelihood that they soon would be fighting. "We didn't know where we were going," Bergman said. "But we knew it was going to be close to the [Japanese] mainland. Football and little things kept us away from all that talk. Plus, we spent a lot of time in that tent censoring the mail." He laughed. "Marines had girlfriends all over the world, and they wrote to all of 'em. We had to read it, and we were supposed to cut things out, but nobody really said anything we had to worry about that way."

Along with many other former college and NFL players, Bergman and Spicer played in a monumental Marine touch football game—matching the 4th Regiment versus the 29th Regiment—on Guadalcanal on Christmas Eve 1944.* A huge crowd of Marines surrounded the rocky field.

Spicer was the starting quarterback for the 4th Regiment. That might seem a curious assignment for a former college guard, considering both rosters included NFL and college stars. But halfbacks threw most of the passes and the quarterback mostly blocked. Wisconsin's Bob Baumann and Dave Schreiner both were on his team.

Bergman was a starting halfback for the 29th Regiment. His team captain was end Chuck Behan, who caught four passes for the Detroit Lions as a rookie in 1942 before entering the Marines. The rough game ended in a scoreless tie, with Spicer intercepting a pass on the final play.

---

* I discussed the game and the fate of its players in great detail in *Third Down and a War to Go*. It was labeled "The Football Classic" on the makeshift programs but called the "Mosquito Bowl" by Marine correspondent Harold Boian, whose dispatches were picked up by U.S. wire services. In a bizarre twist, Harold Boian later became the head of the advertising department at the *Denver Post*.

Spicer, Bergman, thousands of other Marines, and U.S. forces went ashore on the western beaches of Okinawa on April 1, 1945.

"I remember that just as we were getting ready to load on our landing craft, one P-38 [fighter plane] flew over us and I felt like I could reach up and touch it," Bergman said. "I've never forgotten that."

Bergman and the 29th Marines first moved up to the northern end of the island, roughly sixty-five miles long. "The only men we lost were from mines and booby traps in caves," Bergman said. "We lost our machine gun officer and mortar officer going in one of the caves. But then we came back to the lower third, and that's where all the trouble was."

Spicer and Bergman both were in the Battle of Sugar Loaf Hill. Spicer suffered shrapnel wounds in his arm. "I was looking when I should have been ducking," he told me. Bergman, meanwhile, was in heavy action, along with his tent mates, Murphy, the former Notre Dame star; and Mears. On May 15, Murphy was killed, Mears wounded. Suddenly, Bergman was the only tent mate remaining in the battle. Four days later, Bergman helped keep the Marines organized enough to maintain control of Sugar Loaf against major Japanese counterattacks, exposing himself to enemy fire, and he was awarded the Bronze Star.

Spicer went off the lines with his shrapnel wound but returned a week later wearing a bandage. In the final stages of the Okinawa fighting, when he and his unit encountered a trench full of Japanese, he took a grenade fragment in his right eye.

"I got back in the hospital, and my eye started scratching, and it got all puffed up, real big," he said. "They said they had to take it out."

Doctors removed his eye. He was through fighting.

Of the nearly three thousand Marines who died on Okinawa, twelve played in the Christmas Eve touch football game.

"I wondered why it was them and not me," Spicer said. "Nobody could answer that."

Many of the Marine survivors of the battle, including Bergman, were ticketed to serve in an invasion of Japan. Bergman showed me a G-2 summary of the Sixth Marine Division's strategy on Okinawa. In the letter on the first page from Major General Lemuel Shepherd, dated August 1, 1945, the Sixth Division's commanding officer declared: "I believe that the lessons learned at so dear a price on [Okinawa] should be published and distributed for the benefit of combat units who will land again on Japanese soil."

New President Harry S. Truman approved the use of atomic bombs against Japan, and they were dropped over Hiroshima and Nagasaki in early

August. "We were real happy it was going to end the war," Bergman said. "Before that, we knew we were going to go to the mainland."

Instead, the invasion of Japan was unnecessary after the August surrender, and Bergman's unit drew occupation duty in China.

Released from the Marines in January 1946, Spicer learned to navigate with one eye and a limited field of vision. "You have no depth perception, but that doesn't really figure into it where I played," he said.

When Spicer returned to the Boulder campus after a three-year absence, he told CU coach Jim Yeager he wanted to play football again. Yeager didn't ask Spicer many questions. Neither did the team doctors. In fact, as Spicer remembers it, he didn't even have to take a physical. "If you were walking, you were okay," Spicer told me with a laugh.

In the locker room, there was something about Spicer that discouraged extensive interrogation. Some knew he had been a Marine. They didn't know many details. "I didn't want to think about it too much, much less talk about it," Spicer said.

He didn't tell his coaches or teammates that his right eye was a $75 piece of cosmetic glass. He played for Yeager in 1946 and 1947, and then Dal Ward in 1948. Starting at guard in his junior and senior seasons, Spicer also was the Buffs' captain in 1948.

Incredibly, he also played catcher for the CU baseball team. As a right-handed hitter, he could focus with his left, or lead, eye. "The worst thing was, I couldn't follow pop-ups," he said. "My batting average wasn't very high. I either hit home runs or struck out."

After leaving CU, he was a news editor for a Burlington, Iowa, radio station, and then got into the banking field in the Chicago area. "I went in as a trainee and then became an officer," he said.

He and Nancy Spicer had five children and seventeen grandchildren.

"Three times a week, I go to kidney dialysis," he told me shortly before his death. "Other than that, I guard the television set."

In 1946, Bus Bergman returned to Fort Collins and earned his master's degree. He went into coaching at Fort Lewis College in Durango and then moved to Mesa College in Grand Junction in 1950. He coached the Mesa football and baseball teams, and the baseball team three times was the runner-up in the national junior college tournament—an event Bergman helped Grand Junction land as the annual host. He retired from coaching in 1974 and from the faculty in 1980. He was inducted into the Colorado Sports Hall of Fame in 1995.

"They say certain guys are heroes because they did this and that," Bergman told me. "I say the heroes are those guys who never came back. I've thought about that a lot. I think about the sixty or seventy extra years I got on them. I know I was lucky."

Bergman for years didn't volunteer much information about his combat experiences, even to his children—Judy Black of Washington, Walter Jr. of Grand Junction, and Jane Norton of Englewood, who served as Colorado's lieutenant governor from 2002 to 2008 and was a Republican candidate for senator in 2010.

During my visit with Bus, his wife, Elinor, also a Denver native, at times was compelled to point out things Bus neglected to mention. Little things, such as the citation that accompanied his Bronze Star.

On March 25, 2010, Judy Black called me from Grand Junction and left a message, saying Bus was struggling with congestive heart failure and the family had gathered to say its goodbyes to him. When I called her back, we talked, and then she handed Bus the phone. I told Bus he was one of my favorites and how proud I was to know him and to have told his story. I will always treasure what he told me in his response.

He died three days later.

———— ◆ ————

I wrote the book about the Wisconsin team from that wartime era. I could have done the same with the Aggies and Buffaloes, but by the time I got around to researching those teams, available information about the players on both rosters was limited. So I'm certain I missed CU and A&M players who played heroic roles in the war, and the argument still can be made that anyone who served fit that description. If I close my eyes and stab a finger at a page listing all the 1942 college football teams, I probably could write a book about any of them. That's the point. The Badgers, and now the Aggies and Buffaloes, serve as symbols for their generation. They and so many others bring to mind one of General Patton's better-known utterances: "Better to fight for something than to live for nothing."

FRANK SHORTER: FORTY-EIGHT SECONDS BEFORE THE ROAR

WHEN YOU SPEND YOUR FORMATIVE YEARS in track-and-field-crazy Eugene, Oregon, as I did, you at first just assume every other kid in the country has to run a mile every day in junior high PE class—to warm up. You figure that in every college town in the nation, the track-and-field athletes are as prominent—or more so—than football and basketball stars. Oregon distance runner Steve Prefontaine, the subject of not one but two biopics released in the 1990s,* was one of the two most charismatic athletes I've ever seen, behind only Muhammad Ali. I first saw him when he was running for Marshfield High School in Coos Bay. In Eugene, in his collegiate career and beyond, he had rock star status, and although I was in Colorado by then, I knew that his 1974 death in a one-car accident—he lost control of his sports car, it flipped, and he suffocated beneath the steering wheel—cast a pall over the city.

Frank Shorter, the 1972 Olympic marathon champion, competed many times in Eugene, sometimes against Prefontaine, and was Prefontaine's friend. He also was the last person to see "Pre" alive on the night after a meet at Hayward Field. I always felt as if I knew him by extension.

Shorter, raised in New York's Hudson Valley region before winning the 1969 NCAA six-mile run for Yale, has been a full-time resident of Colorado since 1974. He has been a competitive runner, the owner of successful sportswear and athletic supply companies, an attorney, a writer, a television commentator, a race founder, and an anti-doping crusader.

---

* The best was the second, *Without Limits*, cowritten by former Oregon distance runner Kenny Moore, with Donald Sutherland as Coach Bill Bowerman and Billy Crudup as "Pre."

When I put together the list of athletes who made the most impact in Colorado, I wrestled with Shorter because he was neither raised in the state nor attended college there. But the more I looked into it, the more I realized he had become an adopted native son, and his impact was immense on several levels. Because his anti-doping campaign has had an effect on other sports and because he has a Pied Piper status in the running world, he remains influential. I noticed that he wasn't in the Colorado Sports Hall of Fame and successfully advanced his case at the selection meeting. Then and only then did I contact him and interview him, and I did so on a couple of occasions for the paper and then for Fox Sports Rocky Mountain.

Shorter lives in a solar-heated home on the north side of Boulder on the edge of a greenbelt. As he enters his sixties, his most fanatical running days are behind him, but even while talking to him, I sensed pent-up energy and got the impression he would be running across the greenbelt before I had reached downtown Boulder on my return trip.

Shorter graduated from Yale in 1969 and enrolled in medical school at the University of New Mexico. His parents were living in Taos by then. "I didn't have any money, and they didn't want to let me schedule to accommodate my training," Shorter said. "They didn't believe I was serious. The way it is now, the dean of the medical school probably would be a runner. But they just didn't believe me. I've always been one of those people that people kind of underestimate, which is an advantage in a lot of ways." After leaving medical school in Albuquerque, he briefly hung around Taos and then moved to Boulder in 1970.

Why Boulder?

"CU was the only place in the country with an indoor track above five thousand feet," he told me. Although the Mexico City Olympics had been held two years earlier at high altitude, Shorter was convinced training at high altitude at least part time would help him. Also, his girlfriend, Louise Gilliland, was attending CU. He started at the University of Florida law school and the next four years returned to Boulder during school breaks. In Gainesville, he trained with top distance runner Jack Bachelor and made considerable progress.

"By then, my wife and I were married, and she was in school here, so in essence I had a place here because she was here," he said. "So I was going back and forth until 1974 and then in the fall of '74 we moved here [full time]."

Of course, something memorable happened during the time in which he was traveling between Colorado and Florida.

He won the Olympic marathon at Munich in 1972, becoming the first American to win the 26-mile, 385-yard event at the Games in sixty-four years.

"I had decided to take at least one Olympics and see how good I could get," he said. "Not many people go to law school full time and run twenty miles a day."

In Munich, the marathon was contested several days after the terrorist murders of Israeli athletes. "We went through all the stages," Shorter told me. "Our initial reaction was, 'We're all going home, nothing is worth human life.' And then after the memorial service, on the way back, and we could walk back because the Olympic village was that close, we realized you had to keep going, because if you didn't, the terrorists win."

I found it interesting that before Munich, Shorter wasn't even considered a marathoner. He finished fifth in the 10,000 meters eight days before the marathon.

"I was a track runner who could keep running," he said. "The satisfaction of the marathon is being able to endure. In track races, you do run against other athletes, whereas in a marathon, you run against whoever is running next to you. It's a different kind of enjoyment."

An imposter runner sneaked onto the marathon course and entered the Munich stadium first, drawing the traditional ovation from the crowd. Shorter heard the cheers, but he sensed what had happened.

"That's a really interesting situation because I think many of the people had empathy for me," he told me. "They were thinking, 'Oh, my gosh, he thinks he didn't win.' But I had backed off. I was truly aerobic. If somebody had gone by me, I would have known it. And I knew how far ahead I was. I'd done the math from about twenty-three miles in, that if I just maintained a certain effort—in the vicinity of something under 5:10 a mile, or maybe more like 5:05 or 5:00 minutes a mile—someone would have to run 4:20 a mile for the four miles to catch me. And so I would have known.

"The other satisfaction of it is I now know I didn't run for the cheers."

Between the two Olympics, Shorter settled in Boulder.

"I studied for the bar, passed the bar in early 1975, and started to work for the French and Stone law firm here," he said. "But I really had decided at that point to keep training and try to go back a second time."

He suffered a broken foot in February 1976, but kept training, targeting the marathon only. "There wasn't enough time to let it heal and then come back for the Olympic Trials in May," he said. "I kept running. I'd get a cyst the size of a ping-pong ball and get it aspirated every couple of weeks. I was able to be in very, very good shape."

He ran well in the marathon trials at Eugene and seemed positioned for a possible repeat at Montreal. Instead, he finished second to East Germany's Waldemar Cierpinski, who was running only his fifth recorded competitive marathon. That, along with the East German athletic machine's subsequent connection to performance-enhancing substances, raised doubts about Cierpinski's legitimacy as an Olympic champion.

"Don Kardong* put it that I've been in the Olympics twice, and twice I've finished right behind an imposter," Shorter said. "I believe more and more in karma now. I've looked at the film and both times I hit the track forty-eight seconds behind the roar. That just doesn't happen. I remember the second time I heard the roar. I knew I was about the same spot and I said, 'I'm never going to hear this roar.' But that's how I react to this stuff, you know?"

Even then, I told Shorter, there were whispers about the East Germans' tactics.

"Oh, yeah, we all knew," Shorter said. "The irony was when you're running the marathon, it's whomever's running next to you. But I thought Cierpinski was [Portugal's Carlos] Lopes. I had watched Lopes with Erich Segal in the 10,000 meters when I was doing the 10,000 on TV [as a commentator] and he finished second to Lasse Viren. I watched his stride. Cierpinski was wearing a white shirt without the East German logo. I thought it was Lopes. He's short. Lopes is short. I'd only seen Lopes from afar. I ran the whole way thinking this was someone from Portugal. Cierpinski came up to me after and said, '*Sprechen zie Deutsch?*' And I thought, 'That's funny for someone from Portugal to say that.' But if you think about it, what was so odd about that is generally people who are doing drugs—if you really watch how they compete closely—don't know how to compete. They don't appear to be getting tired. The guys on EPO, the blood dopers, I could tell early on. . . .

"You knew. In 1972, we were at the [athletes'] assembly meeting in Maine and I was sitting in the back of the room with the weightmen because I used to hang out with them. They had better parties. The team doctor got up there and said, 'You know, steroids don't work.' I was in the back with the weightmen and they had pictures, before-and-after pictures."

I was operating under the belief—a misconception, as it turned out—that Shorter had sought to overturn Cierpinski's victory and add a second

---

* Another prominent U.S. distance runner.

gold medal to his collection.* "I haven't done anything," Shorter said. "I never did. Again, it's been sort of publicized that I've been on some sort of campaign. Never. Never asked anyone, never called anyone, never did anything. It's sort of like the same thing on the roar going into the Olympic stadium. I know that's not the reason I did it. And since I knew that to ever say anything would be perceived as sour grapes, my view was that if, as part of the deterrent, it would be acceptable if the IOC decided to go back and review [East] Germany." Shorter's point is that more than two hundred former East German athletes received settlements after the dissolution of the Soviet bloc for being placed on steroid regimens when they competed, which involved admissions that cheating was an everyday event in the East German sports machine.

After his second Olympics, Shorter branched out into a business career, founding both an athletic supply and a sportswear company. "I decided to make my living around the sport rather than from the sport," he said. "Over the years, things changed and I sold the companies a couple of times and got them back a couple of times because the lawyer in me is always smart enough to have reversionary clause. I never sold them outright. It's just sort of gone like that for me, with whatever the passion was at the moment."

In Colorado, Shorter perhaps is known as much for his role in founding the Bolder Boulder, one of the nation's top citizen races. "That is the most amount of recognition for the least amount of work I've ever done," he said. "All I had was the idea and I guess that's what America is all about. In three or four years, the community took it over."

Shorter became more directly involved in the anti-doping movement in 1998, writing a memorandum that was used during the formation of the United States Anti-Doping Agency in 2000. He ultimately became one of the leaders in the new organization.

"You take advantage of windows when they open," he said. "So when the window opened after the Tour de France in 1998, I wrote the memorandum. . . . They said, 'Why don't you be on the board?' I said, 'You don't understand, I don't think the USOC wants me on the board.'"

Eventually, Shorter ended up not just on the USADA board, but served as its chairman until 2003.

"I found out that the White House sort of suggested that I be on the board," he said. "I went for a run during the incorporation meeting at lunch and I came back and I was the chairman."

---

* Cierpinski also won the marathon at the 1980 Games in Moscow, which were boycotted by the United States.

Shorter has testified before Congress and remains an outspoken critic of professional sports' relatively belated and passive approach in handling performance-enhancing substances. He said baseball was "trying to appease the press and stall long enough for the people implicated to get out of the pipeline. Baseball's problem is the drugs worked too well and these guys hung around too long. The only solution is to have an independent agency.

"It's a very simple formula. You can't both promote and police. Someone else has to do it. . . . I hope the public isn't lulled, because the fact is, until it's outsourced, there's always going to be that conflict. Whether it's conscious or subliminal, the best job is not going to be done." He is adamant that blood testing, rejected in part because of collective bargaining issues, is the way to go.

If his efforts eventually help USADA-type drug testing become accepted in U.S. professional sports, he deserves a real roar.

PART FOUR

DIAMONDS

Ralph Branca turned and started for the clubhouse. The number on his uniform looked huge. Thirteen.

—Red Smith, *New York Herald Tribune*

Games
3 - 4 - 5

CLUBHOUSE

00594

C   393

WORKING MEDIA
Admit to Press Box,
Field, Interview Room

TERRY FREI
OREGONIAN (SEA)

LOCATION _Aux._
SEC **2**   ROW **4**   SEAT **5**

NOT TRANSFERABLE • SUBJECT TO CONDITIONS ON
REVERSE SIDE • NOT FOR USE BY ANYONE UNDER 18
• NO AUTOGRAPHS • ENTER AT PRESS GATE •
THIS CREDENTIAL MUST BE WORN AT ALL TIMES

GAME GAME GAME GAME GAME GAME
8 4 5   **X**
3   4   5   X

WORLD SERIES
CLUBHOUSE
National
League City

MEDIA
WORLD SERIES

Badge Required for Clubhouse Access

Writer
C

**Terry Frei
Denver Post**

NATIONAL LEAGUE CITY

This credential must be worn at all times. Not transferable. No autographs.
Subject to conditions on reverse side. Not for use by anyone under 18.

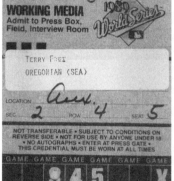

MAJOR-LEAGUE BASEBALL   86th WORLD SERIES

1989 World Series

PRE-GAME NOTES

GAME #3 - Oakland @ San Francisco - Tuesday, October 17, 1989

STARTING LINEUPS

OAKLAND	AVG.	HR	RBI	SAN FRANCISCO	AVG.	HR	RBI
24 R. Henderson, LF (R)	.625	0	0	2 B. Butler, CF (L)	.167	0	0
4 C. Lansford, 3B (R)	.250	0	1	6 R. Thompson, 2B (R)	.000	0	1
33 J. Canseco, RF (R)	.000	0	0	22 W. Clark, 1B (L)	.250	0	0
27 R. Hassey, C (L)	.000	0	0	7 K. Mitchell, LF (R)	.375	0	0
25 M. McGwire, 1B (R)	.500	0	0	10 K. Oberkfell, 3B (L)	1.000	0	0
42 D. Henderson, CF (R)	.000	0	0	9 M. Williams, SS (R)	.000	0	0
2 T. Phillips, 2B (S)	.286	0	1	16 T. Kennedy, C (L)	.167	0	0
7 W. Weiss, SS (S)	.143	1	1	25 P. Sheridan, RF (L)	---	--	--
35 B. Welch, P (R)	.000	0	0	31 D. Robinson, P (R)	.000	0	0

RESERVES

PITCHERS	W-L	ERA	PITCHERS	W-L	ERA
40 S. Bedrosian (R)	0-0	0.00	54 T. Burns (R)	---	---
49 J. Brantley (R)	0-0	0.00	14 S. Davis (R)	---	---
37 K. Downs (R)	0-0	0.00	43 D. Eckersley (R)	0-0	0.00
50 S. Garrelts (R)	0-1	9.00	40 R. Honeycutt (L)	0-0	0.00
14 A. Hammaker (L)	0-0	0.00	21 M. Moore (R)	1-0	1.29
29 M. LaCoss (R)	0-0	0.00	19 G. Nelson (R)	---	---
32 C. Lefferts (L)	0-0	0.00	34 D. Stewart (R)	1-0	0.00
48 R. Reuschel (R)	0-1	11.25	35 B. Welch (R)	---	---
31 D. Robinson (R)	---	---	29 C. Young (L)	---	---
			20 M. Young (L)	---	---

CATCHERS	AVG.	HR	RBI	CATCHERS	AVG.	HR	RBI
18 B. Bathe (R)	---	--	--	36 T. Steinbach (R)	.250	1	3
17 K. Manwaring (R)	---	--	--				

INFIELDERS	AVG.	HR	RBI	INFIELDERS	AVG.	HR	RBI
15 G. Litton (R)	---	--	--	12 L. Blankenship (R)	---	--	--
1 E. Riles (L)	.000	0	0	9 M. Gallego (R)	.000	0	0
23 J. Uribe (S)	.250	0	0				

OUTFIELDERS	AVG.	HR	RBI	OUTFIELDERS	AVG.	HR	RBI
21 C. Maldonado (R)	.000	0	0	28 S. Javier (S)	---	--	--
30 D. Nixon (R)	---	--	--	44 K. Phelps (L)	---	--	--

EARTHQUAKE!

THE PARC 55 HOTEL IN SAN FRANCISCO'S Union Square was thirty-two stories tall, and my room was near the top. I walked down the stairway and outside. On Market Street, one of the first things I noticed was the clock in front of Samuels Jewelers. Both faces of the pillar clock were frozen at 5:04. A plaque touted it as "one of the finest street clocks in America" and pointed out that it was "insured by Lloyd's of London." I wondered if the policy still was in force.

A few steps away, a man wore a sandwich board sign that proclaimed: "Fallen, fallen is Babylon." He would not tell me his name or even speak.

It was the morning of October 18, 1989—the morning after the Loma Prieta earthquake. It also was the morning after Game 3 of the World Series between the Oakland Athletics and the San Francisco Giants was supposed to have been played at Candlestick Park.

After the Athletics romped 5–1 in Game 2 on Sunday, October 15, taking a 2–0 series lead, I noted in my column that they seemed on the verge of ignoring manager Tony La Russa's suggestion that they remain low key and to avoid waking the sleeping Giants. Rickey Henderson stole bases after the game was decided, Dave Parker's home run trot was turtlelike and taunting, and Jose Canseco—remember, this was before he started naming names and when the A's Mark McGwire was a rail compared to what he would become in later years—was strutting everywhere he went.

At least reliever Dennis Eckersley, who had served up the infamous home run pitch to the Dodgers' Kirk Gibson in Game 1 of Los Angeles' five-game victory the year before, was being cautious. He noted that he was on a Chicago Cubs team that blew the 1984 National League Championship Series after taking a 2–0 lead over the Padres. "I've trained myself not to get too carried away," he said after closing out Game 2. "I've played too long and know that anything can happen."

Anything could happen.

Even an earthquake.

Two days later, after the routine interviews on the field before Game 3, we retreated to the press boxes. The regular baseball press box—especially at Candlestick at the time—was far too small to accommodate all of the credentialed writers, and those spots went mostly to the beat writers of specific major league teams. Although I was a Professional Baseball Writers of America member and went to many Seattle Mariners games and also made a couple trips a year to do columns on both the Giants and the Athletics, I joined others in the temporary auxiliary press box constructed in the first rows of the upper deck. It wasn't a bad vantage point, and I was looking forward to watching the games from there.

Some background notes to put the following in context. This was long before cell phones were part of everyday life. We would be rushing to beat the newspaper deadline, so like many writers, I had arranged through the telephone company to have my own line and phone installed at my seat. My computer was typical for the time: it was a tiny Radio Shack TRS-80, the infamous "Trash 80" that operated on either an AC adapter or (and this would become important) AA batteries. It had a tiny four-line screen and transmitted to the newspaper via a phone call. If the telephone cord was modular and could be removed from the phone, we could transmit easily and quickly through the phone line. If it was a pay phone that didn't have modular connections, we had to jam each end of the handset into coupler cups. That worked roughly 41 percent of the time and often led to chunks of copy disappearing. I had a portable radio that could get television sound, too.

When the stadium shook, the reporter next to me, Shannon Fears—a Bay area native—knew what it was. He jumped up and was ready to move. I just sat there. Eventually, I would experience earthquakes in Portland and San Jose, and as strange as it sounds, the one I experienced while in a press box hanging from the rafters of the San Jose arena seemed far more immediately frightening. But the hockey game went on that night. The baseball game didn't start.

Over the next few hours, as did many of my brethren, I talked with fans in the stands and on the walk back to the media bus. I wrote with that tiny Radio Shack on my lap as the bus crawled back to downtown San Francisco.

Here's the column that appeared the next morning in the *Oregonian*. I have resisted the urge to touch it up (I have been teased that my modifiers often aren't just dangling, they are on opposite coasts from the words they modify), and it is word-for-word what landed on the porches the next morning. Even twenty years later, I'm amazed that it actually made it into print. I must have had fresh batteries in that Trash 80.

SAN FRANCISCO—I was sitting in the upper deck of Candlestick Park on Tuesday afternoon, directly behind home plate and about 30 rows from the top of the stadium.

By my watch, at 5:05 p.m., one-half hour before the scheduled start of World Series Game 3, the deck swayed.

For an instant, I thought that one of the airplanes flying over the stadium might have caused a sonic boom.

No, I quickly concluded, that couldn't be it.

An earthquake.

It seemed to last about five seconds.

Then the stands were still, the hearts started fibrillating and the questions began.

Quite a few fans actually cheered when the movement stopped.

There was little, if any, panic.

The public-address announcer quickly said: "In case of an emergency" fans in the lower deck should go onto the field and those in the upper deck should go to an exit.

That was the last we would hear from him for 61 minutes.

Right after that, the power went out.

Few people left immediately.

When the quake hit, I would find out later, three Oregonians—Bob McLeod and Janet Heppner of Portland and Mark Schneider of Eugene—were leaving the IBM hospitality tent on the Candlestick grounds. They all work for IBM and had won the trip and Game 3 tickets in an incentive program.

"My first thought," Schneider said, "was, 'Hey, I haven't even had a beer.'"

Said McLeod: "We thought we had too much beer. I was dizzy."

If that sounds flippant, you must understand: That's the way virtually all of us were taking it. Shaken into gallows humor. And at that time we had only hints of the magnitude of the toll. Nor had we seen it.

Michael Patrick, 38, of San Francisco, was in one of the balcony sections, sitting under the cement roof. "I'm used to earthquakes," he said later, "but the overhang started to bounce up and down. You could hear it. I got out in the aisle. My first thought was that the upper deck was about to collapse."

My telephone worked for one call to the office. Then it went dead and worked only intermittently over the next half hour.

Many of the San Francisco Giants and Oakland Athletics walked out of their dugouts and stood on the field, looking up at the stands. Those of us with battery-powered radios and Watchman televisions listened to the increasingly frightening, mostly unconfirmed, details reported on the fly.

Cars had bounced on the ground in the parking lot. The power was off all over, including in the Bay Area Rapid Transit tunnel under the bay. The epicenter was to the south. There was a major fire in Oakland.

At 5:27, a police car, with its lights flashing, rolled around the warning track, to the home-plate area.

At 5:28, I heard a television report that a 50-foot section of the Bay Bridge had collapsed and that there may be cars trapped underneath. A section of the Nimitz Freeway, the major thoroughfare on the east side of the bay, had collapsed. On the Richter Scale, the quake was 6.5. Or 6.9. Or 7.0.

Andy Lev of Palo Alto was outside the stadium, without a ticket, but $120 in his pocket to buy one from a scalper. A woman came running out of the stadium, he said, and sold him her stub for $10. Lev went into Candlestick. "She was really freaked out," Lev said. "Now I'll get to use this as a rain check."

Incredibly, at 5:39, with about half the 60,000 ticket holders (including Lev) still in their seats, a chant went up. "Let's play ball!"

Fans still were walking into the upper deck, carrying beer and hot dogs. Out on the concourse, the concession stands still were open.

On the field, Oakland third-base coach Rene Lachemann said: "When the quake happened, I saw guys running out of the dugout and I didn't know what had happened. I thought there might be skydivers landing or something. Now I don't know how we're going to get back to Oakland."

At 5:41, there was a mild aftershock. The upper deck had moved slightly again.

At 5:43, the players who had remained on the field gathered up their families and walked toward the clubhouse door in the right-field corner.

Ushers remained on duty, directing traffic. But it wasn't a rush of panic, only general milling.

At 6:05, a man with a bullhorn stood on the field and told the remaining fans to evacuate the stadium "in an orderly fashion." One minute later, the power was restored—at least long enough for the public-address announcer to tell everyone to leave.

U.S. Highway 101 was within sight from the concourse and traffic seemed to be moving. However, few vehicles were getting out of the parking lot.

The upper concourse concessions stands still were open. And the souvenir stands were doing brisk business. More than once I head a variation of: "These things are going to be collectors' items."

We walked to the media bus. Again, there wasn't much panic. Just concern. The Giants' radio network still was on the air, and reporter Bruce McGowan was interviewing a few Giants' players.

"It's just too weird, man," said San Francisco catcher Terry Kennedy. "They're talking about how important this series is. We're finding out now where the priorities are."

Amen.

I'm writing this on a bus riding through darkened streets, hoping to be able to transmit when we make it to the first downtown stop, the Meridien Hotel.

One man on the bus just got ill.

"Be extremely careful," the bus driver just said. "They are doing a lot of looting down here. So be careful."

Update: Sixty-three minutes after the bus started moving, we pulled up at the Meridien. The lobby was dark, but the bar was open and cocktail waitresses were serving drinks. The makeshift pressroom was open in a restaurant.

If you're reading this, the phone worked.

If I had to do it over again, I'd delete the "Amen." Over the next few days, I was reminded how sickening it gets to hear "This sure puts sports in perspective." Fact was—and still is—that most of us do have sports in perspective, and it doesn't take disasters to force us into reassessment.

After filing the column and probably having a drink at the Pierre Restaurant, the temporary media work room in the Meridien, I walked a mile through the darkened downtown—three blocks down Battery Street and then the rest of the way on Market to the Parc 55. The power was out, but a freight elevator and hallway lights were operating on a backup generator. I waited my turn to ride upstairs. On my floor, the darkness was eerie. Most of my fellow guests had their doors propped open to let the limited light from the hallway into the room. The two women in the room next to me were from Missouri, as I recall, and we talked briefly, yet I never saw them. I managed to get ready for bed in the dark and went to sleep.

The next morning, I did a radio interview by phone with Scott Lynn of Portland's top station, KEX. I heard announcements in multiple languages through the hotel speaker system about where food and other necessities were available. I left and after noticing the Samuels Jewelers clock and the man with the "Babylon" sign, wandered through downtown feeling a bit guilty because authorities were asking residents to stay put if at all possible.

Traffic moved fitfully without signals. Stores and restaurants were closed. All of them, that is, except for the South of Market grocery on the corner of Fourth and Howard, across the street from the George Moscone Convention Center. Inside the small store, a rack of snack food had collapsed, so packages of Lay's Potato Chips littered one aisle. Beer and soft drinks still were cold in the dark refrigerated cases, but bottled water, orange juice, and packaged food were the best sellers.

A line of about ten people went up one aisle as manager Abe Bateh added up prices with a pen on brown bags. He rounded off prices to avoid using coins, but the prices were near their original levels. He was not gouging his customers.

"Nobody told me to open," Bateh told me. "I came here and when everybody was here and hungry, I decided to open."

Across the street at the Convention Center, a two-tiered social drama was playing out as engineers from around the country who were attending a water-pollution conference mixed with the refugees from the nearby Tenderloin district who had been forced out of their apartments and the hotels catering to transients by the quake's effects. Inside the door, a sign directed the homeless and stranded downstairs to the makeshift American Red Cross disaster center in the exhibit hall. Rodney Bacon, a Red Cross volunteer, told engineers that their conference was canceled. When the bedraggled walked in the door, Bacon pointed downstairs.

Franklin Schutz, an engineer at West Virginia University in Morgantown, wasn't sure when he would be getting home. But he said he had spent the night in his low-rise Cow Hollow hotel in the decimated Marina District. "It was sort of like a block party," he said. "The buses were running. One Mexican restaurant was serving on paper plates for anyone who walked up. When I tried to use a coin phone, somebody walked up and held a light for me so I could see. A lot of people had portable radios."

When Schutz got through to his wife in West Virginia, he told her how he had been on a bus outside the convention center when the quake hit. "We were wondering who was fooling around with the bus," he said.

In the exposition hall downstairs, men and women slept on cots, sat silently, or milled around and quietly talked. Steve Hull, a Red Cross volunteer supervisor, told me that "between 350 and 500 people" spent the night in the center. He said the Red Cross served breakfast to more than 800 refugees from the Tenderloin District and that they had been told they could stay as long as "four or five days."

Barbara Egar, who was staying in a nearby apartment until her gas and electricity went out, sat in a chair against one wall, her arms wrapped around her knees. "It was weird here last night," she told me. "Weird people. They were threatening, too, at times. It was abusive language, the grossest stuff you've ever heard." I asked her if she slept. "No," she said. "No. Too many weird people." Even before the quake, she said, she was planning on returning to her former home in Arkansas. "I don't have any money to go home on now, though, to tell you the truth."

Twenita Jones, thirty-two, was five months pregnant. When the quake hit, she was at the Episcopal Center shelter, four blocks away from the convention center. "We were getting ready to eat," she said. "The floors and everything were moving and when it stopped, they sent us out in the parking lot. When the aftershocks came, they took us out of the building again. We stayed there in the dark last night, then they brought us here at 6:30 this morning."

Jones said she had been at the Episcopal Center for only three days after leaving her apartment building because she couldn't pay the rent until her next Aid to Families with Dependent Children check arrived. "Now I'm just waiting to get something to eat," she said.

At midmorning, the homeless still filtered into the exposition hall. They signed a sheet at the door. Some carried packs and clothes. Others had nothing. A slight, bent man with a gray-speckled beard spotted my open notebook and the World Series media credential hanging around my neck. He approached me with both hands in his pockets and a not-so-shy smile on his face. "You should talk to me," he said. "I was one of the best lightweight fighters in the state of California. Everybody knows me around here."

He said he was Oscar Smith, a sixty-six-year-old retired construction worker who once had fists of brick and fought out of Newman Gym. "I fought all the good fighters," he said. "I fought for Johnny Monroe. I was a stablemate of Earl Turner." Surely I knew those names, he told me. Well, no, I didn't. But when Oscar couldn't tell me his record, we were even. "I don't know," he said, "but it was good."

When I checked later, he wasn't listed in the sports department's oldest *Ring Record Book*, the 1960 volume, but that didn't mean he was pulling my leg.

Oscar said he was a refugee from the Angelo Hotel on 6th Street. He told me he had been staggering between the ropes in recent years, living on social security and assistance checks totaling $667 a month. He said he had lived in another hotel with a transient clientele for fourteen years, "until they put me out on the street because of a mistake" five days earlier.

"They said I hadn't paid the rent, but I had," he said. "That's the God's truth. The landlord must have gone south with it. I think they just wanted to get me out because they could rent the room for more money from somebody else than I was paying."

After being evicted, Oscar moved into room 331 of the Angelo. He told me that on the day of the earthquake, he was working underneath a friend's car on Eddy Street, near the hotel. "The car was wheeling and rocking," Oscar said. "I thought somebody was rocking the car, jumping on the running board. As soon as I got out from under the car and they told me what had happened, I was frightened to death."

He said the Angelo shut down completely. "There was a housing authority cop or somebody like that standing out front, keeping us out," he said. Oscar said he managed to sneak back into his room "before they came and knocked on the door and told me to get the hell out of there. They said the building was condemned. So I came here. They gave us sandwiches and coffee, and they were real nice to us."

A pregnant woman approached us. "This is my pal," she said, putting her arms around Oscar's neck from behind. "It was pitch-dark and I was one of the last ones out of the hotel. It was so dark and I told this nice gentleman I needed some help. And do you know that he put his hand out to me and I had to slap him silly?"

They both laughed and the woman, who declined to give her name, walked away. Eventually, so did I.

That night, I attended Commissioner Fay Vincent's news conference in a meeting room at the Westin St. Francis. The only lighting was from candles and the limited number of makeshift television lights. The rumors had flown all day about such alternatives for the World Series as finishing in Los Angeles and Anaheim, moving it back across the bay to Oakland for all remaining games, or canceling the rest of the Series altogether. Vincent did the sensible thing, saying Major League Baseball would put the Series on hold until at least the next Tuesday, one week after the earthquake. That seems an obvious decision in retrospect, but at the time there was a lot of that knee-jerk "puts-things-in-perspective" rhetoric flying, and if Vincent had announced the Series was canceled and blathered on about baseball knowing its place, he would have received widespread praise.

I caught a flight home in the next couple of days and was in Portland when the Giants visited the refugees at the Moscone Convention Center after a Friday workout. None of the stories featured my buddy Oscar.

I returned the next week, after Vincent announced that the Series would resume on Friday, October 27. The Athletics finished their four-game sweep with consecutive victories at Candlestick.

The incident I most remember during the resumption of the Series came in the bottom of the ninth inning of the A's 13–7 win in Game 3. The Giants' Candy Maldonado was at the plate, and we were merely counting down the pitches until it was over. Suddenly, one bank of lights in right-centerfield went dark. As the umpires and others began considering what to do, a single light appeared in the section below the bank. It might have been an usher with a flashlight. It could have been a single fan with a lighter. Then there were five lights. Then, faster than you could follow the progress, there were hundreds around the park, far beyond the affected area, individual lights from flashlights, butane lighters, matches. Amid laughter and bobbing points of light, the game went on.

At that point, what were a few light bulbs?

The Series ended on a day when banners in downtown San Francisco heralded "Quake Sales," "Earth-Shaking Bargains," and "Giant Reductions." Souvenir emporiums couldn't restock tables with "I Survived the Quake" T-shirts fast enough. I still have mine.

The dead were not forgotten. Neither were the sensations of loss and helplessness and horror. It was appropriate to remember, yet time to move on. At least in baseball.

THE HONEYMOONERS MEET THE BOYS OF SUMMER

WHEN JACKIE GLEASON DIED in June 1987, I was shaken. I was among the millions of *The Honeymooners* devotees who repeatedly watched the original thirty-nine episodes, set in Brooklyn, and could quote from them.

Adding to my fascination with Brooklyn, I was a retroactive fan of the old Brooklyn Dodgers, although the franchise moved to Los Angeles when I was an infant and my favorite team from my own childhood was the San Francisco Giants, with Willie Mays. I read the juvenile novels by John Tunis about the old Brooklyn Dodgers, starting with *The Kid from Tomkinsville*, and came to appreciate both the Dodgers books and his other works for young adults that gave us credit for intelligence.* Later, I read *The Boys of Summer*, Roger Kahn's classic about the Dodgers, the team he grew up watching and later covered. I still consider it my favorite sports book. I bought a throwback 1955 Dodgers jacket and became a student and fan of those finals years in Flatbush, reading many other books, none of which came close to measuring up to *The Boys of Summer*.

So when Gleason died, I was moved to combine my interest in *The Honeymooners* and *The Boys of Summer* and quickly wrote a column that was a script for a mini-episode. I've played around with it over the years, and after seeing Brad Garrett, best known for his role as Ray Romano's brother on *Everybody Loves Raymond*, do a terrific job of portraying Gleason in a television movie, I picture Garrett as Ralph in the following scenes.

---

* Later, I found out that he had gotten into juvenile fiction by accident, when his publisher announced to him that his *Iron Duke*, about Yale distance runner Jim Wellington, was terrific but would be published as a "juvenile."

Mighty Ralph at the Bat

Fatigued after driving the Madison Avenue bus in Manhattan, RALPH KRAMDEN enters the Chauncey Street apartment in Brooklyn. At the table are neighbor ED NORTON and TOMMY MANICOTTI, a member of the Norton-coached stickball team, plus ALICE KRAMDEN and her mother, MRS. GIBSON. Nobody notices Ralph's entrance. All are listening intently to the radio on the kitchen table.

RADIO ANNOUNCER: Mantle hits a bouncer to the mound! Labine throws to Hodges! The Dodgers have beaten the Yankees 8–5 and the 1955 World Series is tied at two games apiece with Game 5 coming up tomorrow at Ebbets Field!

(All cheer.)

TOMMY: The Dodgers are going to murder 'em, huh, Mr. Norton?

NORTON: Like we say in the sewer, the Yankees are goin' right down the drain. Too bad you won't be able to see it.

MRS. GIBSON: If my Alice had only married that rich Howard Morgan, getting tickets would be a snap.

ALICE: Now, mother . . .

RALPH: Leo Durocher was wrong! (He slams his lunch bucket on the table.) Nice guys don't finish last, they get stuck with mothers-in-law who look like Sal Maglie!

MRS. GIBSON: My son-in-law, the heavy hitter!

NORTON: The heaviest! If he could hit his weight, he could beat out Roy Campanella behind the plate!

ALICE: What do you mean, Ed? The Dodgers do want him behind the plate. They need a new backstop.

RALPH: Haaaar-dee-har-har-har. (Smiling smugly, he walks slowly toward the table.) Now, normally, if you were talking about tickets to a game like this, you'd say, "Fat chance."

NORTON: Then if anybody has a chance, you do!

RALPH: The Yankees' clubhouse man rides my bus. I've told him about that uranium field I'm going to buy and that the first thing I'm going to do after I make my millions is to buy a ballclub. He wants to get on my good side. All I gotta do is go down to the gas station and call him. Two tickets. Like that! (Snaps fingers.)

TOMMY: You mean it, Mr. Kramden?

RALPH: You play hooky and I'll do the rest. (He glares at his mother-in-law.) I'll show you who has pull.

TOMMY: Gee, thanks, Mr. Kramden!

(An hour later, Alice is alone with Ralph, who holds his head in his hands.)

RALPH: Alice, I've got a biiiiiig mouth. I'll have to tell Tommy he has to go to school, after all. Some big shot I am, huh?

ALICE: Why don't you just wait until the morning? Something will come up.

(It's now the next morning. After a knock, Tommy rushes in excitedly. Alice puts her hands on Tommy's shoulders.)

RALPH: (Looking away.) Tommy, there's something I have to tell you.

ALICE: (Smiling.) Yes, Tommy, Mr. Kramden will let you use the tickets only if you promise to tell your teacher the truth about why you're missing school.

TOMMY: Are you kiddin'? She'll be the first one I tell! She loves Duke Snider.

(Alice pulls two tickets out of her apron pocket and hands them to Tommy. He runs out. Ralph is flabbergasted.)

ALICE: Now, you, Mr. Pull Hitter, don't you ever promise Tommy anything like that again.

RALPH: But how?

ALICE: I used to babysit. You don't even know this, but one of the kids was named Sandy. Well, I went over to Sandy's mother's house last night and explained the situation and she said I could have two of their tickets. Besides, Mrs. Koufax said, Sandy's only nineteen and he almost never pitches and he'll have other World Series—if he ever can learn how to control that fastball of his.

RALPH: (Hugging Alice.) Baby, you're the greatest!

BASEBALL IN THE BUSHES

FOR YEARS, THE EUGENE EMERALDS were a Class A team in the Northwest League, and we occasionally would venture to the ancient Bethel Park on the other side of the Willamette River for games. Then, in 1969, when the San Diego Padres joined the National League and the Phillies had to find a replacement for their Class AAA affiliate, the Emeralds jumped two classes, stepped into the Pacific Coast League, and moved into Civic Stadium, previously used only for high school football. That first season, the "Ems" had future major leaguers Larry Bowa at shortstop and Denny Doyle at second base and made the PCL championship series. They slipped considerably the next two seasons, but because South Eugene High was across the street, I worked for the team as everything from batboy to batting practice pitcher to bullpen catcher. I even got to go on a couple of road trips after my summer league games were over, the first time because manager Lou Kahn was angry that the Phillies had him down to one catcher and *somebody* had to warm guys up in the bullpen. In 1970, I roomed during my brief road experience with outfielder Frank DeCastris, who made cameo appearances in the majors, and the Ems' third baseman, who was a vacuum cleaner named John Vukovich. The 1969 Miracle Mets' utility man, Bobby Pfeil, was playing the infield and trying to learn to be a catcher to add to his versatility, so I loaned him my catcher's mitt when he needed it—and I should have had him sign it. I became friends with outfielder Willie Montanez, in part because of my high school Spanish. Greg Luzinski and Mike Anderson were the Ems' teenage phenoms and were tearing up the PCL. On one season-ending road trip to Spokane, I rode with pitcher Lowell Palmer in his new Corvette, and I felt as if we were right out of *Route 66*. The class of the league was the Tommy Lasorda–managed Spokane Indians, whose fluctuating cast of players in those two seasons included Bill Buckner, Bobby Valentine, Bill Russell, Ron Cey, and Steve Garvey.

The Emeralds experience added to my affinity for minor league baseball at all levels. After my career turned out to be as a writer rather than as a catcher, I made several trips to minor league cities for portraits of life in the bushes. I visited Butte, Montana, the rugged former mining town and home of the Pioneer League's Butte Copper Kings twice in a span of twelve years, once to tell the story and once to update it. I also journeyed to Asheville, North Carolina, to spend time with the Rockies' Class A affiliate there. In both towns, I discovered there was a lot to write about beyond baseball, but I came away knowing the sport was part of the summertime fabric of two very different areas.

I started out by spending four days with the Copper Kings in July 1985, taking in four consecutive games against the Helena Gold Sox, their rivals from sixty-four miles to the north. I joined the Copper Kings not far behind another Denver-area resident, Jim Hovorka, a pitcher fresh out of Benedictine College in Kansas. On a Saturday in mid-June, he took a phone call from Butte manager Hal Dyer, who posed two questions: Did Hovorka want to give pro ball a shot? Now that was out of the way, could he get to Butte in time for that night's game?

They compromised. Because of a friend's wedding and reception, Hovorka left Denver in the late afternoon and landed in Butte at nearly midnight. There, he looked out of place in his suit and tie, waiting for baseball equipment to arrive in the baggage claim among the fishing gear of those who had traveled to southern Montana to take advantage of the renowned fly fishing. Finally, Mike Methven, the Copper Kings' assistant general manager, and Marcy Eschenbacher, the booster club president, who had been looking for a ballplayer and not a banker, realized that Hovorka must be their man. Eschenbacher hugged him, kissed him on the cheek, and said, "Welcome to Butte!"

A month later, the Copper Kings and Gold Sox were coming off the teams' only off day of the seventy-game season with a series beginning on a Wednesday in Butte.

Butte catcher Roger Caldwell took it easy the day before, but, still, it was 12:30 in the afternoon when he got out of bed in the studio apartment he shared—along with the $170 monthly rent—with pitcher John Asbell. One of the first hints that this was a maverick operation in the summer rookie league was that Caldwell, who left high school four years earlier and then played a full career at East Tennessee State, was listed as twenty years old in the program. That was one of the many strategies employed by Dyer, who unapologetically would do anything he could to get an organization to take a look at his players, and anything included knocking a few years off their ages.

Dyer was manager of the Tigers' Bristol, Tennessee, affiliate in the Appalachian League the year before, and he conducted clinics at East Tennessee State. Dyer liked Caldwell, the senior catcher, the feisty son of a truck driver from Newberry, South Carolina. Dyer told him if he wasn't drafted, to call. "I was like a million of other kids, sitting around by the phone, waiting—and nothing happened," Caldwell told me. "So I called Coach Dyer and he said to come out here. I just wanted a chance to play."

Caldwell's .333 batting average heading into the games against Helena was the Copper Kings' best. On that Wednesday, after he *finally* got out of bed, he had to decide which of the two lunchtime mainstays—baloney casserole or hot dogs—to make for the roomies' pregame meal. The casserole got the nod, and after he and Asbell watched television for a couple of hours, they headed to Montana Tech's Alumni Field, the converted football field that served as their home park.

The Copper Kings were in the early stages of batting practice when the visiting Gold Sox's bus exited the freeway and headed north up the hill into Old Uptown Butte, the brick-dominated, decaying downtown. On the eastern horizon was a reminder of better times: Berkeley Pit, the copper mine that Anaconda Minerals shut down in 1982. When it closed, it cost more than $1 a pound to produce copper, and the company received about 69 cents a pound.

The closure was another step in the changing economic face of a one-time boomtown. Butte's official population peaked at 70,000 in 1915, when shifts of hungry, hell-raising, and thirsty miners came out of what then was the underground mine every eight hours around the clock. In 1985, Butte's population was about 37,000. Some of the residents were young people who stayed after attending Montana Tech, the expensive and prestigious school officially known as the Montana College of Mineral Sciences and Technology. Tech got about $525 a month for allowing the Copper Kings to use Alumni Field, the football stadium. The Copper Kings put up the fence—for $450 a crack, sponsors could buy one of the advertising sections—and the temporary box seats down the lines, which were folding chairs on platforms.

The Copper Kings had won two straight and were 12–14, decent considering the way the roster was slapped together at the last minute. Most of the others signed shortly before the June 13 reporting date, one week before the season. Jim Hovorka was among the later additions. Why the rush? In 1984, the Kings were affiliated with the Seattle Mariners, who paid all the salaries, travel expenses, and meal money and provided all the equipment. But the Mariners cut back to only one Class A short-season team, Bellingham. When the East Coast–based majority owners, Charlie Greathouse and Fred Nichols, couldn't get another affiliation, Dyer, the former Oakland farmhand who coached both football and baseball at high schools and colleges, including Memphis State and Cincinnati, was hired as the manager and told to line up the team on his own. Fast. By the beginning of the Helena series, the Copper Kings included four players on loan from the Mariners, three from the Dodgers, and one apiece from the Red Sox and Giants. Dyer lined up the other seventeen. There were no open tryouts; this was a roster shaped by referrals and chance encounters. Dyer saw his second baseman, Jim Miller, play center field at Kings College in Bristol but only after Miller had finished earning his scholarship by starring at point guard for the basketball team.

Dyer's best starting pitcher, Steve Gossett, had a 9–2 record at Oral Roberts, but the scouts backed off because they said he didn't throw hard enough, which in part was because he had been born without a middle finger on his right hand. He got the call from Dyer the same day he pitched in a summer league game in San Bernardino, where he allowed four unearned runs and then heard that the scouts in attendance again said he didn't have enough velocity. Those scouts apparently hadn't played catch with him to get a firsthand look at how his pitches moved. "I was pretty dejected," Gossett said. "I went home and my Mom said I had a message to call this man about the Copper Kings."

Gossett gave up a computer job in a hospital that paid him about three times as much as the Copper Kings and came to Butte. Before finding an apartment, he stayed a few days at the Capri Hotel, and a month into the season, he still was trying to convince the dogged hotel manager that he hadn't stolen a pillow and wouldn't pay for it.

Welcome to pro baseball, kid.

All the players Dyer signed came to Butte for $400 a month and $11 in meal money for each day they were on the road. The players under contract to a big-league organization were making up to $850 a month. In the standings, the other city names were followed by the nickname of their parent organizations in parentheses; Butte was followed by (Co-op). But most of all, they came for a chance. "You hope someone sees you and picks you up," Hovorka said.

Gossett was pitching the series opener, so he didn't need to be at the park until 4:30. Marcy Eschenbacher was the self-designated "taxi service" for the players—at any time of day or night. Only two of the players had cars. When she and Gossett arrived at the park, Eschenbacher said hello to Roger Caldwell, who, after some prodding, admitted that his baloney casserole didn't do the trick, and he already was hungry. So Eschenbacher headed to Paul Bunyan's, the submarine shop, and brought back eight sandwiches. While Helena was going through batting practice, Caldwell cut up the sandwiches and passed them around to the entire team.

Eschenbacher was a North Carolina girl who came to Butte in 1974 after marrying a Butte native, Fred, a Marine at Camp Lejeune. After leaving the Marines, Fred returned to Butte and a post office job. With Marcy and Fred attending every game, she oversaw a sponsoring system in which booster "mothers" each were responsible for three players. Eschenbacher's sons for that summer were Caldwell, first baseman Eric Tutt, and pitcher Jim Goldman. "We do have people who will not adopt a black or a Latin," she said. "To me, that's living in the '40s. But it's gotten better. This year, people were begging to get the black kids. Some of us take our kids to church, have them over for dinner. But the main thing is we keep a scrapbook for each one of them, so if they don't make it any further, at least they've got the memories." Marcy told me that among her former "sons," she and Frank were both close to and proud of 1982 Copper King Cecil Fielder, who was playing for the Toronto Blue Jays' Class AA affiliate at Knoxville.

Several players told me how they had become accustomed to early-morning knocks on their doors from their sponsors, asking if they had any laundry to be done. The booster club also offered a lending library of linen and kitchen utensils, run out of the Eschenbachers' garage. Each year, the boosters stocked the players' apartments; at the end of the summer, the players returned the sheets and pots and pans to be handed out to the next year's Copper Kings.

Near game time for the series opener against Helena, the wait at the single ticket window wasn't more than a minute—just enough time to decide between the $2.25 general admission and the $2.75 box seat. Since there were no ushers, it was the honor system. Inside the door, you could look at the pictures of the four former Copper Kings in the major leagues at the time—Milwaukee's Bill Schroeder, Randy Max Ready, and Dion James and Cleveland's Julio Franco.

Kathy Cash, the twenty-three-year-old general manager who began as a Copper Kings' program seller in the franchise's first season, 1978, came out of her tiny office behind the third-base dugout. While Dyer was the baseball man, Cash and Mike Methven oversaw the business operation for the ownership, which consisted of Charlie Greathouse and Fred Nichols, local resident Rich Taylor, and the Lockett family of Helena.

There was an air of fatalism throughout the organization, because without a major league affiliation, it was impossible for the franchise to break even. The hope was that the co-op approach would be a one-year stopgap. Cash told me that the season before, when the Copper Kings drew an average of 850 fans, the team made money. "But now," she added, "we have to pay seventeen players, plus all the concessions people, the official scorer, the batboys, Hal, Mike [Methven], and the trainer [Bruce Piatt]. You're going to lose money unless you do overly well on advertising and we didn't do overly well."

That night, Gossett was facing a Helena lineup that included two highly regarded Milwaukee Brewer draft choices—first baseman Buddy Haney from Texas A&M and former Arizona State outfielder Todd Brown, who was hitting .510. (Yes, .510.) Gossett gave up an RBI single to Haney in the top of the first but threw a six-hitter and the Copper Kings' first complete game of the season in a 5–2 victory.

A group of young girls sat in the first few rows of the grandstand. Within moments of the final pitch, many of them gathered outside the gate the players passed through to leave the park and head to the nearby field house and its dressing room. Other girls went to nearby cars and waited. There were casual conversations with the players, autographs signed, and a lot of horns honking.

In the locker room—it would be hyperbole to call it a "clubhouse"—the question of the night was, as it was almost every night, "You going to the King?" That was Crazy Clancy's Claim, the bar in the Copper King Inn, and when a handful of the players arrived, the place was packed. They were the house celebrities, sitting down or filtering through the crowd as the live band—the female singer was wearing an imitation leopard skin—covered Top 40 songs. The players knew that if they had no other way of getting back to their apartments, they could call Eschenbacher's shuttle service. "One time, I took ten there," she told me, "and three called me at three in the morning. So seven got picked up—or something."

On the morning of the second game of the series, I had breakfast with one of the Copper Kings' owners. Rich Taylor sat at the counter of the M&M Cigar Store on Main Street, where the waitresses called me (and everyone else) "Honey," and I could watch the cook make my Montana-sized omelet with three eggs, about a pound of ham, and five pieces of cheese. On the other side of the room, the grizzled shot-and-beer boys were at the bar. The *real* fun was in the back of the building, behind the partition formed by the video games. The attractions were Keno, the bingo-like numbers game; Pan, the multideck card game ("Geez," Taylor warned me, "don't get in that unless you know exactly what you're doing"); poker; and a pull-tab type of numbers game somehow tied to the final score of major league baseball games. They were all legal.

The thirty-seven-year-old Taylor was on his break from the nearby Montana Power office, where he was the supervisor of application programs. When the Copper Kings were formed in 1988, he bought nearly 30 percent of the franchise. "When I get off work," Taylor told me, "I take my tie off, drop it off at home, come to the park, get two hot dogs and a Coke, get down the starting lineups, and settle in."

As we ate and talked, Dyer came in and talked with the M&M management, convincing them to upgrade the free dinner players won for hitting a home run or pitching a complete game to T-bones. Dyer's goal was to make one such stop every day during a home stand to line up perks and rewards for the players, and he had a long list of restaurants and businesses that honored the players' team IDs for at least 10 percent discounts.

Before batting practice, Dyer gathered the players in the dugout for his daily "morale" talk. He opened by disclosing the new deal at the M&M. That went over well, but he brought the house down when he told the players they no longer would have to pay the weekend cover charge at Crazy Clancy's Claim. He also got in a bit of purposeful teasing about the players' companionship at the park and at the bar. "I saw one of you leaving with eight twelve-year-olds last night," he said. That brought nervous laughter. Point made.

The Copper Kings had another good night, beating the Gold Sox 11–5, thanks to Helena's *eight* errors and Hovorka's solid pitching. He left with an 11–1 lead in the eighth.

Off the field, though, there were problems. A water main broke, and the periodic announcements that the water was turned on for the next ten minutes set off stampedes to the bathrooms. The scoreboard stopped working.

Many of the faces in the stands were recognizable from the night before, including that loyal group of young girls in the first few rows. John Mulvey, a seventy-six-year-old former miner, was back near the top of the bleachers. I already knew his ritual. After a Copper King reached first base, he raised his plastic horn and repeatedly hollered through it: "There he goes!" "I just like to rib people," he told me. "I don't mean it." He had worked thirty-five years in the mines and pit, and he looked it. "I was a hard rock miner, a coal miner, a copper miner, everything," he said. "This town has changed a lot. It hasn't been the same since they started the pit fifteen years ago. It was all machinery and no miners." In his retirement, the Copper Kings were his recreation. "I've been coming and I've had this horn ever since they started in the Pioneer League."

After the Copper Kings' fourth straight win, Eschenbacher handed out cookies as the players walked through the cordon outside the gate. When I was in the locker room with the team, a player yelled to Bruce Piatt, the trainer, "Hey, Bruce, before you wash my pants, there's a lady's phone number in my pocket. Will you take it out before you wash them?" Piatt was looking at this job as a final bit of fun before he reported for medical school at the University of Colorado at Denver.

I gave Gossett, the pitcher, a ride to Clancy's. We dropped off his roommate, Brian Petty, at the convenience store so he could use the pay phone to call home. Another teammate already was on the phone, so Petty had to wait his turn.

At Clancy's, as I sat with members of the Copper Kings' staff, several of the players jokingly asked where my tape recorder and notebook were. I promised I wasn't taking notes.

The next day, the Copper Kings' bus was scheduled to leave for Helena in mid-afternoon, so most of them slept in until noon. (Gee, I don't know why . . . because I hadn't taken notes the night before.) Among the exceptions were pitchers Lou Griffey and John Columbano, whom I ran into at breakfast at—where else?—the M&M. They both ended up in Butte after attending a camp in Florida, and the director recommended them to Dyer. Columbano, a Brooklyn native, played the previous season in Anzio, Italy, in a league with former major leaguers Joe Ferguson and Lenny Randle. But his team dropped a division, meaning it couldn't carry any American pitchers.

Most of the Copper Kings were living in rentals vacated by Montana Tech students in the summer. Jim Miller, the second baseman, and Steve Diaz, an outfielder getting a second chance after being released by Seattle, shared an apartment they nicknamed the "inferno." "It's about 100 degrees every night, and you have to go down the hall to use the bathroom," Miller told me. Shortstop Dave Castillo, whose status as the younger brother of Tiger Manny Castillo didn't prevent his release by Detroit in spring training, shared half of a duplex with pitcher Bubba Brevell, Greg Swain, and Doug Nelson. Jim Hovorka first had an apartment on the ground floor on Montana Street but moved out because, he said, "it sounded like I was next to a train station." He found a room in a house to rent.

Daniel Sullivan, the first baseman and the Copper Kings' best player, was from Sacramento and played at UCLA before signing with the Red Sox, who loaned him to Butte to ensure he played every day. When he got to Butte, he called all six Catholic churches and asked if there was a parish family he might board with. "I do go out, no doubt about it, but I wanted to stay with a family, coinciding with what I grew up with," Sullivan told me. Nobody could take him soon enough, and after he discussed the problem with Vadine Bosch, a waitress at his hotel, she called her parents. They offered him a room and didn't say a word about rent.

When I asked the rest of the players about Butte, the complimentary answer usually started with "the people." "The people have been unbelievable," said Roger Caldwell. "Besides for someone from Newberry, South Carolina, any place with a mall is like New York City."

I drove to Helena, the smallest town in the league with its population of about 26,000, ahead of the Copper Kings to do some sightseeing—I visited the state capitol—before heading to the park and visiting with Gold Sox General Manager Ward Goodrich. He was bracing for the biggest crowd of the season, thanks to a seventy-five cent beer coupon promotion. (More than 1,300 showed up.) Helena was Goodrich's fourteenth stop in professional baseball. He had lived in Helena since 1980 and worked only part time for the Gold Sox in 1984. "There were 134 days of the fishing season, and I made 99," he told me. "That's because we had thirty-five home games."

Goodrich shook his head about Butte's attempt to survive as a co-op franchise. "I love independent teams, but you have to have at least 100,000 people in your town to make it," Goodrich said. "But the thing is, they're a fighting bunch of sons of bitches in Butte. If World War III ever breaks out, I want to go to Butte. If things ever get too tough, they just throw a guy down the mineshaft."

As Goodrich and I talked in the Gold Sox's office, Cleveland scout Dave Roberts joined us. I immediately recognized Roberts as the one-time University of Oregon infielder who was once the number one overall choice in the draft, taken by the Padres. He had a solid, not spectacular, major league career. He was there to look at other organizations' prospects and to see if any of the Copper Kings who weren't under contract with a big-league team had fallen through the cracks.

The reviews couldn't have been good. The Gold Sox blew out the Copper Kings 14–4, ending the Butte winning streak at four.

In the strangely scheduled series, game four was back at Butte the next night—a Saturday. In his afternoon speech, Dyer first covered a variety of nuts-and-bolts baseball issues. Then he called infielder Brian Petty forward. Dyer grabbed his leg and displayed the bottom of Petty's spikes to the rest of the team. "Do you guys want to make the major leagues?" he asked. "Isn't it worth $30 to you? You can't go to the major leagues wearing shit like that. The spikes are all worn down. You're the most expensive equipment you have. Invest a little in yourself. And don't wear those Kmart things."

Dyer paused.

"Now, we're going to have a little discipline experiment tomorrow when we leave on the trip," he said. He was going to see how much leeway he could give the Copper Kings without regretting it. "You can wear shorts if you want," he said. "No cutoffs. Something with a seam."

Petty asked if he could wear the shorts he had on when he came to the park.

"Those faggy things?" Dyer asked. "Sure, if you want to. And we'll have one other experiment. If you want, you can wear a baseball T-shirt. Do not even consider one of those rock T-shirts with Iron Maiden on it or something like 'Baseball sucks.'"

Dyer preached about not griping behind backs, whether it's about a teammate not paying his share of the rent or a beef with the manager. "And there's responsibility," he said. "You're invited to a picnic, the keg looks bigger and bigger as the day goes along. But we have a rule: no beer during the day. No whiskey, no smoking, beer in moderation and only after the game. A girl at one of our hotels gave us a compliment. She said we were a laid-back group, that when another team was there the maids couldn't even get the drawers closed because there was so much beer hidden. Everything's up-front here. We're adults. I don't want the mushroom technique."

Petty sensed that he was supposed to be the straight man. In a singsong voice, he asked, "What's the mushroom technique, coach?"

"Where you keep me in the dark and spread manure all over me."

In the stands, as game time neared, the big news was what happened that afternoon on NBC's *Major League Game of the Week*. The Toronto Blue Jays recalled Cecil Fielder from Knoxville, and—on national TV—he hit a double in his first major league at-bat. With the Copper Kings, Fielder won the Pioneer League home run and doubles championship in 1982.

"When they announced the lineups, my phone started ringing," said Marcy Eschenbacher.

One more picture for the wall of fame inside the front gate.

Helena won the series-concluding game 16–6.

"We've won four of the last six, and that's the way I have to look at it," said Dyer.

After Dyer and I talked, though, a team staffer finally got around to handing him a letter from the Pioneer League president, chastising Dyer for getting thrown out of a game the week before for the second time this season. He was hereby fined $25 and reminded that the fine would go up each time.

Dyer dropped the letter, shook his head, and took a walk to the showers. Feisty independence had its price.

—◆—

For years, I marveled at the coincidence of having been in Butte, where Cecil Fielder broke into professional baseball, on the day he played his first major league game. As he became a slugging superstar, I wondered if he had fond memories of that summer in Montana or if he barely remembered it. In 1993, I finally had the chance to ask him about it when the Tigers came to Seattle. I was wary about approaching Fielder because I didn't want to be disappointed, but when I told my Butte story to a Detroit beat writer I knew, he exclaimed, "Oh, he loves those people!"

Fielder had been straight out of Nogales High School in Los Angeles when the Kansas City Royals drafted him and sent him to Butte. Sure enough, he lit up when I asked him about Butte and the Eschenbachers. "I'll tell you what," Fielder said. "I don't know how I would have made it that summer if I hadn't gotten in touch with Frank and Marcy. I was away from home for the first time. They basically fed me and the other kids."

Fielder said he survived in Butte because of two things: the help he got from the Eschenbachers and the free M&M Cafe dinners he got for his home runs. He said Marcy kept feeding him "Pork Chop John's."

I called Marcy and asked her what that was all about.

"Every day the team was in town," she said, "I'd go and pick him up and take him to the park. But first, I'd stop at Pork Chop John's and buy him two sandwiches, and he'd eat them on the way to the ballpark."

Until his 1998 retirement, Fielder invited the Eschenbachers to Seattle—the closest major league city to Butte—for annual reunions. The year I talked to Fielder, the reunion was scheduled for the Tigers' next trip later that season. He told me that during the visits, he always would call Marcy "Mom," which would lead to some confusion among his teammates and others who overheard and didn't know the story. But a lot of the longtime Tigers had gotten used to seeing the Eschenbachers at the games and at the hotel in Seattle. They called the couple "Cec's other parents."

———◆———

The 1985 Copper Kings, 14–16 when I left them, stumbled the rest of the season and finished 24–45. Daniel Sullivan, the former UCLA first baseman, hit .331 with a team-high eight home runs, and Steve Gossett— the top pitcher—wound up 4–4, with a 4.70 earned run average. Jim Hovorka, the pitcher from Colorado, was 3–6, with a 6.34 earned run average.

It was the final—and in many cases, the only—season of professional baseball for twenty-eight of the thirty-three players who suited up for the Copper Kings. None of the five who continued playing beyond 1985 ever got higher than Class A. If I had to choose the player who had the best chance, however slight, at reaching the major leagues, I would have picked Sullivan. He spent the next two seasons with the Winter Haven Red Sox of the Class A Florida State League before leaving the game. The only member of the Copper Kings operation who achieved his goal, at least in connection to sports, was Bruce Piatt, the trainer who in 1985 was headed for the University of Colorado Medical School. He is an orthopedic surgeon, handling many sports-related surgeries and injuries in Fargo, North Dakota.

The Copper Kings suspended operations in 1986 before returning to the Pioneer League the next season. I visited them again in 1997; Marcy Eschenbacher still was the mother figure and Rich Taylor still was a part owner. By then, his partners included Mike Veeck, the son of baseball showman Bill Veeck, Miles Wolff, the publisher of *Baseball America*, and actor Bill ("It's in the hole!") Murray. The Copper Kings, then an affiliate of the Anaheim Angels, still got steak dinners from the M&M for home runs, and the town was staging a bit of an economic comeback with Superfund reclamation underway. I had a good time on the second visit, but the Angels were running a tight ship, the players were "prospects" and didn't seem to be having as much fun as the ragtag 1985 group.

The Copper Kings franchise was transferred to Casper, Wyoming, in 2001. Butte has been without pro baseball ever since.

For a few years, before her health deteriorated, a widowed Marcy Eschenbacher traveled to other Pioneer League cities to watch a few games each summer. In 2002, she went to Billings for a Billings–Ogden game and first saw Ogden first baseman Prince Fielder, Cecil's eighteen-year-old son, in her hotel lobby.*

"Did your dad tell you about an old lady named Marcy?" she asked.

"No," Prince said.

"Well, when you talk to your dad, tell him you just met an old lady named Marcy."

A few minutes later, she was still in the lobby when Prince returned.

"My dad wants to talk to you," Prince said, handing her the cell phone.

She had a nice talk with Cecil, and when she was done, she asked Prince, "What did your dad say when you told him?"

"I asked him, 'Do you know a lady named Marcy?' And he said, 'Oh, my God, that's the lady who took care of me in Butte!'"

They have continued to speak periodically on the phone since, and Marcy is largely homebound and on oxygen after extensive heart surgery. She also occasionally hears from other former Butte players.

———

In 1999, I traveled to Asheville, North Carolina, ostensibly to check in with the Colorado Rockies' prospects playing for the South Atlantic League's Asheville Tourists. That was my story, anyway, and I stuck to it for a while, but I also wanted to see writer Thomas Wolfe's hometown, the model for the fictional setting of *You Can't Go Home Again*—a title that has been used in roughly 349,263 bad sportswriting leads. ("Ken Griffey Jr. Thursday found out what Thomas Wolfe meant when he wrote 'You can't go home again.'") It also was the site of the world-famous Biltmore House, the 250-room mansion built by the Vanderbilt family.

Shortly after I showed up at the ballpark, Chris Smith, the Tourists' young assistant general manager, showed me the before-and-after pictures of McCormick Field that spanned sixty-eight years. In a grainy black-and-white shot taken April 3, 1924, the barnstorming Detroit Tigers were meeting the Asheville Skylanders. Ty Cobb was in center field. Huge trees were beyond the fences. On the hill behind the third base line, two large houses loomed. A single tall building, scraping above the horizon, was the locater for the nearby downtown. At the time, McCormick Field was brand new.

When the original wooden structure was torn down after the 1991 season, the firetrap was the fourth-oldest professional park in the country,

———

* This was before Prince and Cecil's falling out.

behind Fenway Park, Wrigley Field, and Yankee Stadium. Ty Cobb, Babe Ruth, and Jackie Robinson were among those who barnstormed through Asheville, and in 1925, there were national rumors that Ruth had died in Asheville when he made the trip with the Yankees for an exhibition game but was a no-show. The official explanation was that Ruth had a stomach problem, but everyone assumed it had more to do with the fact that Asheville had speakeasies and bootleg booze during Prohibition.

Asheville had changed considerably since Cobb and Ruth's appearances, of course. But the "after" picture was of opening night at the hastily constructed new park on the same site in 1992, and Smith pointed out striking similarities. The new park paid architectural homage to the old.

When I watched some players take individual batting practice in the cage underneath the stands, I noticed a huge, hand-painted sign leaning against one wall. "Welcome to Historic McCormick Field," it proclaimed, and it also included drawings of the Tourists in action. The sign looked vaguely familiar. Familiar, as in, *Hey, isn't that . . . ?*

Yes! In the movie *Bull Durham*, the Durham Bulls cut Kevin Costner's character, veteran catcher Crash Davis. Forlorn yet determined to set the minor league career record for home runs, Davis joined the Tourists. He drove his beat-up Mustang convertible through the McCormick Field parking lot and stadium gate, past this sign, and then walked into the deserted and ramshackle clubhouse. In the next scene, Davis hit his record-breaking 247th career minor league home run into the lush, towering trees. Costner's Tourists jersey, signed and still stained with traces of makeup, was framed and hanging in the team offices.

Starting in 1994, McCormick Field and the historic western North Carolina city of 65,000 residents was where the Rockies sent prospects slotted into the second level of Single-A, long-season ball. They came to Asheville shortly after collecting signing bonuses that varied from plane tickets and travel expenses on the low side to the $1.6 million pitcher Jason Jennings, the 1999 college player of the year at Baylor, received. It was advanced summer camp, and it led to the unlikely pairing of Jennings, who had just become a millionaire at twenty, and touted prospect Matt Holliday both sleeping on air mattresses in the apartment they shared with other teammates.

When Jennings joined the Tourists, he became part of a pitching rotation that included a struggling twenty-year-old right-hander, Aaron Cook, Justin Carter, Luke Hudson, and Jermaine Van Buren. "It's been crazy," said Jennings. He had signed in June, made two starts for the short-season Portland Rockies, and then arrived in Asheville in early July. "It's a dream come true for me," he said. "I always wanted to play professional ball at a high level, and I never would have dreamed I would be a first-round pick."

The Rockies had a lot of their hopes under the apartment roof, since Jennings's roommates included Holliday, the infielder coaxed out of playing quarterback at his hometown Oklahoma State University, and outfielder Choo Freeman, nineteen, who was on his way to Texas A&M to play football before signing with the Rockies.

Holliday and Freeman both played for Tucson in the Arizona Rookie League the previous season and became friends, so it seemed natural for them to room together in Asheville. Both had a lot of money and pressure as highly touted prospects—Freeman as the three-sport all-state high school player at Dallas Christian, and Holliday as the star son of Oklahoma State's baseball coach, Tom Holliday.

"I've enjoyed every game we've played here," Holliday said. "The setting is nice, the weather is nice, the city is nice, and the atmosphere is great. The fans are great, too, and we're just trying to win games in the second half and make the playoffs."

Although stocked with some of the Rockies' brightest young talent, the Tourists were only 28–43 in the first half. In the early stages of the second half, they were a little above .500. For players such as Holliday and Freeman, the trick was to jettison the multiple-sport mentality and home in on baseball.

"I'm doing something I like to do every day and having fun at it," Freeman said. "I'm learning a lot about baseball, something new every day about hitting, situations in the game, fielding, whatever."

Holliday had been perplexing to the Rockies, because they thought they were getting a former quarterback who would be a fiery leader on the field. Holliday was hitting .259 with 11 home runs and at times struggling at third base as he played next to nineteen-year-old shortstop Juan Uribe. But the Rockies were hoping to see Holliday assert himself, both at third base and in the dugout.

"I'm nineteen and some of the guys who are older have been through long seasons," he said. "We know what's going on, and with the older guys around, I'm trying to know my place."

Like most of his teammates, he concentrated on baseball in Asheville and had yet to take in the sort of attractions that have made the team's name appropriate. "Tourists" has been the team name, off and mostly on, since 1915.

"I don't know if you can think of a worse name," said a laughing Ron McKee, the Tourists' general manager. "I used to have a car with the name

Asheville Tourists all over it. I was at a hotel delivering some tickets one day, and I came out and there were some people sitting there asking if I could take them to the Biltmore House. I said, 'Well, I guess so. It's a little out of the way, but come on.' They thought I was in the tourism business."

But the Tourists' name was far ahead of its time. It was unique, funky, and made for a distinctive logo. In this case, the logo was a bear wearing a flowered shirt with a camera slung around his neck. Presumably, Ted E. Bear is headed to one of the area attractions, including the Biltmore House and Estate, which opened in 1895 and had a world-renowned winery and daily traffic jams at the entrance, the Thomas Wolfe Memorial, and the wonderfully historic, lively, and hilly downtown.

In Wolfe's autobiographical 1929 novel, *Look Homeward, Angel*, Wolfe is Eugene Gant, the protagonist. Most of the place and character names are similar to the reality. Asheville is called Altamont. George Vanderbilt, who died in 1914, is Goulderbilt. Biltmore House is Biltburn. Patton Street is Hatton Street. So Asheville was hauntingly recognizable to first-time visitors who had read the book.*

Look Homeward, Angel was revered by young Southerners—and still is. Editor and author Willie Morris told in his memoir, *New York Days*, of driving on a whim from his native Jackson, Mississippi, to visit Asheville and pay homage to Wolfe, who died of tubercular meningitis at age thirty-seven in 1938. Morris's admiration was typical of prospective writers of his generation.

As a youth, Eugene Gant unquestionably adopted the racist and anti-Semitic attitudes of the Old South, and while that was an honest portrayal of the times, it causes one to wince today. But Wolfe's emotion, his eyes and ears for detail, and his descriptive power all hold up as monumental.

Here's how Wolfe described Gant's father's arrival in Altamont:

> In the haunting eternity of these mountains, rimmed in their enormous cup, he found sprawled out on its hundred hills and hollows a town of four thousand people. . . . This town of Altamont had been settled soon after the Revolutionary War. . . . And, for several decades before the Civil War, it had enjoyed the summer patronage of fashionable people from

---

* I'm not claiming *The Witch's Season* is on a par with *Look Homeward, Angel*, but I took a similar approach. Eugene becomes the college town of Cascade, Oregon, and the University of Oregon becomes Cascade University. The Oregon Ducks become the Cascade Fishermen. And many of the characters are recognizable as based on real-life men and women, some of them very famous.

Charleston and the plantations of the hot South.... Several rich men from the North had established hunting lodges in the hills, and one of them had bought huge areas of mountain land and, with an army of imported architects, carpenters and masons, was planning the greatest country estate in America—something in limestone, with pitched slate roofs, and one hundred and eighty-three rooms.... But most of the population was still native, recruited from the hill and country people in the surrounding districts. They were Scotch-Irish mountaineers, rugged, provincial, intelligent and industrious.

Wolfe's fans still came by the thousands every year to visit the Wolfe Memorial, the boarding house his mother bought and ran during Tom's formative years. In real life, it was the "Old Kentucky Home," and Tom lived there with his mother. In the novel, it was "Dixieland." When I visited the house, sitting below a high-rise Radisson Hotel, it was closed for repairs after a fire did heavy damage. A high storm fence quarantined the house, but I walked around the perimeter and peered at the Victorian home, guessing where Tom might have read the books he devoured. The adjacent Wolfe visitor center, with exhibits, an auditorium, and a gift shop, still was open. A pamphlet gave directions to the nearby Riverside Cemetery, where Wolfe was buried in the family plot. A tiny arrow sign on the road through the cemetery pointed to the Wolfe plot, and his headstone carried passages from two of his novels.

"Everybody from here had to read *Look Homeward, Angel*," McKee said. "Everybody here then knew who he was talking about in that book. Hey, this is a small town." McKee laughed. "Evidently, the ol' boy had a tough time around here for a few years," he said.

That local resentment provided the material for the posthumously published *You Can't Go Home Again*.

The local legend, one the Tourists cited in their program, was that Wolfe was a batboy for the Tourists at a farcical thirty-one minute, season-ending game against Winston-Salem in Oakes Park on August 31, 1916. At that time, Wolfe was fifteen and just days away from enrolling in the University of North Carolina. Yet Wolfe doesn't have Eugene Gant in that role in *Look Homeward, Angel*. This is Wolfe's description of Eugene Gant:

He played games badly, although he took a violent interest in sports. . . . In the spring and summer, he went as often as he could afford it, or was invited, to the baseball games in the district league, a fanatic partisan of the town club and its best players, making a fantasy constantly of himself in a heroic game-saving role.

That part was timeless and universal. Matt Holliday grew up dreaming that way.

The Tourists drew about 2,000 per home game. It was much better than when McKee took over in 1981, inheriting a $25,000 debt and a chaotic operation playing in a rickety stadium. Woody Kern, who made his fortune in the nursing home industry, became the majority owner in 1982. He lived in Denton, Texas, and ventured to Asheville only occasionally. McKee ran the team and was a part owner.

The Tourists' big draw was Thirsty Thursday. After taking over, McKee decided one night a week would be discount beer night, and it has become an Asheville tradition and much-copied throughout the minor leagues. In 1999, it meant twenty-two ounces of draft beer—and major brands—for a buck.

"Now remember," McKee said, "you're not only in the Bible Belt here, you're in the buckle. But I came up with Thirsty Thursday and it stuck. We're in our second generation now. It's just the place to be on Thursday night in western North Carolina."

On a Thursday night, that didn't seem to be a promoter's hyperbole. The announced crowd was 3,734. The stands were jammed, and there seemed to be perhaps 500 people who never left the concourse. It was a toga party, minus the togas, but with police officers checking IDs just inside the gate and snapping on wristbands.

The Tourists beat the Hickory Crawdads 8–7. The word was that the party continued at Magnolia's downtown well past midnight and that players were known to show up and become the house celebrities for the night. I wondered if it was anything like King Clancy's Claim in Butte.

After the game, the thirty-eight-year-old manager, Jim Eppard, was filling out his nightly organizational report for the Rockies. When he was done writing it out, he would call and read it onto a message machine at the Rockies' Coors Field offices.

"I know I have ten minutes on the voice mail before I have to start all over again," he said. "I haven't had to start over again, but I have come to the end of it. And I have done it in about two and a half minutes. It just depends on what happens in the game, but I have to read from the top all the way to the bottom."

Why not just fax the form?

"Your voice can highlight things and sound excited about things," Eppard said, "and they want to hear that. As soon as I can get this done, I call it in and then it's Coors Light time."

He didn't even have to wait in line.

———

The Tourists had a cumulative record of 64–77 in both halves that season. In retrospect, it's even more shocking, considering nine of the players—Choo Freeman, Matt Holliday, outfielder Juan Pierre, infielder Rene Reyes, Juan Uribe, Aaron Cook, Jason Jennings, Luke Hudson, and Jermaine Van Buren—made the major leagues. Holliday finished the year hitting .264 with 16 home runs, and several of the folks I talked with were concerned he was going to be a complete washout because of what they considered his lack of passion for the game. Freeman turned out to be the disappointment, playing 151 games over three seasons for Colorado, and he was done after playing for AAA Las Vegas in 2007. Pierre hit .320 for the Tourists, but he seemed such a punch-and-judy hitter to me that I didn't buy into the possibility that he would end up with the Rockies—or anyone else. I was wrong on that one, too.

What of the pitchers? Aaron Cook had the look of a guy who stayed in the Asheville rotation only because the Rockies had a lot of money invested in him. He was 4–12 with a 6.44 earned run average that season. Jennings finished 2–2 in twelve starts for the Tourists. Their best pitcher by far that season was Justin Carter (13–6 with a 3.51 earned run average); he never got higher than Class A and was done with baseball by age twenty-five.

I doubt if Matt Holliday is sleeping on an air mattress nowadays.

PART FIVE

DANCING HALL OF FAMERS

Dancing with the Stars became a major hit on television in the mid-2000s. Retired Hall of Fame–caliber players I had visited and written about kept popping up on the show. Emmitt Smith. Jerry Rice. Michael Irvin. The producers also have tried to coax John Elway into giving the competition a try, but he has resisted. Maybe they'll wear him down eventually.

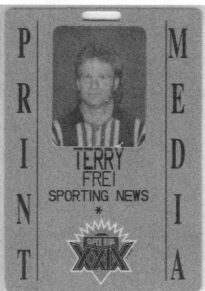

PRINT MEDIA

TERRY FREI
SPORTING NEWS
*

SUPER BOWL
XXIX

Terry ⚹ Frei
The Sporting News

National Football League
MEDIA WORKROOM ID

SUPER
XXVIII
BOWL

JERRY RICE: MISSISSIPPI YEARNING

TO VISIT THE SAN FRANCISCO 49ERS wide receiver in the off-season, I flew into Memphis and drove 185 miles southeast to Starkville, Mississippi, at night. I lost track of how fast I was going while looking at a map to make sure I wasn't lost when I saw flashing red lights in my rearview mirror. *Great*, I thought, *a rural Mississippi speed trap. I'm going to spend the night in jail because I don't have cash on me.* The officer was nice, asking what a guy with a Colorado driver's license was doing there, and I just blurted out that I was there to meet Starkville-area native Jerry Rice, who was visiting his parents. I had a business card, too, which backed my story. The officer handed me the ticket but told me that if I got him an autographed Jerry Rice jersey and sent it to him by the end of the month, he'd "take care" of the ticket. I wasn't thinking so much about the money—I think it was $75—but about points on my license and insurance rates. So I said I'd see what I could do.

I continued on to Starkville and the State House Hotel, one of those old-world hotels on a southern Main Street that had me feeling as if I should join William Faulkner for drinks at the bar. The next morning, Rice parked his red Thunderbird across the street, got out, stretched, and then greeted me. We spent several hours together, and I also visited his nearby hometown of Crawford. There, I drove on the unpaved road he had told me about just outside town, the one that ran past his childhood home. In his childhood, the dust was subject to the swirling influences of the occasional hot Mississippi wind and passing cars on the verge of overheating.

When he started his childhood running rite, he was almost twelve. Rice would leave his house and run down the highway, past spectators on porches, past the trees. He ran stubbornly through the dirt blowing in his nose, eyes, and hair. He ran through the heat. He ran until he decided he had gone far enough, at least in that direction, before he turned around. Sometimes he ran about forty-five minutes, all the way into Crawford, the hamlet with a population of about five hundred and a Main Street one block behind the U.S. Highway Alternate 45.

In Crawford, young Jerry Rice was drenched as he met friends and talked, hung out, wandered. Drenched is a universal human condition in the Mississippi summer, even for those whose major exercise is getting up from their chairs in front of the little grocery store. Yet when Jerry got home, he was worse than drenched. He looked as if he had fallen in a lake and rolled in the dust.

Years later, as Rice drove me to the Mississippi State University track, he confessed that he had turned into a golf fanatic—only a year after taking up the game—and gotten his handicap down to 15. He was invited to tournaments in the past and said: *Sorry, don't play.* By 1995, he did, with a passion, all over the country, and I wondered how he found the time. In the summers, some of Rice's workouts lasted longer than an eighteen-hole round. Rice worked out every day—no matter where he was.

Starkville is about twenty miles northwest of Crawford, a short drive from the sprawling one-story home of Rice's parents. From the perspective of tiny Crawford, nearby Starkville is big enough to be the most convenient city of upward mobility, and since it is the site of the county's hospital, it is listed in all the guides as Rice's birthplace. Rice had the Starkville home built for his parents when he signed his first NFL contract with the 49ers in 1985. No, "had built" isn't quite right. Jerry's bricklayer dad, Joe Nathan, insisted on doing a lot of the work himself.

On that July morning, I watched as the best receiver in NFL history ran on the track and worked out in football cleats on the infield grass. We talked before, during, and after the workout. While this was going on, Rice, who was thirty-two, admitted with a laugh that he also was arguing with the demons whispering: *Take it easy, Jerry. Nobody's pushing you. Take it easy.*

Rice didn't always work out alone. Other NFL players would join him in the San Francisco area, and on some days, Mississippi State players showed up to try and knock off Rice in the pyramids of 220-, 100-, 80-, 60-, 40- and 20-yard sprints. Solo workouts tested his resolve, not his sense of competition. He passed. "You have to play games with yourself," he said, barely puffing. "I'm in the best shape of my life right now. It's like the older I get, the better I get at this."

He told me that he occasionally found himself thinking of that twelve-year-old runner. Of the dust and the sweat. Of Eddie B., his mother, waiting when he got home. "My mom would wonder why I was doing it," Jerry said.

I challenged him to answer her question.

"I don't know why," he said. "It was not like I thought I was going to make it to the pros or anything. For some reason, I had to go out there and train hard. I had no interest in football then. None. For some reason, I had to go out there and train hard."

The "why" for Jerry Rice often was: because. Just because.

"I've had the urge to go back and run those unpaved roads," he said. "I think before my career is all over, that's what I'm going to have to do. They're calling me, saying, 'Jerry, come back, this is where you got your start.'"

As a teenager, he worked with his father and his brothers in the summer, catching bricks passed to him on a scaffold and handing them off to his father. A brick snagged in a standing position is not akin to a football caught on the run. There was a lesson, though. "It taught me the meaning of hard work," he said. "We were very disciplined."

He went to B. L. Moor High School, outside Crawford. Moor drew from areas of rural poverty and had very little money for classroom necessities, much less football extravagances. "We would play the football games on Fridays, and I would stay after school without a ride home," he said. "We would wait. I think we had maybe a ham sandwich. That was our pregame meal." He paused. "But we had so much fun," he said.

When I visited Crawford, the election campaign was heating up. Among the many signs jammed into the ground at one corner of Main Street were those on which Henry (Backbone) Robinson and Willie Saunders pleaded for votes as constable. The Jones Boutique was boarded up and shut down. Crawford City Hall was a steel building, painted light green, with a little park in front. The city office was open only Wednesday through Saturday, from eight until noon.

Residents worked on cars in driveways on Martin Luther King Street, which led from Main Street to the highway. Some of the homes would have blended into subdivisions in more prosperous towns; others were deteriorating. The major businesses were out on the highway, including the Crawford Package Store, Crawford Mini-Mart, and Tonio Domingo's Drive-in.

Back on Main Street, Fannie Alexander was in the tiny post office's parking lot. She gave directions to B. L. Moor High School that even I— capable of getting lost anywhere, even in this town without a stoplight— could follow. "Go past both churches, go to where the pavement ends," she told me, pointing north, "and then turn left and you'll run into it."

I passed the Crawford Methodist Church and Oakland Missionary Baptist Church. Gravel and dirt were straight ahead. I took a sharp left, following the pavement. After another mile, B. L. Moor was on the right. It was a brick building with peeling paint on the aluminum roof trim, with eight modular trailer-type structures aligned next to the permanent building.

It didn't take long to find the picture of the class of 1980 on the main hallway's wall. J Rice, looking every bit the teenager, was between G L Brown and B McGee, and he was a member of the class with the motto, "If there is no struggle, there is no progress."

In the main office, Principal Lillian Thomas was dressed casually as she prepared for the academic year. "You tell Jerry we can use all the help he can give us," she said. Ed Dukes, the athletic director and assistant football coach, was my tour guide. The gym ("Home of the Eagles") where Rice also played on the basketball team was presentable, but the girls' and boys' locker rooms were tiny. The lockers were hooks—one per player. Behind the gym, the football building was an oversized shed locked with chains fed through holes where doorknobs could go—and maybe once went. The Universal weight machine was old and rusted. Dukes said the showers hadn't worked in years. "The kids come in right after practice, take their stuff off, go home, and hopefully shower," Dukes said. The locker room was a barren open room with a cement floor, and the rough plywood-paneled walls were unpainted— except for graffiti. There were no lockers.

The football stadium behind the school had ten rows of bleachers on each side. The boards were sagging and warped, and I wondered if a spontaneous, enthusiastic ovation would cause the bleachers' collapse. The scoreboard in one end zone had a Coca-Cola emblem, but it was so old and faded that I had to assume it was once red. The grass was high and pocked and would take considerable care to get into game condition.

Starkville is the seat of Oktibbeha County, yet Starkville has its own school district; Moor is in the Oktibbeha County School District. Largely because most of the corporate tax base is within the city limits, the Starkville schools' budget was $36 million at the time of my visit; the county schools' was $6 million. Mississippi had 82 counties and 151 school districts, and the financially disparate two-districts-per-county was the norm. James Smith was assistant superintendent of schools for the Starkville School District. Through Rice's junior year at Moor, Smith was an assistant football coach and teacher. "Jerry was an excellent kid, a good student," Smith said. "He was never a discipline problem. He'd always do what we asked him—or break his neck trying."

———————

While stretching at Mississippi State's track, Rice smiled at the twists fate takes. MSU didn't offer him a scholarship out of high school. In 1980, Rice went off to Mississippi Valley State, about seventy-five miles to the west in Itta Bena. Three players from B. L. Moor went to Mississippi Valley together. Two of them, William Gillespie and Joe Thomas, quickly left. "I watched those guys get on the Trailways bus," Rice said. "It was hard for me at first. But I had a purpose and I stayed."

With schools such as Grambling and Jackson State, football in the Southwest Athletic Conference had a proud tradition. But the facilities were Spartan and support was minimal, especially when compared to reality in the Southeastern Conference.

"I'm not going to say it was racism," Rice said of Mississippi State's lack of interest. "Maybe it was just the small school I came from. That's not something I'm going to make an issue of or an excuse. I get along with them now, and I have nothing against them. I come out there, I use their facilities, and we treat each other with respect.

"Look at this," he said, smiling and gesturing to the empty football stadium, Humphrey Arena, and the track and field building. "It's paradise here. I had it hard at Valley. Having it hard is having one uniform, taking it in and washing it after practice on your own. I wouldn't trade those days for anything. You had to work for everything. Nothing was given to you. I didn't get spoiled."

After his senior season, he was at a Valley basketball game when he was introduced to a high school senior from Greenville. Her name was Jackie, and she had no idea who he was and why they were making all this fuss over him. She didn't seem all that impressed, but Jerry promised to call her at noon the next day. When I visited Rice, Jerry and Jackie Rice had two children—Jacqui Bonet, eight, and Jerry Jr., four.

After his 49-catch rookie season with the 49ers in 1985, Rice returned to Mississippi, humbled. "I dropped so many balls, I couldn't wait to get out of California," he said, smiling. After that, though, Rice spent much of his off-season in California, honing that legendary workout discipline. If a passer were around, he would run routes and go through some catching drills. It could last as long as five hours.

Although he became a Californian, Rice returned to Mississippi for family visits. And he didn't forget.

"The amazing thing is that I can walk into any bank and get about anything I want," he said. "Whereas before. . . . Well, life is strange. I was the same person back then. It's just the recognition, I guess. I have the funds now, they don't mind socializing with me, being a part of me, and sometimes even going overboard at times. I think if I wanted a key to this town here, I could easily get one. That's something I couldn't have done a long, long time ago. So that's something I've had to deal with. Racism, stuff like that. You're always going to encounter some of that. I was not brought up to be a racist person, and I believe we are all the same."

"We claim Jerry Rice, I guarantee you," Starkville Mayor Jesse Greer told me. "When he's down here, he comes to [MSU] basketball games, and he's as nice and friendly as can be. He's not flamboyant at all; he's not looking for attention. I'm sure Jerry Rice has all the attention looking for him. Everybody here thinks he's a great person and athlete, and I can tell you that his family is well thought of in this community."

The game, and his considerable talents and resolve, brought him prominence. Riches. Respect. Rice was one of the athletes to whom that latter word was the pinnacle, even if the definition was cloudy.

He loved the rush of accomplishment. Yet he sometimes frowned as he considered what it did to Jerry Rice on the field, and he was adamant he wouldn't allow his son to play football. The realization crystallized after an exhibition game in 1994, when Jerry Jr. walked off the field with his father. "He wanted my helmet, he was getting upset and he wanted to put it on," Jerry said. "The photographers were saying, 'This is our opportunity here.' Well, I'm saying to myself, 'Son, you don't know what you're doing. There's no way I want you to play football.' Football is violent. When you go out there, you can't be a nice guy. You have to have an attitude. I don't like that sometimes. I'm not a nice guy when I pick up the helmet. I'm not. You see so many guys socializing before the game. I cannot do that. It's like I'm a madman. I want him to just not play football. Swing the golf clubs. Tennis racket. I think, too, there's always going to be so much added pressure on him if he does play football. Because Jerry Rice is always going to be his father."

Jerry Jr.'s father was destined to leave the game with records that could stand—well, forever. "I would like to put everything out of reach," he said. "I think the reason I'm hungry is that I'm really afraid of failure. I don't care who you are, if you start feeling comfortable with yourself and saying, 'Okay, I have made it now, I can relax,' that's when you dry up, and they're going to find reasons to bring you down. That's why I've worked so hard."

———

During my visit, I bought a replica Rice 49ers jersey at a Starkville store. I put it in my trunk and confessed to photographer Tom Roster that if I got it autographed and sent it to that rural Mississippi county police officer, I might get out of a speeding ticket. When we were finishing up, Roster signaled to me: *Get out the jersey!* I waved him off, indicating that I had decided against it. It was too embarrassing and a bit unprofessional, and even the timing didn't seem right. Rice noticed this byplay, and Roster spilled the beans. Rice laughed and told me to go get the jersey.

I mailed the autographed jersey to the officer at the address on the ticket, marveling that he didn't even seem concerned about trying to hide his payoff. And I never heard another word about the ticket. I spent more on the jersey than the fine would have been, thinking I was avoiding drivers license points and insurance costs, but I soon learned that Colorado and Mississippi didn't have a reciprocal program to recognize tickets and levy points for tickets at that time.

The joke was on me.

———◆———

I was disappointed when Rice, at age forty-two, tried to hang on for what would have been his twentieth NFL season, signing with the Broncos in 2005. He spent the 2004 season with Oakland and Seattle after three full seasons with the Raiders. I don't subscribe to the tarnishing-legacy school of thought; mostly, it was disconcerting to watch the man who had been so thoughtful about the effects of the game and so full of pride about his role in it insist that he still could keep pace. Mike Shanahan, his former offensive coordinator at San Francisco, gave him that chance. I remembered what he told me on my visit with him in his prime: "When everything starts to slow down, when I'm not as explosive, when I don't have that fire in me, I will break away and let go."

He didn't back that up. The greatest receiver in NFL history, I'm convinced, was seduced by his own training regimen and what he saw when he looked around and saw younger and tremendously talented receivers who didn't come close to his work ethic. He thought he could hang on through guile, desire, and his tremendous conditioning. His one-year deal with the Broncos came with no promises, not even of a roster spot. I was at Dove Valley the day he spoke by conference call to the Denver media about his signing. He sounded very much like a man who wanted a farewell tour.

"For so many years, I keep telling people, there was so much pressure on me, and I had to set a certain standard, and I had to carry that standard," he said. "I had a lot of weight on my shoulders and I had blinkers on. I couldn't hear the crowd; I couldn't hear people chant my name. I couldn't see little kids in the stands. I was so focused on what I had to do. . . . I feel that it's not going to be hard to walk away from this game. But I want to get everything I can out of this game. You can't retire from football and all of a sudden say,

'Look, maybe I should have played another year,' and try and come out of retirement. When I walk away, I'm done."

The end came on September 5, 2005. After realizing that he was going to be the Broncos' fourth or fifth wide receiver at best and likely acting on the advice of his friend Shanahan, Rice announced his retirement in Denver. "I've pushed this body for twenty years," he told reporters that day. "A lot of guys here were three when I started playing. I think those guys are pretty much amazed that I can still run the way I can run."

When he retired, he held thirty-eight league records, among them for career receptions (1,549), receiving yards (22,895), and touchdown receptions (197).

Jerry and Jackie are now divorced.

After football, Rice moved on to other things, including his 2006 appearance on the second season of *Dancing with the Stars*. He and professional partner Anna Trebunskaya finished second to entertainer Drew Lachey and partner Cheryl Burke.

EMMITT SMITH AND THURMAN THOMAS: HALL OF FAME FRIENDSHIP

I N JANUARY 1994, DALLAS TOOK ITS second consecutive Super Bowl victory over Buffalo, this one by a 30–13 score in Atlanta. Many of us covering the game noticed that rather than staying with his celebrating teammates, Cowboys running back Emmitt Smith—named the game's most valuable player after rushing for 132 yards and two touchdowns—sought out and consoled the Bills' Thurman Thomas. They had talked all week about their developing friendship, and it seemed on display after the game. In fact, when they met on the field, Smith was carrying his goddaughter and told her of Thomas, "This is the best running back in the National Football League." Thomas responded, "Naw, being second to you, I don't mind at all." Smith told Thomas to keep his head up and "get ready to come out and play great again."

Corny? Yes. A bit refreshing? Yes.

Smith and Thomas, along with the Lions' Barry Sanders, were the elite runners of the 1990s. The consensus was that in their Super Bowl matchups, Smith shined, but Thomas was so much the epitome of the "agony of defeat" that he outdid the hapless ski jumper tumbling down the hill in the opening credits of *The Wide World of Sports*. We forgot that Thomas's earlier performance in the Super Bowl XXV loss to the Giants in January 1991 was so compelling, he should have been the MVP—and he would have been if Scott Norwood's potential game-winning field goal hadn't gone wide right. Thomas had 135 yards rushing and five catches for 55 yards in that game against the Giants, the first of four consecutive Super Bowl losses. Rather, he was remembered for being unable to find his helmet after it was moved during the pregame pageantry and subsequently missing two plays at the outset of the Bills' second Super Bowl loss the next year, this one to the Redskins. Then came the two desultory performances against the Cowboys in Buffalo's third and fourth Super Bowl losses in four seasons.

To both experience and discuss their friendship, I checked in with both in the off-season, first at Smith's birthday party to benefit the "I Have a Dream" Foundation in Dallas. It was shortly after Thomas spent a week visiting Smith and his family in Pensacola, Florida. Then I attended their teams' training camps—the Bills' in Fredonia, New York, and the Cowboys' in Austin.

The birthday party was quite a soiree. Actress Dawnn Lewis, one of the stars of the television series *A Different World*, warbled "Happy Birthday" on the stage of the Iguana Mirage, a glitzy and upscale Dallas nightclub. As the impeccably attired Smith and Thomas stood, slightly embarrassed, on each side of Lewis, the crowd began to sing along. Smith and Thomas were mute, except for each time Lewis and the audience came to the words "to you." Then the low-center-of-gravity, high-profile running backs cranked up the smiles, pointed at each other and joined in.

Smith said, "to you, Thurman."

Thomas said, "to you, Emmitt."

Smith's twenty-fifth birthday actually was the day before the party—and Thomas's twenty-eighth was that day. At the party, I was struck that their physical similarities were more apparent when they were in street clothes than in pads. They were illusionists, like other diminutive great running backs before them. Tony Dorsett could pull it off. So could Walter Payton. Smith, five feet nine inches and 209 pounds, and Thomas, five feet ten inches and 198 pounds, played much bigger, standing in huddles next to huge men, taking hits from linebackers, all the while making us forget—or rarely notice—just how small they were. With their squat physiques, they both had a low center of gravity and great sense of balance, and they both were extraordinarily adept at anticipating rather than reacting. They had quick feet, quicker reactions, and great acceleration. They ran with intelligence and instinct, sensing the hole, the seam, the movement, whatever gave them their opportunity, and they were there in time to take advantage of it—and then they were gone.

At one point at the party, Thomas and Smith disappeared to another side room for a couple of beers. Thomas later told me it was mostly a Smith interrogation about his off-season plans. Thomas laughed and added, "It was like the guy wanted to make out my schedule for me." One reason Thomas's affection for Smith—and even his acknowledgment that the Cowboys' tailback might have been the better athlete—was uncharacteristic was that

Thomas had the artist's requisite ego, which sometimes made him look ridiculous. At one point in his career, he was the NFL Player of the Year and whined about not getting sufficient respect because some folks still had the audacity to say that Smith or Sanders, a fellow former Oklahoma State player and another friend, might be better. Actually, Smith was the best runner; Thomas was the best combination package of runner and receiver. "I take a lot of pride in that," Thomas told me. "I don't want to be just seven yards deep on every play."

The way they tried to anoint each other the best and complimented each other, it almost seemed as if they still were "arguing" on that field in Atlanta or pointing at each other while singing "Happy Birthday."

"Because of the things that Thurman does, he definitely can be considered the best back in the NFL," Smith told me. "I admit the versatility he has, getting downfield and catching the ball deep. And the way he makes people miss! He's an all-around back. You don't see too many all-around backs in the league anymore. I don't look at myself as the best back." Then he got to an important point. "That's just me. If I don't consider myself the best, I always have something to strive for."

Thomas on Smith: "I think what I admire about him most is he's a tough little son of a bitch. He's tough and he doesn't have a lot of speed, but he makes up for it with his quickness and his ability to cut on a dime. We're pretty much the same size, but he's a little bit heavier than I am. People didn't think that small backs could make it in this league. I think that Emmitt and Barry and I have proved a lot of people wrong."

That belief certainly wasn't paranoia. The question marks about small backs involved strength and durability, but the diminutive great talents of the NFL of their era—from Tony Dorsett and Walter Payton through Smith, Thomas, and Sanders—withstood the pounding. Better yet, they were adept at slipping, sliding, or scooting at the last instance to avoid the direct hit while fighting for the extra yard. Neither was the fierce blocker that Payton was, and neither could approach Payton's unparalleled strength for a man that size. Yet they both were above the small running back norm.

Smith had won three consecutive NFL rushing titles, and he was heading for his fourth under new coach Barry Switzer, who took over for the departed Jimmy Johnson. Amid what clearly would be a circus, Smith was determined to run on. "I've still got the high standards for myself," Smith told me. "Nothing changes. Once you've accomplished something, you've got choices. You can be happy or satisfied with what you've done. I'm neither happy nor satisfied. There's so much more for me to accomplish."

After the teams reported for work, I caught up with Smith at the Cowboys' camp at St. Edward's University. He had just come off a well-publicized golf cart accident that drew breathless coverage in Dallas, although he was unscathed. "We're along the same lines," Smith said in a St. Edward's dormitory cafeteria. "We're both Taurus and we're both stubborn. It's not like we can hang out every day, or we talk every day, or that we're buddy-buddy all the time. But I think we've found out that when we get together, it's a good time."

When I told him that I next was headed to the Bills' camp, Smith good-naturedly asked me to remind Thomas that he had bought a painting for $1,000 at the "I Have a Dream" Foundation benefit and the check still hadn't arrived.

On the Fredonia State campus, about forty-five miles southwest of Buffalo, Thomas laughed when I brought up the painting. "Hey," he shrugged, "sometimes you forget." He said of Smith, "He understands me, really understands me." Thomas leaned over and smiled, and it reminded me of the way he looked as he listened to Dawnn Lewis sing at the party in Dallas. "I think we're getting to be almost like twins," he said.

When Thomas and I adjourned for the day in Fredonia, the Buffalo running back jumped into a golf cart, started it, backed it up, then stopped, looked over at me, and said, "I can drive a cart."

It took me a second to realize that he was poking fun at Smith.

At the time, Smith was active on the endorsement front, in commercials and ads. At only twenty-five, his every off-field move—his hook-up with a marketing group, an autobiography, a clothing line, and a sports memorabilia store—seemed to already involve positioning himself for strengthening his image and looking ahead to retirement. He also had his own eponymous foundation and worked with such organizations as the Salvation Army, the "I Have a Dream" Foundation, and a foundation involved with abused children. Thomas also had a foundation and regularly donated monetary awards— such as the $30,000 he won for being named Player of the Year—to charity. He also donated $125,000 to Oklahoma State.

Remaining amazingly durable for his size up until the end, Thomas played a total of twelve seasons with the Bills and part of one with Miami before suffering a career-ending knee injury. He was inducted into the Pro Football Hall of Fame in 2007, his second year of eligibility, and now lives with his family in Buffalo, where he runs his own company, Thurman Thomas Sports Training.

Smith, meanwhile, broke Payton's record for career yards during the 2002 season. He retired at the end of the 2004 season after a lackluster two-season stint with the Cardinals and 18,355 career yards. In retirement, his broadcasting work with ESPN was much criticized, and his contract wasn't renewed for the 2009 season. He has been more successful in other endeavors and managed to pull off what Jerry Rice hadn't—winning the *Dancing with the Stars* with partner Cheryl Burke in 2006. He also is majority partner and co-chairman of a Dallas-based commercial real estate firm. He made it into the Hall of Fame along with Jerry Rice in 2010, the first year they became eligible.

Smith and Thomas are still friends.

MICHAEL IRVIN: GETTING OPEN

I N THE NFL, ESPECIALLY WHEN THERE was less player movement, opponents on divisional rivals often went up against each other twice a year for as long as ten years. The positional confrontations fascinated me.

In one case, I chronicled a left offensive tackle versus right defensive end matchup, the one most crucial in pass protection because it's at the right-handed quarterback's blind side. That was Green Bay's Ken Ruettgers versus Chicago's Richard Dent. I enjoyed spending time with both players the week before a 1993 Packers–Bears matchup in Green Bay, then attending the game at Lambeau Field.*

In another, it was the "showcase" wide receiver versus the "shutdown" cornerback. That was Dallas' Michael Irvin versus Arizona's Aeneas Williams. Williams was so low-key and humble, it diminished his profile, but he might have been the top corner in the game. He invited me to attend a 5:45 a.m. Bible study group—I passed—and asked a photographer to refrain from using foul language after he said he didn't want to do a "half-assed" job on pictures. His play and personality reminded me a lot of former Bronco Louis Wright, another great corner who merited Hall of Fame consideration but hadn't gotten it due to his refusal to call attention to himself with anything other than his play. With a Deion Sanders personality, Williams would have been perceived as one of the league's brightest stars. But that wasn't him.

By the time I visited the two players in Phoenix and Dallas before a 1995 game in Texas Stadium and then watched them go against each other, Irvin had toned down since his wilder early seasons in the league. But he remained

---

* When the story ran, with a picture of Ruettgers and Dent going at it on the cover, it was billed the "Headbangers Ball," a reference to the hit MTV series.

a mix of ego ("my greatest asset"), flashiness, and often talked at a speed that reminded me of 4.2-second 40-yard dash.

Irvin was in the whirlpool at the Cowboys' headquarters. I sat at the side. I had been forewarned that the trick with Irvin was to assess his mood—good or bad—each day and to react accordingly. On this day, he was in a good mood, which meant I mostly listened.

"I think the biggest thing I've learned over the years is that this is a game of inches and 90 percent of it is played above the shoulders," he said.

Irvin had watched tape the night before on his big screen in his den, focusing on Williams in several Cardinals games, including the one a couple of days earlier at Detroit. The plays were all first downs; each night during the week, Irvin advanced to another down. He was expecting the Cardinals to have Williams take him man-to-man as much as possible without fouling up their schemes, because that's what they had done in earlier games against elite receivers.

"He's very good, and I'm not saying that because I'm about to play him," Irvin said of Williams. "Now that I know that he's supposed to follow me all over the field, I look forward to it a little more than I usually look forward to it. It's a personal challenge. Aeneas has good speed, good reaction. You try and attack a corner's weakness, but it's hard to find a weakness in Aeneas. He ain't no fool. Usually, I study both corners, but I haven't even looked at Patrick Hunter. I've looked at their games and I've looked at Aeneas. I saw him when he followed Henry Ellard* and Herman Moore. You look at those things and you say, 'That's how he's going to play me right there.' I think he did a great job on Herman, and I know how he did it, but if I told you that and he finds out that I told you, he might change things and trick me."

————◆————

At their home in the Golden Heights neighborhood of Fort Lauderdale, Pearl and Walter Irvin raised seventeen children. Walter had two, Pearl six when they met, and then they had nine together. Michael was number fifteen, the second youngest of seven sons in the merged families. Michael sometimes ate mayonnaise or ketchup sandwiches. His clothes were hand-me-downs. He wore $3.99 tennis shoes called Cat Heads—and when they were too small, his father extended their lives by cutting off the shoe's toes.

The Irvins had air conditioning in the three-bedroom house, but they couldn't afford to use it. Instead, they had a fan. One fan. "It wasn't good

---

* The Redskins' best wide receiver.

then, but it's funny when I think about it," Michael told me. "We couldn't afford two fans. How much do fans cost? I always would have to be the one to go steal the fan from the girls' room. You had to 'call' the fan after six in the morning, like, 'We get the fan tonight.' My sisters always seemed to be able to call the fan, and I always would go steal it. We'd get it going, now we're okay, and we sleep. Of course, my sisters start to get hot, and they come in and steal it right back."

Walter, their father, was a roofer and a lay preacher for the Primitive Baptist Church, which was big on sermonizing but opposed choirs altogether. Two weekends a month, Walter drove to preach in Americus, Georgia, and Fort Myers, Florida. The rest of the time, he worked. "He was as dark as I am, but he would come home just white from all the cement and everything," Michael said. "He would come out and play marbles with us. It'd be right before it got dark, and we'd be out there, playing. He always cheated! He'd always try to shoot with the hunk, the big marble."

Irvin sighed. "You know, my days are pretty busy, and I know now that he had to be tired. He'd still find time to be with us, and it wasn't just us. It was all the kids in the neighborhood."

Michael admitted that he was no angel at Piper High. At the end of his sophomore year, he was suspended. He swore he never would disclose why, but the incident angered both him and his father. They decided he would transfer to a Catholic school, St. Thomas Aquinas. Piper officials cried foul and "recruiting," then refused to sign his athletic release, so he couldn't play his junior year of football.

Suddenly, Walter Irvin was diagnosed with cancer. Michael drove his father to the hospital for treatment. Father and son talked. "Even when he was suffering and he was in pain," Michael said, "all he could worry about was family. He'd say, 'Doc, I don't know how long I can take this.' The doc would say, 'Is the pain that great?' He'd say, 'It's not the pain; it's the pain of my family seeing me in this position.' That was the biggest lesson of my life. That's why we're here, to be with the people we love. My father did something a lot harder than what I do, and he was always thinking about his family. I go out and play football. It's a fun game. There was no glorification in roofing, man."

The week of Michael's first game in his senior year, Walter told Michael, "Mike, I feel I'm going home on the morning train." He made Michael promise to take care of his mother. Walter died the next day, and Michael ran five miles to St. Thomas Aquinas and collapsed, sobbing, into the arms of a priest.

Michael wanted to quit school and go to work. Pearl Irvin said, "No way." Michael previously carried roofing cement in the summers and on weekends and cooked French fries at Burger King but was fired for trying to take food home. He and neighborhood friend Lorenzo White, eventually an NFL running back, also ripped down wallpaper at hotels. Heavily recruited, Michael decided to stay home and play for Jimmy Johnson at the University of Miami.

At Miami, as part of the nation's most brassy program, Irvin became the "Playmaker." When the Cowboys took him as the eleventh pick in the first round of the 1988 draft, he immediately proclaimed that he and quarterback Danny White were going to be "the hottest combination to come along since butter and bread." He signed a three-year, $1.8 million contract, bought Pearl a car and a house in Plantation, Florida, and became the informal Michael Irvin foundation for his family. He guaranteed business loans for several siblings, doled out allowances, and decreed that all males in the family would attend St. Thomas Aquinas, at his expense, where he also endowed a scholarship fund in his father's name.

He played for a terrible team in Tom Landry's last year and then suffered a torn anterior cruciate ligament in his right knee in 1989, his second season. He spent most of 1990 trying to regain his stride physically, and his great 1991 season (93 catches, eight touchdowns) meant he wouldn't be written off as a bust. The big contracts and even greater fame followed.

Irvin's temper and mercurial nature occasionally flared up. He got into a shouting match with the NFL Players Association's Gene Upshaw in a team meeting over the collective bargaining agreement. He had a run-in with 7-Eleven clerks and was accused of punching a referee at a charity basketball game. He stormed out of coach Barry Switzer's first team meeting out of loyalty to Jimmy Johnson.

Each year before Irvin reported to the Cowboys' camp, his family had a picnic. The year I visited him, he handed out envelopes at the picnic. For each brother and sister: $1,000. For each niece and nephew: $500. "I wouldn't even want to tell you how much that was," Michael said. "There are so many of 'em!"

Irvin's Aunt Fannie, his mother's sister, asked for help in getting her old car fixed. "She doesn't ask for much," Michael said. He told Fannie he would take care of it, which he did by buying her a new Mercedes. Michael laughed when he told of trying to talk Fannie and Pearl, the sisters, into taking only one car on the ninety-minute drive to the Primitive Baptist Church in Fort Myers. (Long sermons, long drive.) Nope, on those Sundays in Fort Myers,

Pearl pulled up in the Cadillac Michael bought her, and Fannie pulled up in the Mercedes. Sometimes, they had to scramble to get home in time to watch Michael's games.

———◆———

In the game at Dallas, the Cardinals played more zone than they had in the first three weeks of the season. On one occasion, Williams locked in on Irvin, who got a step on Williams down the sideline. Bingo, Troy Aikman dropped the ball in for the 50-yard completion that put the Cowboys on the Cardinals' 2 and set up their first touchdown in a 34–20 Dallas win. Irvin finished with five catches for 105 yards. In the final minute of the first quarter, Emmitt Smith ran six yards for another touchdown, and Williams suffered a knee injury when he got tangled in the end zone pileup.

In fact, when I met with Irvin again the Monday morning after the game, the first words out of his mouth were, "How is he?"

He meant Williams.

At that point, I hadn't heard, but it turned out that the knee injury wasn't serious and Williams didn't miss any games. In the teams' second meeting of the season, Irvin again had five catches, this time for 82 yards, and Williams's 48-yard interception return accounted for the Cardinals' only touchdown in a 37–13 loss. When they played against each other in other games as their careers progressed, Williams most often took Irvin man-to-man or at least had primary responsibility for trying to control him. Three years later, in fact, Williams had two interceptions when the Cardinals beat the Cowboys in the playoffs.

Williams traveled to Denver in 1999, following the Columbine shootings, with a group of Christian NFL players that also included Reggie White, and they visited victims—including Patrick Ireland and Sean Graves—at Craig Rehabilitation Hospital.

The Cardinals traded Williams to the Rams in 2001, and he not only had two interceptions against Brett Favre and the Packers in the divisional round, but he also returned both for touchdowns. In the NFC championship game, he had the game-clinching interception of the Eagles' Donovan McNabb. When he retired in 2005, he had 12 career defensive touchdowns and 55 interceptions, and he had been an All-Pro four times. He is a minister in the St. Louis area. He now is eligible for the Hall of Fame and deserves to get in eventually.

Irvin, whose personal behavior has continued to be mercurial, was forced to retire after suffering a spinal injury on the cement-hard turf in Philadelphia. He had 750 receptions for 11,904 yards and 65 touchdowns.

The "Playmaker" also had forty-seven games with 100 or more reception yards, leaving him behind only Rice and Don Maynard. He made the Hall of Fame in 2007 and is a broadcaster. He and partner Anna Demidova finished ninth among the fifteen couples in 2009 on *Dancing with the Stars*, but he got a measure of revenge on the closing night of the competition. Wearing Cowboy blue and up against Rice in 49ers colors, Irvin won a dance-off between the two great wide receivers and their professional partners. His Dallas radio talk show ended in early 2010, only days before his contract was set to expire, following a civil suit by a Florida woman who accused him of a 2007 sexual assault. Irvin filed a countersuit, the Broward County State Attorney's office said it had investigated the charges and wouldn't pursue prosecution of Irvin. The former wide receiver continues to work for the NFL Network.

PART SIX

COLLEGE FOOTBALL

I want a university the football team can be proud of.
—George Lynn Cross, president, University of Oklahoma,
1943–1968

PENN STATE

4

VS. NEBRASKA

Beaver Stadium, University Park, PA

Saturday, Sept. 25, 1982

PRESS

Booth/Seat

_____ № 135

1995
ROSE BOWL GAME
PENN STATE
VS.
OREGON

JANUARY 2
1995

216

PRESS BOX

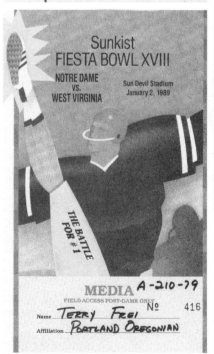

Sunkist
FIESTA BOWL XVIII

NOTRE DAME
VS.
WEST VIRGINIA

Sun Devil Stadium
January 2, 1989

THE BATTLE
FOR #1

MEDIA A-210-79
FIELD ACCESS POST-GAME ONLY № 416

Name TERRY FREI
Affiliation PORTLAND OREGONIAN

Sunkist
Fiesta Bowl
XVI

Catch a rising star!

Sun Devil Stadium
January 2, 1987
6:00 p.m.

THE BATTLE FOR #1:
MIAMI
VS.
PENN STATE

WORKING PRESS
NO FIELD ACCESS

AUX. B

ROW 1

SEAT 26

"THERE IS A PLACE CALLED NEBRASKA . . . ."

MIGHT GET KICKED OUT OF THE University of Colorado Alumni Association for saying this or have my sanity questioned by those who sing the praises of game-day atmospheres involving Georgia's hedges, Ohio State's horseshoe stadium, and Notre Dame's Touchdown Jesus. Yet I've always felt that the top college football Saturday experience in the country is in Lincoln, Nebraska. I've been there many times, but one time I took great care to sample and chronicle the entire weekend in 1994. As near as I can tell, not much has changed since.

The Cornhuskers, 5–0 and ranked second nationally, were playing Oklahoma State. It was star defensive tackle Terry Connealy's "Senior Day," and much of the population of his small Nebraska hometown, Hyannis, made the 320-mile drive southeast to Lincoln for the game. The Bank of Hyannis passed out T-shirts honoring Connealy. Hyannis, so often overlooked by selective atlas publishers, was the only dot on the shirt's Nebraska map. Connealy's name was in block letters. His number—99—was superimposed across Nebraska, stretching from South Dakota into Kansas. The message: "HOMETOWN PROUD!"

Coincidentally, the travelers from Hyannis were part of the Cornhuskers' 199th consecutive sellout, extending a streak that began in 1962, when Memorial Stadium's capacity was 31,080. To the residents of Hyannis and the other towns of northwest Nebraska, it is irrelevant that they are closer to the University of Colorado campus than to Lincoln or that they tend to be fans of the Denver Broncos and other Colorado professional franchises. If you live within the borders of Nebraska, the Huskers are your major college team. Your only team.

The night before number 199, after checking in at the athletic department, I renewed acquaintances with Nebraska athletic director Bill Byrne. He promptly took me around the offices and asked everyone to toss out suggestions about where I might go that night to get the true feel for a Nebraska football weekend. I'd already planned a couple of stops I had made in previous trips to Lincoln, but time after time, I saw wry smiles and heard the same comments: *Oh, you have to go to the Sidetrack! What? You've never been to the Sidetrack?*

A little later, I stopped by Byrne's house, adjacent to the country club on Lincoln's east side. He had been the athletic director at Nebraska for only two years, and his hiring was a tough sell. There were in-house candidates, and Byrne was an outsider. When I visited, he was trying to shepherd a plan to build skyboxes at Memorial Stadium, again expanding capacity and giving the athletic department a significant new source of revenue.

Even for teams that regularly sell out their home games, the financial pressures are immense. Byrne wasn't being merely the gracious athletic director–host as he and his wife, Marilyn, put on a dinner party and served the best salmon that can be flown into Nebraska. Some of the Huskers' boosters were mingling among the athletic department staff, guests from Oklahoma State, and Jim Barker of the Orange Bowl committee.

When I told the woman from the catering service that I eventually was headed for the Sidetrack, she told me conspiratorially, "That's where I'd be if I weren't working."

At the time, Connealy and most of his Nebraska teammates were at a Sylvester Stallone–Sharon Stone movie, *The Specialist*, at the Plaza 4.

After leaving Byrne's, photographer Doug DeVoe made an intermediate stop at Misty's restaurant, Lincoln's slightly more wholesome Friday night tradition for both Nebraska and visiting fans. The restaurant served a cut of prime rib some offensive linemen couldn't finish. The display case in the waiting area had helmets from every Division I-A program. Sports banners and the logos of all Big Eight schools were on the walls. The bar in the bustling lounge was shaped like a football, and a gold statue of Jerry Tagge, quarterback of the 1971 national championship team, rotated over the shelves of liquor stock.

At nine o'clock, right on time, thirteen members of the Cornhuskers' marching band strutted down the stairs, belting out the fight song. They wore white tux shirts and red bow ties. After parading through the eating area—diners put down their forks to stand and clap—the musicians adjourned to a stage in the lounge. For the next thirty minutes, they put on a mini pep rally and concert. A contingent of Husker yell leaders (Nebraskan for "cheerleaders") led—yes—cheers. One poor girl stood on the shoulders of a yell king, and she had to be careful not to scrape the ceiling with her fingernails as she raised her arms overhead. After a couple of renditions of the fight song, and even a quick rendition of the Oklahoma State fight song, the band marched back to a meeting room. The second set was scheduled for eleven that evening.

Jay Hoffman, twenty-three, was in his third year in the Friday night band and was the leader for the season. He said the Misty's assignments went "to the committed group. These people have been in band three or four years and this is kind of their reward." A senior economics major, Hoffman was a Lincoln native. "You can't grow up here and not know about the Friday night tradition," he told me. "It's not like you live here and there's a football team. It's you live here and you're part of the football team, part of the tradition. When you play for the Colorado game or the Oklahoma game, it's absolutely nuts around here. Of course, they're hammered beyond belief. The crowd is pumped up, it's standing room only wall to wall."

But I asked, wasn't this a combustible mixture, especially when the Big Eight rivals come to town? Alcohol, rivalries, the band playing both fight songs? What about this newly virulent rivalry with the hated Colorado Buffaloes?

"We don't talk about the Colorado fans," Hoffman said. "They're pretty much a bunch of whiners. They come out here and think it's going to be a Colorado pep rally. It's like, 'Wake up, this is Nebraska, this is our pep rally.' We say, 'Yeah, we'll play your stupid fight song, but. . . .' They're a bunch of whiners. If you get them hammered enough, though, they'll pay you twenty bucks every time you play their fight song." He smiled and reconsidered. "I guess there's something good to say about Colorado fans."

Bob Milton, the owner of Misty's, told me the pregame tradition began back in the late 1960s. "I got acquainted with Bob Devaney," he said of the former Huskers coach and athletic director who by that point probably was eating dessert at Byrne's house. "He brought a lot of football players out here. He'd bring recruits. At that time, you could hire football players to glad-hand people, to shake hands and wear red sport coats. Now you can't do that. But I stayed involved."

Many of the visiting teams had their Friday night squad dinner in a Misty's meeting room. Oklahoma did it every time. The hated Colorado Buffaloes did not.

After the movie, Connealy and the Huskers were bused back to the Nebraska Center, the on-campus hotel where they stayed the nights before home games. Connealy was counting them down—three home games left in his career.

His father, Marty, was a rancher in the sandhills-dominated area of the state and a former Nebraska scholarship player who didn't play a down because of a heart murmur. Marty first bought season tickets in 1968 and was the president of the Big Red Cattle Club, which annually donated a "beef" to be auctioned off to benefit the athletic development fund. Marty's brothers, Jerry and Jack, played for the Huskers in the 1970s.

At the Huskers' eighty-seventh consecutive sold-out game, when they met Alabama on September 17, 1977, Terry's name was announced on the Memorial Stadium public-address system for the first time. He was five. "They announced: 'Marty Connealy, you're lost and your son Terry is looking for you at gate so and so,'" Marty told me.

Terry was a multisport athlete at little Hyannis High. "I never let him know that there was any place other than Lincoln to go to college," his father said.

Said the six feet five, 275-pound Terry, "As long as I can remember, it's been an obsession. I think every little boy in Nebraska wants to play Nebraska football. I never took any other official [college scouting] trips. I did go to Wyoming for a few games"—again, Hyannis is closer to Laramie than Lincoln—"and I was talking to some other schools. But I committed early, and after I committed, I didn't take any trips anywhere else."

Of the Huskers' twenty-two position starters against Oklahoma State, three came from both California and New Jersey, with one apiece from Texas, Kansas, Alabama, Maryland, South Carolina, Illinois, Wyoming, and Florida. That left eight starters from Nebraska, including Connealy; over the years, a surprising number of Huskers' regulars had come from within the borders.

Both in terms of recruiting and financial resources, the Huskers clearly benefited from the single-program obsession. The attraction for those coming from out of state was winning and being the focal point of not merely the campus but of an entire state.

When I visited, the concern was that starting quarterback Tommie Frazier was out following surgery to remove blood clots from his right leg. Backup Brook Berringer still was affected by a lung problem. Behind him was walk-on Matt Turman. It seemed likely that the Huskers might be able to overpower Oklahoma State with a water boy taking the snaps, but fans were concerned the Huskers might be headed for problems down the road. They were thinking ahead to Kansas State the next week and especially to Colorado. Even in early October, the odds seemed good that by the time that the Colorado game arrived, both teams still would be undefeated, and the stakes would be the Big Eight title and continued national championship contention. Then, of course, national press would flock to Lincoln and ask coach Tom Osborne for the 1,373rd time if he wouldn't feel complete as a head coach until one of his teams had finished number one.

As curfew approached for the players, Terry Connealy's family settled in at the Airport Inn, where they'd had a standing reservation on game weekends for twenty-six years.

At the Sidetrack Tavern, they were just getting rolling.

Sidetrack owner Joyce Durand looked matronly but had a voice that could peel paint and a vocabulary that would make a hockey player blush. She doubled as the piano player in the house band in the cavernous warehouse-style building that was packed and raucous most nights and downright riotous the night before a game. Paul Newton and Fred Meyer joined Joyce in the band.

Occasionally—oh, no more than once every eleven minutes—the band broke into the Nebraska fight song and got the crowd really going:

There is no place like Nebraska
Dear old Nebraska U

The rest of the time, students and others in the mixed-age crowd handed Durand notes written on napkins, and she read them all aloud, making the most fuss over those from self-proclaimed "Sidetrack virgins" and those that made obscene references to the opponents and media. Then we heard familiar tunes, many of them adapted for the football crowd, with rewritten lyrics. One song was an obscene biological suggestion for ESPN commentator Craig James, who apparently was anathema in Lincoln because he knocked the Huskers in the previous season. Caught up in the spirit, I told Joyce that if she ever ran into James, she should ask the former Southern Methodist running back how many games his alma mater has won since the Mustangs—the only football program to receive the NCAA death penalty, in part because of elicit payments to players from a slush fund provided by a booster—had to institute a salary cap, so to speak. I apologized to James in my story, saying it was a real cheap shot and that Lincoln had rubbed off on me.* But it wasn't just James. The Sidetrack songs and banter-filled

---

* Perhaps the enmity guaranteed that James's son, Adam, years later wouldn't consider attending Nebraska and—unfortunately for coach Mike Leach—went to Texas Tech instead.

interludes from the musicians included barbs directed at just about every college football media personality, network, and publication in the country.

The big hit of the night was Durand's "I love/I hate" song. Guess which applied to "Coach Bill McCartney and the Colorado Buffaloes?" She described her affection or contempt in words that largely had to go unreported, but when someone in the audience tossed a paper missile at the stage, Durand said, "You keep throwing stuff like that, people might think you're from Colorado!"

Newton introduced a parody to the tune of Billy Joel's "The Longest Time" with this admonition to me over the microphone: "Feel free to reprint this song, but only in its entirety." Entirety? It was so obscene, I couldn't even get in an entire line or even begin to describe what Durand pantomimed to match the words. In wholesome Lincoln, Nebraska, of all places!

By then, I was thinking: *My story was supposed to be about the most wholesome college football weekend experience in America.* I was shaking my head, thinking, *this is just awful,* but laughing at the same time because I knew I would be right back here the next Friday night I was in Lincoln for a game weekend.

The next morning, Terry Connealy and the Huskers got their wake-up calls at 8:00 and were in chapel or mass by 8:30.

I did find something wholesome! I went to the Big Red Breakfast on Saturday morning in the packed Ramada Inn meeting room. Former Cornhuskers play-by-play man Dick Perry held court at the head table and was broadcasting live on KMEM-AM, Lincoln's big-band music station. Originally, I guessed that DeVoe and I were the only ones in this room who were at the Sidetrack the night before. But then when I mentioned where we had been, enough folks laughed to make me wonder if they hadn't been there singing along with Joyce, after all.

I was invited to the head table to talk with Dick Perry live on the radio. I revealed that I was working on a story about a unique college football weekend and that I knew I would find that in Lincoln, despite the fact that I had gone to the University of Colorado. My secret was out. I was one of the hated Colorado Buffaloes.

Perry, a true gentleman, said I seem like a nice guy but asked what the *Sporting News* had against the Huskers, because even from our magazine, they didn't seem to get enough . . . well, you know. It was what Aretha Franklin sang about. His broadcasting partner, Bill Wood, asked on the air if I couldn't put in my vote for *Sporting News* to run all the major-league box scores again.*

At the Nebraska Center, the Huskers went into group meetings at 9:30, about the same time that student Denny Franks ran pass patterns across 16th Street in front of the Sigma Nu fraternity, amid traffic, then turned his attention to trying to coax drivers into pulling into his fraternity's driveway. Nineteen-year-old Franks jumped in the path of cars, waved, begged, screeched. The Nebraska fight song was blaring from a boom box.

It was three hours to game time.

"We have to try to get cars to park in our lot and get money," said Franks, from Omaha. "We can't let 'em by. We gotta stop 'em."

Football parking was five bucks a pop, with the money going to Sigma Nu's pledge function. Franks and twenty-year-old Ryan Anderson, also of Omaha, were the chief parking recruiters while some of their fraternity brothers played catch in the front yard. Jason Rohrs of Syracuse, Nebraska, was sitting on a second-floor ledge, outside a window, shirtless, and wearing a huge red foam cowboy hat. Greg Metschke also was bare-chested, but he was wearing a red cape. Metschke also was adept at recruiting parking customers but has backed off a little since the time he "stiff-armed a bus."

I asked, "How did last night go, guys?"

"It was the normal Friday night, staying up all night and getting ready for the Saturday morning of a game," Franks said. "We don't sleep Friday nights, otherwise we wouldn't be this wound up."

Franks paused to holler at cars.

"Some of the people pass out," he said, "but we try and make people stay up all night, by keeping 'em up, making 'em go crazy, running around, blasting the stereos, screaming."

I observed that it sure was a good thing that Nebraska fraternities officially were "dry."

"That's why we have cups," said Metschke, who indeed was holding a paper cup.

I said I assumed this was all a dry run for that game against the hated Colorado Buffaloes. "I think Colorado's doing all right now," Franks said, "but as soon as they come here, we'll see if they can really play."

There was a time when Oklahoma was the Cornhuskers' number one opponent, and Colorado—though a rival—didn't trigger such indignant

---

* In my years at the *Sporting News*, at one time the Bible of baseball, I heard that a lot.

reactions in Lincoln. Before the rivalry died down again, it clearly picked up after the Buffaloes' resurgence in the late 1980s. Bill McCartney anointed the Cornhuskers the Buffaloes' chief rival, and he asked Colorado fans not to sell their tickets to Nebraska games to anyone who might wear red to Folsom Field. Yes, Nebraskans overreacted to that, and at times Husker fans deserved the number one ranking in a poll about paranoia. McCartney never suggested that Nebraska should be nuked or that residents were subhuman slime. Arguably, he was paying a compliment to the depth of Nebraska loyalty and the Huskers' winning tradition. But I'll concede this: the Denver media, both then and since, often has portrayed Nebraska fans as hayseeds at best and straight from the banjo scene in *Deliverance* at worst. Many of Colorado's fans at Folsom Field have treated Nebraska visitors with rudeness that goes beyond the usual Saturday stadium jeering of folks wearing the wrong colors. So when I asked the Sigma Nu boys why they didn't like Colorado, the answer didn't surprise me. "Because they suck," said Metschke, the man with the cape. "They decided they didn't like us, so we don't like them. Hey, what's his name—McCartney?—wanted to make it into a rivalry, so we'll take it to the end. He picked us as his rival, so they could rise to our level. But they can't."

At the nearby Nebraska Center, the Huskers took turns having their ankles taped and then pulled their socks back on. They wouldn't be leaving for the nearby stadium for a few more minutes.

Despite the predictable game week rhetoric from the Cornhuskers, nobody expected the Oklahoma State game to be much more than a warm-up for the bigger games later on, when the Huskers would find out whether their abundance of talent could balance the loss of a superlative quarterback, Frazier. The Huskers still had a tremendous offensive line led by All-American tackle Zach Wiegert, a six feet five, three hundred pounder from Fremont, Nebraska, an electric sophomore I-back, Lawrence Phillips, and a solid defense.

When I arrived at the stadium, Rich Stanwiak, who worked in mail advertising in Omaha, was standing outside, decked out in a red Nebraska hat, a white Nebraska sweatshirt, red Nebraska sweatpants, and red-and-white shoes. He had been holding two fingers aloft for about forty-five minutes and had already turned down the scalpers who wanted $50 for $22 tickets. Finally, he closed a deal: $25 apiece. He knew he'd have to pay more for tickets to the Colorado game.

A thirty-four-foot Pace Arrow was parked at the base of the footbridge adjacent to the stadium. Blue Iowa plates were the most common evidence of out-of-state support for the Huskers in the season-pass lot, but the Pace Arrow was from South Dakota. The owners, Donna Vader and her husband, David, who had retired after a career in marine construction, lived in Pickstown, South Dakota. "I'm D. Vader, like Darth," Donna said, "and I am spacey most of the time." The Vaders once lived in Omaha and had been going to Huskers games since the 1970s.

The Vaders left home Friday morning. They stopped in David City, Nebraska, on Friday night, hooking up to Pat Comte's garage—"so we could have electricity and keep the beer cold," Donna said—and then visited Pat's establishment, the Comte Bar. Pat was aboard Saturday morning when the Pace Arrow left again at 6:30, and the final stop was in Osceola to pick up Donald and Doris Ostberg, who had the coveted pass for the prime parking lot. "That's what friends are for, to use each other," Donna said. "We have the mobile home, and they have the parking spot. We hate each other, but we get along for the Nebraska games."

For the record, Doris Ostberg was aghast when that quote was read to her—and Donna Vader was kidding. In a few minutes, Muffy, the tiny dog with red ribbons around each ear, would be shut into the mobile home, and the trailer contingent would enter the stadium. They joined, among many others, Isabelle Lampshire of Lincoln. Isabelle was in section 30, row 42, seat 3, above at the north goal line. Isabelle, ninety-one, had been sitting there since the second year of the sellout streak, since she and her husband, Wesley, obtained the season tickets in 1963.

"I've missed only two or three games," Isabelle told me. "I don't remember which ones, except I know one was against Washington State and we lost."

That was sellout game number eighty-six, on September 10, 1977.

"When I came back the next game," she said, "my buddies all around me blamed me for the loss because I had been gone."

That next game, by the way, was the Alabama game—the one at which five-year-old Terry Connealy's name boomed over the public-address system. Isabelle didn't remember that, but she had forgotten very little about the Huskers and her game day experiences, both at Memorial Stadium and at the Devaney Center, where she had attended all but a handful of the men's basketball games since the building opened in 1976.

Isabelle went to the games with friends, her son, retired dentist Earl Lampshire, or her daughter, Virginia Hagerman. Wesley, Isabelle's husband, was a contractor. In November 1969, he was in considerable pain with leukemia but was determined to attend the last home game of the season against Iowa State on November 8. "They gave him a transfusion," Earl told me, "just so he'd be able to walk up to his seat. Devaney got him a special parking permit for under the stadium and he went to the game."

Wesley died twelve days later.

Isabelle was so good-natured that I thought she might say something good about the hated Buffaloes. "I don't like Colorado," she said sharply. *Oh.* "I've been to all the stadiums in the league except the Kansas ones. I was at Colorado one of the times, enjoying a good game, but three seats in front of me, I saw a Colorado fan pour a can of beer over some Nebraska people, and I thought that was terrible. Another time, we were going along the street and Earl had one of those nice red hats on. We had the window down and a guy reached in and stole his hat. So I didn't like Colorado."

Against Oklahoma State, Connealy got a sack on the first defensive series and got up pumping his arms in emotion. The Hyannis contingent went nuts. The Huskers won 32–3, but Berringer left the game because his lung had partially collapsed again. Turman, the walk-on, played a mistake-free game and the Huskers got three second-half touchdowns. Phillips, one of the Californians, ended up running for 221 yards and three touchdowns. I decided that the score might end up looking good enough for the poll voters, but I didn't think I had seen a national-championship-worthy team in the wake of the loss of Frazier.

The fans were having fun with the latest saga of a walk-on hero. Turman was being called the "Terminator" and treated as if he were Rocky Balboa after fighting Apollo Creed for the first time. Turman, poised and glib with the media, said quarterbacks coach Turner Gill—himself a former Nebraska quarterback who later would become the head coach at Kansas—"told me to get in there, call the play, line up, and take a deep breath and pretend like it was just another scrimmage."

Fans and families waited outside the main door to the athletic complex at the south side of the stadium. Players greeted their families, signed autographs, or both.

After showering, dressing, and briefly meeting with the media, Terry Connealy headed straight to the Ramada, where the meeting room—the same one used for the Big Red Breakfast—was jammed. Every man, woman, and child from Hyannis seemed to be there. Half of them were wearing the T-shirts. This was a town meeting, 320 miles from town.

When he arrived, Terry made it about eleven feet into the room in the first fifteen minutes, looking like a U.S. Senate candidate attempting to wade through the crowd before claiming victory at the podium.

"I hope we don't have any prairie fires," Marty Connealy told me. "We won't have anybody there to put them out."

The next home game, sellout game number two hundred, was against Coach Bill McCartney and the hated Colorado Buffaloes. Berringer was back in the lineup at quarterback. The Huskers beat Colorado that day, 24–7, and it turned out to be the 1994 Buffaloes' only loss. The Huskers jumped to number one in the polls after that and stayed there. Frazier returned to the starting lineup, but Berringer came off the bench to lead the Huskers to a 24–17 comeback victory over Miami in the Orange Bowl.* The next day, Penn State also remained unbeaten, getting past Oregon 38–20 in the Rose Bowl. I was in Pasadena covering the game for *Sporting News*, and in my story and a companion piece to Steve Marantz's story on the Huskers and the Orange Bowl, I wrote about what I later discussed in greater depth in *Horns, Hogs, and Nixon Coming*:

> That show in Miami made you wonder that if Richard Nixon were still alive, NBC might have brought him to the bowels of the Orange Bowl to present the Cornhuskers with some sort of national championship plaque, again angering an otherwise loyal Republican named Paterno. Remember, Nixon anointed Texas the No. 1 team in the nation after Texas defeated Arkansas in December 1969. That came after Paterno and Penn State had just completed its second consecutive undefeated, uncrowned season.
>
> On New Year's night, here was Bob Costas and the rest of the NBC crew, talking about the power of being No. 1 entering the bowl season, acting as if the national championship had been decided. Hmmm. Wonder how NBC would have reacted if it (and not ABC) had been carrying the Rose Bowl the next afternoon? It's a good guess that the NBC promotional announcement would have sounded something like: "Tune back in for Act II of this national championship drama tomorrow!"

Years later, Costas brought up what I had written in a conversation with me. He was very nice, but it also was clear he had considered it a bit of a cheap shot. I didn't even remember what I had written and had to go back and look. I had gotten a taste of one of the things that makes Costa peerless—his amazing memory.

---

* Tragically, Berringer was killed in a 1996 plane crash. He was at the controls of a Piper Cub when it crashed in a Nebraska alfalfa field. He was twenty-three years old.

The voters heeded Costas: Tom Osborne finally had his national championship.

The Huskers went 12–0 the next season, routing Florida in the Fiesta Bowl, and repeated as national champions. That was the year when Osborne was criticized for allowing the troubled Lawrence Phillips back on the team for the Fiesta Bowl in the wake of his brutal assault on his girlfriend. I covered that game, and I laughed when a Florida fan on the flight to Phoenix told me to "support your Cornhuskers—leave your car unlocked." The night after the Fiesta Bowl, David Letterman joked that the Huskers were being treated unfairly, because if given the chance, they could grow up to be "model prisoners." Osborne's decision was debatable, but considering that Phillips's backup was Ahman Green—who already had proven he could pick up the slack and eventually became the Green Bay Packers' all-time leading rusher— it was and still is ludicrous to argue that Osborne did it only to enhance the Huskers' chances of winning the national title. He really did think he was giving Phillips a chance to straighten out his life. It didn't work, because Phillips remained a thug, but we couldn't have known that at the time.

Byrne left Nebraska to become athletic director at Texas A&M in December 2002. Some scratched their heads over his departure, given his continued reputation as one of the top athletic directors in the country, but the main reason was that Osborne and his supporters never stopped considering him an "outsider," and Byrne got tired of it.

Osborne coached through 1997 and served three terms, beginning in 2001, as a U.S. Congressman from Nebraska. In the wake of his and then Byrne's departure, the Cornhuskers' program went through some relatively tough times. Athletic director Steve Pederson fired Osborne's protégé and successor, Frank Solich, and hired former Oakland Raiders head coach Bill Callahan. Pederson himself was fired during the 2007 season, and Osborne took over as interim athletic director. He fired Callahan at the end of the season and hired Bo Pellini, who presided over a turnaround.

The Sidetrack band plays on. Joyce Durand sold the Sidetrack recently, but the new owners insisted that she and the band return to perform at least on game days.

THE TEAM YOU LOVE . . . OR LOVE TO HATE: NOTRE DAME

LOU HOLTZ'S REPUTATION FOR WHINING about how he didn't know how the Fighting Irish of Notre Dame were going to be able to hang in there with that gritty (but also winless) opposing squad, whether Navy or another struggling team, was well-established. So it didn't surprise me when I walked into his office in the Joyce Athletic and Convocation Center, stuck out my hand, shook his, and only got a few words out of my mouth about how I was in South Bend because of the Fighting Irish's number one ranking in the upcoming 1994 College Football Preview issue of *Sporting News* when he interrupted me.

"I don't want to insult you starting off, but I've never seen a greater display of ignorance than you all have displayed this preseason," Holtz said, settling back in his chair. "I mean that sincerely. I wish somebody could explain it to me. I wish someone could explain to me how you picked us number one."

For the next five minutes, Holtz ran down his list of doubts, ticking them off with his fingers. And going through both hands. They included, but were not limited to (woe is Lou): going into the season with an untested quarterback, Ron Powlus; losing seven defensive and six offensive starters and a total of ten players to the NFL from the previous season's 11–1 team; and replacing four assistant coaches.

Holtz's style was to lobby for a higher ranking during and especially after the season. Yet before seasons, he was careful to discourage high expectations, and that could be counterproductive because preseason rankings always were the reference point before teams moved up and down. The lower you were ranked at the start of the season, the harder it was to get to the top, unless you were the only undefeated team in the country. I liked Holtz and would enjoy this visit with him, too, but found it all contradictory and not very credible—even before he advanced his conspiracy theory.

"What you all try to do each and every year is to put tremendous pressure on us hoping we won't live up to the expectations of people," Holtz said. "That's the only logical explanation."

Well, I told Holtz, if we talked about that at a *Sporting News* strategy meeting during one of my eight visits to the office in St. Louis each year, I must have been at the copying machine. But I understood his paranoia in the sense that, yes, Notre Dame tended to polarize the public—even members of the allegedly objective media. Years later, that's still the case. That was one of the reasons my challenge was not just to write the "Irish are number one" story. I was to explore the largely deserted campus with school not in session, to research the Notre Dame archives, soak up the atmosphere, attend media day at the opening of fall practice, and write a piece that combined the present with a look at the myths and mystique of the program.

At the time of my visit, from Knute Rockne to Holtz, the Irish had won eleven consensus national championships and seven Heisman Trophies. I had covered the 1989 Fiesta Bowl, where the Irish beat West Virginia to clinch their eleventh national championship. Holtz's woe-is-us filibuster in the private audience with me sounded familiar for a lot of reasons, and one was because I remembered what he told us in his news conference. Within minutes of winning that national championship, Holtz was asked about the Irish's prospects for the next season. It almost was like a straight-faced smart-aleck asking a hypochondriac how he was feeling.

"We've really got some problems!" Holtz said, triggering laughter. "I don't know how we can replace that senior leadership."

Earlier in the Fiesta Bowl week, I heard Holtz address the issue of trying to live up to the Notre Dame legends as the game approached. "I don't wonder about that anymore," Holtz told us. "I know I don't. One of the great books I've read is *Shake Down the Thunder*, which is basically a biography of Frank Leahy, about his total dedication and total commitment, his positive belief in the university. I don't believe there's any way in this world [to measure up], nor did I come here to do that."

The Irish still have won eleven consensus national championships and seven Heisman Trophies. Something else hasn't changed. They remain the lighting rod for fervent attention and acrid hatred. They've had the television deals, from the Dumont Network in the black-and-white days of television's infancy in 1951, to the Sunday morning condensed replay of the Saturday game, to the modern-era sweetheart arrangement with NBC that was arranged controversially, with its defection from the College Football Association's package after a new deal had been negotiated.

The intriguing mix of mystique and myth is among the reasons why teenage football players decide to go to the campus of the small Catholic university to the north of South Bend, Indiana. It's why a young Brian Kelly dreamed of being associated with Notre Dame, so much so that an older Brian Kelly's opening remarks, when introduced as Notre Dame's new coach in December 2009, were both extemporaneous and heartfelt. I watched the clip online shortly after the news conference. Kelly said,

> Growing up as an Irish Catholic in Boston, Massachusetts, I'd come home from church after driving my parents crazy and listen to the reruns and replays of Notre Dame football. Indelibly etched in my mind and my vision was the great Lindsay Nelson talking about, "As we move further into the third quarter. . . ." That was all that was on the TV in the Kelly house. So when you have those types of memories, of Ara Parseghian, Joe Montana, Father Hesburgh, it makes today seem like a dream.

The truth—warts and all—is compelling enough.

Mystique: "Notre Dame Victory March"

No contest. Notre Dame has the best fight song in America.

In 1945, James Riehle arrived on the Notre Dame campus as a freshman. Nearly fifty years later, after his short career as a salesman, after his ordination as a priest, after his long service to Notre Dame in a variety of administrative and spiritual roles, one annual moment still could choke up the Reverend James Riehle C.S.C.

"The band comes back before school starts and before the season," Riehle, who was in his nineteenth season as the athletic department chaplain, told me. "They start practicing, just like the football team.

"The first time they walk across the campus, the first time they play that 'Victory March,' I get a tingle. Still. Every year."

Here's the chorus:

> *Cheer, cheer for old Notre Dame,*
> *Wake up the echoes cheering her name,*
> *Send a volley cheer on high,*

Shake down the thunder from the sky.
What though the odds be great or small,
Old Notre Dame will win over all,
While her loyal sons are marching
Onward to Victory

It's simple. Stirring. Hummable in the shower. Adaptable, which means generations of high school players have run through butcher-paper pep banners as sophomore flutists butcher the song.

Like many Notre Dame stories, the origin of the "Victory March"—credited to the Notre Dame graduate/brother team of Michael (music) and John (lyrics) Shea—has gone through considerable permutation. The most credible and seriously researched book about the early days of Notre Dame football—Indiana University professor Murray Sperber's impressive *Shake Down the Thunder*—concluded that Michael Shea almost certainly wrote not only the music, but also most of the words. Michael, a priest, eventually was a prominent church musician, for a time playing the organ at St. Patrick's Cathedral in Manhattan. John, who copyrighted the song in his name, became a politician in Massachusetts and seemed to claim more credit for the "Victory March" every year.

Mystique: The Fighting Irish

When I was at the *Oregonian*, the paper unilaterally banned the names Redskins, Braves, Indians, and Chiefs from its pages. With that experience in mind, I kept waiting for someone to point out that "Fighting Irish" initially was a derisive term used by anti-Catholic fans of the Notre Dame opposition. But it has survived. So a leprechaun continues to be the mascot, parading the sidelines on a campus with a justified reputation for having an affluent student body, as well as endowments and alumni contributions that most other universities eye with great jealousy.

When Notre Dame opened, its bent wasn't Irish, its student body wasn't affluent, and it technically wasn't even Catholic. The first native language of the campus was French. Notre Dame du lac was founded in 1842 by a French priest, Edward Sorin. The Vatican didn't recognize his religious order—the Congregation a Sancta Cruce (C.S.C.) or the Congregation of Holy Cross—until fifteen years after Notre Dame opened. In the early days, Notre Dame didn't turn away any men who wanted to attend the school, as long as they could work off or barter for their tuition, and that brought working-class men to the campus, many from immigrant families.

Given the occasional historical enmity between Irish Americans and Italian Americans, who both were battling anti-Catholic prejudice and often each other, it's surprising that Italians neither rebelled against the Irish nickname nor adopted another school. But to this day, Italian Americans are fond of pointing out that they have contributed many of the Irish's stars.

The Holy Cross order also founded other schools, including the University of Portland, St. Edward's in Austin, and St. Mary's, the onetime women-only school adjacent to Notre Dame. But Notre Dame was the flagship, with its subway alumni and appeal for Catholics who never were able to attend college.

Myth: Saint Knute

Listen to the legends, and you might reach the conclusion that Knute Rockne was a saint—and not because he coached the Irish to three consensus national championships in his thirteen-season reign. No, Rockne is supposed to be a saint because he scrupulously ran a clean, exemplary, and highly moral football program.

As Edward Sorin might have said: "*Au contraire.*"

Rockne was a great coach and innovator and certainly a superb and highly inventive motivator. But he constantly was pushing the envelope of even the looser collegiate football standards of the 1920s, when Notre Dame's mandate to Rockne was to abide by Western Conference (Big Ten) guidelines in an attempt to gain admission. That's myth within a myth. Notre Dame was not a feisty independent by choice; the Big Ten repeatedly rejected the Fighting Irish.

From 1918 to 1930, Rockne oversaw a system under which Notre Dame football players got the majority of on-campus jobs to pay their way in an era when full rides were against the rules and bird-dog alumni financially sponsored talented recruits, as was legal and common nationally. Rockne chafed against academic eligibility restraints and tried to circumvent them whenever possible. He ruthlessly manipulated newspapermen, for years hiring influential sportswriters to officiate Irish games while they also wrote about the team. Walter Eckersall of the *Chicago Tribune* was a Rockne favorite. That seems incredible, but that was part of the system in those days, and Rockne was by far the best at using it to his advantage. He also, in essence, bribed writers by supplying them valuable complimentary tickets, at times by the dozen, knowing they would be scalped. Free tickets for sportswriters lasted until the ethics policy revolutions, as late as the 1970s, but Notre Dame tickets provided an extraordinary opportunity for profit. Rockne even was known to skip Notre Dame games to make money as a print commentator at other big college games. A Notre Dame man forever? He talked with other schools, including Columbia—with which he even signed a contract—and Southern California.

Rockne's "Win One for the Gipper" speech for the 1928 Army game was bunk; there is no indication that George Gipp ever made such a request or that Rockne was even in a position to hear it from a dying Gipp in 1920. Moreover, the words used in *Knute Rockne, All American* apparently were the invention of Rockne's ghostwriter for his autobiographical articles in *Collier's* magazine, which were turned into a book after his death. But hand this to Rockne: Notre Dame upset Army, 12–6, in that 1928 game in part because Eckersall—the journalist/referee—whistled the game over with Army within one foot of scoring the tying touchdown and having a chance to win with the extra point. That game was played the Saturday after Herbert Hoover routed Al Smith, the Catholic governor of New York, in the 1928 presidential election. To many, the election showed that an America in which the Ku Klux Klan was powerful wasn't ready to jettison hateful anti-Catholic prejudice. So Rockne's speech came when Catholics needed a boost.

After Rockne's fatal 1931 plane crash, university officials tightened the reins on subsequent coaches, worked harder to dispel the image that the university was a football factory, and created what Sperber labels the "Fortress Notre Dame" concept of trying to operate not only under national rules, but under more stringent standards.

So the change began: the Irish, once portrayed as renegades and "Ramblers" under Rockne because they seemed to be on the road more often than the Chicago Cubs, evolved into a program that drew resentment because it had higher standards—and they weren't afraid to brag about them.

Mystique: The Game Weekend

Before every game, team managers mixed gold dust, lacquer, and lacquer thinner and repainted the helmets. The helmets are a tribute to the famed Golden Dome atop the administration building, which was built after an 1879 fire destroyed most campus buildings. Sorin, the university founder, said, "Tomorrow we will begin again and build it bigger, and when it is built, we will put a gold dome on top with a golden statue of the Mother of God so that everyone who comes this way will know to whom we owe whatever great future this place has."

On the day of games, Riehle conducted Mass for the players and team personnel. All the players were required to attend. In the Catholic Church, only members of the church are supposed to take Communion, and Riehle told me that roughly half of the players did so at the game day Masses.

"After the Mass, the captain leads the team in the litany of the Blessed Virgin Mary," Riehle told me. "And I give them all a medal, a different medal for every single game. I have a relic of the true cross, and each player comes up and kisses that relic, and the manager gives them the medal."

Mystique/Myth: Hooray for Hollywood

One day during my visit, Rudy Ruettiger was signing copies of his book in the campus bookstore. Normally Hollywood wouldn't have touched a script for a fact-based film about a walk-on football player. But somebody said the magic words—"Notre Dame"—and next thing we knew, Rudy was in a theater near us.

Rudy was the only movie filmed on campus and with university cooperation since *Knute Rockne, All American* brought us Pat O'Brien as Rockne and Ronald Reagan as George Gipp. Various attempts to do another Rockne/Gipp movie failed over the years, perhaps in part because America would be so reluctant to see the truth about Gipp and Rockne. Gipp was an indifferent student, once expelled but reinstated when the administration gave in to alumni and football staff pressure; he was a professional gambler who played pool, bet on his own team, and acted as the squad bookie; he was a hard drinker who might have brought on his fatal illness—probably strep throat—with a three-day bender. Wonder what would have happened to American political history if the screenwriters hadn't so bent the truth, partially because Rockne's widow, Bonnie, insisted on a sanitized, glamorized story? Portrayed accurately, the Gipp role might not have been so . . . well . . . presidential for the young actor who landed it.

Mystique: Four Men on Horses . . . or a Poster

When I was at the stadium, Holtz pulled up to the parking gate outside the Fighting Irish locker room, got out, and joined the four 1994 captains for a poster photo.

It fit with tradition.

Seventy years earlier, the school set up another camera session with four Irish players—Don Miller, Elmer Layden, Jim Crowley, and Harry Stuhldreher. They were the Four Horsemen astride livery stable horses lined up by student sports publicist George Strickler. It was Strickler's baby all the way, since he planted the "Four Horsemen" idea in the head of *New York Herald Tribune* sportswriter Grantland Rice with an offhand remark in the press box during the 1924 Army–Notre Dame game at the Polo Grounds. Strickler had just seen the silent movie version of the Vicente Blasco Ibanez novel, *The Four Horsemen of the Apocalypse.*

The Four Horsemen were great college players. But this was Rice's hyperbolic prose at its best—or worst, depending on your perspective about an era of gushing sportswriting:

> Outlined against a blue, gray October sky the Four Horsemen rode again.
>
> In dramatic lore they are known as famine, pestilence, destruction and death. These are only aliases. Their real names are Stuhldreher, Miller, Crowley and Layden. They formed the crest of the South Bend cyclone before which another fighting Army team was swept over the precipice.

Rice wrote that this "set of backfield stars . . . ripped and crashed through a strong Army defense with more speed and power than the warring Cadets could meet."

So this mighty Notre Dame offensive cyclone must have blown away the Cadets, right? Notre Dame won 13–7. What would Rice have written had the Irish cracked twenty points? Woody Paige many times pointed out to me that to see the players outlined against the sky, Rice would have had to be lying down on the sideline, looking up.

Stuhldreher went on to be the head coach at Villanova and Wisconsin, and my father was on his 1942, 1946, and 1947 Badger teams. Late in my father's life, I found a used copy of the book Stuhldreher wrote about Rockne shortly after the Notre Dame coach's death. The book was called *Knute Rockne, Man Builder* at publication but later retitled *Knute Rockne, All-American.* My dad read it and then told me he felt he had played for Rockne, because everything Stuhldreher said Rockne said or did while coaching at Notre Dame was what Stuhldreher himself said or did while coaching at Wisconsin.

Mystique/Myth: Holier Than Thou

Why is it that we don't throw out that holier-than-thou accusation when a coach at, for example, Your State University says his program is going to do it "right"—make players go to class, point them toward graduation, recruit within the rules, keep the boosters under control, the whole package? Every once in a while, though, Notre Dame leans into the holier-than-thou punches. For a long time, Notre Dame bragged about not redshirting players. It actually did redshirt for many years, though on a very limited basis before getting around to publicly admitting it. The school usually uses the term "preserving eligibility" and does it more often now. They still target players for graduation after four years and try to have eligible fifth-year seniors taking graduate school courses or pursuing a second bachelor's degree.

The Notre Dame reality should be impressive enough: my belief was that Notre Dame was as close to the noble collegiate model as a national power could have been in 1994, and I still believe that today—even after the inglorious reign of Kelly's predecessor, Charlie Weis, who had the vocabulary of a longshoreman, even when dealing with young men he had recruited, and who was far more arrogant than he had a right to be. It was interesting, too, that I know folks who swore that Weis was a great guy, while others detested him. That's not unusual for coaches, but I'm not sure I've ever seen the opinions vary so dramatically.

Over the years, a few of the Notre Dame players have gotten into trouble. But keep in mind that you don't read about it when the lead in the student production of *My Fair Lady* fouls up. That applies at any school, by the way.

With its very selective admissions policy, Notre Dame has been known to reject valedictorians, but it accepts football players who are not academic All-American threats. But even major public schools allow "special admittance" for a limited number of athletes who don't otherwise pass muster at the admissions office. It's not a level field, because the degree of "flexibility," shall we say, varies depending on mandates from the university administration. Notre Dame still rejects, or doesn't even bother to approach, football players who easily gain entrance elsewhere. Notre Dame recruits good players it can get into school and sometimes does it with the basic underlying knowledge common to every school: a roster full of future Nobel Prize winners couldn't beat anybody.

The Irish took a lot of heat for having admitted quarterback Tony Rice, a Proposition 48 student who soon led the Irish to that national championship in the 1988 season. It even was fodder for a book or two that capitalized on the widespread Notre Dame resentment and sold well. The Rice furor was ridiculous for several reasons. Rice was a decent young man who didn't deserve to be labeled an academic freak for being the kind of student Miami or Florida would have admitted in a heartbeat and without apologizing for it. Still, Notre Dame tightened up its standards.

Clearly, as the critics gleefully pointed out, some Notre Dame players were caught up in the steroid craze of the 1980s—and despite one of the most rigorous testing programs in the country, the Irish sent mixed messages by hiring strength coaches in the 1980s from the steroid-plagued Nebraska weight room. But that was a nationwide plague at the time, and, heck, you might even use the stuff and end up the governor of California if you played your cards right.

No, I haven't yet gotten to athletes' graduation rates. Here's why: they're overrated. By no means is this an indictment of Notre Dame, which routinely has one of the highest graduation rates for football players in the country. Especially before the College Football Association championed standards for academic progress toward a degree and not just toward hours, getting players' degrees, at Notre Dame or anywhere else, wasn't always a sign of academic commitment. It could be the product of nursing some students through the system regardless of whether they deserved it.

Is Notre Dame perfect? Of course not. Never has been, despite the myths. Never will be, despite the recruiting advantage of the mystique.

But above all, Notre Dame claims to be different. And it is. That's undeniable.

FIRST-YEAR COACH CASE STUDY: NICK SABAN

NICK SABAN HAS BEEN THE HEAD COACH of two national championship teams at two different schools—Louisiana State in the 2003 season and Alabama in 2009. Those were his third and fourth stops as a collegiate head coach, following a one-season stint at Toledo and then a five-year stay at Michigan State.

I hadn't expected him to move around that much.

In the months I spent visiting him off and on, chronicling his first year at MSU, he seemed sincere that he wanted to be with the Spartans program for many years to come ... or as long as MSU officials and fans would have him. On an early visit to East Lansing, we walked across the campus together. He waved his hand for emphasis and brought up his initial impressions of the place after joining George Perles's MSU staff as a young assistant coach in the early 1980s.

"I thought, 'Now this is what a college campus should be like,'" Saban told me. "The trees. The river. It's like a national park with a college in it."

Even fifteen years later when his tendency to become restless seems indisputable, I'm convinced I read him correctly at the time. I'm also convinced that his approaches and principles haven't much changed if at all since that season at MSU, and they have served him well in his odyssey.

I had targeted the MSU coach even before we knew whom the MSU coach was going to be, because I wanted to write about the challenges that head coaches face in their transition years after taking over programs. It turned out to be Saban, who had been the Cleveland Browns' defensive coordinator under Bill Belichick.

Perles's firing was announced as the 1994 season was winding down. He did a good job early in his tenure, but the program had deteriorated, both on and off the field. The players' reputation for academic underachievement and general indifference was an embarrassment. That wouldn't have mattered if the Spartans went to the Rose Bowl every season. But this genuinely was a case where the overall impression of a program in decay involved more than the record. Perles and the administration agreed he would coach the Spartans through the rest of the season, which ended with a November 26 game at Penn State.

Saban was a natural candidate, meaning his name was mentioned from the start. He was Perles's defensive coordinator for MSU's 1987 Big Ten and Rose Bowl championship team, was the Oilers' defensive backs coach for the next two seasons, and then spent the one year at Toledo, going 9–2 before moving on to the Browns.

Five days before the MSU–Penn State game, Saban met the MSU selection committee at a Detroit hotel. The committee had six other members, but MSU President Peter McPherson was in charge. Saban had two strikes against him: the perception that he might be an NFL coach at heart because he had left both Michigan State and Toledo to go to the pro game and that he was closely tied to Perles and wouldn't represent a completely fresh start.

Saban told the committee he didn't want just any head-coaching job; he wanted this one.

The coach and his wife, Terry, met at a junior high science camp, and their relationship overcame a rough start when Nick stood up Terry on their first date—bird watching at 5 a.m. They were married for more than a decade before Nick Jr. and Kristen arrived, and by the mid-1990s, Terry and Nick were concerned about where their children would be raised. A college town would be nice; the Lansing area would be ideal. The Perles issue? Saban argued that his extensive resume spoke for itself: he was his own man and not Perles's or anyone else's. It was safe to assume, too, that Saban implied that he had differences of philosophy with Perles that contributed to his decision to leave East Lansing for the Oilers and the NFL.

One problem was that McPherson was impressed with Fran Ganter, Penn State's offensive coordinator.

I went to University Park and saw Penn State steamroll MSU 59–31 in Perles's final game. Afterward, Perles conducted a rambling filibuster before anyone could even ask a question, but his bottom-line point resonated with me. "I worry about the young coaches because there's so much pressure on them to win because the dollar is so tight nowadays with gender equity," Perles said.

Saban was the runner-up in the search, but as often happens—whether it comes out publicly or not—the runner-up got the job. Five days after the final game, Gantner told McPherson thanks, but no thanks; he was staying at

Penn State. That was a Friday night, and shortly before midnight, McPherson called Saban and offered him the job.

This time, the answer was yes.

Saban's five-year contract called for a starting base salary of $135,000, plus a $150,000 bonus in the year 2000 if:

- The team's grade-point average improved from 2.3 during Perles's last year, to at least 2.55 during the 1999–2000 academic year.
- The Spartans stayed clean in the eyes of the NCAA.
- Saban's teams won two-thirds of their games.

Of course, if he accomplished the first two points but not the third, chances were Saban would be fired before 2000. He knew the rules of the game. Hell, we all did. And they're still the same rules, including the most important one of all: win.

The week after the announcement, Cleveland beat the Dallas Cowboys in Texas Stadium. Saban traveled that night to East Lansing and met with the MSU players. The room was silent. Players were afraid to exhale too loudly lest they get marked as troublemakers, and it was said that Saban didn't smile once.

"This is the way we're going to do things around here—my way," Saban told the players. Saban told them that he still was coaching two starting Browns linebackers who played at MSU, and he held them up as examples. "I love Michigan State," Saban said, "Carl Banks loves Michigan State, Bill Johnson loves Michigan State, and I sit in a room with them every day. If one of you guys does something to embarrass yourself and this program, it hurts every one of us. But you hurt yourself worse, and you're responsible for your actions."

He brought up the classroom, asking, "So what happens if you aren't interested in getting a legitimate education?" Then he answered it. "We probably will have some problems down the road."

That was the start. Over the next year, I periodically returned to East Lansing. I never meant it to be about just Nick Saban and Michigan State. They would serve as a case study, representing all first-year head coaches and programs in transition.

Like all new head coaches, Saban sifted through the mixed messages about what we want out of college football. He did it in the style of a man who neatly orders his life as if it were divided into periods, announced by an equipment manager with a blowhorn. Or by a coal mine's end-of-the-shift whistle.

In 1968, Saban's senior year at Monongah High School in West Virginia, seventy-eight men died in an accident at the nearby mine. Saban had run across some of the coal miners during his hitchhiking travels around the sparsely populated region where an upturned thumb turned any spot into a bus stop. Saban, the son of a service station owner, was Monongah High's quarterback. He was a defensive back and shortstop at Kent State, and he was a horrified freshman on May 4, 1970, when members of the Ohio National Guard shot and killed four students.

Reflecting the calendar's relentlessness, the generation of men of the 1960s and 1970s who questioned authority later became authority, telling college students: *you will do this*. When they happened to be major college football coaches who had just gotten their reputation-defining opportunities, they faced the challenges about honor. Specifically, when taking over a program in a down cycle, can you afford to have honor?

I wasn't so sure. I looked around a college football landscape in which it seemed as if known renegades were getting ahead and even landing NFL coaching jobs. The truth was—and still is—that if a coach wins—even with players who barely pass the registrar's muster, then take money from boosters and steal stereos from dorm rooms, and manage to remain eligible only through sleight of professors' grading hands they will be stamped a "winner." I've always wondered whether we are telling coaches that honor didn't really matter.

Saban was insistent that it did.

"It's almost like I have a lot of money but I stole it all, so do I feel good about being rich?" Saban told me at the Browns' offices in Berea, Ohio, after he had accepted the MSU job but still was working as Belichick's defensive coordinator. "Or is it better if I worked hard, earned every cent, and developed financial security for myself because of my work ethic and willingness to do things correctly? I'd rather do it the second way."

Every new coach, then and now, says something like that, doesn't he? All but the most deceitful probably believe it. But then comes the test. Knowing that we ultimately judge by the scoreboard standard, do coaches begin to rationalize the dilution of their ideals?

When I met with Saban the first time, Cleveland had two games remaining, the first a Central Division showdown at Pittsburgh. On Wednesday morning of that week, Saban drove to the Browns' headquarters in the dark. He dialed area code 517 on his car phone. The ringing awakened Gary Van Dam, one of the holdovers from the Perles staff. Before he could wipe the sleep from his eyes, Van Dam heard his new boss rattle off what he wanted done in East Lansing that day.

It was 6:15.

"I'm basically the head coach at Michigan State when I'm in my car," Saban said.

Saban coordinated the academic program during his stint under Perles, and he was unapologetic about his belief in giving academically questionable players chances to prove themselves in school—but also not letting them skate through. His first financial request of the Downtown Coaches Club, MSU's football booster club, was for the club to buy five desktop computers for the players. That request was ahead of the curve; in the upcoming years, computer labs would become important elements in recruiting. "I've recruited too many guys who have been willing to make the commitment to improve the quality of their life," Saban said, "and they got the education. Right now we're saying in the NCAA that those guys shouldn't get the opportunity, and I don't necessarily agree with that."

In early January 1995, the Steelers ran over Saban's Cleveland defense in a Saturday playoff blowout. Saban was in East Lansing that night, eating with fifteen high school prospects. On Monday, he returned to Cleveland, cleaned out his locker at the Browns' offices, and spoke frankly with Belichick about the defense. He was in East Lansing the next day. He finally was Michigan State's head coach, full time.

For the next few weeks, or until the February 1 letter of intent signing date, Saban felt like a "hot potato" tossed around by his staff. One day, he visited six prospects in their homes—five in Detroit and one in Toledo. The new staff's first twenty-player freshman recruiting class included nine linemen, where the Spartans needed the most help.

During the next few months, Saban learned that an alarming number of Spartans were having academic problems. He also discovered that the conditioning program had slipped in the seven years since he left Perles's staff. "George gave me a great opportunity professionally in 1983," Saban said. "We took over a 2–9 situation and in five years built it to a top-ten team, a Big Ten championship, and a Rose Bowl victory. I think George did an outstanding job. What has happened since that time, I really don't know. I wasn't here, but we certainly don't have the quality of players."

Saban met with every holdover scholarship player. As the new staff established its authority, there were some grumbles, but the players seemed to gradually come around. "He kind of shocked us because the strength and conditioning programs were so intense," Tony Banks, the holdover quarterback, told me. "A lot of us weren't in very good shape. We were a lot bigger. Guys were rebelling, talking about transferring, about not playing. But then we started seeing a difference in the way we looked. A lot of the linemen dropped a lot of weight."

The Sabans commissioned a builder to construct their dream home. While waiting, they lived in the home offered to them by MSU faculty member Jim Cash—a screenwriter who cowrote *Top Gun*. Cash's mother-in-law usually lived in the home, but she visited Florida in the winter.

Mindful of the post–NFL season family routine, young Kristen Saban kept asking, "Daddy, when are we going to see Mickey and Minnie?" Nick had to say there would be no Disney vacation for the Sabans that spring.

In late February, Saban strayed from his normally cautious character by announcing on the public-address system at a Michigan State–Michigan basketball game that the Spartans needed the help of the home crowd in the second half "to kick Michigan's ass." It both drew a lot of attention and sent a message. He would pick his spots, but he would ignore protocol when it served his purpose.

I returned to East Lansing during the Spartans' spring practices. One of the most interesting aspects was to walk through packs of fans and eavesdrop. Generally, it seemed to be: *This guy means business!* I also was struck by the fact that he had been Perles's defensive coordinator only a few years earlier, but it had been at a time when assistant coaches—even coordinators—could stay somewhat under the radar.

At the first Saturday open practice, Saban wore khaki pants and a green windbreaker, and during the stretching and calisthenics, he seemed nondescript—so nondescript that I heard some fans trying to make sure they were looking at the right coach.

"The little guy."

"Without the hat."

"Yeah, he's not a big man."

Fifteen minutes into practice, Saban was actively coaching the defensive backs, but he also made points to the whole team. He caught fullback Robert Dozier trash-talking and hollered at him: "I don't want to have that out here, understand?" Then he turned to the entire team. "Understand?" he yelled.

At the end of the practice, Saban made a surprisingly soft-spoken speech to the players about how much more they have to accomplish during the remainder of spring practice. Dozier approached Saban, then walked toward the locker room with his new coach. Dozier tried to explain the trash-talking incident. Saban quietly listened, and said something along the lines of: *It's all right, no big deal, don't worry. Just don't let it happen again.*

I left East Lansing thinking that the cupboard was bare, that recruiting had slipped significantly in Perles's final seasons, and that Saban was going to take his lumps in his first season. I guessed the Spartans would win three or four games, max, but the important thing would be creating the impression that Saban was the right man in the right place to ultimately get the program turned around.

As spring practice wound down, Jim Cash's mother-in-law returned from Florida, and the Sabans moved into an apartment near campus. But Saban still wasn't around much. He was involved in early spring recruiting and met—or reacquainted himself—with Midwest high school coaches.

May 4, shortly after spring practice ended, was the twenty-fifth anniversary of the Kent State massacre.

The school's ROTC building had been burned down on that Saturday night in 1970, and Governor James Rhodes dispatched the Ohio National Guard to Kent. "Martial law was declared," Saban recalled. "It was a war zone. I mean, the place looked like Saigon, with all the damage that had been done and the choppers circling overhead."

Demonstrators planned a protest of the U.S. invasion of Cambodia for that Monday. Saban had an 11 a.m. class in the education building. His friend and teammate, Phil Witherspoon, wanted to watch the protest on Blanket Hill; Saban lobbied for lunch. They went to the cafeteria. At 12:24 p.m., thirteen young people were shot. At about 12:30, as Saban and Witherspoon approached Blanket Hill, they heard sirens. "It was shocking to see the people hurt and the large pools of blood," Saban said. Four of the wounded died; one, Allison Krause, was in Saban's English class.

On June 1, linebacker Ike Reese, the Spartans' leading tackler as a freshman in 1994, was involved in a fight outside an East Lansing club. He eventually pleaded no contest to disorderly conduct in August and spent two days in jail. Saban allowed him to remain in the program. "People make mistakes in this world," Saban said. "The question is, do I think he'd do it again? But you can't change your value judgment based on how good any player is."

Over the summer, Dozier (the former trash-talker) and guard Jason Strayhom—both backups—were charged with conspiracy to distribute marijuana. After reading the police reports and talking to the players and their parents, Saban indefinitely suspended both players. Neither was on the roster for the 1995 season.

"The most frustrating thing for me as a college coach is if a guy does something wrong socially, however minimal it is, it's almost like it's your responsibility, because he's a part of your team," Saban told me. "I don't think you can control anyone's behavior to that degree. I mean, I don't know what my four-year-old is going to do when she goes down the street on her bicycle, and she's done a few embarrassing things. I don't think you should tolerate those things either, but at the same time you have to have compassion for the people involved."

In the summer, the Sabans moved into their quickly constructed new home and made their annual trip with friends to Myrtle Beach, South Carolina. Saban also appeared in Chicago for three days at the Big Ten Conference kickoff. "No offense," he said, ruffling some feathers, but the day of golf and two days of media sessions were keeping him away from football preparation, and he looked very much like an impatient man. By then, Saban was working under a new athletic director. Merrily Dean Baker was out, replaced by Merritt Norvell Jr., who played for Wisconsin's 1963 Rose Bowl team. In Chicago at the Big Ten kickoff, Norvell told reporters that he was "comfortable" with Saban. But the mandate was familiar.

"It's important to win," Norvell said. "It's also important to make sure your kids graduate, important you get leadership within the department from the coaches, and important that people conduct themselves properly. But if winning wasn't important, we wouldn't have a stadium that seats 72,000 people."

The Spartans got off to a 2–2–1 start under Saban, recovering from a 50–10 season-opening loss to Nebraska. Game six was on the road at Illinois. On the plane ride to Champaign, Saban played checkers with little Nick. Little Nick won. Big Nick insisted he didn't throw the match. And he wondered, could this be an omen?

In Champaign, Saban made his weekly pregame speech to the team.

"When I was a kid in West Virginia, I went fishin' a lot," Saban said. "One time, there was this old man fishin' nearby. He was catching them right and left. Big ones, little ones. But I noticed he was throwing all the big ones back and keeping only the little ones. Drove me nuts. So finally I went over and asked him, 'Why do you throw back all the big ones?' He looked at me and says, 'I only have a ten-inch frying pan.'"

The players laughed.

Saban waited.

"That's the way you guys think sometimes," he said.

He challenged them to set their sights higher.

The players made that story their tongue-in-cheek rallying cry the next afternoon: "Win one for the small frying pan." And they knocked off the Illini 27–21.

Big Nick won the checkers match on the way home.

The next week, the Spartans faced Minnesota at home. During the week, Saban said he was enjoying his return to college football—and MSU— almost as much as anticipated. "Here, you try and instill a positive attitude, get them some goals and objectives," he told me. "Most pro guys, regardless of what the motivation is, you don't have to instill that. They might want to do it for the wrong reason, but they still want to do it. If they don't? You find another player. Here, you have to develop the player you have, all the way around—physically, mentally, emotionally. But I think that's the fun of college coaching."

Perles, still living in the Lansing area, called his own news conference and announced he had dropped his lawsuit against MSU, one he filed because the university was dragging its feet on finalizing a settlement on his contract. The speculation was that MSU was stalling because after Saban took the job, the news broke that the NCAA was investigating the football program for more than sixty possible violations during the Perles tenure. If the NCAA imposed sanctions, then MSU could try to say that Perles—who was being paid in the interim—wasn't owed another dime.

Could the NCAA investigation hurt the Saban program? "I think it could," Saban told me. "I don't know how to say this without . . ." He paused. "I don't really know of anything [against NCAA rules] of a significant nature that had happened here. Of course, I wasn't here for part of the time, and I know there's nothing that has happened since I have been here. . . . The only thing I feel bad about is if there's some punishment for the university and the program now, it's not really justified for the people who are here now who would be punished."

On Friday, Saban slipped into his seat next to the podium at the Downtown Coaches Club meeting at 12:15 p.m., moments before the program began. Downtown Coaches President Gary Thomas, a retired fireman and a Saban fan, told me that Saban was "so businesslike. From week to week, I don't even know if he's going to make it here. He's got the most disciplined schedule I've ever seen. Some guys are hour to hour; he's minute to minute."

The room at an East Lansing restaurant was packed: 239 paying customers at $11 a head for lunch and a raffle ticket. (I didn't win.) When Ike Reese, the linebacker, nervously accepted his defensive player of the week plaque and mentioned that the Spartans had "another good game plan" for Minnesota, Saban leaned over, smiled, and said something to Reese. In his turn at the microphone, Saban said, "It's very encouraging to me that Ike has approved the game plan for the week." The audience laughed. "Better get laughs now," Saban said, looking at Reese, "because when we watch the film on Monday, I'll either approve or disapprove of the execution of that game plan."

On Saturday, the Spartans trailed Minnesota, 31–21, after three quarters, but rallied for the 34–31 victory. Banks returned to the lineup after missing time with an ankle injury, throwing for 309 yards and two touchdowns. Saban had to caution his players not to look ahead to bowl possibilities. "I guess the attitude of the players has progressed to the point where we really believe we can win," Saban said. "I don't think we had that kind of character as a team earlier in the year."

They came back to earth on week eight, falling 45–14 to Wisconsin. That didn't instill a lot of confidence heading into the rivalry game at home with Michigan. All week long, Saban reminded his players: *You know, there aren't going to be very many days in your life when you don't run across somebody from the University of Michigan. Wouldn't you like to be able to talk about the year you beat their asses?* It was the kicker to his message at the Michigan–MSU basketball game.

Michigan scored with 3:38 left to take a 25–21 lead. MSU drove 88 yards, and Banks threw the game-winning, 25 yard touchdown pass to Nigea Carter with 1:24 remaining.

The raucous celebration lasted into the wee hours in East Lansing.

Saban was the eightieth head coach in MSU history; he was the first to beat the hated Wolverines in his first season.

A 35–14 victory over Indiana in week ten made the Spartans bowl eligible, at 6–3–1. Some seemed concerned that Michigan and Penn State might get more coveted bowl slots despite subpar seasons because of their programs' reputations. But the important thing in East Lansing was that the Spartans were going to go to a bowl, period.

At the regular-season finale against Penn State, one Spartan Stadium end-zone sign proclaimed to ESPN viewers: *Saban is God.* I was thinking: a year ago, when these teams met, the Michigan State coach already had been told he wasn't wanted any longer and the top candidate for his job was coaching the Penn State offense. Now, much to my own surprise, given my preseason expectations for the Spartans, the second choice for the MSU job was within reach of a seven-victory season, a third-place Big Ten finish, and a mid-rung bowl berth.

Trailing 20–17, Penn State started on its 27 with 1:45 to play. Finally, on a third-and-goal from the 4, quarterback Wally Richardson dumped an inside screen to Bobby Engram, who stretched the ball across the goal line with eight seconds remaining.

"It's just like the guy who had a gold mine and worked it for two years," Saban said. "He stopped one foot short of the vein. And the next guy came in and struck it rich. They struck it rich. And we didn't."

Still, Saban said that he was proud of a team that was favored just twice all season and came so far since that opening-week embarrassment against Nebraska. The Spartans lost to Louisiana State in the Independence Bowl and finished 6–5–1. That kind of season most likely wouldn't be good enough for a fifth-year coach, but it was praiseworthy under the first-year circumstances at Michigan State. It was the best first season for a Spartan coach since Biggie Munn (7–2) in 1947.

Saban seemed to have won over the Spartan constituency. He managed to overcome NCAA sanctions levied for the Perles regime's transgressions, but he stayed only five seasons. It was his choice, though. After the Spartans went 9–2 in the 1999 regular season, giving MSU a 34–24–1 record under him, he let Louisiana State know through the grapevine that he would listen to an offer. He subsequently accepted the job and didn't even coach the Spartans in the Citrus Bowl against Florida. His reasons? A huge contract and his disillusionment with what he viewed as MSU's halfhearted commitment to the football program. He won that 2003 national championship at LSU, spent two seasons as the coach of the Dolphins, and then bailed out again to go to Alabama. He took considerable criticism for denying interest in the Alabama job during the Dolphins' season, then taking it, and he deserved it, especially given his previous emphasis on integrity.

But as we've seen after an instant turnaround in the Alabama program and a national championship, the guy *can* coach. Albeit with better facilities, resources, and support than he had at Michigan State. I'm still convinced that he has struck that delicate balance between doing everything he can to win and trying to do it with a program that both takes chances on young men of marginal academic qualification and maintains integrity.

PART SEVEN

PUCKS

To see the three Chiefs make a scoring rush, the bright colors of their jerseys flashing against the milky ice, was to see a work of art in motion.

 —Dickie Dunn, Charlestown *Times Herald*

ROCKY . . . REALLY ROCKY . . . HOCKEY

I N '77: *DENVER, THE BRONCOS, AND A COMING OF AGE*, I weaved in the story of the first part of my first season as the young beat writer assigned to follow and chronicle the NHL's Colorado Rockies in 1977–78. Denver oilman Jack Vickers, who went on to gain greater recognition in the sporting world as the patriarch of The International golf tournament, had purchased the NHL's Kansas City Scouts in 1976 and moved them to Denver. Only two seasons old when it came to Colorado, the franchise had been undercapitalized and ineptly run in Kansas City. Vickers quickly realized that Denver wasn't going to fill McNichols Sports Arena just because it was the NHL. The Rockies sneaked into the 1978 playoffs as the twelfth and final qualifier in the seventeen-team league, lost to the Philadelphia Flyers in an entertaining two-game mini-series in the first round, sold out the home game, and seemed to kindle hope for the future. But soon, Vickers agreed to sell the Rockies to New Jersey trucking company operator Arthur Imperatore. At the news conference announcing the sale at Mayor Bill McNichols' office, Imperatore said he was hoping to operate the team in Denver until the new arena was open in the New Jersey Meadowlands complex and then to gain approval to move it to East Rutherford. Standing next to Vickers, Imperatore told us: "I'm buying the team with the expectation of brining it into my home area, which is New Jersey. I was born there, grew up there, and became a hockey nut there." I even stood on a chair to ask whether they really expected Colorado fans to support a lame-duck franchise, and the fact that Imperatore was genuinely surprised at the impudence of the question indicated to me that nobody involved in all of this had completely leveled with him. I sincerely admired how open he was, but it was incredible that it had gotten to this point without someone at the NHL saying: *That won't work!*

227

Sure enough, the NHL quickly made it clear it wouldn't commit the Meadowlands to Imperatore. It was planning to award New Jersey as an expansion market. Imperatore went through with the purchase of the team and put his stepson, Armand Pohan, in charge. Pohan was brilliant, and one of the reasons I liked him was that he pretty much admitted that he and his stepfather had been naive when they bought the team. They tried to make the best of it; they really did, in part because to do otherwise would have been financial lunacy.

Early that next season, on October 25, 1978, an on-ice incident in Detroit's Olympia Stadium could have heated up a Colorado–Detroit rivalry—if the teams had been any good. I wasn't there; the *Post* decided to have me skip the two-game trip that started in St. Louis. In Detroit, Wilf Paiement, then the Rockies' twenty-three-year-old star winger and captain, nailed Detroit's pesky Dennis Polonich in the face with a swing of his stick. The attack came behind the play after a Polonich pass and, at least in Paiement's mind, was an instinctive retaliation for Polonich carelessly—or purposefully—following through on the pass with relish and hitting Paiement in the face first. Few saw it, and this was a different era: no video footage of the incident existed. Polonich suffered a broken nose, cuts, and a concussion.

Paiement was suspended for fifteen games. Two years later, while still playing, Polonich sued Paiement, who by then was with the Toronto Maple Leafs. In 1982, Polonich received an $850,000 award in federal court.* But that was all in the future.

Coach Pat Kelly was fired during that 1978–79 season and affable team executive Aldo Guidolin finished it out as the interim coach. The record was an abysmal 15–53–12, erasing all the momentum of the previous season's playoff berth. Arthur Imperatore, Armand Pohan, and general manager Ray Miron decided they needed to do something dramatic.

To fill the coaching vacancy, the Rockies hired Don Cherry.

Today, Cherry—also known as "Grapes"—is a legend in Canada. A fixture on *Hockey Night in Canada*'s "Coach's Corner," the bombastic Cherry spouts off, in both loud voice and loud suits and sport coats. His *Rock 'Em Sock 'Em* videos are huge sellers in Canada. He's a watchdog for old-fashioned, old school Canadian hockey values and is variously revered or ridiculed for his reluctance—no, his *refusal* to evolve with the game and the times. His fame is international and his influence immense.

---

* Polonich played for the Red Wings until the 1982–83 season, but his goal totals dropped drastically.

None of this might have happened if his stint with the Rockies had gone better. I enjoyed covering him, and I have to say that he was a beat writer's dream. Cherry had just left Boston, where he and general manager Harry Sinden had a venomous relationship that led to Cherry's exit after a semifinal round playoff loss to Montreal—one that included a too-many-men-on-the-ice penalty on the Bruins in the final two minutes of regulation in the deciding Game 7. The Bruins were ahead by a goal at the time, but the Canadiens tied it up on a power play and won the game in overtime.

Regardless, Cherry's record at Boston was impressive. The belief that the players universally loved him was misleading. Those who were among his favorites indeed embraced him. Those on his bad side bit their tongues and played on.

He got into coaching by accident. After a journeyman's career in the minor leagues—he got into one playoff game with the Bruins in 1955—he tried his hand at construction. "My specialty was the jackhammer," he told me. "I liked it. It was a good honest job. But I got laid off in the recession there, and I couldn't find any other job. I tried selling cars, but in my estimation, I was the world's worst car salesman."

When he was laid off, Cherry didn't have a nest egg from his playing days.

"People on welfare were getting more than minor league hockey players in those days," he said. "I was getting $4,500 for nine years. And in the tenth year, they cut me to $4,200."

Because of his need for a job—any job—the stocky defenseman went back to the Rochester Americans at age thirty-seven in the fall of 1971. "Halfway through that season, the coach and general manager bailed out because the team had such a rotten record," Cherry said. "That's why they made me the coach. I didn't get a raise in pay or anything. The next year, I was the general manager and coach. We took all the players no one else wanted and then made the playoffs. The next year, we were the only independent team in hockey, and we finished first."

The Bruins hired Cherry in June 1974. In five seasons, he was the NHL's coach of the year once and got the Bruins to the Stanley Cup finals twice, where the Bruins lost to the Canadiens both times. His accessibility and shoot-from-the-hip style increased his popularity. "It seems like I served my apprenticeship in the minors as a general manager and coach," said Cherry. "As a general manager, I had to give good press. I really worked at it. The easiest thing about coaching is to coach and then go home. That way, there might be no pressure on you—not as much, anyway. Let's face it: I've made a lot of enemies. I've said a lot of things. I've gotten myself in a lot of hot water. But I don't regret any of it."

He brought his beloved wife, Rose, and his famous white pit bull terrier, Blue, a gift from the Bruins' players, with him to Denver. He also came with a reputation for sartorial excellence, and this was before his wardrobe tastes took bizarre turns. "Honest to God, people used to tune in the TV games just to see what I was wearing," he told me of his days in Boston. Cherry said he had "always dressed pretty good. Other kids would wear sneakers and jeans, but I would wear Oxfords and pants like knickers. And when I was playing, I played for Joe Crozier, and he used to dress pretty nice. I think the players look up to that. Maybe I go a little overboard."

The Rockies signed Cherry to a two-year, $180,000-per-year contract. "I'm just a guy who likes to go out and have a good time with the players," he said. "Somebody asks me how we win so much. It's the players. First and foremost, everything's got to be for the players. If the players aren't with you, you're dead. I don't know; if I knew what I was doing, I'd probably screw it up.

"I have my own style, and it's very simple. It's so simple that [defenseman] Dennis O'Brien came up to me before a game and asked me to explain my style of game and my philosophy to him. So we went to a bar, and I drew it on a napkin. It's as simple as that." Diagramming that system, he said, it took him "ten minutes at the most, between sips of beer. Only five, if I'm not drinking beer."

Cherry immediately was a sensation in Denver. Much of it was his flamboyance, and he had most members of the media in the palm of his hand. (Including me.) He was a great sound bite for the local television folks, who started showing up at games. I appreciated that he offered colorful quotes, was always cooperative, and actually enjoyed having a few beers with the scribes on the road occasionally. I was wide-eyed when he took Fred Pietila of the *Rocky Mountain News* and me to Toe Blake's tavern in Montreal and told stories for a few hours.

The Rockies still were rotten. They had the first overall pick in the 1979 draft, an incredible opportunity because four World Hockey Association teams—Edmonton (with a teenage Wayne Gretzky), Quebec, Hartford, and Winnipeg—finally were coming into the NHL. The two WHA teams that didn't make the cut and were folding, Cincinnati and Birmingham, also had players who had been too young to play in the NHL under its previous twenty-year-old cutoff, so they were included in the NHL draft pool. Four of Birmingham's "Baby Bulls" went in the first round, including defenseman Rob Ramage to the Rockies, the number one choice overall. Ramage had a solid career, and the consensus at the time was that it was the wise choice. In retrospect, it was a major foul-up. The other Baby Bulls who went in the first round were Rick Vaive, Craig Hartsburg, and Michel Goulet. Goulet and former Cincinnati Stinger Mike Gartner, who went to Washington, are in the Hockey Hall of Fame today. So is a young defenseman from the Verdun Eperviers named Raymond Bourque, who went to Boston in the number eight slot.

Cherry didn't have the patience for a step-by-step team-building effort. Before long, the coach was sniping at Miron, both in public and private. Miron acceded to some of Cherry's requests, acquiring a couple of veteran players who fit his style. One of the ironies of his stay was that despite his image—cemented during his days on television—as being suspect of French Canadian players, he was all for the preseason acquisition of Rene Robert from Buffalo. Robert had been on the Sabres' famed "French Connection" line, and he quickly became one of Cherry's favorites. But the Rockies' approach was misguided, primarily because they didn't decide on a coherent strategy and stick with it. Instead, they were stuck in a no-man's-land with a hybrid and capricious philosophy, including periodic attempts to pacify Cherry or quiet his complaining with the acquisition of hard-working journeymen with more grit than talent or aging veterans.

After a 1–7–2 start, the Rockies traded their best young player—intimidating defenseman Barry Beck—to the Rangers. For Beck, the Rockies got a package that included defenseman Mike McEwen and Dean Turner, plus wingers Lucien DeBlois and Pat Hickey. Beck had been the Calder Trophy winner as the league's rookie of the year in 1978. Shoulder problems later slowed and then ended his career, but trading a cornerstone defensemen who could score goals—he had a dynamite shot from the point—and help shut down opponents was a sign of panic. Cherry supported the trade, saying that if the Rockies didn't get some goal scorers, there was no hope. The day the deal was announced—ironically, the day before the Rockies played and beat the Rangers in Denver with a stunned Beck, a western Canadian boy who was having a home built near Evergreen, going through the motions—I saw Cherry and Miron walking down the hall in front of me. Cherry actually patted Miron on the back. That might have been the last time that ever happened.

On December 2, 1979, Cherry returned to Boston Garden with the Rockies. Incredibly, the Rockies led 4–2 with fifty-three seconds left. With a faceoff about to take place in the Colorado zone, the Bruins brought goalie Gilles Gilbert to the bench—and Cherry called a time-out. During the time-out, Cherry didn't huddle with the Rockies to talk strategy. He let them rest and get drinks of water. He stepped to the end of the bench and began signing autographs for the fans who had gathered there; that, of course, brought more fans in their wake. It was one of the funnier scenes I've ever witnessed in sports, in part because it was so brazen. I was just across the ice, because the hockey press box at the Garden was a front row appendage to the low balcony.

A "Cher-ry, Cher-ry" chant began and continued through the time-out. After Colorado had won 5–3 to get to 6–14–3 for the season, Cherry got in a few digs at his Boston successor, Fred Creighton. He said the Bruins had "as much or more talent as anybody in the league. There seemed to be an awful lot of times when they weren't all there." The Bruins still were 15–6–3, but Cherry admonished the Boston press not to forget that the Bruins had gotten off to a 16–2–2 start under him the previous season. "When they lost their third game, Blue told me, 'They can't match your record for the first twenty games, anyhow.' Blue is doing handstands all over the place now, I imagine."

Later in December, the Rockies traded Pat Hickey and Wilf Paiement to Toronto for star winger Lanny McDonald and a young defenseman named Joel Quenneville. Although Paiement—the franchise's first-ever draft choice when the team was based in Kansas City—was talented, it was a good deal, primarily because cantankerous Maple Leafs owner Harold Ballard despised McDonald and wanted to trade him to Siberia. And that's what NHL traditionalists thought the Colorado franchise was at the time.

McDonald was a leader and a terrific player who played with passion and heart, and his bushy moustache made him hard to miss. Soon, McDonald was the Rockies' most prominent player ever, and—aside from Cherry—its most eloquent spokesman. But on the ice, little went well. The goaltending indeed was bad, but in retrospect, I probably concurred too easily with Cherry's position that Hardy Astrom, who was acquired from the New York Rangers and making decent money, was the worst NHL goalie of all time. A handful of others in the league who played twenty or more games that season had worse goals-against averages than his 3.75, and there were even a couple who played more than half their teams' games—Hartford's John Garrett and Los Angeles' Mario Lessard. Regardless, Cherry held his nose long enough to use Astrom—yes, management and ownership wanted him out there, but Cherry could have defied them—in forty-nine games, while also trying Bill McKenzie, Michel Plasse, and Bill Oleschuk in the net. In February, the Rockies had to settle for a 4–4 tie at Hartford when Plasse had only 17 saves. Cherry had let loose many times, but he got into high gear that night. "Our goaltending was horseshit," he said, standing a few feet from the trailer where I had done a between-periods interview with a fledgling Connecticut-based cable operation called ESPN. "Let's face it. Come on. Let's be honest. We're not going to go anywhere until we get a goalie. I've tried everyone except the guy who works in the confectionary store."

I felt as if I were covering the Washington Generals, the Harlem Globetrotters' foils and straight men, when the Rockies were the opposition in the March 1, 1980, game that was "Miracle on Ice" goaltender Jim Craig's NHL debut for the Atlanta Flames in the Omni.* In Atlanta, the Flames had their first sellout of the season (15,156), everyone waved American flags, and the Flames probably could have beaten the Rockies using Cherry's "guy who works in the confectionary store" as their goaltender. In the story, I said they could have used Eric Heiden, who had just won a big haul of speed-skating gold medals but probably wouldn't have been helpless in the net. The Rockies' first shot didn't come until 12:50 of the first period, and McDonald took it from near the red line. The Flames won 4–1. Craig seemed fazed by only one thing: the Confederate flag one fan waved behind one goal. "I'm a Yankee," Craig said, laughing. "This has been unbelievable," he added. "There was the governor's visit yesterday, and they made me an honorable colonel of something. I was fortunate enough to have my brother and father here tonight. I just hope they all go like this."

Surely Craig was on his way to NHL glory, right? He wasn't. He wasn't playing the Rockies every night.

The breaking point in the Cherry era was the coach's falling-out in early March with McEwen, the defenseman acquired in the Beck deal from the Rangers. Imperatore and Pohan had been Rangers fans and they liked McEwen. When McEwen stayed out on the ice too long and took an extended shift, and Chicago scored the game-winning goal, Cherry shook him on the bench. The next day, McEwen skipped practice and he didn't come to the next game, also at McNichols, leaving the Rockies with only four defensemen. Cherry was surprisingly conciliatory, saying after that game that he had just talked with McEwen on the phone and told him he would be welcome back. "What more can I do?" he asked us. "I made a lot of mistakes when I was his age. Lots of them. I'm not vindictive."

I also called McEwen, and he agreed with Cherry's version of the conversation but said he wanted to be traded and wouldn't go on the team's

---

* On the night the Americans knocked off the Soviets, on February 22, the Rockies beat Wayne Gretzky and the Edmonton Oilers 3–1 at McNichols.

next road trip. McEwen said he couldn't fit Cherry's style, so I asked Cherry about that. "Sure he can," Cherry said. "That's what Brad Park thought when he came to Boston, and he was an all star the next year. I don't want him to do a lot of things. I just want him to pass the puck a little more. What I'm trying to do is help him. He thought I was on him all the time. I have an abrasive nature. Some guys respond to it. Some don't."

Next, I called Pohan. "I don't understand why things reached this point," he said. I asked him if this was a sign of a deteriorating relationship between the team and Cherry. "No comment," Pohan said.

McEwen did come back to the team and finish out the season.

The incident in Boston when Cherry signed autographs during the timeout was funny. What happened in Denver in late March was bizarre. The Rockies were playing the Quebec Nordiques when Quebec's Paul Stewart and Colorado's Bobby Schmautz, a former Bruin and one of Cherry's all-time favorites, drew minors for high-sticking in the first period. They served their penalties and then were given game misconducts when they waved their sticks at one another in a faceoff. Before the game could start again, other players raced off the ice—the exits at McNichols were in the corners, across the ice from the benches—because they had figured out Stewart was chasing after Schmautz in the hallway. So the crowd was left wondering what was going on as the game was delayed. Stewart and Schmautz had a brief stick-swinging duel in the hallway between the two locker rooms.

That night, when I went back and forth to talk with the combatants, Stewart admitted he had gone after Schmautz in the hallway. "I've only got two eyes, and I'm not going to let anyone take a run at them with his stick," Stewart said. "Hey, even the guys on [Schmautz's] own team in Boston said he high-sticked his Thanksgiving turkey to death."

Schmautz was scornful of Stewart. "This is the guy who came up earlier this year and got beat up and sat in the penalty box giving the 'V' sign because he'd fulfilled his dream to play in the Boston Garden," Schmautz said.

By the time the Nordiques became the Colorado Avalanche, Stewart had found another line of work. He was an NHL referee.

Before the Rockies' final home game of the season, the players raised their sticks and formed a cordon for Cherry, wearing a cowboy hat (a gift from the players) and boots, to walk through to the bench. Rene Robert, by then the Rockies' captain, came into Cherry's postgame news conference— the Rockies had beaten Pittsburgh 5–0—to explain the reason for the raised sticks. "It was to show people how much we love him and where he stands in our book," Robert said. Robert patted Cherry on the back and headed to the dressing room, and the coach turned to us and said, "Just like I told you!" The crowd that night was 11,610, a respectable figure considering we were in the midst of a major spring snowstorm. "The franchise is here," Cherry said. "With ten more wins, we'd be in the thick of the playoffs, and you couldn't buy a ticket."

The fans also had chanted Cherry's name in the final minutes. "Just like Boston," Cherry said. "'Cher-ry, Cher-ry.' What more can I tell you? There'll be a lot more like that. As long as I've got the players with me, that's all I need. You stick with the players, and they'll stick with you. The fans love me. The players love me. That's the most important thing."

The Rockies finished 19–48–13, and their 51 points were the lowest in the twenty-one-team league. Their average home attendance was only 9,754, but that was a huge increase over the average of slightly more than 6,000 the season before. On the ice, the good news was that McDonald, then only twenty-eight, had 25 goals in only 46 games for Colorado and an aura of leadership (and the moustache) that seemed to stamp him as the franchise's public face—at least among the players—for years to come.

The day after the season ended, I called Pohan to do a season wrap-up and casually asked if ownership was considering firing Cherry. Despite the fact that the strains between ownership and Miron on one side and Cherry on the other were obvious and well documented, I really didn't think the Rockies would fire the popular coach. Much to my surprise, Pohan said, yes, he was considering doing just that, emphasizing he was in the process of evaluating the entire operation, including Miron, as well. "If we had eighty points right now," Pohan said, "I'd put up with anything."

Cherry dared Pohan to fire him. "If he doesn't want me back, there's nothing I can do about it," he said. "I intend to fulfill my contract. If not, *c'est la vie*. I've never backed out on anything yet. I don't want to leave anything unfinished here. I want to come back. But that's up to them. They're the bosses. I'll tell you, if you think people have forgotten about me around hockey, let me give you an illustration. I'm going to go back and film twelve hockey-tip things for *Hockey Night in Canada* during the playoffs. They picked five stars from the NHL to do United Way commercials, and I'm one of them. I've already been approached to do five banquets back east in May alone. And you're asking me if I'm worried about a job?"

Cherry also said he didn't think the Rockies were that far off from being contenders; they were heading in the right direction and had made huge inroads both at the gate and in gaining attention in the marketplace.

It took seven weeks for Pohan to announce his decision. He fired Cherry. It did take courage, considering Cherry's support was vocal and widespread. My biggest criticism was that Cherry's track record for being uncontrollable and outrageous was well-known when the Rockies went after him, so they should have known what they were getting and tried to ride out at least the final season of his contract to see what happened.

After trying to let the furor die down, Pohan had decided that the situation was just too toxic. Imperatore and Pohan deservedly had the reputation for being great employers in the trucking business, and they expected loyalty in return—not realizing that professional sports often didn't work that way. "He's said he could get another job in ten minutes," Pohan told me. "I'm not going to hold him to that, but. . . ."

Cherry threatened to take a year off, which would have forced the Rockies to pay him.

He did that work for *Hockey Night in Canada* in the playoffs, started out as an analyst the next season, and then was moved into a role that better suited him—the studio pundit's role on *Coach's Corner*. His ridicule of his Rockies' goaltender, Astrom, has made the man the former coach calls the "Swedish Sieve" one of the working definitions for ineptitude in the net—as Mario Mendoza and the "Mendoza Line" became references to bad hitting. Even thirty years later, Cherry occasionally takes shots at Miron, long-ago retired and living in the Tulsa area after making a fortune as one of the founders of the revived Central Hockey League, which now awards its champion the Ray Miron Presidents Trophy.

———◆———

Arthur Imperatore owned the Rockies only a few months longer.

I had lunch with Imperatore and Armand Pohan during the 2003 Stanley Cup Finals at the Imperatore-owned New York Waterway's port station in Weehawken.

"We bought that team to bring it here," Imperatore again acknowledged. "Know what would happen? Usually, I'd work half the day because I'm a workaholic. I'd get off the airplane, get a headache first thing. A bad headache. Then I'd get a nosebleed. I'd go the arena and meet the guys and talk to them about how well we were doing. And then came the clincher. You're tired, it'd be nine here when the game started in Denver, and it's about to begin, and I'm looking around asking, 'Where are the fans?' They'd come trickling in. All I can see are the empty seats. Then, the game would start, the other team scores the first goal, and I think of how many more empty seats there are going to be the next game. And, sure enough, that's what happened."

"I loved that sport and I enjoyed the experience. But what absolutely confounded me was why the Denver people didn't take too much to hockey then."

Imperatore smiled again and provided his own answer.

"I guess we didn't have much of a team," he said.

No, he didn't.

"In life, you can't do everything and do it well," Imperatore said. "We're guys who try to do something and do it well. There's no other way. We tried. We tried."

Pohan laughed about being one of Cherry's *Coach's Corner* foils.

"I'm his Inspector Clouseau figure or something," he said. "At the time, the team needed credibility in the Denver market. Strictly as a coach, it was a mistake to hire him. He was a *dis*organization man. He wasn't an organization guy. Everybody knew that before we knew it. But at the time, it was a statement to the fans that we were trying to do something meaningful. Should I have let him go one more year and then fired him? Maybe. But we would have had to, because you couldn't build with him."

To replace Cherry, the Rockies hired Billy MacMillan, a former player and assistant coach with the then-successful New York Islanders. Miron stayed on as general manager.

On November 30, 1980, the Rockies played at Buffalo. Pohan attended the game, and he later confirmed what happened in the VIP room after the first period at Memorial Auditorium. Sabres owner Seymour Knox introduced him to Peter Gilbert, a Buffalo cable television magnate and Sabres' season-ticket holder.

"I have two questions for you, if I may be blunt," Gilbert said. "Number one, is your team for sale?"

"Yes," said Pohan.

"Number two, how much do you want for it?"

Pohan named his price.

"You've got a deal," Gilbert said.

The news of a tentative deal broke within days, and the NHL approved the sale in January. I asked Gilbert why it could work under his ownership and not under those of Vickers and Imperatore. His answer: "We'll be running it." He added, "I'll make people feel about the Rockies how people in Buffalo feel about the Sabres."

Gilbert was born in Austria, and he said his family had gotten out of that country in 1933 and made it to British-controlled Palestine. He joined the British Army late in World War II, served in the Israeli Air Force after the postwar founding of the modern state of Israel, and moved to the United States in 1950, when he was twenty-four. In a Brooklyn machine shop, he started out as an office boy and ended up buying the company and turning it into an electrical components company. That company merged with Alloys Unlimited, and Gilbert made a considerable profit. In 1970, he bought a bankrupt Long Island cable company from a bank, and it exploded when he talked Madison Square Garden into awarding his system the rights to Knicks' and Rangers' games—in the forerunner of the Madison Square Garden Network. He sold that cable network to Viacom for $12.5 million and reinvested in another struggling cable company, this one in Buffalo. That also boomed. So he had a lot of money to play with, and there was considerable speculation at the time that he hoped his purchase of the Rockies might help give him the inside track on acquiring the soon-to-be-awarded exclusive cable franchise in the City and County of Denver or that he planned to make cable a centerpiece of the Rockies' future. When I asked him about that, he responded, "Let's not get the cart before the horse."

Late that season, with Gilbert in control of the franchise, the Rockies finally acquired a good goaltender in a trade with the Islanders. Colorado picked up Glenn "Chico" Resch and young center Steve Tambellini for Cherry's favorite, Mike McEwen.*

At one point, Gilbert taped television commercials for tickets with McDonald. In them, Gilbert said to McDonald, "Hey, Lonnie. . . ." Nobody had the nerve to correct him, nor saw anything wrong with putting ads on the air in which the team owner gets his star player's name wrong. In the macabre and pointed sense of humor of the locker room, I heard a teammate holler at McDonald at least once a day, "Hey, Lonnie!"

Nothing much changed under Gilbert, at least on the ice.

In the wake of a fifteen-win season in 1980–81—a season that made the Cherry season look good—Miron was fired. MacMillan, despite his lack of success as the coach, had impressed Gilbert, and he was championing the successful model of the "Islanders Way." MacMillan stepped up to become GM and hired a former Islanders teammate, Bert Marshall, as head coach, with University of Denver coach Marshall Johnston coming aboard as an assistant coach and assistant general manager.

I rode with Gilbert on his private plane from Denver to Winnipeg for an exhibition game and got to know him better. He still was cocky about how he was going to get the franchise turned around, believing if he could do it

---

* As of this writing, Tambellini is the Edmonton Oilers' general manager.

with two bad cable companies, he could do it with the Rockies. His bluster wasn't for everyone. The Rockies' employees—other than the players and the famous coach—had been loyal to Imperatore, primarily because Pohan, who was in Denver more, was universally liked; Gilbert rubbed many of them the wrong way. At one point in the subsequent season, the Rockies played the Red Wings in the new but already obsolete Joe Louis Arena in Detroit, and I came back to the new Renaissance Center Westin after the game, realizing that my plan to meet several team employees "in the bar" wasn't specific enough. They weren't in the hotel bar and the "Ren Cen" then had many restaurants with bars in them. As I approached one of them, though, I could hear a Rockies' employee blasting Peter Gilbert—"that son of a bitch"—from the hallway. So I knew my search had ended. (Years later, I still see that former Rockies' employee and occasionally tease him about it.)

Gilbert hadn't reacted well to the realization that he had a fiasco on his hands or that he was losing money by the bushel.

By November, Lonnie . . . er, Lanny McDonald was refusing to talk to me because he felt I violated a confidence. He came to Denver with a contract from Toronto that ran through 1982–83, but much of it was based on the assumption he would be playing in Canada, where he had made a lot of money on endorsements. He also maintained that Imperatore and Pohan had promised him the deal would be renegotiated after the 1980–81 season if he performed well. I heard that he was asking Gilbert and MacMillan to honor that commitment, and McDonald said he had no comment on the record but confirmed it off the record and asked me not to write about it because he expected it to be taken care of quietly and soon. He said he would let me know when that happened. His agent, Alan Eagleson, initially wouldn't talk about it, either. The problem was that the grapevine was hard at work. It was common enough knowledge and soon I had heard it from enough people to feel as if I had to write about it, and I told him I was doing so. Then Eagleson, also the head of the Players Association and eventually shown to be a crook, confirmed it publicly. McDonald didn't like it when I wrote about it, and he also was perturbed that I had called Pohan, who said the promise had been vague and in part designed to react to McDonald's anger over Cherry's firing. He said he had told McDonald that the team would consider renegotiating the contract in the 1981 off-season if McDonald proved he deserved a raise and if the team's financial condition had improved. The airing of that dirty laundry didn't please McDonald, and he gave me the silent treatment for at least another month.

The Rockies reacted by trading him. On November 24, 1981, the Flames—by then playing in the 8,700-seat Calgary Corral while the Saddledome was under construction next door—blew out the Rockies 9–2. The next morning, we went to Winnipeg—and I say "we" because in the fashion of the time, I traveled with the team on buses to and from airports and on commercial flights. Noticeably, Billy MacMillan and Bert Marshall weren't on the team bus to the Calgary airport or on the flight to Winnipeg. Marshall Johnston told me they were coming on a later flight. I was the only writer on the trip—the *Rocky Mountain News* was being more selective about following losing teams—and I asked Johnston if that meant a trade was in the works. He was vague, and I went to the pay phone and tried both MacMillan and Marshall's rooms back at the Calgary hotel. They didn't answer.

At the Winnipeg airport, McDonald, who was sitting near the back of the plane, was one of the last ones off. An Air Canada agent met Johnston with a message. As the other players headed for the baggage claim area, I saw Johnston intercept McDonald and take him to a pay phone. Soon, the other players were all on the bus, waiting, when they noticed that McDonald and Johnston weren't aboard. Tambellini was designated to find out what was going on, and when he went back in the terminal, he saw Johnston struggling to get his phone credit card number to work and get his call through and McDonald sitting, waiting, and looking forlorn.

That was Rocky Hockey in a nutshell.

Finally, Johnston reached MacMillan and handed McDonald the phone. He had been traded to Calgary, along with a fourth-round draft choice, for Flames forwards Bob MacMillan—Billy's brother—and Don Lever. When he got off the phone, he filled in Tambellini, who was noticeably distraught. McDonald looked at me and said, "I guess I have to talk to you now."

His reaction?

"I'm stunned," he said. "I'm serious. I just can't believe it. I think you know I'm not a quitter, that I'd never ask to be traded. All I can say is that I wish them the very best. I think there are a lot of class guys here."

We agreed that I'd ride with him in a taxi to the Winnipeg Arena, where he was going to pick up his equipment, and talk to him there before he headed back to the airport to catch a flight to Calgary. He boarded the Rockies' team bus, and he later said in his autobiography that when he broke down talking to his teammates, Rob Ramage told him to shut up because he would figure out this was the best thing that ever could have happened to him.

I rode in the cab with McDonald and Rockies' radio broadcaster Norm Jones to the Winnipeg Arena. Norm and I both did interviews with

McDonald, and Lanny went out of his way to take the high road. "Bitterness has no place in hockey, as far as I'm concerned," he told me. "Trades are part of the game. Billy is trying to turn this franchise around. I don't agree with him on the trade because I don't think I was the problem. If you take the time to feel bitter about every little thing in life, you're in a pretty sorry state."

I asked McDonald if his request for a contract renegotiation was the cause of the trade.

"If it did, they're crazier than I thought," he said.

It wasn't long before he figured out that Ramage was right. He was a Medicine Hat, Alberta, native. He was going home. But on that day, McDonald was crushed to be leaving the Rockies. He and his wife, Ardell, truly did love living in Denver.

The trade itself didn't seem as ridiculous at the time as it might seem in retrospect—and it especially looked ridiculous when McDonald scored 66 goals for Calgary only two seasons later. Bob MacMillan and Don Lever were solid all-around forwards. MacMillan had 75 goals in a two-season span for the Blues early in his career, and Lever was coming off a 30-goal season. But the fact that one of the players acquired for the franchise's most visible and best player was the general manager's brother raised a lot of eyebrows, as it should have.

In retrospect, I came to the conclusion that, after all the other trials and tribulations, Rocky Hockey finally lost any chance of surviving in Denver the day McDonald was traded.

Gilbert barely had owned the team for a year when it was obvious he didn't have the stomach for the continued losses. To his credit, he kept writing the checks and the franchise never was in danger of folding, but at meetings in Washington held in conjunction with the early February All-Star Game, he officially told the league he wanted to move the Rockies to New Jersey. That was an issue again because the new Meadowlands arena finally was on the verge of opening. The meetings went so long and Fred Pietila and I had so much to write that neither of us made it to the All-Star Game itself. The league put Gilbert on notice that at the very least, he had to exhaust all avenues in finding a buyer who would keep the team in Denver.

In the final month of the 1981–1982 regular season, St. Louis businessman Robert Hutchings, who had made his money selling high-risk insurance policies, was advanced as a possible owner who would keep the team in Denver. He met with Gilbert and was championed by a Colorado-based member of the Rockies' board of directors—a group that was largely window dressing as Gilbert attempted to defuse the issue of absentee ownership. One day, though, I took a call from St. Louis, and the caller suggested I check out Hutchings's companies, including United States Central Underwriters and a holding company called Eagle Pacific. With a lot of help from folks in the Missouri Secretary of State's office and other sources, I ended up with mountains of material about the companies and lawsuits and about the Missouri Division of Insurance accusing U.S. Central of misappropriating $166,595 in premiums. I also came up with photocopies of two $150,000 U.S. Central checks to a lawsuit plaintiff that bounced. I went to St. Louis and visited Hutchings at his offices, and he was cordial, downplaying the significance of the checks, saying one was a mix-up and the other involved a stop payment. I was able to get confirmation from the bank involved that the stop payment on the check came *after* it had bounced. Amazingly, through all of this, Hutchings remained civil and insisted that he still was interested in buying the Rockies. I wrote smaller news stories about all of these findings and had a major Sunday package, including a question-and-answer piece with Hutchings, ready for publication when he sent a telegram to Gilbert and the Rockies "withdrawing" his offer. We still ran the Sunday package on March 28, 1982, including a picture of one of the bounced checks, under the headline: "The Man Who Almost Bought the Rockies." That probably wasn't accurate, though. It was obvious to me that he never would have been able to pull off the purchase. Even if I hadn't written a word about his business dealings, that still would have been the case. So I never felt that I had anything to do with "scuttling" a deal that would have kept the team in Denver. The mess was typical of the Rockies' fiasco.

The Rockies beat the Flames 3–1 in the final game of the season at McNichols. Goalie Chico Resch was the number one star. By then, most NHL observers assumed the franchise was leaving, but Resch said, "I'd just like to thank the fans who came out and the ones who thought about coming out but didn't. We gave them a lot of reasons not to. We think we can improve next year. If people will have a lot of faith and maybe buy season tickets."

It was too late. Edmonton furniture and real estate magnate Bill Comrie was the major figure in a group that talked about buying 70 percent of the franchise with local ownership retaining the remaining 30 percent. That deal also fell apart and for a bizarre reason. With the deal under discussion in mid-April, an armed intruder burst into the home of Edmonton Oilers owner Peter Pocklington, who was trying to broker the sale, and demanded $1 million in ransom. Police eventually shot the extortionist, but Pocklington was grazed in the arm in the crossfire. Shaken, he had better things to do than to help close the sale that would have kept the Rockies in Colorado.

At least I got a couple of trips to New York out of it. In mid-May, the NHL's board of governors met for two days in Manhattan, failing to agree on the Rockies' fate or what to do with the Meadowlands market. Gilbert proposed simply being allowed to move the Rockies there, but it was obvious the NHL wasn't going to allow that to happen. Millionaire John McMullen wanted either the Rockies or an expansion team for the Meadowlands, and the debate mostly revolved around how the league could allow the Rockies to go to New Jersey and still get the same amount of money it would get from expansion fees if an expansion team went there. Every time Gilbert walked out of the room, I was in the mob chasing him down for comment, even if he was just taking a restroom break. Part of the comedy was that he was willing to talk to me on the phone from his Buffalo home or in his hotel room at these sorts of meetings, whether it was an official on-the-record comment or a background briefing. So I was part of the mob out of self-defense more than anything else. When the meetings adjourned, board of governors chairman Bill Wirtz—who I have to say was always helpful to me, despite his spendthrift and curmudgeonly image as the Blackhawks' owner—confirmed that there wasn't anything under discussion that would keep the Rockies in Denver. Gilbert said the same thing. I marveled at how quickly he had gone from being the blustery self-professed savior of the NHL for Denver and even a possible buyer of the Nuggets to a harried, even hapless man trying to get out without losing his shirt.

The official end came at another meeting in New York on May 27, 1982. The league approved Gilbert's sale of the Rockies to McMullen, who at the time also owned the Houston Astros, and two minority partners—Brendan Byrne, former New Jersey governor, and John Whitehead, senior partner of Goldman Sachs. The league also approved a franchise shift to New Jersey. Because it wouldn't be getting an expansion fee for the New Jersey territory, the NHL forced McMullen to pay compensation to the New York Rangers and Islanders and the Philadelphia Flyers; he also had to pay a transfer fee to the league. Gilbert, who had paid $7.6 million for the team, got $10 million. He said the franchise losses were greater than his profit on the sale. In announcing the league approval of the moves, NHL President John Ziegler said the league tried to come up with owners to keep the team in Denver but failed. "To operate the team in Colorado, based on the financial record, someone would have to be willing to lose a lot of money until the team was turned around," he said.

The day after the league's board of governors approved the sale and move of the franchise, I went to the Meadowlands on the other side of the Lincoln

Tunnel for the news conference at the new arena. Everyone involved predicted the NHL immediately would be a hot ticket in New Jersey, and we'd see such phenomena as season ticket rights being fought over in divorce proceedings and passed on through wills. New Jersey Governor Thomas Kean put it this way: "I can assure the management as well as the players that the seats in this arena will be filled game after game." McMullen said that sounded good to him. "I'm convinced the stadium will be filled every evening," he said.

In reality, the Devils would "underachieve" at the gate, even after Lou Lamoriello had taken over as general manager and built the franchise into one of the league's elite teams.

Back in Denver, we were left to wonder if we'd ever get another shot at the NHL.

AVALANCHE GLORY DAYS: SAKIC, FORSBERG, ROY, AND THE STANLEY CUP

I WAS WORKING FOR THE *Sporting News* and had moved back to Denver when the news broke in June 1995 that the Quebec Nordiques were being sold to COMSAT and relocating to Denver. The real plan had been for the Nuggets' ownership, COMSAT, to help provide leverage for Nordiques' ownership as it sought a new arena to replace the undersized and out-of-date Colisee in Quebec City. COMSAT would earn the gratitude of the league and move to the front of the line for an expansion franchise, preferably to begin play after the opening of a privately financed Denver arena on the drawing board at the time. But Quebec officials wouldn't be bullied into building the Nordiques a new arena and Denver suddenly was back in the NHL after a thirteen-year absence.

I attended the Avalanche's home opener, against the Red Wings, as a *Sporting News* staffer and wrote a short piece for the front of that week's magazine about the return of the NHL to Denver. A few weeks later, I agreed to return to the *Post*, to cover the NHL at-large and also to help Adrian Dater cover the Avalanche but with the additional understanding that I would be the relief columnist and operate as a feature writer and versatile reporter deployed on virtually all sports and beats. We also agreed I would remain affiliated with the *Sporting News* and get spot assignments from the magazine. In the next few years, I was called out of the *TSN* bullpen for events such as the Fiesta Bowl and Super Bowl and to write other pro and college football stories before I signed on with ESPN.com.

Meanwhile, I—and everyone else—knew right off that this wasn't Rocky Hockey. In the lockout-shortened 1995 season, the Nordiques had the best record in the Eastern Conference but lost in the first round of the playoffs to the New York Rangers. Center Joe Sakic was the young captain. Baby-faced Swedish center Peter Forsberg had just won the Calder Trophy as the league's rookie of the year and already showed his ability to take over games while refusing to be knocked off the puck. Marc Crawford, a feisty former utility forward with Vancouver, had just won the Jack Adams Trophy as the league's coach of the year in his first year as an NHL coach.

COMSAT officials hadn't expected to find themselves with a hockey team so soon. The situation reminded me of Robert Redford at the end of *The Candidate*. As a newly elected senator who has compromised his idealism during the campaign, he asks, "What do we do now?" COMSAT wisely took advantage of the marketing staff already in place for the Nuggets and let general manager Pierre Lacroix, only a year removed from his long career as a player agent before moving to the other side of the table, operate as if the hockey team was his—within more budgetary constraints than some of Lacroix's critics acknowledged.

I still was on the *Sporting News* payroll and working on a story about Ohio State football—I was supposed to advance the argument for the Buckeyes being the number one team in the nation, an argument made moot when they lost to Michigan in the final regular season game with the issue still on the newsstand—when Avalanche official Jean Martineau called me in Columbus. He introduced himself and informed me that Colorado had traded winger Owen Nolan to San Jose for defenseman Sandis Ozolinsh, whom I soon came to think of as the "Wandering Latvian." The deal was billed as providing the Avalanche a sorely needed second-wave offensive contribution from the blue line, and it turned out to be perhaps the most underrated deal of Pierre Lacroix's tenure.

Given my background with the Rockies, I always was convinced that a winning NHL team would be a big draw in Denver—both in the days of yore and in the mid-1990s. Yet I was a bit surprised by how fast the Avalanche caught on. When they drew a full house of 16,061 for the ninth home game of the 1995–96 season, little did we know that it would be the start of the longest recorded sellout streak in NHL history. The undersized McNichols Sports Arena had something to do with it, but there was no question that the new NHL team quickly became a hot ticket.

For my first story, I profiled Claude Lemieux, the controversial winger who had joined the Avalanche in early October in a trade with New Jersey, for whom he had won the Conn Smythe Trophy as the league's playoff MVP for the champion Devils. I laughed after I asked Forsberg about his new linemate. "He's a little dirty player, and I like that," Forsberg told me. "He's a goal scorer and a defensive player, and I can't complain about playing with him. He gets people upset and all that, eh?" One of the reasons I laughed was that although Forsberg had been in North America less than a year, he had started to sound like a Canadian.

Even then, with Lemieux playing on the line with Forsberg and Russian Valeri Kamensky, I found Lemieux to be one of the most interesting athletes I had encountered, mainly because of the conspicuous contradictions. Then a soft-spoken, thoughtful thirty year old, he was known to yap on the ice in the manner of the playground brat we all hated and to take cheap shots and run. He often was considered as selfish and annoying by his Montreal and New Jersey teammates ("Le Me" was one of his dressing room nicknames) as he was by his disdainful opponents.

The Avalanche got off to a good start that first season, but the major question mark remained their goaltending, with young Stephane Fiset and Jocelyn Thibault alternating. Then came the infamous Patrick Roy implosion in Montreal. Roy, who twice had won the Conn Smythe Trophy as the playoff MVP, was the best "money" goalie in the game and at the time had just turned thirty. The Canadiens got off to a horrible start that season, leading to the firings of general manager Serge Savard and coach Jacques Demers. The new coach was Mario Tremblay, whose relationship with Roy had been rocky (there's that word again) as teammates when Tremblay was a veteran winger playing in front of Roy. With the Canadiens struggling, Roy was impatient and cranky and couldn't hide it, so much so that even Roy backers wondered if his temperament made him intolerable in losing situations.

Before the Canadiens' December 2 game at home against Detroit, Roy was angry when high-scoring winger Vincent Damphousse showed up only ten minutes before the warm-up and Tremblay let it slide. Roy challenged Tremblay about it, asking if he would treat rookie winger Yves Sarault the same way. A little later, Tremblay left Roy in for the first nine Detroit goals in an 11–1 Montreal loss, and Roy—backed by the conventional hockey wisdom that dictated that you remove your goalie amid such onslaughts— took that for the affront it was. On the bench after finally being yanked, he squeezed past Tremblay and approached Canadiens president Ron Corey.

"I've played my last game in Montreal," Roy hissed.

The incident was Roy's Montreal exit visa. He issued a semi-apology, but the Canadiens were adamant: he would be traded. Opinion leaders in the Montreal media, including respected columnist Red Fisher, acted as if Roy had burned the Canadian flag. General manager Rejean Houle told him he would be traded to a Western Conference team.

Lacroix was Roy's former agent and longtime friend. The Avalanche were in the Western Conference. There was no way the Canadiens would have traded him to their divisional rivals, the Nordiques, especially because Roy was a Quebec City native and that would have rewarded him.

The trade was announced on December 6: Roy and Mike Keane to the Avalanche for wingers Andrei Kovalenko and Martin Rucinsky, plus Jocelyn Thibault.

Roy played his first game in a 5–3 loss to Edmonton at home on December 7. He acknowledged he hadn't played very well—an admission I would come to learn was rare, even when he stunk out the arena. That night, I watched and tossed out questions as he patiently answered all of us, including those who hadn't known how to pronounce his last name a week earlier and a couple of Montreal writers who had come to Denver for his Colorado debut.

Next, the Avalanche went on a multigame trip to eastern Canada, and I accompanied them. Roy had been gone only a few days, but with the attention he drew, it was as if the circus was in town, even when he got the night off and didn't play against Ottawa on the first game of the trip. I met with him at the Ottawa Westin on the afternoon of the game for our first lengthy talk. Patrick and his wife, Michele, had three young children—sons Jonathan and Frederick and two-year-old daughter Jana. He said the major concern about the trade and the move for him was how it would affect his family.

"That's what scared me the most," he told me, "but I believe it will be a good experience for my family at the same time. My wife's pretty strong. None of them speaks English very well, and the kids will learn, though."

Keane that day told me something that stuck with me. "He's hungry to prove a lot of people wrong," Keane said. "When Patrick says he's hungry, you know he's going to play up to another level and that could be scary."

From then on, I'm convinced, every save Roy made was a way to stick it to not only Tremblay, but also to those who endorsed the trade as a good-riddance move. Quickly, I came to recognize that he had the sort of touchy egoism and stubbornness so common to artists, complete with tendencies to come off as spoiled, hypersensitive, and selfish. Roy wouldn't plead for forgiveness in Montreal, even when on the brink of being traded. "It was clear from the organization that they had made their decision," he said that day in Ottawa. "I said, 'Okay, I'll accept my mistake.' I agree I was the one who made that thing happen on that Saturday, and both parties agreed it was in the best interests of us that we go different directions. I understand that you can't put ten years aside and give it a little tap and it's all gone. I lived through lots of good things in Montreal, but, again, it's a turn I accept. This will be a very nice experience for us."

For the most part, it was.

The Avalanche piled up 104 points in the regular season, beat Vancouver in a tough first-round series, and advanced to meet the Chicago Blackhawks in the Western Conference semifinals. Colorado was trailing 2–1 in the series when Game 4 went into overtime at the United Center, and Ozolinsh so blatantly tripped Chicago's Jeremy Roenick from behind on a breakaway that the play could have been used as an instruction video for calling penalty shots. Referee Andy Van Hellemond, destined for retirement at the conclusion of the 1996 playoffs, not only didn't award Roenick a penalty shot, but he didn't even call a tripping minor on Ozolinsh. So play continued, the Avalanche won 3–2 in overtime to tie the series, and they then went on to win the fifth and sixth games as well to advance. Had they lost that Game 4 in Chicago, they would have been down 3–1 in the series.

So the issue, both on that night and later, was: what would have happened if Van Hellemond hadn't swallowed his whistle, going along with the veteran referees' standard of not "deciding" a playoff game? After the game, the Blackhawks, including Roenick, were vocal in their criticism of Van Hellemond, and knowing that was the reaction, Roy said it was moot because he would have stopped Roenick on a penalty shot anyway.

This didn't come out until ten years later, when I heard Roy talk about it at a fan forum in connection with his Hall of Fame induction in Toronto. Roy recalled that on their ride together to the Denver arena the next day for practice, he and Keane talked about a possible response to the Blackhawks. Roy said Keane told him: "You have two Stanley Cup rings! I think that will be so much better. Tell them you have your Stanley Cup rings plugging your ears!" That's how it started.

The Blackhawks' media session in Denver came first on that day between games. Having read Roy's postgame remark, Roenick fired back, bringing up his breakaway goal on Roy earlier in the series. "I like Patrick's quote that he would have stopped me," Roenick said. "I just want to know where he was in Game 3. Probably getting his jock out of the rafters of the United Center."

I was standing near Roy a short time later when team broadcaster Norm Jones played the tape of Roenick's comment for the goalie. Then Roy went to the microphone to speak at the off-day news conference. So he not only had been fed a line by Keane, he had heard Roenick's specific remark from the earlier media session that day.

When a reporter asked him what he thought of Roenick's words, both after the game and on the off day, Roy pounced. "I can't hear Jeremy because I've got my two Stanley Cup rings plugging my ears," he said.

On the VHS tape of Avalanche playoff highlights from that season, the loudest laugh you hear is mine. It completely cracked me up.

The Avalanche went on to knock off the favored Red Wings, who had won sixty-two games in the regular season, in the six-game Western Conference finals, with Lemieux's hit from behind on Detroit's Kris Draper fueling what was becoming the NHL's most venomous rivalry of the 1990s. Draper suffered a broken jaw and other facial injuries when he slammed into the boards, and it caused the famous lament from Detroit's Dino Ciccarelli after he—and the rest of the Wings—went along with protocol and shook hands with Lemieux in the postgame, postseries lines. "I can't believe I shook his freakin' hand," said Ciccarelli.

I've seen a lot worse hits with no injuries sustained. But it indeed was a careless hit, and Lemieux's reputation for cavalier play added to the reaction. Plus, his lack of sufficient public regret, much less contrition, and his subsequent failure to apologize directly to Draper was indefensible. In that sense, the Wings' crusade—or at least Darren McCarty's crusade—was understandable and, to a point, even justifiable.

The Avalanche identity was taking hold. This no longer was the team dropped into Denver from Quebec. It was Colorado's team. At age twenty-seven, Joe Sakic stepped into the forefront of the local sports scene. Even the previous September, right before the Avalanche opened camp, Sakic walked up to the Broncos' ticket office at Mile High Stadium, picked up some tickets left for him at the will call window and was a little surprised that his name was recognized. Yet when he went to the Broncos' game, he could walk through the crowded concourses at will. No autograph requests. No heads turning as he walked past, no instances of his name being murmured—or yelled—in his wake. No "Hey, that's . . ." Less than a year later, that had changed. He scored two goals in that series-clinching win over the Wings.

"It's been fun, not only for the players, but for the fans," Sakic said the night the Avs clinched the series against Detroit and prepared to move on to the Stanley Cup Finals. "I think it's just great for the city. Early in the year, we weren't recognized as much. But obviously right now, with the way things are going, everybody is turning into a hockey fan. It's just great."

Sakic was a North American success story. His father, Marijan, and his mother, Slavica, journeyed separately from their native Croatia to Canada, where they married and started a family. When he began attending school in the Vancouver area, Sakic already was known for being a young boy of few words, and those few words were in Croatian.

"Everybody knew English, and I was just starting to learn it," Sakic told me. Beginning to play at the local rink, a ramshackle complex then known as 4 Rinks, he discovered that hockey was Canada's Esperanto—a universal language. "It was the worst place in the world," he said, jokingly, of the rink.

Marijan, a stonemason, built a rink in the Sakic backyard. He and Slavica rounded up $300 to buy a family membership to the North Shore Club so their daughter, Rosemarie, could practice figure skating. As part of the deal, Joe and his brother, Brian, also were able to play hockey in the club. Before long, Joe was a prodigy, and he ended up with the Lethbridge Broncos of major junior's Western Hockey League at the end of the 1985–86 season, then with the relocated Broncos at Swift Current, Saskatchewan, the next season.

On December 30, 1986, the Broncos were headed to Regina on the team bus when the driver lost control in icy conditions. In the resulting crash, four Broncos playing cards at the back of the bus sustained fatal injuries. Sakic, sitting up front, climbed out of the windshield. The rest of that season, the Broncos received standing ovations at every WHL stop.

In June, the Nordiques took Sakic in the first round of the entry draft, and he joined Quebec for the 1988–89 season. Within a few years, he was the captain. In Quebec, he was "Giuseppe" or the "Croatian Sensation" and the face of the franchise.

As captain, he always considered another of his nicknames—"Quoteless Joe"—to be a compliment. His captaincy was leading by example and with a barbed sense of humor he turned off when the tape recorders and cameras came on. That was the case during that first playoff run and until the day he retired.

———————

After the victory over the Red Wings, the sweep of the Finals against the overmatched Florida Panthers was anticlimactic. The series-ending Game 4 went into three overtimes until defenseman Uwe Krupp finally scored the game's only goal. When it suddenly ended, I was in the makeshift press area at ice level, writing and not watching. I didn't even see a replay of the shot that finally beat Florida goalie John Vanbiesbrouck, because when it happened, I had to plug in a score for an early edition, send that story, then hustle to watch the on-ice celebration, then attend the news conferences, and go to the Avalanche dressing room.

The scene was eerie. The dressing room was tiny and it would have been jammed even if it were only the players, coaches, team staff, and their families. With the media in there, it was wall to wall, and several players—including Mike Keane and Adam Deadmarsh—at one point sat on top of their lockers, looking down as they swigged champagne and in Keane's case smoked a cigar. The Stanley Cup was a goblet. The players were making no moves to take off their uniforms and head to the showers. First, I approached Sakic, whose 18 goals in the postseason were only one short of the NHL record.

"You dream about this moment, and it's unbelievable," he said. "We've come such a long way in this organization, from the time we started rebuilding in Quebec."

Two days later, the Avalanche rode in a parade through downtown and then an estimated crowd of 200,000 in the Civic Center Plaza watched Sakic hold the Stanley Cup aloft on the steps of the City and Country Building during the rally and celebration.

As this went on, there were many snide remarks made internationally about Denver's long-suffering hockey fans waiting several months to celebrate a Stanley Cup, but unless those were made tongue-in-cheek, they overlooked that the area's hockey tradition didn't begin when the Avalanche arrived. The area's hockey history included powerhouse University of Denver programs, a parade of minor-league pro franchises, and the NHL's Rockies, plus youth hockey programs that would grow even more popular after the Avalanche stoked interest in the sport. Absolutely, there was a bandwagon aspect to the celebration. Yet I'm convinced that even as the Avalanche deteriorated into one of the worst teams in the league in 2009 and attendance plummeted, the fact was that there was more interest than ever in the team and the sport because of the foundation that was laid in those early seasons. The Avalanche nurtured a huge base that continued to follow the team with passion, often with more knowledge and hardened cynicism, even if that didn't translate to continued sellouts at high prices in a down economy. That's the Avalanche legacy, too. It started that first season and built from there.

———————

The next season became famous for intensifying the rivalry that developed in the 1996 Western Conference finals and was heightened by Lemieux's hit on Draper. It's been covered many places, including in *Denver Post* colleague Adrian Dater's book, *Blood Feud*, and as ESPN and other television networks played and replayed the same videos over the years, they almost became clichés.

But I'd be remiss if I didn't at least make mention of the most toxic game in the rivalry—the March 26, 1997, meeting in Joe Louis Arena. Adrian stayed home, I took the trip, and in subsequent years, we joked that if all hell was going to break loose, it was going to break loose on one of the trips I was on. It was the Avalanche's second appearance of the season in Detroit, but the first game, in November, was relatively calm—primarily because Lemieux was hurt and didn't play. Detroit's all sports radio station had been selling "Screw Lemieux" T-shirts and treating the return as a monumental event. The morning of the game, the *Detroit News* added to the hysteria by running a mock Lemieux "Wanted" poster as a graphic accompaniment to a column castigating the Avalanche winger. In the column, Darren McCarty was quoted as saying, "I was taught the best time to get revenge is when they're not expecting it. He's [Lemieux] played long enough, he knows eventually something will happen. The trump card is, he doesn't know when."

The "when" was late in the first period. It got started in unlikely fashion—when Peter Forsberg and the Wings' Igor Larionov, the veteran Russian, got in a skirmish along the boards. It was mere jostling, but it provided McCarty an excuse to go after Lemieux and start throwing punches as the officials were preoccupied with the Europeans. Lemieux "turtled" and didn't fight back, and McCarty kept throwing punches. Other fights broke out. It got out of hand, but the NHL had progressed from the Broad Street Bullies days because the benches didn't empty. The fines and suspensions would have been prohibitive, and everyone understood that.

As Lemieux covered up, Patrick Roy skated out of the crease to come to Lemieux's aid, but he was intercepted by—and collided with—Detroit winger Brendan Shanahan, and Roy suffered a cut when he hit his head on the ice. Then he got in a fight with Detroit veteran goalie Mike Vernon, who had answered the call by coming out of his crease to even the numbers. Years later, when I visited Roy in retirement, when he was part owner and general manager of major junior's Quebec Remparts, Roy had a huge poster of himself with blood dripping down his face, being escorted off the ice by a linesman, displayed in the equipment room. It was supposed to be inspiration for his young players, reminding them that he had been a warrior. That night, he quickly took some butterfly stitches from trainer Pat Karns and then returned to his crease.

Referee Paul Devorski fouled it up, giving McCarty only a double minor. I'm an advocate of discretionary officiating and of leagues empowering its officials to make what amounts to "power of God" decisions in situations such as this. Heading off further trouble, Devorski should have given McCarty a game misconduct, regardless of how much he did or didn't see, and announced that if anyone so much as coughed the rest of the game, they'd get tossed, too.

And, yes, he should have found a way to toss Lemieux, too, although all he did was take punches then return to the game in the second period. That first period melee was just the start of things, and the upshot was that the Red Wings, trailing 5–3 with eleven minutes remaining in regulation, ended up winning 6–5 in overtime—on a McCarty goal.

In the visiting dressing room, Lemieux didn't speak, but it was almost comical to see Keane positioned at his stall, obviously ready to get some things off his chest. To wave after wave of reporters, he repeated the same speech. One of his points was that Lemieux had played against the Red Wings in Denver ten days earlier, but the Red Wings hadn't tried to get retribution there. "I think that team has no heart," Keane said. "Detroit had the opportunity to do that in our building, but they didn't. They come home and played it rough. That's fine. I think they showed their true colors tonight. Everyone's gutless on that team and I'd love to see them in the playoffs."

I walked down the hall and found Pierre Lacroix in the visiting bench area pacing with his hands in his pockets. He told me that McCarty had "sucker-punched" Lemieux and also delivered a knee to the head. He argued that some of McCarty's pregame comments about retribution were evidence of premeditation and that he not only deserved to be tossed from the game with a gross misconduct, but that he deserved a suspension.

Next, I headed to the Detroit dressing room. McCarty took so long to emerge and talk with the media that I caught his entire session. I actually like McCarty, but his comments, while candid, were also disingenuous. If he was proud of what he did, he should have just said so. Instead, he strained credibility by saying he hadn't targeted Lemieux.

"No, it just sort of happened," McCarty said to those of us crowded around him for comment. "Guys just square off. You gotta get a partner, eh? He was the closest one to me. I didn't really realize it was him."

Was it a sucker punch?

"No, because he was looking at me," McCarty said. "I didn't hit him from behind. It was face to face."

McCarty scoffed when the subject of a possible suspension came up. "I don't see why," he said. "It was boys having fun out there, that's what it is. They started it, anyway."

Told that the Avs were talking about the Red Wings lacking heart, McCarty said, "They can say whatever they want. They're the Stanley Cup champions and they can say whatever they want until we dethrone them or somebody dethrones them."

He delivered a filibuster about why fighting is the ultimate accountability.

"Hockey's an emotional game," he said. "We're not stupid in here. We're not going out of our way. I don't know what you expect. You want real retribution right away. . . . Crack a stick across the face, is that it? No. You might knock his eye out. No matter how bad it was to Kris [Draper], he's all right now.

"If you believe in the Bible, it's an eye for an eye. Fist on fist. That's another reason you have to keep that in the game. . . . In this game, you have a long memory. We've played this game since we were six or seven years old, and you remember things kids did to you when you were eight, and you don't get them back until they're twelve. You have a long memory."

A Red Wings official called McCarty away from his locker, but he did have one more comment when he was asked about getting the winning goal.

"That's the best thing," he said. "We won the game."

———◆———

Two months later, the Red Wings got revenge for the previous year's loss to the Avalanche in the playoffs, beating the defending champions in six games in the Western Conference finals.

After the Wings' clinching 3–1 victory in Game 6 in Joe Louis Arena, even the civilized tradition of shaking hands after the conclusion of a playoff series was a casualty of the animosity. Dino Ciccarelli wasn't with the Wings any longer, so he didn't have to worry about shaking anyone's "freakin'" hand, but there were other decisions made.

Traditionally, as opponents, you might have carved each other up on the ice, but you walk through the reception line, grit the teeth you have left, and even with blood dripping down your face and hatred in your heart, you shake hands. But on that night in 1997, Draper wouldn't shake hands with Lemieux. Lemieux stuck out his hand, Draper conceded, but Draper said he passed because Lemieux wasn't looking him in the eye.

It was catching. Seconds later, Lemieux refused to shake hands with McCarty.

"I was gonna, and he didn't want to," McCarty said. "So I think it just shows his immaturity. I was brought up better than that, so I didn't go out of my way. That's all I have to say about that."

———◆———

Despite bizarre ownership situations—COMSAT's corporate ownership evolved into Ascent, which then had deals to sell the teams and arena to Bill

Laurie and then Donald Sturm fall through before Liberty Communications bought all of Ascent's properties and sold the sports teams and arena to Stan Kroenke—the Avalanche remained one of the elite franchises in the league under Lacroix's control.

The biggest blip was in 1998, when the Avalanche blew a first-round series to Edmonton that cost Marc Crawford his job. It was one of the most bizarre coaching changes I'd ever covered, even more so than Cherry's exit from the Rockies. After several weeks of what Lacroix called "allowing the dust to settle," Crawford left. He had a year left on his contract and officially resigned. (The media jokingly referred to his exit as a case where the coach "got resigned.") The Avalanche declared they wouldn't have to pay him, yet they would be entitled to compensation if Crawford went to another team during that year. Colorado's position was that Crawford, with a year remaining on his contract, had been maneuvering to go to the Toronto Maple Leafs, his dream job, and that let the Avalanche off the hook. The NHL backed the Avalanche, and if Crawford later seemed to harbor much resentment against Lacroix and the organization and react accordingly, it was a bit—note that I said "a bit"—understandable. He joined Vancouver in the middle of the next season, and the Avalanche got their compensation.

In 1998–99 and 1999–2000, Colorado twice lost to Dallas in seven-game Western Conference finals, the second time after acquiring Ray Bourque from Boston near the trading deadline. By then, Bob Hartley was the coach, and Lacroix came close to firing him after the second loss, theorizing that he had been given the parts to win a championship, but he hadn't done it. The fact that the Avalanche had beaten Detroit both years in the conference semifinals might have saved his job.

It all came together the next season. Bourque, a step slow but still an inspiration, returned for one more shot. But before they went after the Cup again, there was the little business of Roy completing his obsessive quest for Terry Sawchuk's NHL record of 447 career wins. It had taken me awhile to completely comprehend how important Roy considered that chase. He made no apology for it. He trashed video equipment after a game at Anaheim in December 1998 because of a Hartley coaching strategy that *worked*. Hartley briefly sent in backup Craig Billington to buy some rest for his skaters on a power play, and Billington consequently was on the ice when Colorado got the game-winning goal and got credit for the win without facing a shot. That anomaly "stole" a victory from Roy. The video equipment could be repaired and replaced. The relationship with Hartley could be repaired. But the prideful competitiveness, even if it has an element of selfishness, was indispensable. Roy couldn't tone down that selfishness and remained effective.

The number in Roy's sights was directly tied to team success. His point: preoccupation with other numbers, such as goals-against average, is more selfish. Wins are the measure, because when your teammates skate toward the crease at the end of the game, they are coming to congratulate and celebrate, not to commiserate or follow protocol. "Why is it important?" Roy asked. "Because when I started, I had one objective. It wasn't to have one very good year. It was to have a career where I would play consistently throughout. And the only way to reach that record is to have done that. That's why it's important."

We also talked a lot about how changing conditions in the sport made statistical goaltending comparisons between eras even more risky. Even in the wins category, the addition of a five-minute, sudden death overtime in the regular season changed the equation.* But Roy's point always was that the best way to measure a goaltender was whether his team won. It was both a selfish measurement, taking credit for team success, but also realistic, because we all know that goaltending is that important. Forget the number of shots, the power play distribution, the good and bad bounces. Did he allow fewer goals than the guy at the other end?

The quest ended at Washington on October 17, 2000, when Forsberg's overtime goal against the Capitals gave the Avalanche the 4–3 win—and Roy his 448th. During his postgame news conference—he had showered and dressed and was at a podium in the pressroom—Jean Chretien, Canada's prime minister, called Roy to congratulate him. I was a few feet away, and there were perhaps twenty reporters in the room in *our* nation's capital.

"I think that all Canadians at this moment are very proud of you," Chretien said.

"I just wanted to get it over as soon as possible," Roy said. "I didn't want my family and my friends to have to keep following me around the country."

Roy went on to have his first 40-victory season and a 2.21 goals-against average that season.

As the 2001 playoffs were about to begin, I took a trip to Hartley's hometown of Hawkesbury, Ontario. I saw the site of the paper mill where the Avalanche coach went to work as a teenager, forsaking college, after his father

---

* As would the addition of shootouts and a guaranteed winner later, when Martin Brodeur was chasing and eventually breaking Roy's record.

Avalanche goaltender Patrick Roy is the most competitive professional athlete I've ever covered. Here, he's holding the commemorative puck after his three hundredth career victory, which was over Edmonton in Denver on February 19, 1996. He would go on to break Terry Sawchuk's NHL career record of 447 and finish his career with 551. *Source*: Photo by Jerry Mellman.

died suddenly. I visited the windshield factory where he ended up working after the mill closed and saw the rink where he got his start in coaching as a part-time goaltending coach for the local junior team, the Hawkesbury Hawks. I noticed that the arena had undergone a name change and now was the Robert Hartley Arena. I saw the ranch-style, brick home he and his wife had bought after convincing the owners that these two "kids" who had ridden their bikes to the appointment were bona fide buyers. I talked to his friends, neighbors, and fellow Hawkesbury residents who felt they were a part of the Avalanche run. That type of story couldn't happen in any major league sport other than hockey, which allowed for unconventional coaching backgrounds.

But with such a proven, veteran-laden roster, Hartley had little safety net because expectations were so high that anything short of a championship would have been considered failure.

On the night the Avalanche finished off Los Angeles in a tough seven-game, second-round series, Colorado lost Forsberg for the rest of the playoffs when he had to undergo an emergency operation to remove his spleen. But they beat St. Louis—coached by Joel Quenneville—in the conference finals and advanced to face the New Jersey Devils in the Stanley Cup Finals. If nothing else, I could say that I was the only person in the building who had covered both franchises.

Roy had a major Game 4 puck-handling gaffe against the Devils that was crucial in enabling the Devils to even the series. New Jersey also took Game 5 in Denver and could have closed out the series with a Game 6 win at home. It looked as if that might happen when New Jersey decisively outplayed the Avalanche in the first period, but Roy was spectacular in keeping the Devils off the scoreboard. The Avalanche won that game 4–0 and then clinched the Cup with a 3–1 win at home with Alex Tanguay scoring twice and Sakic once.

That's when Sakic had his signature moment as captain, making a quick pass after accepting the Stanley Cup from commissioner Gary Bettman and handing it to Bourque, the veteran who had waited so long for the thrill, and as everyone expected, had played the last game of his twenty-two-season career. I know some thought we got carried away with the sentimental Bourque angle, but I don't know how anyone could see those pictures of the veteran defenseman who had waited so long enjoying the visceral thrill of raising the Cup overhead and not be affected. It was about the power of sport's most storied championship trophy and the perseverance of one of the game's best players in seeking it out.

This time, the crowd in the Civic Center Plaza was even larger than in 1996; it was estimated at 250,000.

A few days later in Toronto, I watched as Sakic had an incredible one-day haul of hardware. In the afternoon at the Hall of Fame, he accepted the Lester B. Pearson Award as the NHL Players Association's MVP, and then that night at the Air Canada Centre, he was named winner of the Hart Trophy and the Lady Byng Trophy as the league's most "gentlemanly" player.

In Toronto, Sakic told me, "I couldn't imagine a better week in the game of hockey."

CHRIS DRURY
AND STEVE MOORE

R AY BOURQUE RETIRED AFTER COLORADO'S second Stanley Cup championship, and he was watching from afar as the Avalanche blew the 2002 Western Conference finals to the Red Wings, taking a 3–2 lead and then dropping the final two games. Patrick Roy made a notorious "Statue of Liberty" gaffe in Denver in Game 6, trying to show off with a wave of the glove on a save and dropping the puck into the net. The Red Wings blew out the Avalanche 7–0 in Game 7, a game in which Bob Hartley mercifully pulled Roy.

That was an inglorious ending, but it was Roy's best regular season ever. He was a finalist for the Hart Trophy, along with Montreal goalie Jose Theodore and Calgary winger Jarome Iginla. Roy deserved the award more than the man who won—Theodore. I had Iginla as my first choice and make no apology for that, but in retrospect I wish I had put Roy there. It became apparent that some voters' pettiness swung the vote to Theodore. Voting for the "other" Canadiens' goalie, Theodore, was a combination of the traditional bias in the game toward eastern Canada and a way to spite Roy, who had rubbed so many of them the wrong way. Among other things, he had announced early that season that he didn't want to be included on the 2002 Olympic team roster, citing a sore hip and the desire to watch his son play in the famous Quebec Pee Wee tournament during the break. A major reason likely was that he wasn't certain of being the number one goalie, as he was in Nagano in 1998, but so what? This was his decision to make, and I'm convinced that if the Hart Trophy vote had been entirely on merit, Iginla or Roy would have won. Theodore had a terrific year, lifting a mediocre team into the postseason, but the combination of circumstances led to him getting an award he didn't deserve. All of this, of course, would turn out to be a bit ironic after he joined the Avalanche a few years later.

The deterioration of the Avalanche continued on October 1, 2002, when Pierre Lacroix blundered and dealt Chris Drury to the Calgary Flames. Drury and checking line center Stephane Yelle were sent to the Flames for defenseman Derek Morris and forwards Dean McAmmond and Jeff Shantz. Drury's value was impossible to quantify with anything that showed up in his career statistical log. He won the Calder Trophy as the NHL's top rookie in 1998–1999. He had eleven game-winning playoff goals in his four seasons and a total of eleven goals in twenty-three games during the 2001 Cup run. He was a huge fan favorite, despite his soft-spoken demeanor. Lacroix and the others seemed to consider Drury some little American college kid who paled in comparison to Sakic and Forsberg and was just a spare part who could take advantage of having great players on the ice with him. I still consider Hartley a terrific coach, but his background in coaching both junior A and major junior in Canada on his unlikely climb contributed to his tendency to downgrade U.S. college players and question their grit.

I first spoke with Drury in April 1998, when he was a senior at Boston University and the Avalanche traveled to Boston to meet the Bruins. He had just finished his college career with a loss to New Hampshire in the NCAA quarterfinals, and it was a week before he was named the winner of the Hobey Baker Memorial Award as NCAA hockey's top player. I was surprised that the team hadn't tried to set up a meeting when the Avalanche was in Boston, and that was a foreshadowing of how they would take him for granted down the road. The Nordiques drafted him in 1994, after he graduated at Fairfield Prep in Connecticut, shortly after Lacroix took over as general manager, and the organization watched and waited through his career at BU.

"I've followed them a lot," Drury told me in Boston. "But it's got more to do with them being such a great team than the fact that they drafted me."

At the time, despite his accomplishments in college hockey, Drury was best known for helping lead the team from Trumbull, Connecticut, to the Little League World Series championship in August 1989. His team's starting catcher, Drury doubled as a pitcher and was on the mound as Trumbull shocked the heavily favored team from Taiwan—which we all suspected had players old enough to legally drink beer in the Williamsport bars—in the championship game. In the ensuing years, ESPN and other networks carrying Avalanche games showed the clip of a chunky Drury pitching, spitting, and jumping in the air after the final out roughly as many times as the stock footage of Red Wings–Avalanche mayhem at the height of the rivalry.

"We knew we weren't supposed to win," Drury told me. "I mean, we knew the combined scores of the past few championship games before that was 100–3 or something like that. Then you just looked at them physically, and there was no comparison between them and us. None. Nobody gave us a shot. I think we had looked at the other Americans and we were hoping, 'Gee, we hope we don't lose that bad.'"

Drury, then five feet one and 126 pounds, knew a worldwide television audience was watching. In the United States, Al Trautwig and former Baltimore Orioles pitcher Jim Palmer were the announcers for the game broadcast on ABC's *Wide World of Sports.*

"I was pretty excited when I went out to the mound," Drury said. "We had one other pitcher and we each pitched eight of our sixteen games, but he had started the first one, so I guess you could say I was our number two pitcher. There were 40,000 people there, and most of them and most of the country wanted us to win, and that really got the adrenaline going."

Taiwan led 1–0 after the first inning, but a two-run bottom of the third gave the Americans a 2–1 lead halfway through the scheduled six-inning game.

"That seemed like a miracle in its own right," Drury said. "People were happy that they didn't have to leave early because we were getting killed."

Ken Martin, Drury's best friend both then and now, drove in a run with a single and later hit a home run. Drury also drove in a run and ended up jumping up and down when he got the final out. He had thrown a five-hitter.

"I think part of it was that in the years before, the U.S. teams had worked it so they'd have their big, hard-throwing kid ready for the championship game," Drury said. "I didn't even have a fastball. I threw curveballs and changeups and I think that threw them off. Plus, they had been so dominating, I don't think they were ready for us."

After the upset in the championship game, the Trumbull boys were invited to the 1989 World Series, and Drury threw out the ceremonial first pitch before Game 2 in Oakland—two days before the earthquake struck at Game 3 in San Francisco. They also appeared on *Good Morning America* and at the White House, where President Bush honored them.

So what happened to Drury's baseball career?

"After that, I was playing both baseball, mostly as a catcher, and hockey," Drury said. "Actually, I got hurt playing hockey my junior year of high school and wasn't able to play baseball for a year, so it worked out that the decision was kind of made for me. I got checked in a hockey game and broke my wrist. I was able to play hockey with my hand in a cast, but not baseball."

Drury eventually signed with the Avalanche in 1998. In Drury's first training camp scrimmage, journeyman winger Pascal Trepanier drew him into a fight, and it was a safe bet that Trepanier had done Bob Hartley's bidding to "test" the college kid. I wondered whether Hartley would have been held accountable if Drury, unaccustomed to fighting, had suffered a significant injury. (And, yes, hockey players do get hurt in fights.) Soon, Drury was renowned as a clutch player and fan favorite in Colorado, and his trade to Calgary immediately drew a firestorm of criticism.

The Avalanche rationalized it as the only way they could have acquired Morris, then considered one of the better up-and-coming defensemen in the league. The day of the trade, when I talked with Drury, he was trying to find positives about going to what then was one of the troubled small-market Canadian franchises that hadn't made the playoffs in six seasons.

"It never really bothered me too much, but I was behind Peter and Joe and some other world-class forwards in this organization," Drury said. "I never really cared about that. All I cared about was winning and going deep in the playoffs and trying to win a Stanley Cup. Now that the deal's been done, without Joe, without Peter, and without the other guys in front of me, maybe it's a good move for me."

Drury went from Calgary to Buffalo, then signed a lucrative five-year free agency deal with the Rangers in 2007 and became their captain in 2008. The Avalanche like to point out that a draft choice acquired in one of the Drury trade's offshoots enabled Colorado to draft star center and 2010 Olympian Paul Stastny, but that's a red herring. Colorado could have taken him six choices earlier, when it claimed Ryan Stoa. Granted, nobody knows how things would have worked out if Colorado had kept Drury, and the franchise was headed for a salary-cap crunch in 2005, when the cap was instituted. But I'm certain of this much: they didn't sufficiently appreciate Drury, and trading him was a mistake.

———◆———

That 2002–03 season was bizarre. A slow start (10–8–9–4) cost Hartley his job thirty-one games into the season, though it was one of the rare instances where a coach's firing came out of nowhere. There wasn't any speculation about a move being imminent or pressure on Lacroix to oust the coach who had raised the Stanley Cup seventeen months earlier. I've always suspected there was a smoking gun incident involved—perhaps an influential veteran telling Lacroix something had to be done. I've repeatedly been told that wasn't the case, but I still wonder. The team was underachieving, and Hartley's tendency to play both Sakic and Forsberg up to thirty minutes didn't thrill either of those star centers, and while Sakic liked Forsberg, he didn't think they should be playing in the same line—an occasional Hartley strategy. But there was no clamor or even buzz that Hartley was about to go. In stepped his first-year assistant, Tony Granato, the recently retired journeyman winger who had turned feisty toward the end of his career. The Avalanche recovered, in large part thanks Forsberg's play: he was amazing, with a league-high 77 assists and 106 points and play that went beyond those numbers. His run over the final half of that season was the best individual performance I've seen in more than thirty years of covering the sport. With all due respect to Sakic, and even to his Hart Trophy season, when healthy, Forsberg was a better all-around player. Yet because of Sakic's relative resiliency, leadership, and circumstances that enabled him to remain with one organization for his entire NHL career, he has to be considered the top skater in Avalanche

Patrick Roy and Avalanche center Peter Forsberg, wearing the "A" for assistant captain, celebrate another victory. The triumvirate of Roy, Forsberg, and Joe Sakic (on the cover) led the Avalanche through the franchise's wildly successful first years in Colorado. Forsberg and Sakic eventually will join Roy in the Hockey Hall of Fame. *Source*: Photo by Jerry Mellman.

history—and, yes, that qualification is because Roy was Colorado's top overall player.

But the 2003 playoffs were a fiasco, with the Avalanche taking a 3–1 lead over Minnesota in the first round and then losing three straight. Andrew Brunette's overtime goal for the Wild on a partial breakaway in Game 7 ended the series—and, as it turned out, it also ended Roy's career. Until that point, he was leaning toward retirement; that goal clinched it. He had another career awaiting him in Major Junior hockey, where he already was the co-owner of the Remparts. Give him credit: he was thirty-seven, and he could have hung on for at least another couple of seasons, made a lot of money, been a decent number one goalie, but he needed to be more than that.

Shortly after he announced his retirement, the Avalanche pulled off a remarkable coup, signing unrestricted free agents Paul Kariya and Teemu Selanne, who shared an agent—Don Baizley—with Sakic and signed "bargain" one-year contracts to be able to play together and perhaps position themselves for killer long-term deals after that. The signings were banner headline material in Denver and beyond, and the prospect of Sakic centering the two terrific wingers was exciting. I was thinking the Denver city administration should be planning on a third Stanley Cup parade, assuming that Roy's successor, David Aebischer, could give Colorado decent goaltending. The problem, as it turned out, was that Selanne was playing on a horrible knee that eventually required reconstructive surgery and Kariya was apathetic even when he was healthy, which wasn't often. But when that season started, hopes were as high as they could be given Roy's retirement. Despite getting disappointing contributions from Selanne and Kariya, the Avalanche had a 32–11–10–4 record when they faced Vancouver at home on February 16.

In the second period, Avalanche rookie winger Steve Moore, a Harvard graduate from the Toronto suburb of Thornhill, delivered an unpenalized, open-ice hit on Vancouver captain Markus Naslund. Until that point, Moore was having a nice, if unspectacular, rookie season, showing that he probably could have a journeyman's career in the league as a third- or fourth-line center. Naslund suffered facial cuts and a minor concussion. The Canucks won 1–0 and all but announced after the game that they would seek revenge. I was among those in the Canucks' dressing room that night and was part of the questioning of Canucks winger Todd Bertuzzi.

Bertuzzi noted that the Canucks and Avalanche meet twice more "so hopefully, they keep [Moore] up. . . . It's called respect in the league. Players like that kid coming up, just shows what kind of respect we have around this league. Here's a guy reaching out, and the puck's not even there, and a guy blindsides a guy like that. It's unfortunate that the game was where it was at, because it would have been a different situation."

I asked him if he meant the Canucks might have retaliated if the game hadn't been close.

"Absolutely," Bertuzzi said. "That's the best player in the NHL. That's for the refs to police. They didn't do it."

Canucks winger Trevor Linden, who doubled as the president of the players' association, called the play "a blatant attempt by a marginal player to hurt our guy."

Nearby, Canucks winger Brad May made what turned out to be an infamous remark to Vancouver *Sun* writer Iain MacIntyre, referring to a "bounty" on Moore.

Outside the locker room door, Canucks coach Marc Crawford delivered a stinging rebuke to Moore and the referees. "They talk about players not having respect for players. How about the officials?" the former Avalanche coach asked. "Should they not have respect for the leading scorer in the league? When does that come? It could have been an obstruction call, it could have been an elbow call, and it could have been anything. Instead they call absolutely nothing. That was a cheap shot by a young kid on a captain, leading scorer in the league, and we get no call. We get no call. That is ridiculous. How does that happen? That's got to be answered. Why is there no respect from those referees for the leading scorer in the league? I do not understand that for the life of me. I don't care if they fine me. I really don't. That needs to be answered."

After that tirade, Crawford stormed off. I was told that his smirk when he came into the dressing room made it clear he had been performing and making a point: his stars needed protecting, too. If there was any irony, it was that Marc Crawford the player was a lot more like Steve Moore than Markus Naslund.

After hearing all that, I scrambled over to the Avalanche dressing room to get Moore's explanation and his reaction to what we had just heard.

"I came out of the zone and the puck looked like it was going to come out to the neutral zone," Moore said. "It went right to their guy, and I just came out and finished my check. I didn't even know who it was. I just finished my check the way we always do, and I guess it ended up being Naslund, and I guess they weren't too happy about that. I'm certainly not looking to hurt him or anything, just a clean body check with a shoulder."

He added, "People can look at the tape and see what they think. The refs didn't call a penalty and I heard them yelling, 'It was a clean check, it was a clean check.' Certainly, I just hit him with my shoulder. If that's a cheap shot. . . ."

Frankly, nothing that happened or was said that night in response to the Moore hit was all that objectionable. Crawford took the same stance when he coached the Avalanche and called for officiating respect and protection for Forsberg and Sakic. I considered his rant lobbying, the sort I heard all the time in decades of being around the sport. At times, it seems contradictory because it runs against what the culture proclaims as the all-for-one, one-for-all fabric of the sport. But it wasn't getting Michael Jordan to the line every time he was touched or looking the other way when he didn't dribble for five strides on the way to the hoop. It's physical protection in a tough sport.

Although I didn't hear it directly, I assumed May's "bounty" remark was a dark and slightly tongue-in-cheek reference to *Slap Shot*, the movie every NHL player has seen repeatedly. In the film, Paul Newman's character, Reg Dunlop, says, "I am personally placing a $100 bounty on the head of Tim McCracken. He's the coach and chief punk on that Syracuse team."

The teams met again in Denver two weeks later, and I talked with Moore about the upcoming game following a morning skate in Columbus and also set out to tell readers more about the player who, until the Naslund hit, had stayed under the radar.

The youngest of three hockey-playing brothers from the Toronto suburbs, then age twenty-five, Moore seemed an unlikely villain. "We played just about every sport you can imagine growing up," Moore said. "We played a lot of tennis in the summers, and our dad was on Team Canada in his age group. But, obviously, academics were important in our house."

All three boys gravitated to hockey. One by one, they attended Harvard and played for the Crimson. Mark was a defenseman who signed with the Pittsburgh Penguins' organization. A year behind Mark, Steve starred for four seasons, becoming the Crimson's all-time scoring leader. But his record only lasted two years—until his younger brother, Dominic, broke it. By then, Steve was the only player in the Avalanche organization with an Ivy League degree in environmental sciences and public policy.

"It was liberal arts, so you take a very wide range of courses," Steve said. "So while it was a concentration in environmental sciences and public policy, it was kind of a general degree. It's not necessarily something geared for a vocation. It may or may not translate into something in that area down the road."

Moore played twelve games for Colorado in times of injury sieges in the previous two seasons, but he wasn't viewed as much more than an organizational insurance policy. In 2003–04, he got the summons from Hershey of the American Hockey League again because of the Avs' recurring injury problems, and by late season, he seemed to have cemented a spot on the playoff roster.

Meanwhile, the storm was continuing to build. In the wake of the hit, Vancouver general manager Brian Burke—who, ironically, received his law degree from Harvard after playing hockey at Providence—labeled it "a head-hunting shot on a star player by a marginal player." This was even before the American-born Burke in later years as general manager at Anaheim and Toronto seemed to increasingly adopt the Canadian backwoods macho ethic in piecing together a team and in his public pronouncements.

"I'm just doing what I'm supposed to do out there: finish checks," Moore said. "I understand that when a player the stature of Markus Naslund gets hurt, maybe some questions are going to be asked. I understand that. He's a phenomenal player. You don't want him hurt. I don't want him hurt. I understand that he's their best player, he's their leader, he's a huge part of their team. I can understand why they're upset. I'm not going to comment on the rest."

So what happened during that March 3 game in Denver? Nothing. It was a 5–5 tie and gratuitous stupidity would have been potentially costly. Also, NHL commissioner Gary Bettman and discipline czar Colin Campbell were at the game. Bettman told us after the first period that he was on the way to an appointment on the West Coast and just felt like stopping in Denver to watch a game. Yeah, right. Bettman played down the Canucks' remarks about Moore.

"More often than not, the remarks in the heat of the moment dissipate by the time the actual game is played," said Bettman. He smiled and added, "Although we still have two periods to play."

Five days later, the teams played again in Vancouver, and again it was my turn to be there. With the game still scoreless at 6:36 of the first period, Moore was challenged to a fight at a faceoff by Vancouver forward Matt Cooke and held his own. By some standards, he had answered the call, and that should have been it. Moore had one of the goals as the Avalanche roared to a 5–0 lead early in the third period. Then it happened. With Bertuzzi stalking Moore coming up the ice, Bertuzzi threw a roundhouse punch from behind to Moore's head, drove him to the ice near the red line, and kept punching. The most ridiculous thing to come out of the incident was the contention that Moore suffered his injuries when teammates joined the pile, trying to break it up. It could have been worse if Avalanche center Andrei Nikolishin hadn't interceded and pinned Bertuzzi's arms. Bertuzzi wasn't going to stop punching on his own.

In this era of "homer," ridiculously slanted broadcasts—at the teams' insistence—the Vancouver radio crew showed a lot of courage. Play-by-play man John Shorthouse saw it happen and immediately called it a "cheap shot, sucker punch from behind." Analyst Tom Larscheid, a former Canadian Football League player and certainly not a shrinking violet, exclaimed, "Oh, I hate that!"

I wasn't watching the ice when it happened. We face tough deadlines on all West Coast games, and with the outcome not at all in doubt, I was writing. So was Aaron Lopez of the *Rocky Mountain News*, who was next to me. Plus, this was the eve of the trading deadline, and the Avalanche had announced after the first period that they had acquired forward Matthew Barnaby from the New York Rangers, and we met Lacroix for a briefing. So we were writing that sidebar story, too. We were like everyone else who hadn't been focused on the incident, which happened behind the puck: we had to catch up by watching replays.

In the ensuing mayhem, with Moore down on the ice amid blood, Crawford was shown on television behind the bench, smirking. That remains a blot on his image. I've often been asked how I can remain civil with him, and I continue to say I still like Crawford. A lot, in fact. Here's why. He's a walking representation of the traditional Canadian mind-set. To focus on excoriating him as the single culprit ignores the larger issue. I thought back to when I visited him in Chicago to do a story on him shortly after he took over the Canucks. In a gym workout in downtown Chicago, I noted that Canucks center Dave Scatchard had a black eye and got caught laughing about it. Crawford looked at me and said, "My dad always told me you don't have to worry about the guys who look like that. You have to worry about the guys who don't."

This all happened at 8:41 of the third period. In the mess that ensued, Granato stood on the bench and yelled at Crawford. Moore was down on the ice for about ten minutes before he was taken off on a gurney. Because of the subsequent skirmishing, Avalanche enforcer Peter Worrell drew a game misconduct, and as he headed toward the tunnel to the dressing room, he paused and needed to be restrained from trying to get in the stands.

Another ridiculous view aired in the wake of the incident was that it was somehow Granato's fault for having Moore, the player in the eye of the storm, on the ice at that stage of the game in a blowout. What was Granato supposed to do, double-shift Sakic? Wouldn't keeping Moore on the bench have been considered cowardly, anyway?

After the game, with Moore off at a hospital and with no information regarding his condition available, the atmosphere turned somber. Crawford wasn't smirking any longer. In the Avalanche dressing room, the rhetoric was restrained. In a sport that prides itself on team togetherness, only defenseman Derek Morris—who until then was most notable for being the guy the Avalanche obtained for Chris Drury—had the nerve to take off the muzzle.

"We're not supposed to say," Morris said. But he went on to call it "the worst thing I've seen. . . . That was a premeditated act. We got a guy hurt because of that. It was disgusting. There's no other word for that. I haven't seen anything like that in my seven years of playing hockey."

Granato said, "It was a game where a team was up 5–0, and obviously something was said on their side to instigate, initiate the physical part of it. When we're up 5–0, there's no need for us to do anything, to get involved in something like that."

Granato was asked who he thought might have said "something."

"Something was said on their side to provoke that," he said. "I don't think you just go out and start fighting for the fun of it. . . . I'm going to stand up for my players." He said Crawford was "responsible for their players and their actions. I didn't like the body language. I didn't like the way he was standing there when the whole thing transpired."

After the game, Bertuzzi didn't speak to the media, but Crawford was subdued.

"First of all, our concerns are for Steve Moore, and we're hoping he's okay," Crawford said. He added, "Obviously, that's not an incident anybody likes in the game. It's very unfortunate. Todd feels terrible. He's very upset right now."

The reason the Canucks were upset, of course, is that everyone suddenly realized the potential consequences. I'm not saying there wasn't concern for Moore, who at that moment was in the hospital, and an acknowledgment that things had gotten out of hand, but that was secondary. The Canucks figured out that this wasn't going to go away. Another of the twists was that Crawford and former Avalanche winger Mike Keane, who on that night was playing for Vancouver, both had been so disdainful of the Red Wings waiting for a home game to target Claude Lemieux.

The Avalanche stayed overnight in Vancouver. The next morning, the team put out a release that Moore had suffered fractured neck vertebrae, a concussion, and cuts. The term "broken neck" also informally was used, and that raised the specter of possible paralysis. The NHL announced Bertuzzi was suspended indefinitely, pending a disciplinary hearing.

Also, the Avalanche announced that morning that Morris and the rights to prospect defenseman Keith Ballard had been traded to Phoenix for veteran center Chris Gratton, defenseman Ossi Vaananen, and a second-round draft choice. The Avalanche also acquired veteran goalie Tommy Salo, who had led the minor-league Denver Grizzlies to a championship in 1995, from Edmonton. With all that going on, Lacroix and Granato appeared at a news conference at a Vancouver hotel.

"It's the cheapest shot I have ever seen," Lacroix said of Bertuzzi's hit. "All those shots are bad and no good for our business."

Lacroix said he was able to see Moore in the dressing room during the third period.

"I came down to the medical room after the injury happened," Lacroix said. "I shook his hand, I looked at him, he looked at me. His eyes were clear, so in a way I felt he was recovering. How long he was out [cold], I can't tell you."

Granato said the incident cast a pall over a significant road win.

"You saw it after the incident," Granato said. "You could see it on our bench, in our faces, in the manner after the game. That's your warrior, that's your brother, that's the guy you're going to bat with every night. Unacceptable. Best way to say it is, it was unacceptable. It doesn't matter what the score was, what the time was, what the history of it was. There's no room for that in our game."

As a player with the Los Angeles Kings, Granato underwent brain surgery in February 1996 after suffering head injuries after being driven into the boards.

"As [Moore] was being wheeled off, I thought of the history that I had with the head injury," Granato said. "I thought more of his family, his parents. For his parents to go through something like that, that's the thing I thought of first."

After the news conference, Aaron Lopez and I spoke with several players outside the hotel. Nikolishin, the Russian center who first came to Moore's aid and tried to pull Bertuzzi off his teammate, said, "I saw Bertuzzi grab him from behind and I just jumped in right away, and that was it. I saw blood spill out and spread out. I don't even want to talk about it. It's tough to see."

Significantly, the Avalanche said Worrell wouldn't be able to talk with me until later that day in Edmonton. The Avalanche had decided to make an exception on the trip and invited Lopez and me to be in the traveling party for the day. Our bosses agreed to it. That meant that rather than take our ticketed commercial flights to Edmonton, where the Avalanche was playing on March 10, we went with the team to the Vancouver General Hospital to visit Moore and then joined the team on its chartered flight to Edmonton.

When the team visited Moore, all were conscious that Aaron and I were there and would write about the exchanges. I'm not saying the reactions weren't sincere, but there was a bit of a scripted feel to it, too. We waited in the hospital's fourteenth floor rehabilitation gym. Players leaned on workout equipment, talking softly, and watching the double-door entrance. Moore, sitting up in a raised bed, his neck in a long cervical brace, was pushed into the room. His teammates applauded. If they had sticks, they would have tapped them on the floor. There were some positive signs. He was conscious and coherent, had the use of his limbs, and managed to smile. Avalanche trainer Pat Karns gave a quick briefing on Moore's condition. Moore, he told his teammates, had cuts, a concussion, and two chip fractures in the C-3 and C-4 vertebrae in his neck.

"Looks worse than it is, though, right?" Moore asked.

In a voice not everyone in the room could hear, Moore briefly addressed his teammates. He told them again he was going to be all right. "I just have to wear this stylish brace for a while," he said.

Granato approached the bed. "On behalf of the boys," he said, "we just wanted to stop and let you know how much we think of you. We'll win some games while you're laid up for a while." Granato said Moore would be in everyone's prayers and that they knew his family was worried and supported him. "This part of your family," Granato added, "is going to win a game in Edmonton."

One by one, teammates approached Moore, spoke with him, smiled, and grasped his hand. Moore was wheeled out, and the Avalanche players filed out.

After the visit, Sakic said, "It's just nice to see him doing well, or as good as you can expect. To see him last night after that hit, it didn't look good. To see him today, he had good spirits."

Next, the team, plus Aaron Lopez and I, traveled to Edmonton. At the Hotel MacDonald, I patiently waited to speak to Worrell. The reason I had to wait was that Granato pulled him aside and had a long conversation with him. Standing close to the huge winger and looking up at him, Granato seemed to make several points. Worrell nodded and when I talked with him, said nothing beyond the benign. When I asked him point-blank if the fans or the Canucks had been directing racist comments at him, as I had heard from some folks within earshot, he said no.

I've always assumed that Granato told Worrell the situation already was stormy enough and that it would serve no useful purpose for him to add to the turmoil. I don't know that, but it's my guess.

The firestorm was international in scope. I even appeared on National Public Radio's *All Things Considered* to talk about it, and I also cranked out an ESPN.com column. As usually happens when the NHL is involved in a controversial incident, over the next few days I saw many prominent newspaper columnists trotted in front of cameras to discuss it. Most of them hadn't been to an NHL game in five years or couldn't have named five players on the team in their own market. They kept waving their arms and yelling. They certainly had the right to express their opinions, and one of the NHL's mistakes is pretending not to care when "outsiders" knock the sport, but it was laughable how ill-informed many of them were.

There was plenty of blame to go around, as Moore's legal team later recognized with lawsuits that sought at various times to include Brian Burke, Brad May, and Marc Crawford as defendants. The man we let off the hook was Markus Naslund. I'm not saying he is to blame, but he could have headed off trouble. He's a nice guy who comes from Ornskoldsvik, Sweden, the same hometown as Forsberg and several other NHL players. He was the Canucks' captain. For team-oriented reasons, he should have seen that the preoccupation with Moore was counterproductive. At any point, he could have stepped in and said, "Guys, I appreciate this, but enough's enough. Let's get on to the business at hand." That especially could have been the case after Moore fought Cooke and as it became apparent that there might be some ugliness in the third period. I've even wondered why Trevor Linden, the president of the players' union, wasn't more of a voice of reason. Crawford's actions were unconscionable, but as I've said, I think he's more a product of his background. To me, the highly educated and erudite Burke's rhetoric and attitudes were the most bewildering.

What about Bertuzzi? He has to be held primarily accountable for his own actions, because, let's face it, not even Brad May was thinking, "Hey, let's take a cheap shot from behind, break the guy's neck, end his career, *and* completely screw up this team." Because that's what it did to the Canucks. Yet as disdainful as I am of Bertuzzi, he was a dupe to some extent, caught in the crosscurrents of events and rhetoric that other, more intelligent men in positions of power and influence could have influenced.

The Avalanche response was one of the major blots on the team's tenure in Denver. Steve Moore wasn't popular among his teammates primarily because he was quiet and he was a Harvard boy.* (I'm not saying he was unpopular, either.) The Avalanche initially showed considerable concern and helped both Moore and his family. But beyond that, especially after Moore showed signs of taking legal action, it was as if Moore never played for the team. When the Avalanche signed May for the post-lockout season, 2005–06, it was the single most stupid public relations move the franchise made. May was a major league schmoozer with the media and even folks in the league, and to me the issue wasn't him personally as much as the perceptions and what the signing represented. Plus, in the Colorado dressing room, it was as if they took down Moore's nameplate and he ceased to exist. Part of that was player turnover, but it was more than that. When Sakic in his final season told me that he had taken vacations with May and Bertuzzi and that Bertuzzi actually was a "nice guy" who had paid for his mistake, I admit I was taken aback. Sakic said it so casually, in fact, that he didn't seem to have a clue that anyone would be offended. I stifled the urge to ask, "Are you sure you want to say that?" Instead, I just wrote the story, and it indeed offended a lot of Avalanche fans, among others. Yes, Moore was suing Bertuzzi and the Canucks, and it doesn't take an Einstein intellect to figure out that the league wouldn't have been thrilled if the Avalanche held a Steve Moore Night or otherwise honored him. The Avalanche had neither guts nor class when they didn't just go ahead and do it, the league be damned.

The short-term reaction highlighted some of the contradictions about the NHL and its fans. Much of it was the knee-jerk and brainless reaction of the loud fringe, arguing variously that: (A) Moore had it coming, and he should have dropped the gloves and fought every Canuck that night, or (B) Bertuzzi got a bit carried away, but do you want guys playing in skirts? Of course, any attempt to argue rationally with that segment of fans was futile, because it responds to any disagreement with the intellectual equivalent of sticking out tongues: "aw, you don't know the game!" Some of the criticism and even grandstanding about this incident, as I've admitted, absolutely came from folks who didn't know the color of the blue line. Yet that also ignored the fact that by far the most intelligent discourse and analysis about what this meant about the fabric of the sport came in Canada, including from

---

* Later, the Avalanche would have former Dartmouth players David Jones and TJ Galiardi on their roster, but neither graduated from the Ivy League school.

some former NHL stars. *Macleans*, the Canadian news weekly, did a scathing story on the incident, showing Bertuzzi holding Moore's jersey and winding up for the sucker punch *on the cover*.

As time went on, the mindless wing usually resorted to saying, "Let it go!" We were supposed to pretend that because the NHL reinstated Bertuzzi after a seventeen-month suspension that ran through the lockout season and because Bertuzzi received only probation and a slap on the wrist from legal authorities, his assault on Moore should be like a driving violation and wiped off his record.

This was about a sport unwilling to hold itself up to ruthless self-examination. The NHL didn't forget the lessons learned; it never learned them at all. The Avalanche's indifference was the most curious, of course, but it was part of a league-wide collective shrugging of shoulders. Even Hockey Canada, which aired wonderful television ads promoting respect in its sport from the stands to the rink itself, sent mixed messages by inviting Bertuzzi to its 2006 Olympic orientation camp after the NHL reinstated him and then including him on the team that didn't win a medal at Turin. The desire to move on seemed to have more to do with amnesia and rationalization than forgiveness and a feeling that Bertuzzi had been penalized enough.

In August 2005, I visited Moore in Thornhill. I talked with him on the phone for several weeks as he visited the Cleveland Clinic periodically for testing but didn't write anything as we laid the groundwork for a visit. When I got to Thornhill, he wouldn't discuss the specific incident. His attorney, Tim Danson, told him not to. We did have long talks and also visited the local rink where he had played as a youngster. At the time, he still, officially at least, was hoping to get clearance from doctors to play.

"The concussion is more the issue, for sure," he told me. "Most of the time I'm positive that I'm going to get better. I've come a long way and I'm gaining. Things pop in my head every once in a while that shouldn't, but to be honest, I don't think like that very often."

I was convinced that even if he was pronounced physically able to play, the chances of the Avalanche or another NHL team signing him were slim. He would have been marked as physically suspect, and he had violated the "code" with his lawsuit.

"I think anybody who understands the situation that I was in, and that I am in, would probably do the same thing," Moore said. "I'd like to think that part of putting this whole ugly incident behind me is that I would hope to be back with the Avalanche. And I hope that they realize I've done everything I can to make this not more of a spectacle. I've been trying to focus on getting better, and I hope that they're aware of that."

Eventually, Moore gave up on attempting to return to the game. His lawsuit against Bertuzzi and the Canucks was filed in Ontario. In late 2009, Danson told me that all the pretrial maneuvering finally was winding down and that he was hoping the lawsuit ended up assigned a court date of late 2010. (And we thought *our* court system was slow.) By then, Bertuzzi's camp successfully maneuvered to have Crawford added as a defendant. All along, I was ambivalent about the lawsuit. Part of me believes there's an implied consent involved in playing professional sports, and you're agreeing you'll leave issues up to the leagues involved. Part of me wants the courts to stay out of sports, period. But this ended a career. I've come around to the appropriateness of the lawsuit. It wasn't so roundly criticized when Dennis Polonich sued Wilf Paiement, as I recall, and Polonich even came back and played several more seasons in the NHL.

The Avalanche, meanwhile, continued to pretend Moore had been deleted from the team's annals.

———◆———

The franchise's slide wasn't immediately after the lockout ended. Both because of bad luck tied to the expiration of contracts and also because of insufficient foresight, the Avalanche essentially *had* to let Peter Forsberg and Adam Foote leave. Forsberg and Foote eventually made it back, but it wasn't the same. Colorado had 95 points in each of the next three seasons under Joel Quenneville, who returned to the franchise he had served as Crawford's assistant before getting the job at St. Louis. Granato went back to his former role as assistant coach. Twice, 95 points were good enough to make the playoffs, once it wasn't. The acquisition of Jose Theodore had mixed results; for much of his time at Colorado, he was stealing money. But in his contract year, he was spectacular down the stretch of the 2007–08 season and probably had the best single playoff series of an Avalanche goalie ever in the first round against Minnesota. Everything fell apart for the overmatched Avs in the Western Conference semifinals against Detroit, including when the team claimed Theodore came down with the flu. He ended up signing with Washington in a pox-on-both-houses development. Theodore should have admitted that although the Avalanche had paid him $11.5 million in his two full seasons with the team, he had delivered a half season of quality work. Thus, he should have been willing to grant the Avalanche more of a "hometown" discount in the negotiations. But the Avalanche were equally intransigent on the other side of the table. There was middle ground there, but neither side would budge.

With Quenneville giving off vibes that he didn't believe in the organization's young talent nearly as much as General Manager Francois Giguere and others, he was fired and Granato was re-elevated from assistant coach back to head coach. After the Avalanche finished last in the conference, Lacroix, who had had severe complications following knee replacement surgery, fired his successor as general manager, Giguere. Then after failing to coax Patrick Roy into taking over as general manager, coach, or both, Lacroix fired Granato, who would have had no credibility in the wake of the negotiations with Roy. I felt bad for Granato, but he had two years left on his contract. He would eventually go to Pittsburgh as an assistant coach. Lacroix promoted the affable Greg Sherman, like Giguere another former accountant who would amount to a chief executive officer, from assistant general manager to general manager, and promoted Joe Sacco from head coach at Lake Erie to the Avalanche. Also, after taking center Matt Duchene with the third overall pick of the 2009 draft, after unloading their second best player (Ryan Smyth) to Los Angeles to clear payroll, and after Sakic's retirement, what almost everyone believed would be a difficult rebuilding job was on. With the teenage Duchene immediately becoming a star, the Avalanche's unlikely surge to a playoff berth in the 2009–10 season was one of the more shocking developments in Colorado sports in many years.

It was almost as if Colorado was positioned for a return to the Glory Years.

PART EIGHT

BOXING

I can't help it. Boxing has me hooked. I don't rationalize that by making boxing into something it isn't, either. So I won't offer any attempt at "sweet science" rationalization.

It's a dirty, grubby, often crooked sport—and that's *before* you get to the seamy underbelly. I have very foggy memories of watching the Gillette-sponsored *Friday Night Fights* as a youngster, before NBC dropped the long-running series in 1960. Two years later, I was watching television the night when Emile Griffith dealt a fatal beating to Bennie "Kid" Paret, who died ten days later. I've covered it at several Olympics and was in the arena when Roy Jones Jr. was robbed of a decision in Seoul and Evander Holyfield was victimized by a bizarre disqualification in Los Angeles. On the professional level, I've covered everything from the virtual club fights at Rodolfo "Corky" Gonzales's *Escuela Tlatelolco* in central Denver in the 1970s to many championship and high-profile bouts in Las Vegas.

TYSON VS. TUCKER

Saturday, Aug. 1, 1987

Las Vegas Hilton

N? 322

Good for Admission to Center

RINGSIDE

TERRY FREI   5 7 7
PORTLAND OREGONIAN

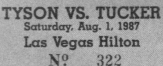

Press
Ringside

2662

TERRY FREI
PORTLAND OREGONIAN

SEC III
ROW 3
SEAT 20
A WRITER

CAESARS PALACE

THE WAR.
Leonard · Hearns II
World Super Middleweight Championship
June 12, 1989

THE SUPER FIGHT.

World Middleweight Championship

HAGLER vs. LEONARD

Presented by Top Rank, Inc. and Caesars Palace
April 6, 1987

TERRY FREI
PORTLAND OREGONIAN

2117

SEC   I
ROW   2
00/00/00   SEAT   23
A WRITER

CAESARS PALACE
LAS VEGAS

CAESARS PALACE
Presented in association with Victory Promotions, Inc.

LEONARD. LALONDE. NOV. 7, 1988.

2096

TERRY FREI
PORTLAND OREGONIAN

SEC   1
ROW   3
SEAT 20
A WRITER

MUHAMMAD ALI AND THE HEAVYWEIGHTS

UNFORTUNATELY, I NEVER GOT TO COVER Muhammad Ali in his prime. I did in his twilight, though. I had to reconcile what I saw with the memories of the late 1960s, when I saw him dominate the division, put on shows, talk up a storm, and ultimately refuse induction into the U.S. Army. Later, especially after reading Dave Kindred's excellent dual portrait of Ali and Howard Cosell, *Sound and Fury*, I came to understand that Ali was more compliant in following orders from his Islam cabal than principled in refusing induction. But in 1979, when Ali signed to fight an eight-round exhibition in mid-July against Broncos defensive end Lyle Alzado at Mile High Stadium, I still was capable of awe.

Ali hadn't fought since regaining the heavyweight title from Leon Spinks in August 1978, and he was claiming to be retired. Alzado—angling for a new contract with the Broncos and pretending that a pro boxing career was a viable option—assumed that the chance to see the "The Greatest" in person against a Broncos star who had fought in the Golden Gloves would be a box office hit. He mortgaged his own house betting on that. He was wrong. The fight turned out to be a financial disaster, but it went on. At times I seemed to be the only person in the world who thought this, especially among the media, but as long as it wasn't taken too seriously and was accepted for what it was (an exhibition), it was an interesting afternoon at the stadium.

Ali breezed through town a couple of times trying to promote ticket sales. Because I nominally was the *Post*'s boxing writer, I got to spend some time with him. One of the more fascinating elevator rides I've ever had was the one from the upper level of the International Athletic Club downtown, after the weigh-in, down to the street level. Behind the closed doors, Ali was soft-spoken, making small talk. When the doors opened and a crowd waited in the lobby, he immediately was "on." Outside the ring, his act had slipped a bit since his prime, but he still was animated.

The news conference at the Marriott Hotel two weeks before the fight was chaos. Chairs were arranged in neat rows and Ali was going to speak to us from a podium. As a result of the various hangers-on ignoring the seating arrangement and crowding the podium, few sat in the chairs and he was virtually surrounded as he went through his spiel.

He told Alzado: "Let me tell you something about this game. We're friends now, we smile and we laugh. But when the bell rings, we rumble. You've got some nerve. You're a crazy white boy . . . and I'm a crazy nigger."

He took off his coat and demonstrated the "Ali Shuffle" onstage. He was puffy and overweight—a trend that wouldn't be reversed—but his hands still were fast in pantomime. "I'm not in shape to fight no Joe Frazier or Foreman," he said. "But I'm in shape for a football player."

He recited a long poem about sending Alzado into orbit, and nobody seemed to mind that he had used most of those lines before. He called himself "the greatest thing in the history of the world," and promised us he would stick to his announced decision to retire—an announcement that for the moment seemed to be at least mildly credible because he had given up the World Boxing Association's version of the heavyweight title.* Since beating Spinks, Ali had fought only two five-round exhibitions in Denmark.

He went through the obligatory pushing and shoving match with Alzado while the cameras rolled and clicked. "I've never heard of you before," he told Alzado. "After this fight, you're going to be known all over the world. I'm going to give you a worldwide whipping."

For one live segment on a noon television news show, he insulted Alzado again and then after they were off the air asked, "Did we sell some tickets?"

By the day before the fight card, when it was apparent that it was going to all but ruin Alzado financially, maybe Ali realized the way to sell the fight was to emphasize what should have been emphasized from the start. Any pretensions that this was a real test for either Ali or Alzado were ridiculous, and it should have been treated as a lark, a fun way to see them both in the ring. The Alzado camp, of course, had been trying to convince everyone it was a way for Alzado to prove he could make a living at boxing—if it came to that.

"Let me tell you something," Ali told us the day before the fight when he got to the International Athletic Club. "After all I've done—I destroyed

---

* It soon came out that promoter Bob Arum paid him $300,000 to renounce the title early, before the WBA declared it vacant due to Ali's inactivity, so Arum could bill the John Tate–Gerrie Coetzee fight as a championship bout.

Frazier; I destroyed George Foreman; I came back and danced fifteen rounds on Spinks—and then you believe that he has a chance? It's impossible, after all I've done, after the greatest I've been, that I'm going to go up against a football player and you're going to build it up like it's a real fight. I'm not going to add to that by coming out there and taking a weigh-in like I'm serious."

Finally, though, he consented to go through the motions of stepping on the scale, and his weight was announced as 235 pounds, 13 pounds more than he weighed for the latest Spinks fight. "I'm going to make one prediction," he said. "They called me up and they said, 'We want you to fight this guy.' I said, 'Are you serious?' They wanted three rounds. I said no, the guy might be in shape to go three. I might forfeit two rounds, might beat him the last round. He might land a punch, might get lucky. I'm gonna suggest we go eight rounds. Because eight three-minute rounds are enough to tire out Superman. So I want eight rounds in case he knocks me down, or anything can happen. This way, I've got a chance to come back. I'm telling you all this: if this goes five rounds at the pace I'm going to put him under, I'm crazy. If he's not puking and vomiting, and not stumbling around after round four, I'll be surprised. Boxing is a tiresome sport. You can't just train for it and go three rounds with a man like me. I'll be dancing and sticking, and popping and hooking.

"I can't play football. No matter how great I am at boxing, I can't do nothing but box. He's a football player, and I'm telling y'all that this is going to be a terrible annihilation. I'm gonna have to lighten up on this man. I'm gonna have to go easy, because I feel sorry for him. He's gonna be bleeding, puking, hollering, [choking]. I'm telling you: he's going to get a whuppin', and you all will get a lesson."

The exhibition itself? I've told a lot of people in the years since that it all depended on expectations. They at least carried off an appearance of seriousness, maybe even too much so, and if the fight was scored, Alzado, mostly punching off the ropes, might have won one round and one might have been even. Ali never smiled. Not while trying to put some "fun" in the exhibition, and not while exulting over a flurry, as he so often had done in the past. Attendance was announced as more than twenty thousand but *Post* columnist Steve Cameron—who panned the fight—and I guessed that it was actually around fifteen thousand. NBC bought the television rights late, so that mitigated some of the damage. Ali was subdued afterward and played along with the leverage angle for Alzado, saying he was "good enough, with some conditioning, to turn pro. He's got the potential to be a great fighter." He said Alzado's strengths "are his defense and his sense of judgment. He's not easy to hit, and you can't jab him." Cameron, my close friend, wrote that watching Ali that afternoon "was seeing a memory, like visiting a museum."

I asked him what was wrong with museums.

———◆———

On the Ali–Alzado undercard, Leroy Jones, one of the most unheralded undefeated heavyweights of all time, waltzed through a decision victory over a journeyman named James Beattie. There were several problems with Jones's act: he naturally was a butterball and couldn't get his weight down. Technically, he was an excellent fighter who frustrated opponents and piled up points with jabs and a workmanlike style. But he had no power and his fights were boring. He came to Denver to work with trainer Bobby Lewis, and because of a combination of careful opponent selection and his strange set of skills, he *was* undefeated, which landed him a World Boxing Council heavyweight title fight at Caesars Palace against Larry Holmes on March 31, 1980, three days after the Colorado Rockies played what turned out to be their final home game under Don Cherry. The *Post* sent me to promoter Don King's production, and I now can look back and laugh at my naivete. The fight probably drew as little media coverage as any bona fide heavyweight title fight in twenty-five years. Caesars was so glad to get someone from a major paper that my room—I'm guessing I paid something like $39—was one that I later came to realize was reserved for "whales," or high-stakes gamblers. For subsequent, more hyped fights, I discovered that the media not only didn't get prime rooms at the major hotels, but we were shipped off the Strip altogether to less glamorous hotels. But I was thinking: *Wow, what a great sport to cover!*

The fight was inside, in the Pavilion behind Caesars. It probably was the least exciting of the major championship fights I covered over the years, but I came away from the experience starting to feel what I became certain of as time passed. There's not a more exciting atmosphere in sports than one at a title fight, especially in Las Vegas. Toss out every cliché you can think of. Electricity. Excitement. Anticipation. The introductions of the celebrities. (*I didn't know Sylvester Stallone was that short!*) The ebb and flow of a fight itself. The involuntary roars when punches land. Even as titles became fragmented and true champions harder to find, the title fights remained glamorous.

It's impossible to adequately explain in words. You just gotta be there.

Referee Richard Green stopped the Jones–Holmes fight with four seconds left in the eighth round. Holmes didn't have any trouble solving Jones's style, and it was a pummeling. For all his defensive skills in the past against lesser fighters, Jones couldn't keep Holmes from repeatedly scoring with his left jab, softening him up for what became a final-round onslaught that left him helpless. When I went into Jones's dressing room—I'm pretty sure I was the only reporter who cared enough to go talk with him, and I don't believe he even went to a formal news conference—he was putting on a pair of dark glasses. "Things are a little blurry, but I can see," he said. "You guys might have to lead me around a little bit, though." I knew Jones fairly well by then, and he quickly opened up to me.

"I had bronchitis and the flu and missed a lot of training," he said. "I tried to get out of the fight for now. But Don King came to Denver and let me know the position he was in and said how he had stuck his neck out for me to get me this shot and that television contracts were signed. He stuck his neck out for me and I just returned the favor. He put it out there for me. Yeah, we put our neck on the line. And nobody got the worse of it, except the people you see in this room. We're the ones who got the short end of the stick."

Of Holmes, Jones said, "Larry's a good fighter. But he's also a dirty fighter. He was thumbing me when he threw the jab. Then he'd lace me when he was pushing me off."

King was in a great mood after the fight, because the card had been one of dueling heavyweight championships that night. In Knoxville, on rival promoter Bob Arum's card, challenger Mike Weaver upset World Boxing Association champion John Tate, and Holmes was viewed even more as the consensus people's champion. King appeared with Holmes at a news conference, and when he left the arena building behind Caesars and started walking back, I followed him and repeatedly asked if Jones indeed had tried to get out of the fight. "I don't remember now," King said. "I'm not going to knock Leroy. My job is to build up my fighters, not tear them down. I'm not a Bob Arum, the type that casts aspersions on fighters. I think Leroy is a great challenger. If he gets himself into shape, I'll use him again."

As we walked, I asked the same question about four times. King patted me on the shoulder at one point and said, "You're a persistent young man!" When I finally tried asking him why he had come to Denver to see Jones if there hadn't been a problem, he said, "I went to Denver to ride back to Las Vegas with him. I like to make them feel like champs, like first-class fighters."

As it turned out, Jones suffered a detached retina that night. He had only one more fight that made the record books, a 1982 second-round technical knockout victory over Jeff Shelburg in Gary, Indiana. He finished his career with only one loss—to a great heavyweight champion. Yet as near as I can tell, he not only didn't gain fame and fortune from boxing, but nobody knows where he is thirty years later.

———————

Six months after that victory over Jones, Holmes fought again—against Muhammad Ali, who indeed came out of retirement. Holmes officially was credited with an eleventh-round technical knockout when Ali was slumped on his stool and beaten after the tenth round. *That* was sad, especially since Holmes was Ali's former sparring partner and a man who respected the former champion, yet Holmes so decisively beat Ali that it bordered on pathetic. But, still, when Ali came through Denver again in July 1981, he was defiant, saying he had at least one more great fight left in him. Hadn't we counted him out before? I again spent time with him when he came to the Regency Hotel to plug an upcoming charity dinner. I met his entourage in a suite, spoke with Ali, and then went with him to the meeting room for a full-fledged news conference. He used the occasion to deliver a filibuster about why he should be allowed to fight again. He knew it might be an uphill fight to get a license from a boxing commission, any boxing commission.

"I don't like the boxing commissioners," he said that day. "They retired me. Joe Frazier got knocked out. Nobody retired him. George Foreman got knocked out. Nobody retired him. Ken Norton's always climbing into the ring. Nobody retired him. I've never been knocked out. Even at my worst, against Holmes, I wasn't hurt. And they're going to tell me, 'You had a bad night, we're going to retire you.' So I'm going to fight for spite. If the lords of boxing won't let me fight in this country, since the world is my home and they've put curtains over this room, I'll just go into another room. Jamaica. Switzerland. Australia. Sweden. Costa Rica."

He said he was going to go back into training, aiming to fight Holmes again and prove everyone wrong.

"I never lose twice to a fighter," he said. "Joe Frazier couldn't beat me twice. Ken Norton couldn't beat me twice. Spinks couldn't beat me twice. They say I'm getting too old. I saw an old lady in Russia, 125 years old. A man ran across Canada, one thousand miles, on one leg.* And they're going to tell me I can't fight. People give up too easy. People on welfare can go to work if they want. People are stealing, into crime because they're too lazy to get a job. People are dropping out of school because the work is too tough. I'm going to be an example to all those who are catching hell. They told me I can't do it. I love challenges. They told me I can't do it, but I'm gonna come back, get my

———————

* Cancer victim Terry Fox.

license, get in shape. And I promise you: I will come back dancing and I will straighten out this whole thing."

At the end of his rant, though, he became a bit more reflective. "If I can't do it, I'll be the first to say I can't do it," he said. "If I can, I shall return."

Five months after that Denver appearance, he got back in the ring for one more fight. Indeed, it had to be in the Bahamas, and he lost a lopsided ten-round decision to Trevor Berbick. He couldn't do it.

The next time I saw him in person was in Atlanta, where with quivering hands, he lit the Olympic flame to officially open the 1996 Summer Games.

———•———

By June 1982, two years after his victory over Jones and four years after he took the WBC title from Ken Norton, Larry Holmes should have had little left to prove. At age thirty-two, he was an active champion with eleven successful defenses. But the public still held him at arm's length. He was no showman, no beloved champion. There were still some doubts about his ability, raised by what was perceived to be a dearth of quality fighters in the heavyweight division and perhaps even encouraged by his persecution complex. He reacted to any slight, real or imagined, with the tiresome lament about "respect," yet it also served as part of his motivation. As his twelfth title defense approached, his biggest money fight to date, he was resentful of the attention the undefeated challenger—"Irish" Gerry Cooney—had received, as well as the fact that Cooney was in line to make as much as the champion for the fight. Depending on the gate and closed circuit receipts, that might be as much as $10 million for each. Cooney had fought only three times in two years, defeating a parade of over-the-hill fighters including Jimmy Young (fourth round), Ron Lyle (first), and Norton (first). He was the next "Great White Hope," an issue not so much of racism as identification. Cooney was twenty-five, from a working-class family on Long Island, and in some ways he reminded me of Alzado. I got to Las Vegas in time for the weigh-in the day before the fight and heard a clearly resentful Holmes say, "I feel sorry for a lot of the people who came all the way from New York, because they surely will be disappointed. I promise that I will knock Gerry Cooney out, and I stand by my prediction of seven rounds. And if he acts foolish, it won't go four rounds."

With the temporary stadium packed, the fight didn't seem all that much different than the beating Holmes had given Jones. Cooney went down for the first time in the second round and apparently proved that he had the courage to take a punch—or two hundred. I say "apparently" because it's entirely possible Holmes carried Cooney for a while to deal out more punishment. I got my first taste of the curious Nevada judging, because when Cooney's trainer, Victor Valle, stepped through the ropes and stopped the fight with eight seconds left in the thirteenth round, Cooney would have been ahead on two of the three judges' scorecards if referee Mills Lane hadn't deducted three points from Cooney for low blows. I was writing when the photocopies of the scorecards were passed out in the pressroom and didn't believe what I saw. Holmes punished Cooney from beginning to end.

"Once again, I've done it again," Holmes told us. "It seems like every time I go to the stage, I have to continually prove myself. I don't have to prove it to you or the world. I have to prove it to myself, my family. I don't fight for blacks, whites, Spanish. I fight for the people. I still say, I still believe in what I do, what I say. I believe we're all God's children. When I see Gerry Cooney, I see a heavyweight boxer trying to take my head off, and I was trying to protect myself. I'm very sorry I can't be what you expect. I'm very sorry I can't be a Muhammad Ali, a Joe Louis, even a Leon Spinks. I wasn't born to be those people. I was born to be myself, Larry Holmes."

The next day, appearing at a joint news conference with Cooney, Holmes was mostly civil and complimentary to Cooney. But then he boiled over again, referring to the fact that the challenger—and not the champion—had been on the covers of many major magazines the week before the fight. "You can take my money, my cars away from me, but you cannot take my pride," Holmes said. "You can take *Time* magazine and shove it, and *Sports Illustrated* and shove it, and all the writers and all the criticism and shove it. I have proved again that I am the heavyweight champion."

Holmes diminished his own legacy with a ridiculously prolonged career. Absolutely, that followed the sport's tradition, but what made this puzzling was that Holmes not only made a lot of money, he was a savvy businessman who seemed to always be positioning himself for a comfortable retirement. He didn't need to fight so much as he couldn't stop fighting. The losses mounted after his pair of defeats to Michael Spinks. He also lost to Mike Tyson. Evander Holyfield. Oliver McCall. Even somebody named Brian Nielsen.

But in the two Holmes fights I saw, when he was thirty and thirty-two, he was one of the best ever.

———◆———

I also covered two Tyson title fights in Las Vegas—against Tony Tucker in August 1987, when Tyson's victory unified all three titles, and Englishman Frank Bruno in February 1989. For a while, at least when he fought Tucker, who held the IBF title, I bought into the Hollywood angle for Tyson—juvenile delinquent taken under Cus D'Amato's wing, shown the error of his ways, rehabilitated, channeled into what passed for a constructive use of his violent tendencies. There has been a lot of revisionist history written since his fall, but the fact was, there was a time when he seemed a refreshing story of redemption, and he actually was fun to talk with, on a one-on-one basis, as I did a couple of times when he simply plopped down at a table in a hotel meeting room and answered questions for the writers in town before the fights.

In the Tucker fight, he went against a good fighter who probably was a better athlete than most other heavyweights of recent history. But a great boxer, Tucker wasn't. At the time, Michael Spinks was persona non grata to Don King because he had pulled out of the heavyweight tournament to unify the titles for a fight with the warhorse Gerry Cooney. King told us it was treachery, pure and simple, so Spinks could "make megabucks in a racist fight." (When King's champion, Holmes, made megabucks fighting Cooney, presumably it wasn't a "racist fight.") The IBF took away Spinks's title for pulling out of the unification tournament and bestowed it on the winner of the Buster Douglas–Tony Tucker fight, which turned out to be Tucker.

"I'm beating, in order, the best fighters in the world," Tyson told us that week. "Whatever criticisms people have in their minds doesn't matter." A key issue was whether his much-publicized relationship with Robin Givens, then in its early stages, and the other sideshows would distract him. "Cus told me everything that would happen and how it would happen," he said of his late legal guardian and trainer, D'Amato. "You can't let it get the better of you or it will drive you crazy."

Tucker frustrated Tyson, going the full twelve rounds, but the outcome never was in doubt, not even with the unpredictable and unreliable Nevada judges involved in rendering a decision. Tyson reduced a decent heavyweight to a man hoping to hear the final bell on his feet. "When you're in there with a good fighter, and they're holding you to survive, there's nothing you can do," Tyson told us, shrugging. "If they have their mind set that they're going to survive, you're not going to knock them out."

By the time Tyson fought Bruno, Givens was his ex-wife in the wake of a celebrated breakup. He was coming off a broken hand suffered in his on-the-street bout with Mitch Green. He had fired manager Bill Cayton and trainer Kevin Cooney, who filed a $10 million breach of contract suit against Tyson. All of this made it clear that he still had demons lurking. Yes, he lost at love, so much so that *National Lampoon* ran a cartoon the month of the Bruno fight showing Givens kneeling on Tyson while his former mother-in-law counted, "One million, two million, three million . . ."

"People say, 'Poor guy,'" Tyson told us that week. "That insults me. I despise sympathy. So I screwed up. I made some mistakes. 'Poor guy!' Like I'm some victim. There's nothing poor about me."

At the Bruno fight, I sat next to the reporter from the *London Mirror* on press row. He said the only way his paper would get a bulletin in the Sunday edition would be in the event of a first-round knockout. When Bruno went down only fourteen seconds into the fight, the writer seemed assured of making his deadline, but also of losing his wager on Bruno making it through four rounds. That's what's known in the business as "mixed emotions." Bruno ended up lasting until 2:55 into the fifth round, mainly because he got down and dirty, holding on at every opportunity.

That night, in fact, I wrote, "Barring the premature ruination of Mike Tyson by forces outside the ring—such as wine, women, and the song and dance of Don King—if there is a man alive who will beat Tyson, he is not yet a man. He is maybe eleven years old."

Tyson lost his titles fifty weeks later, suffering the monumental upset knockout at the hands of Buster Douglas in Tokyo. He won back two of the three, including the WBC title he reclaimed with a second victory over Bruno in 1996, before his consecutive losses to Evander Holyfield and his slide into sideshow caricature.

I'm convinced I was right, and the retroactive belittling of his in-the-ring talent is off target.

Forces outside the ring beat him.

LEONARD VS. HEARNS VS. HAGLER

I N HIS PRIME, SUGAR RAY LEONARD was the best fighter I covered.

In June 1981, five years after he won Olympic gold at Montreal, he was in training for a fight with World Boxing Association middleweight champion Ayub Kalule when promoters offered a handful of major newspapers in the West opportunities for private interviews with Leonard if they sent reporters to Phoenix, where Leonard was training. He was a year removed from his pair of fights with Roberto Duran—the first a decision loss, the second the infamous "*No mas, no mas*" concession from Duran. The idea of the interviews wasn't only to promote the Kalule fight, but to start building interest in another fight he already had taken—against Thomas Hearns that fall in Las Vegas.

Leonard joined me on the mezzanine level of the Hyatt Regency in Phoenix. A small entourage stood behind and around him, but it wasn't bothersome. The only problem was that word got around that he was there, and a small gallery gathered. The inevitable backlash was starting to set in, encouraged by those in the sport who believed his public image was a sham or by those who were jealous that he was on a commercial roughly every twelve minutes in prime time. He had the smile. The familiar baby face. The soft-spoken sincerity. The charisma. I asked him about the difficulty of maintaining that image for such folks as those gawking at him.

"I think, fortunately, when I go to bed each night, everything's pretty settled, and I feel pretty good when I get up in the morning," he told me. "I've been very fortunate to maintain my composure for such a long period of time, dealing with the press, public, and people in general. But it's okay as long as you are yourself. See, I'm accepted for what I am. So it's not difficult. They say, 'Sugar Ray, maintain that image.' But that image is me."

This was easy to forget later, but in the aftermath of his gold medal performance at Montreal, when some questioned whether he was gritty enough to be able—or want—to make the transition from the relatively soft amateur version of the sport to the professional level. He had even promised his mother he wouldn't become a pro fighter. Some hardened boxing traditionalists argued that Leonard should just go into acting because their sport wasn't some pretty-boy pastime. But among other lures, there was the fact that boxing was guaranteed money for the young man from Palmer Park, Maryland. His family was poor. His girlfriend, Juanita, whom he later married, had given birth to their son, Ray Jr., and there was a fuss when county officials issued a petition of paternity after she applied for welfare. So Leonard told his mother, sorry, he didn't have much choice. By the time I talked with him, ten-figure purses and the endorsements had him set for life—or so it seemed—and he was fighting on for more money, but also because he was enjoying the spotlight.

"After Duran number one, I said I wanted to retire," he told me. "I think anybody who has someone beat on your head like Duran did to me in Montreal, that would make you want to retire. But after coming back and regaining my title, I saw something I really wanted to do, and that was capturing three titles. I can pretty much envision 1984 as the year I leave the ring as an active fighter. Every time I go into training, the question comes up, 'How much longer do I want to take this?' But I realize now that boxing is near its highest peak as far as being a commodity or being marketable. I think boxing has taken a whole new step into the entertainment field. You can look at the endorsements, the commitments to the personal appearances, the specials, that sort of thing. It all means boxing has opened a lot of doors for me."

With the fight with Hearns on the horizon, the debates already had begun. Especially those who didn't like Leonard's "cute" style and preferred Hearns's power and straightforward malice were saying that Leonard again, as in Leonard–Duran I, would be exposed as overrated. Some of that buzz was artificially generated to begin selling the fight, but a lot of it was genuine.

"I never will be accepted, maybe, as far as saying I have met *the* supreme fighter," Leonard said. "Duran was the supreme fighter, and now that I've done away with him, now it's Tommy Hearns who's the invincible, supreme fighter."

In September 1981, I covered the much-anticipated Leonard–Hearns fight. I also had company from the *Denver Post*, since the paper hired Woody Paige away from the rival *Rocky Mountain News* and sent him to the fight with me.

Whoever planned and coached the fighters for the media breakfast two days before the fight did a great job of ensuring that it accentuated the story line of the slick Leonard versus the menacing Hearns. Leonard arrived first, completely relaxed, wearing a sweat suit and a captain's hat that made him look as if he could work one of the showrooms with Toni Tennille. Hearns, wearing a suit and tie, arrived after Leonard had left, and the first question he was asked was why he had been late. "Because I wanted to be late," he said, triggering much laughter. At their final public workout sessions that day, Hearns seemed to go out of his way to prove he was loose, too. Leonard jumped rope to "Sweet Georgia Brown" and addressed the crowd on the public-address system himself. Later, Hearns worked out, then called Magic Johnson into the ring, along with a television broadcaster, an overweight fan from Detroit, and his own brother. Hearns directed all of them in calisthenics and boxing agility drills and even "sparred" with a young boy for a round. It was funny, and Hearns was almost Leonardesque.

"I'm not proving anything," Hearns said later. "Basically, I just enjoy working with kids. As a child, I didn't get all the attention I wanted." He also said that Leonard's "psych" job hadn't worked. "Ray has tried everything he possibly can do to put me down," Hearns said. "He's said I don't have the knowledge for boxing. He's done all he can, but he sees it's not working. He's a very nervous man right now."

Leonard said of his strategy, "The main thing I'm going to do is jump on Thomas Hearns, not give him a stationary target, but be there. I just want to make him think, and when Thomas Hearns starts to think, he's in trouble."

Yes, it was all about frustrating Hearns, staying away from him, but scoring points. That's the way the fight turned out, and it was a blueprint Leonard also used in other big fights. The amazing thing about this was that we later found out that the judges weren't impressed.

In the ring in Caesars's temporary stadium between the Pavilion and the hotel that night, Leonard couldn't have known that all three judges had him trailing Hearns after thirteen rounds and by margins that probably were insurmountable if the fight went the fifteen-round distance. Instinct saved Leonard. There was the boxing instinct that not only enabled him to throw punches in staccato combinations, but also let him know that the judges couldn't be trusted to get it right. After driving Hearns through the ropes twice in the thirteenth round—only the second was ruled a knockdown, and referee Dave Pearl was motioning the fighters back together just as the bell rang—Leonard finally finished up the job in the fourteenth when Pearl stopped the fight with Hearns again helpless along the ropes.

"I didn't ever feel that Hearns had an edge," Leonard said after the fight. "But I felt the fight was getting too close for comfort, and I had to put him out."

The three judges had Hearns leading after thirteen rounds—124–122, 125–121, and 125–122. He had done a lot of damage, especially in the early rounds, and Leonard had a puffy eye that was starting to close. Hearns started to move around more himself in the middle rounds, and Leonard seemed willing to let him. "I had to take a breather," Leonard said. "The heat, the lights were factors. But my conditioning, my stamina paid off."

Barely. If it had gone the distance, Leonard could have won with a pair of 10–8 rounds in the fourteenth and fifteenth rounds and earned a draw with a 10–9 and a 10–8. Otherwise, he would have lost, although I was among the majority at ringside who assumed he was leading on the scorecards when the fight ended.

It was a terrific fight, a contrast in styles made more interesting because Hearns, after hearing Leonard needle him about his ring acumen, adapted and adjusted in a fight that while curiously scored, did come down to issues of interpreting styles. That would be a recurring theme in subsequent big Leonard fights, too.

The next day, Hearns asked for another chance. "I feel Ray can give me a rematch," he said. "I feel I can put on a much better show this time. I know Ray's style now, and after that fight, I learned quite a bit. You can't win all your fights. To be a great champion, you have to prove you can come back."

Hearns got his rematch. But it was eight years later.

Leonard retired in 1982 because of a detached retina, but—surprise, surprise—couldn't stick to it. He had one fight in May 1984, against Kevin Howard, and quit again. He emerged from the mothballs to take an April 1987 fight with Marvelous Marvin Hagler, the longtime middleweight champion. I was there for that, too.

By then, the big question for Leonard, as it always was with fighters, was why? The answer usually was money, but in this case, it didn't seem to apply.

He'd had the detached retina in one eye and a weakened retina in the other. He had undergone surgery on both. He knew that his namesake, fellow Olympic gold medallist Sugar Ray Seales, was nearly blind due to similar problems. In Las Vegas, his camp passed out a written statement to reporters, essentially saying the eye problem would be off limits but that doctors had given him a clean bill of health. In it, Leonard asked us to "give me credit for not underestimating the seriousness of the situation."

He needed the spotlight. He had been a *People* magazine commodity and didn't like being a young has-been in retirement. As a ringside commentator, he was unexceptional at best, a tuxedo, a voice, and a name with nothing particularly illuminating to add. When he came to fights at

Caesars or other venues, he knew people pointed at him and said, "He *was . . .*" When he looked into the ring, he knew the men couldn't carry his Everlasts. He was pushing and hitting thirty, yet he still looked and felt like a prime-time athlete. With the glaring exception of his eyes, he was probably right. Before there was no chance of retrieving his fire and the physical gifts, Leonard came back to Caesars as a *fighter* again, to see his larger-than-life picture draped from the facade, to experience the excitement mounting for his confrontation with Hagler. As the fight approached, Leonard repeatedly referred to the middleweight champion as his personal "Mount Everest."

Hagler was resentful of the way he seemed to have been admired but taken for granted and certainly not beloved. (He was sounding a lot like Larry Holmes.) His longtime and loyal trainers, Goody and Pat Petronelli, relentlessly pushed his hardscrabble story and their role in it. As a teenager, Hagler moved to Brockton, Massachusetts, with his mother, brothers, and sisters, to live with other relatives to get out of the roughest neighborhoods in Newark, New Jersey. High school was a luxury, so he quit and worked in a tannery to help to support his family.

One day, he walked into the Petronellis' gym, which had been open only about a year. Brockton had given the world Rocky Marciano, so neighborhood tradition was on the brothers' side. Goody Petronelli had been in the Navy for twenty years. Pat had been training fighters at night after sweating through the day at his small construction business. The sons of Italian immigrants, they still could remember owning one pair of pants apiece, waiting for the welfare checks, and realizing there were folks in that era who didn't like them, if only because their names ended with vowels.

Goody Petronelli told Hagler that if he was serious, to bring his gear the next time. On his first day working out, Hagler fought from both stances, threw both hands. "This kid was a switch-hitter the day he walked into the ring," Pat Petronelli told us. "He boggled my mind. Left, right, left, right!"

Within two years, Hagler was a national champion. He turned pro and stuck with the Petronellis. The road to a title shot was difficult and ridiculously long, but he ultimately knocked out middleweight champion Alan Minter in London and had twelve title defenses before facing Leonard, the man he had so resented for years. One of those defenses was a legendary three-round knockout of Hearns in 1985 in a middleweight title fight of such compressed fury and wild momentum swings that many considered it the short fight of the ages. I regretted missing that one, but now I was getting to see Hagler in person against Leonard.

"This is everything I worked for in my life," Hagler told us at his final appearance before the fight. "It gives me good peace of mind knowing I can walk away, having defeated Sugar Ray Leonard. I know he wanted to get hold of me. Plus, I brought him out of retirement for the public, for the fight of the century."

I was seated near Juanita Leonard, who was in the first row of public seats. After the fourth round, one of Hagler's cornermen and advisers, Ollie Dunlap, turned around and hollered at her: "This is worse than Custer!"

Leonard stole the fight. He stole it with style and cunning. To this day, many are convinced that the split decision in Leonard's favor was another case of highway robbery or judging incompetence. I didn't agree at the time, and I still don't. Like most at ringside, I kept my own scorecard.

That night, I wrote (hurriedly, of course):

> It was almost as if Leonard could sense it. He knew each time it seemed that the dance was being squeezed out of his legs. He knew each time the punches of Hagler, the natural middleweight, seemed to be starting to wear down the natural welterweight. He knew each time it seemed the inevitable was about to start unfolding in the ring.
>
> Now, he seemed to tell himself.
>
> That's enough.
>
> Time to show them it isn't going to happen.
>
> Then he would explode with the quick combinations, the showy and flashy bursts. The magic is there, easily summoned.
>
> Leonard sold the judges, although he probably couldn't have seriously hurt Hagler in twenty-five rounds.
>
> He sold me. I had Leonard winning by one point, 115–114.

When the announcer said it was a split decision and read Judge Lou Filippo's two-point nod for Hagler, Juanita Leonard stood on her chair, momentarily quieted. Then we heard that judge JoJo Guerra of Mexico had Leonard winning by eight. (Even I thought that was out of line.) Finally, when we were told that judge Dave Moretti scored it 115–113 in favor of the "new"—as in "new middleweight champion"—the secret was out and Juanita jumped off the chair into the arms of one of Leonard's handlers. Sugar Ray was back on top of the world.

The Associated Press's card had Hagler winning 117–112, giving Leonard only four rounds. In the years since, I've heard HBO analyst/judge Harold Lederman refer about a million times to "effective aggression" in justifying his scoring of televised fights, and even that can be a matter of interpretation. Absolutely, Hagler was the more relentless aggressor that night. Leonard was on the verge of grogginess at least twice, in the fifth and seventh rounds, and also probably the ninth.

"Marvin didn't hurt me," Leonard said after the fight. "He kind of shook me up."

I gave Leonard the decision because he effectively moved and astutely picked his spots. He let Hagler stalk and lunge. He stood and stuck just enough. "My tactic was to stick and move, to hit and run, to taunt, intimidate, and frustrate," Leonard said.

A key issue, often overlooked, was that with several major sanctioning organizations' middleweight titles on the line, promoters had to choose between scheduling the fight for fifteen or twelve rounds. Fifteen long had been the universal title fight standard until renewed criticism sprang up after the death of lightweight champion Ray "Boom Boom" Mancini's Korean challenger, Duk Koo Kim. Referee Richard Green stopped the Mancini–Kim fight early in the fourteenth round, but Mancini had been battering his opponent for several rounds. The World Boxing Council stubbornly stuck with fifteen rounds for title fights, while the rival World Boxing Association cut back to twelve. The Leonard camp successfully fought to have this fight scheduled for only twelve. Leonard's fight strategy was based on that distance, and if the officials suddenly had announced it was going another three rounds to clear up any disputes, Hagler would have won all three and the fight.

"I beat him," a disgusted Hagler told us. "I beat him, and he knows it. I told you about Vegas. They stole it. I was aggressive. I stayed aggressive. I won the fight."

As it turned out, the sport would have been better off if the decision had gone to Hagler, who at the time of the fight was only thirty-two. He was so disgusted with the decision and what he perceived to be the objectionable politics involved in the sport—it's hard to argue with him there—that he not only retired from boxing, but he stayed retired.

Leonard fought on. I covered two more of his fights, when he defeated Donny Lalonde, the WBC's light heavyweight champion in 1988 and fought to a draw in the anticlimactic rematch with Hearns in 1989. The fight with Lalonde actually was entertaining. Although he had a championship belt, Lalonde, the Canadian "Golden Boy" looked more like a magician in the Hilton's midnight show or a guy out of a *So You Think You Can Fight* smoker at a local tavern than a boxer. Even at the time, I said his name looked as if it should be on the back of a Quebec Nordiques hockey sweater and not on a robe.

Leonard won on a ninth-round technical knockout after knocking down Lalonde twice. Lalonde looked terrible for the first three rounds, then put Leonard down with a stunning punch in the fourth, reminding all of us that a light heavyweight indeed had a puncher's chance against the former welterweight. Leonard's only previous knockdown was in his victory over Kevin Howard, two comebacks earlier. "Anytime you're in a fight of this caliber," he said, "if you get hit right, you can go. Obviously, I got hit right. He tagged me with a right hand, a counter right hand. I wasn't hurt at all. It was similar to the Kevin Howard experience."

Leonard opened his postfight news conference with a lengthy monologue about Lalonde's championship legitimacy, and two things seemed obvious. One, he was on the defensive. Two, he was angling for a rematch against Hearns as a sort of "Thrilla in Manila" throwback to Muhammad Ali's classic victory over Joe Frazier, when both men were past their prime.

Leonard didn't fight again until that 1989 rematch. In his previous two fights, Hearns was knocked out by Iran Barkley and beat James Kinchen on a controversial decision. He was only thirty but seemed far over the hill. Leonard had gotten around to giving Hearns a rematch when he thought Tommy had sufficiently slipped. Hearns knew that. "I feel I have to prove that I'm a better man, a better fighter than Ray Leonard," Hearns said. "I don't want to go through my life thinking about that fight over and over. It's been a definite nightmare, over and over again."

"We were two different people, two younger people," said Leonard of the earlier fight. "I think now I'm more economical, although that's perceived as being slower and older. I hit harder, although that's been perceived as compensating for my legs not being able to carry me. As far as Thomas Hearns, I think everyone should look back at that last fight, because that's all he remembers—that last fight."

The major reason the two fighters were expected to get a record $26 million—Leonard $14 million and Hearns $12 million—was the burgeoning pay-per-view industry. "You have fight fans who pretty much determine who they want to see fight," Leonard said. "It's all relative. It's like Michael Jackson. It's like Eddie Murphy. People pay for who they like."

Leonard–Hearns again was controversial. It could go only twelve rounds this time, and Leonard never came close to duplicating that thirty-four-punch flurry that ended their first fight. It was close and competitive, and even before the decision was announced, the consensus was that this one could go either way—and no decision, as long as the scorecards were close, would be ridiculous.

It came out a draw. One judge had it 112–112 and the other two had it 113–112—one for each fighter. Those were hard to argue with. The Associate Press card had Leonard winning by one; I had it as a draw and had to show the full card to friends later to prove it. I didn't claim to be smart; nothing in line with the often-absurd Nevada judging is anything to brag about. Leonard had been knocked down twice, in the third and the eleventh, but closed with a spectacular twelfth. Although skills clearly had eroded in the eight years since their previous encounter, it was a thrilling fight to watch—and it's even a bit puzzling that it didn't approach "Thrilla in Manila" status.

Leonard went on to beat Roberto Duran (again) later in the year. He should have left well enough alone, but he returned to the ring to lose to Terry Norris in 1991 and to get knocked out by Hector "Macho" Camacho in 1997.

Hearns fought sixteen more times, and as late as 2006 earned a technical knockout over Shannon Landberg in the Palace of Auburn Hills.

When the three men—Leonard, Hagler, and Hearns—fought one another, it wasn't always boxing at its best, but with the accompanying sideshows and atmosphere, it was boxing at its most thrilling.

PART NINE

OLYMPIC FLAMES

The Olympics long ago became professionalized. There's no turning back. But there's still something to the notion that the Olympic flame can warm even hard-bitten professional athletes, and not only because they have an eye on the possible endorsements or other rewards that can come from representing their nations.

Qualification standards have been tightened in most sports since I first covered an Olympics, in 1984 in Los Angeles, but there still are plenty of cases of athletes showing up wide-eyed and awed with little chance of winning medals but thrilled to be there.

Even at the approach of the 2012 London Summer Games, there still are many athletes taking part for whom this is the highlight of their careers—and perhaps their lives. That atmosphere, plus some quaint and interesting settings, fascinated me at the handful of Olympic Games I've covered more than the triumphant moments of individual athletes.

Calgary 1988
Olympic Winter Games

Calgary 1988
Jeux Olympiques d'hiver

E

TERRY FREI
OREGONIAN USA
UNITED STATES OF AMERICA

∞   6

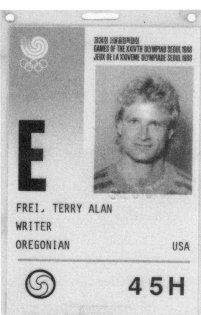

제24회 서울올림픽대회
GAMES OF THE XXIVTH OLYMPIAD SEOUL 1988
JEUX DE LA XXIVEME OLYMPIADE SEOUL 1988

E

FREI, TERRY ALAN
WRITER
OREGONIAN   USA

45H

XVIᵉˢ Jeux
olympiques d'hiver
8-23 Février 92

XVI Olympic
Winter Games
8-23 February 92

E

26664

TERRY FREI
THE OREGONIAN (USA)
ETATS-UNIS D'AMERIQUE

4

Jocs de la XXVa Olimpiada
Barcelona 1992
Jeux de la XXV Olympiade
Barcelona 1992

Juegos de la XXV Olimpiada
Barcelona 1992
Games of the XXV Olympiad
Barcelona 1992

E

174280/01

FREI, TERRY
REDACTOR
PORTLAND OREGONIAN

∞ MEDIA MPC   USA

5 8

SAN MARINO, MY SAN MARINO

AT THE 1988 WINTER GAMES IN CALGARY, I sat with Michael Knisley at the frigid opening ceremonies. We decided to make it interesting that day and throughout the Games by adopting a country we had never heard of during the opening ceremonies and following its athletes' progress.

I adopted San Marino.

Now, you're probably making fun of me for not knowing where San Marino is located . . . or maybe you're not. But after watching its athletes— all five of them—march in the opening ceremony, I went back to the press center on the Stampede grounds and discovered that San Marino is a tiny independent republic within Italy, northwest of Venice and near the Adriatic Sea. I also discovered that San Marino's five competitors all were skiers.

A few days later, I attended the super giant slalom at the Nakiska ski area near Calgary and watched the skiers from "my" nation compete. Near the finish line, I introduced myself to one of the skiers, Fabio Guardigli, and explained that I had adopted him and his team. In exchange, he gave me a history lesson.

"We are the oldest and smallest republic in the world," Guardigli, wearing the powder blue ski outfit of his nation, told me.

Founded in the early fourth century as a refuge for persecuted Christians, San Marino's population was twenty-two thousand. The longest distance from border to border is eight miles. Its total area is twenty-three and a half square miles. The capital city, San Marino (population five thousand), is on the side of Monte Titano. Stone walls on three sides of the town and medieval castles on the mountain's three peaks are tourist attractions.

"I think that today all of San Marino was watching us on television," Guardigli said.

That didn't do much for the ratings.

All of the San Marino skiers in the super giant slalom made it across the finish line. Nobody got hurt. That was about all they'd hoped for. Among the sixty finishers, Nicola Ercolani was forty-sixth, Fabio Guardigli was fifty-second, and Riccardo Stacchini was fifty-third. Stacchini went so wide at one stage of the race that he almost ran into the boundary fence. The public-address announcer told the crowd that Stacchini "has abandoned the course" before sheepishly issuing a correction about thirty seconds later. The only finishers with slower times were from the skiing hotbeds of Puerto Rico, Mexico, Monaco, and Taiwan.

In the United States, Americans were wondering why our skiers, who didn't do well, couldn't beat the rest of the world down a stupid hill. In San Marino, though, nobody denounced the tiny nation's athletes for a "disappointing performance." Nobody tried to guess how the low finishes would affect their future marketability.

"We ski for fun," Guardigli told me. "We try to get better every day. The time we have for training is not that much, so that's all we can expect of ourselves."

I contrasted him with another "inept" competitor at the Calgary Games, British ski jumper Eddie Edwards. Edwards had hired a Calgary attorney to act as his liaison and agent, was making well-publicized appearances at a Las Vegas–style nightclub in his hotel, and was positioning himself to take financial advantage of his notoriety. The San Marino skiers weren't following the lead of the Jamaican bobsled team and selling sweatshirts for $28 to defray expenses. The men from San Marino were legitimate recreational-class skiers who drove four hours to train in the Alps. Only five hundred San Marino men, women, and children participated in the sport. The national program had ten skiers. Elena Matous was a prominent alpine woman skier in the 1970s, but she was a nomad who competed for San Marino only because she needed a national affiliation to be eligible for the Olympics. Unlike the heavily sponsored skiers on the World Cup circuit and their competitors at Calgary, the San Marino men had jobs and wedged training into their leisure time.

"We are not professionals," Guardigli said. He laughed and looked at Stacchini, who added, "Less training, less results."

Guardigli, who worked in a factory, and Stacchini, an accountant, were twenty-two, lived in the capital city, and spoke English as their second language. In addition to the distance they had to drive to ski in the Alps, their training obstacles included convincing their employers to give them time off.

"They are proud that we are here at the Olympics," Stacchini said. "They are not so proud for our training."

Needless to say, perhaps, San Marino's medal count at Calgary was zero gold, zero silver, and zero bronze. I also wrote about flamboyant Italian skiing superstar Alberto Tomba, figure skaters Debi Thomas and Katarina Witt, and the Soviet Union's gold medal in hockey, which was won with a deep roster that included future NHL stars Igor Larionov, Slava Fetisov, and Alexander Mogilny. But the story that stuck with me was the men of San Marino.

AN OPENING STROLL

AFTER MY FREEZING EXPERIENCE IN CALGARY, I decided to take a different approach during the Opening Ceremonies of the 1988 Summer Games in Seoul. I wanted to see what "real" people were doing during the ceremonies.

That morning, in the Chomdam Dong section of central Seoul, the automobile repair garage was quiet except for the reverberating sound of two televisions. A huge replica of a WD-40 can loomed over the iron-spired fence that separated the dusty yard—blacktop poked through in a few places—from the bustling street. From the scattered boxes and tires, to the sleepy dog, to the dilapidated clock hanging over the door, the station could have been the only one for two hundred miles on a two-lane Nevada highway. But it was in the middle of one of the world's largest cities, frozen in inaction as the ceremonies began less than two miles away in Olympic Stadium.

The televisions were precariously balanced on a stand of three boxes and an old wheel. Three men stood behind a woman who was seated in a swivel chair. The woman spotted me, smiled, and gestured to one of the old swivel-style chairs next to her. At first, we didn't speak. The Olympic credential hanging around my neck advertised why I was in town, and my blond hair hinted that communication would be difficult. On the television, we watched the colorful dancers for a few minutes. The men washed a well-dressed customer's Hyundai, but they watched the television as they sprayed. I thumbed through my phrase book, told the woman I was an American, and asked her name. Park Nan He. I said thank you, handed her my business card, and left.

A few doors down Tosandaero Street, several taxis were parked outside a little restaurant. Woks were on each table. Blue-shirted drivers stabbed lunch with chopsticks, continuing to watch the television in the corner. The waitress put a glass of cold tea in front of me. Just as I had on the walk up the

Yongdongdaero from the press center, I could feel the eyes. Not necessarily unfriendly eyes, but unquestionably curious eyes in turning heads.

In the restaurant, as I took notes, a voice came from behind me: "Excuse me, what are you writing?"

A man in an expensive long-sleeved polo shirt asked if he could be of any help and handed me his card.

S. H. YOON
MANAGER
PHILLIPS-VAN HEUSEN COMPANY

He and a friend were eating a concoction of bean curd, noodles, vegetables, cabbage, ham, and "lots of hot spices." He offered a pair of chopsticks and reflections. "We have been talking about the Olympics for many years," he said. "It seems to me that we got a little tired of the Olympics. But as we got closer to the opening ceremonies, as we were realizing we were hosting an event for the whole world, people are feeling very proud. We hope this is a good chance to show the real Korea, the progress of the Korean economy."

Nearby, a little alley branched off Tosandaero. About two storefronts up, two elderly women were sitting in a tiny five-table cafe. As I paused to look through the door at the television, they waved me in. The oldest woman was peeling garlic in a blue vat, smiling when I found the word: "*manul.*"

"*Kimchi,*" she said, meaning the garlic was going into the evening's batch of pickled cabbage. She wrote her name on my pad in Korean script. Only later did I find out from a Korean Associated Press worker that the woman spelled out "Lee Young-Rae." On the tiny black-and-white television on top of the refrigerator, the Nigerian team marched into the stadium. Mrs. Lee's friend brought out two bottles. The unspoken, smiling question was, "Coke or orange?" I took the Coke and between sips pointed to the television and asked, "*Ku kot chousimnikka?*" (Do you like it?)

Mrs. Lee nodded and clapped rhythmically. We "conversed" for about fifteen minutes without expressing much except good feelings. She waved her hands, and I nodded.

Two more blocks to the west, a skinny diagonal street off Tosandaero looked like a farmer's bazaar or a European street market. In one of the jewelry stores, owner Shin Kie Bom was watching with his father. As I came in, he got off the couch, told me to sit there, and pointed toward the plate of Korean pastries. What a guy has to do for a story, I thought. Not only did Shin have Seiko watches at a bargain price and a wall full of hypnotically swinging pendulums in his Chong Shin Dang shop, he spoke "a little" English. He was forty-nine years old, wearing sandals and white socks. The Olympics? He beamed. "Good!" he said repeatedly.

As the Antiguans took their turn on the camera, I started the walk back, this time taking the street called Samsongno.

I considered the flame lighted.

In the upcoming weeks, I found myself in the dressing room of the Soviet Union's winning basketball team, both because of lax security and because I knew center Arvydas Sabonis, who had come to Portland to rehabilitate his torn Achilles' tendon and who eventually would join the Trail Blazers. Later, I would realize that the players from Baltic republics, such as the Lithuanian Sabonis, had mixed feelings about competing for the Soviet Union, but that day I laughed and felt like a comrade as the players guzzled OB beer and Sabonis interrupted his halting attempt to describe his feelings to me to pose with a group of young Korean volunteers who also had crashed the dressing room. Canadian Ben Johnson was disqualified after winning the 100 meters, and my suitemates and I got word the morning after the race and spent the rest of the day scrambling to document the world's first steroids splash. I was there when Greg Louganis cracked his head on a diving board and still won a gold. I was in the arena when Roy Jones Jr. lost to a South Korean boxer on a decision that later was proven to be fraudulent.

But most of all, I still remember that walk through Seoul.

A FRENCH VILLAGE AND A PIN TRADER

AT THE 1992 WINTER GAMES IN ALBERTVILLE, France, the press, Olympic volunteers, and competitors—like the athletic events themselves—were scattered all over the region. About twelve hundred of us drew Brides-les-Bains, a little mountain spa village twenty miles from Albertville. The townspeople were accustomed to having visitors, but not this sort of multinational, multilingual onslaught. The tiny village had twenty-two small hotels, the type where guests were expected to drop off their room keys, anchored to huge chains roughly the size of anvils, at the front desk each time they left.

Across the street from my hotel, on the other side of a huge storm fence erected down the middle of the street, the figure skaters—including Tonya Harding—and skiers were among seven hundred athletes in a handful of hotels that formed a temporary Olympic Village, one of the six such facilities scattered in and around Albertville. That also meant a huge contingent of blue-uniformed gendarmes guarded the Olympic Village. Nobody guarded the media hotels, but I came to believe that the biggest hazard we faced was dodging the huge *Tourisme Verne* busses that roared in and out of town, taking us to and from the Olympic venues.

When the three groups—security forces, athletes, and media—had free time, we often mingled in the village's restaurants or encountered one another on unguided tours.

On the day I set aside to sightsee before covering nighttime events, I laughed to note that some things probably didn't change, even when the world came to visit. Outside a boutique, a little dog wearing a scarf around its neck was tearing at a piece of denim and wagging her tail. In the doorway, a man in a beret—I was all but certain I had seen him arguing with Maurice Chevalier in several movies—was in an animated conversation with the proprietor. I could tell they'd had this argument before.

Thanks to the pull of world-renowned *Denver Post* outdoors and skiing writer Charlie Meyers, I was able to join him and Woody Paige at the starting gate of the Olympic downhill at Val d'Isère, France, during the Albertville Winter Games in 1992. This was taken shortly before the race, and shortly after I looked down the course from what seemed to be the top of the world and decided those downhill racers were nuts. *Source*: From the author's collection.

I discovered that most of the shops closed for two and a half hours at midday. The town had one main street with a handful of winding, tiny tributaries leading to it. My first thought was that if they moved the few cars, filmmakers could have shot a movie set in the 1950s, especially on the side streets. My second thought was that they didn't really need to move the cars after all, because they looked as if they had been sitting on the street since 1954.

It was a tourist town of contradictions, one with the feel of old and new Europe, with sounds of huge stereos and accordions, with the looks of another century and, especially in the heart of the main street, a little shopping plaza that could have been current-day Vail. Which world I saw depended on which way I turned.

The modern shops in the plaza generally were busy. However, when talking to the proprietors—they almost all spoke English—I got occasional shrugs about the business bonanza not materializing during the Olympics. They told me that the nightclubs, *Cythere* and *Phoque*, had been periodically busy, but it seemed clear that nobody had explained in advance to the good folks of Brides-les-Bains that journalists would be working until late at night and that the athletes would find it easier to stay in their fenced-off athletes' village across the street, which had areas for socializing.

The big lunchtime customers of the Parisien Bar, for example, seemed to be the Games volunteers in their silver coats embossed with the five Olympic rings. I had heard a rumor that eight or nine adults in France didn't smoke, but none of them seemed to be among the volunteers staying in Brides-les-Bains. The bartender sold me a Loto card, writing out and smiling that if the right numbers came up in the *Tirage du Loto*, I could win 40,000 francs! The small *Poste* outlet was selling a lot of stamps for postcards, and the *Presse* store displayed souvenirs and multilanguage newspapers. Everyone was nice, but the little mom-and-pop grocery stores, creperies, and bakeries didn't seem busy at all, and I half-wondered if the French discussions around me centered on tearing down the fence and bringing back the regular, money-spending vacationers.

I went through the red tape to arrange a visit to the athletes' village. They were about two hundred feet away, but in some ways, they were in another world. I walked down the stairs from the main street toward a river. I came to a trailer at what we dubbed "Checkpoint Charles de Gaulle." I obtained a day pass, enabling me to wander on that side of the street but not into the athletes' residences. I had to promise to depart by nightfall, which wasn't a problem. At the hotel in the athletes' village, the *Hotel des Thermes*, different flags hung from the balconies, advertising the nationalities of the occupants—or the nationalities of new friends from whom the flags were obtained. Trading was a big sport in the village.

Outside the Pharmacie, a condom machine was attached to the wall, like an automatic teller machine. A few steps away, a bandstand was set up in the plaza. A mini-Olympic flame burned in a cauldron on the plaza wall. The cinema was showing *Robin des Bois* and *Point Break*. The library had become a lounge, stocked with books and newspapers. The outdoor, open-air pay phones were like the rest in France—amazingly efficient. You could buy phone credit in advance, slide in a card and punch 237 to get Cameroon in nothing flat. I passed two athletes talking on the phones, one in Spanish and one in German.

The little church inside the athletes' temporary complex was unmistakably Catholic, with confessionals and stained-glass window images of St. Francis and Pope Innocent and statues of the Virgin Mary. During the Olympics, though, it was also holding Protestant and Ecumenical services. Pope John Paul II, the former alpine skier, signed off on that radical departure from protocol. How did I know that? Copies of John Paul II's letter to the area's archbishop and bishops were posted at the entrance in two languages. (The English translation: "I wish in these historical moments to assure the athletes that my thoughts as well as my prayers will unite with theirs.")

An elderly priest walked past the "Statue Pro Patria" of a sword-wielding Joan of Arc. The plaques below reminded his parishioners—and visitors— that Jean-Baptiste Blanc-Talleur, twenty-two, was killed at the Somme in the war that was supposed to end all wars on September 4, 1916. There were four other names below the statue and more on another statue outside honoring the dead of World War II—the war that for a time seemed to mark the end of the world for France.

On one of my trips down to Albertville, I came across an American who embodied the pin-trading craze that had become more prevalent with every Olympics I attended.

Many French citizens attending the Olympics knew how to say three things in English, which I admitted was about three more things than I could say in French. The French people said: (A) "God bless General Eisenhower"; (B) "We tried to tell you about Vietnam"; and (C) "Excuse me, do you have any Olympic pins for me?" My response: (A) "I like Ike, too"; (B) "We should have listened"; and (C) "NO, I'M SORRY, BUT I DON'T HAVE ANY PINS!"

They were just souvenirs, but they could make folks go a little nutty in their pursuit. At the Albertville Games, French policemen took back parking tickets for a pin. Any pin. In fact, one time, an officer pulled up next to me and our photographer in our car (with a press parking pass in the window) at a light, got out of the police van, knocked on the window, and asked for a pin. The waitress asked for a pin. The barber asked for a pin. Photographers, amateur and professional, had them sticking out of their hats. Women had them all over their aprons. Companies put them out, Olympic Committees put them out. This was baseball card trading gone platinum, but the positive side was that it was possible to strike up friendships while exchanging the pins. It was part hard-nosed capitalism, part trading post, and part ice cream social.

The vendors, many of them English speaking, were set up all over Albertville and the Savoy venues, just as they were in Seoul, Calgary, and Los Angeles.

Victor Cornell set up his table in the alley leading from the main shopping street to one of Albertville's top auto shops. He was buying, selling, trading, and talking—in one of seven languages. He wasn't a hustler. He was just willing to talk and show and tell. If a deal came of it, it was a bonus.

"You know what my mother used to tell me?" Cornell asked me, with a trace of an Eastern European accent. "Bad business is business, too." He told me his first Olympics was at London in 1948 and that he had been at every one since, "except Moscow in 1980 because I didn't want to break the boycott."

Victor was a Czechoslovakia-born, sixty-six-year-old former-cabbie-turned-owner of a small New York taxi company. On the card he gave me, he called himself a "collector of materials relating to the Olympic Games" and listed a Riverside Drive address. He told me he had about five thousand pins and legions of friends.

Atlanta businessman and Olympic regular Bob Cohn, who walked by and talked pins, knew Cornell's story. "Victor is the undisputed king of pins," Cohn told me. As I stood with them, he and Victor got into a friendly argument about which Olympics they met. Was it there? Or there? They both laughed, and Cornell told me: "Just say we met someplace." They met someplace. Years earlier.

Victor's eyes opened wide in excitement when he talked of his pastime but became misty when I finally prodded him to tell me of his past. Most of Victor's customers didn't know his story. To most of them, this was their one Olympics and he was just a character, that old guy with the pins sticking to his sweater and his hat, with the amazing collection on his table, with hammer and sickle pins from the Soviet Union team, with the little numbered medallist pins that were issued to the gold, silver, and bronze winners, with participants' badges from the Mexico City Games, with just about anything Olympic you can imagine.

He told me he was born in Skotarsko, a part of Czechoslovakia that now is part of Russia. During World War II, he said, he ended up in a concentration camp at Bor, Serbia, and also did forced labor in copper mining and then helped build the railroads and the tunnels in the system that brought the copper out. He told me he worked for "thirty decograms of bread a day." Some survived. Many died.

"The Croatian collaborators were worse than the Germans," he told me. He said he escaped while on a work detail away from the camp, in part because he was "able to speak the Slav language and was able to communicate with the farmers. They helped me get away. I worked with the resistance the rest of the war." When he finally made it home after the war, he said, "I saw the writing on the wall and said this was a good time to take a powder." The colloquialisms were spoken without humor, and they sounded a little awkward, but his meaning was clear. He wanted a fresh start. "I was able to contact my aunt in the States, and she sent me a ticket for the boat," he said.

Cornell started driving a taxi, and he ended up selling his small service in 1984. In between, he got serious about pins. "My first pin was a football pin, a soccer pin, a Hungary soccer pin, in 1938," he said. "My first Olympics was London, 1948." For a while, he thought about skipping the Albertville Games. "I lost my wife, and I lost my spirit," he said. But he decided to show up anyway, getting a room in a small Albertville hotel and talking to the garage owner about letting him do business at the end of the alley.

"All he wanted was a couple of pins," Victor said. "I asked whether he could sell me a table. He said he could lend me one about two meters long. I said, 'Perfect.'"

Victor loved dealing with people, not just the money—if there was money to be made. That's why he kept coming back. I thought that was as much a part of the Olympic spirit as anything that went on in a medals competition.

THE DREAM TEAM AND THE MARATHON ROUTE

THE 1992 SUMMER GAMES in Barcelona featured the U.S. basketball Dream Team, among other athletic heroes. Because I was at the *Oregonian* at the time, and the Trail Blazers lost in the 1992 NBA Finals to Michael Jordan and the Bulls, and I covered the Tournament of the Americas Olympic qualifying competition in Portland, I felt as if I was on the ground floor in covering the Dream Team. It was hilarious to see opposing players from some of the especially overmatched teams in the Tournament of the Americas scramble after the game to take pictures with the Americans and get autographs.

In later years, when the rest of the world temporarily surpassed the United States in basketball, or at least better displayed fundamentals, team play, and even jump-shooting, this tended to be shoved into the background: in 1992, the U.S. team assembled was a band of superstars considered—and proven to be—head and shoulders above the rest of the national teams. The rest of the world quickly would close the gap, both because the U.S. Dream Teamers retreated into retirement and because their innate ability to understand and play the game didn't seem to be handed down to the next wave of NBA stars. That next wave was more athletic and talented than ever, but those players couldn't carry the Dream Team's jocks.

Although this was in advance of much of the technology and online advances that could make the rest of the world seem as if it was just around the corner, I was a bit taken aback by the gushing reception the Dream Team got after arriving in Spain. At the very first news conference, a Japanese journalist stood at the microphone stand in the aisle of the packed auditorium and read his question in English, carefully and slowly, from a legal pad.

"How do you feel," he said to Michael Jordan, "to be called as a god?"

It was a Beatles reunion tour, times four. "I thought the stampede in the village was the most frightening thing," said Coach Chuck Daly. And the team

317

wasn't even living there; this stampede was when the team arrived at the village to go through the accreditation process. At the news conference, the twelve players sat at a long table and took questions, one by one, in order, down the line. The usual procedure at such events was for everyone to sit together for a short time, providing the sound bites, and then to break apart so each player could be interviewed separately by surrounding groups of reporters. U.S. Olympic Committee officials decided that wouldn't be wise for security and safety reasons. At first, that seemed a ridiculous overreaction. After a few minutes of this mass hysteria, it seemed reasonable. Jordan gee-whizzed himself through that "god" question and most of the others. But Charles Barkley made a point of referring to it later, when he was asked to address the issue of why the team wasn't staying with the rowers and gymnasts and everyone else in the athletes' village. They would be mobbed, he said. Besides, he said, looking at Jordan, "We got God on our team!"

As expected, the Americans stormed through the Olympic tournament and ultimately won the gold medal game in another rout, 117–85, over Croatia. During the medal ceremony, there were so many flashes going off all around the Palau d'Esports that the teams almost looked as if they were playing under flickering, freeze-frame strobe lights. The man across the aisle from me was doing the television play-by-play in Swedish, on a Finnish television station that serves his country's Swedish-speaking minority. "Magic Johnson" sounds the same in Swedish or any one of the dozens of languages in the broadcasting section. Even the law-enforcement types paid the championship game a compliment of vigilance, because the Americans won the gold medal on a night when the arena resembled an armed camp, much more so than usual at an Olympics that would have been an inviting target for Basque or Catalonian separatists. With dozens of extra police trucks and tanks parked around the arena, with more vigilant searches, with frowning officers everywhere taking little care to blend in, it seemed obvious that authorities had decided that if something was going to happen, this was the night—and the event.

At the end, and this is an Olympic cliché offered without apology, there really were no losers on that elongated medal stand as Juan Antonio Samaranch, the International Olympic Committee's president, prepared to do the honors.

On the left were silver medallists, the Croatians, proud claimants of their own land after the splintering of Yugoslavia. On the right were the bronze medallists, the Lithuanians, in their wild, tie-dyed T-shirts donated by the Grateful Dead. They were so grateful to be a part of a reborn nation, especially Arvydas Sabonis and Sarunas Marciulionis, who played for the Soviet Union in 1988 in Seoul but didn't love much about it except the gold medals. And in the middle, a step above and a world apart, the team that so many seemed to think we should have felt sheepish about sending to Barcelona. The team with a sense of accomplishment not so much involving the results on the floor—what did anyone expect?—but the impressive display of ego subjugation.

"It's awesome to see twelve Americans come together," said Utah Jazz forward Karl Malone, "and play together for their country and do something that's positive."

They didn't seem to worry about minutes. They didn't seem to worry about who was the focal point. They just played, played together and with an almost incredible lack of selfishness. Magic Johnson was so effective that you forgot that he sat out the season and that he was presumed to be under a death sentence because of his HIV diagnosis. Under the circumstances, Portland guard Clyde Drexler, who was asked if this made up for coming close but not winning an NBA championship at Portland or an NCAA title at the University of Houston, appropriately said the comparisons were not valid.

"A gold medal is a gold medal," he said as the medal hung on his chest. "You're playing for your country. You're not playing for one university or one city. I'm not saying those other situations aren't very important. They are. That's what puts bread on the table. This is special because it's the first time ever."

Nobody seemed to be bringing up the "apology" business. It had come up, again and again, in Barcelona. At least when I caught parts of games on television, the Pakistan men's field hockey players made their opponents look as if they were trying to play on ice skates. Cuba's boxers should have been fighting behind Caesars Palace for millions, not medals, and Cuba's baseball team hadn't lost in international competition approximately since Castro closed the casinos in Havana. And those Icelanders seemed to smash everyone else out of team handball. Yet nobody was screaming that those nations "should just send their kids!" That had even been one of the popular themes for the cadre of American columnists who covered the Olympics by sitting in the Main Press Center and either writing about what they watched on monitors—something they could have done back home—or about the weather and the media village laundry service. The truth was, the rest of the basketball-playing world wanted the United States to send its best pros and was willing to accept the routs as the price. In retrospect, I'm absolutely certain it helped accelerate the improvement in European basketball. They knew how far they had to come.

After spending three weeks in Barcelona, among Catalonians shopping for Bulls and Spurs and Dream Team sweatshirts at el Corte Ingles, among kids in Lakers shorts speaking French or German on the subway, among Japanese who saw "USA" on press credentials and said "Magic," and after seeing the starstruck players on other teams, I could add this: almost everybody loved it.

I had heard all this business about the worldwide popularity of the NBA. I had been to Europe a couple of times before and even watched the NBA Finals on Italian television while on vacation. Yet I wasn't quite prepared for the intensity in Spain.

By the end of the gold-medal game, in fact, I was beginning to wonder if there was an additional reason for all the added security that night. The officers might have also wanted to be a part of basketball history.

———

On the closing day of the Games, when the men contested the marathon through the streets of Barcelona, I wanted to find a vantage point in or near the Parc de la Ciutadella, the site of the city's Universal Exposition of 1888. I got off the subway and headed south to the Arc de Triomf. It sits at the top of the Passeig Lluis Companys, a promenade that leads to the park. Adolf Hitler didn't visit this arch in triumph, but it did look like the one in Paris. Just through the arch, a group of men, perhaps ten of them, were playing a game with little balls slightly larger than baseballs. It was a cross between croquet, minus the wickets, and bocce, the Italian lawn game, but the surface was sandy rock. One of the balls—only one—was tiny and red. The men had handkerchiefs out, and they wiped their foreheads between each toss. They had drawn a small crowd, and a woman said this game was "Petanca." (Scores later, on *SportsCenter*.)

I went to the south end of the Passeig to the park entrance. I found the painted blue line the runners were supposed to follow through the park. It turned from the street into the park. I came to the Umbracle, a brick shell structure that resembled an arboretum. The roof and much of the sides were wooden slats, spaced far enough apart to let light and air in. The plaque on the outside said these were Fontsere's gardens, and the inside was a tropical jungle. There were benches inside, but the doors were not open. Outside, as I circled the building, I came across a slight woman carefully reaching into a grocery-type cart. She brought out newspapers and cat food, and within a few seconds, cats surrounded her. They came down the angled roof, they came out of the bushes, and they came from all over. She put the food on the paper and she watched them eat. She put paper on a low ledge, and another cat climbed down to eat. Then she climbed on that low ledge, perhaps three feet high, and reached up to put food on a higher ledge, maybe eight feet high, for the shyest cat of all.

The catwoman wanted to know why I wanted to know her name. As best I could, in Spanish and a bit of Catalan, I explained and showed my Olympic credential. Her name was Antonia Traga. I asked her age. "Sesenta y ocho." I wrote down seventy-eight. That was why I received a C in Spanish. She didn't like that. I corrected myself. Sixty-eight. She has been feeding the cats of the park, she said, for ten years. Every day? Every day. How many are there? Not possible to say. They come, they leave, they die, and they are born. She lives *cerca*. Nearby.

The marathoners were getting close.

I walked past the statue of General Don Juan Prim, ventured out the park gate and quickly walked through the Estacio de Franca, the older of Barcelona's two major train stations. In this one, residents took refuge from the Fascist bombing when Barcelona was the seat of the Republican government during the Spanish Civil War.

I took up position at the thirty-four-kilometer (about twenty miles) banner, just across the Avenguda del Marques d l'Argentera from the station. I was right against the police-line tape. When I looked at the Guardia Civil car parked there and started taking more notes, the officer—they were still nervous about terrorists—asked me what I was doing. He did not ask in a civil tone. I tried to answer in Spanish and I pulled out my credential again, and I think we got it all straightened out.

The press buses rolled by. Those bums. Then the Red Cross truck. Then police cars, with lights and sirens. Then dozens of motorcycles, with two officers on each. The second officer on each pointed a semiautomatic gun skyward. Then a SWAT team truck, with side doors open. I didn't make any sudden moves. Then more of all of the above. Then electric vans and slow cars with the Barcelona Olympic Committee emblem on the sides.

Two runners came into view. Applause escorted them. I wrote down their numbers, 1087 and (about a half stride back) 1147. I had no clue who they were. I forgot to bring a start list. We clapped. Later, I determined that Koichi Morishita of Japan was barely leading Hwang Young-Cho of Korea. And I learned that Hwang took the gold and Morishita the silver. They passed me at 8:18 p.m. The others arrived in flurries. They were greeted with more applause, with fanning waves of the Catalan flag, with shouts of encouragement. They came for a half hour. Finally, for a long time, there were no more.

I walked back into the park and sat below the Prim statue. Oops. Here came number 1221—Hussain Haleen of Moldavia. He was limping and hurting but still running. It was 8:53. Children skated down the blue line, and yet officers still were in place. I wondered why. I walked over to one of them along the course. It was 9:10. Were all of the runners done? He said there were three more.

A group of curious English-speaking tourists walked past. I told one man what the policeman had said, and he passed it along to the rest. A woman in the middle of the group turned as she walked and pointed to the east, in the direction of the Placa de las Armas, saying, "What is that? It's beautiful."

I was 99.9 percent sure it was Mary Tyler Moore, in part because if you tell me the title of any *Dick Van Dyke Show* episode, I can tell you the plot. I would have been 100 percent sure if she had said, "Oh, Rob!"

The other two stragglers must have quit.

At 9:24, another artillery division and armada of buses came past, both in front of and behind a struggling number 1251, a lonely man in short-sleeve T-shirt.

He was Pyambuu Tuul of Mongolia.

One hundred and ten men started the race. Eighty-seven finished. Tuul was eighty-seventh, in 4:00:44. He was more than fifty-five minutes behind the limping Haleen, who was eighty-sixth. Tuul was 107 minutes behind the winner. He finished after the closing ceremonies began in the stadium, so, unlike the others, he didn't get to finish with a lap around the Olympic track in front of the full house.

He finished, virtually alone, at the adjacent practice track.

It was his private Arc de Triomf.

INDEX

ABOUT THE AUTHOR

Award-winning journalist Terry Frei writes for the *Denver Post*. He also has worked for the *Rocky Mountain News*, the Portland *Oregonian*, and the *Sporting News*. He is a graduate of the University of Colorado at Boulder with degrees in history and journalism. His previous books include *Horns, Hogs, and Nixon Coming: Texas vs. Arkansas in Dixie's Last Stand*, *Third Down and a War to Go* (with a foreword by David Maraniss), *'77: Denver, the Broncos, and a Coming of Age* (with a foreword by Ron Zappolo), and *The Witch's Season*.

Terry and his wife, Helen, live in Denver. For more information, visit his Web site: www.terryfrei.com.